"*Big Vegan Flavor* is Nisha's best work yet! She shares tons of insanely delicious vegan recipes along with techniques and tips to make you a confident, creative plant-based cook. This book is an incredible resource for anyone who wants to make vibrant, nourishing meals that are PACKED with flavor."

—**Jeanine Donofrio,** *New York Times* bestselling author of *Love & Lemons Simple Feel Good Food*

"*Big Vegan Flavor* marries stunning photography with a master class on plant-based cooking. With her trademark precision and palpable joy for food, Nisha delivers not just big flavor, but big heart in this must-have addition to every cookbook collection."

—**Joanne Lee Molinaro,** James Beard Award–winning author of *The Korean Vegan Cookbook*

"A glorious celebration of the diverse world of vegan cooking and a wonderful resource."

—**Nik Sharma,** James Beard finalist, IACP winner, and author of *Veg-table*

"Nisha has a gift for creating incredibly satisfying and approachable dishes. In this book, she offers a mountain of useful information and insight, helping any home cook to maximize flavor and texture. The end result is a magnificent collection of recipes that you'll want to run to the kitchen and make."

—**Timothy Pakron,** author of *Mississippi Vegan*

"You can trust Nisha for thoughtfully composed and meticulously tested recipes. In *Big Vegan Flavor*, Nisha showcases the full breadth of the vibrancy and diversity that vegan cuisine has to offer. It is a must-have resource brimming with stunning photographs and practical tips that are accessible to any vegan home cook, from the early beginner to the seasoned professional."

—**Sheil Shukla,** author of *Plant-Based India*

Big Vegan Flavor

Big Vegan Flavor

Techniques
and 150 Recipes
to Master
Vegan Cooking

NISHA VORA

AVERY

an imprint of Penguin Random House

New York

AVERY

an imprint of Penguin Random House LLC
penguinrandomhouse.com

Photographs by Nisha Vora, edited by Rosana Guay
Lifestyle photographs on pages 5, 8, 10 (far left, third from left), 11 (third from
right, far right), 26, 29, 55, 56 (top right, bottom left), 59, 74, 83 (top right),
112 (top left), 129, 130, 144–47, and 590 by Niki Cram
Photograph on page 217 by Rosana Guay

Most Avery books are available at special quantity discounts for bulk purchase
for sales promotions, premiums, fundraising, and educational needs.
Special books or book excerpts also can be created to fit specific needs.
For details, write SpecialMarkets@penguinrandomhouse.com.

Library of Congress Cataloging-in-Publication Data

Names: Vora, Nisha, author.
Title: Big vegan flavor: techniques and 150 recipes to master vegan cooking / Nisha Vora.
Description: New York: Avery, an imprint of Penguin Random House, 2024. | Includes index.
Identifiers: LCCN 2023050411 | ISBN 9780593328934 (hardcover) | ISBN 9780593328941 (ebook)
Subjects: LCSH: Vegan cooking. | Cooking (Vegetables) | LCGFT: Cookbooks.
Classification: LCC TX837 .V669 2024 | DDC 641.5/6362—c23/eng/20231220
LC record available at https://lccn.loc.gov/2023050411

Printed in China
3 5 7 9 10 8 6 4

Book design by Ashley Tucker

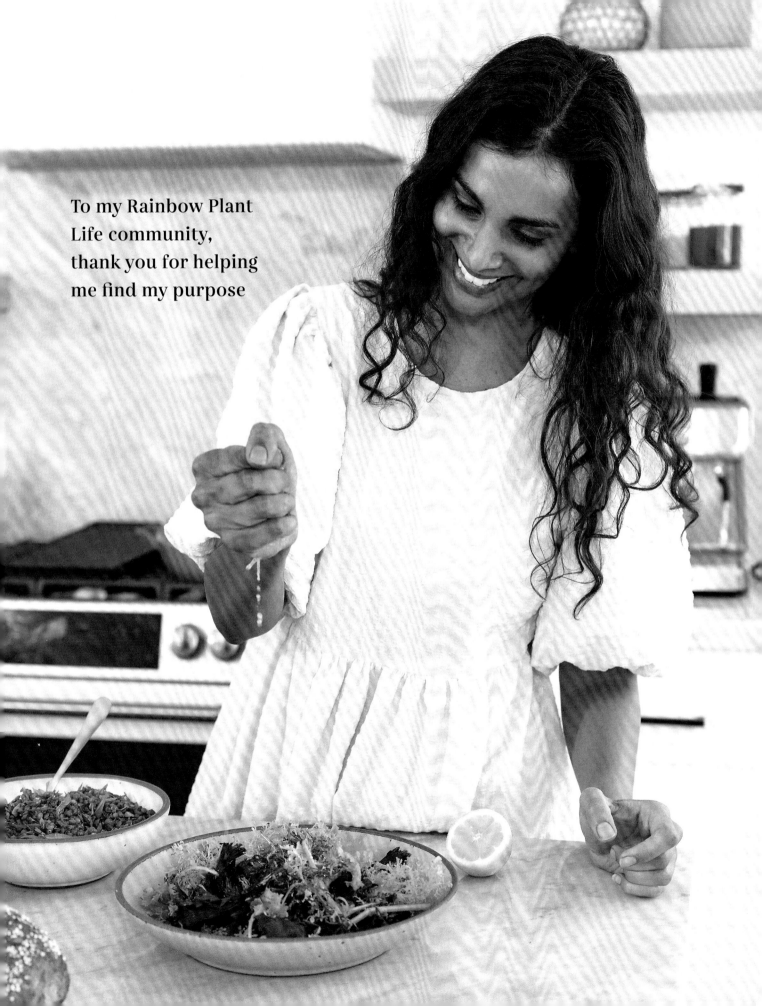

To my Rainbow Plant Life community, thank you for helping me find my purpose

Contents

Introduction

I have loved to cook for as long as I can remember. Well, at least since I was fourteen years old. That's around the time I traded in the usual teen hobbies (sulking and generally being emo) for cooking and baking. Most afternoons, I'd race home from school to watch the Food Network, pen and notepad in hand, ready to take notes. On the weekends, I'd turn down tantalizing invitations to garage parties and instead curl up in the cookbook section of Barnes & Noble (I was very popular in high school, thank you).

Over the next decade, I fell in love not just with cooking but with sharing food with others. I'd host decadent eight-course feasts with my friends and family, and regularly wow my college peers with meals that didn't resemble Hot Pockets. Later, I charmed my law school classmates with fancy baked goods.

So when I went vegan for ethical reasons at the age of twenty-eight, I assumed my love affair with food would come to an end. No more creamy pastas or cheesy concoctions, no more gooey chocolate desserts. I even gave up the pints of ice cream I ate to console myself after a stressful day in court (I was a lawyer back then).

From then on, I imagined I'd be sipping smoothies and eating quinoa bowls, salads, and whatever else Instagram circa 2016 was serving up. I planned to replace my seared slabs of meat with black beans, and that would just have to do. The values I was embracing were more important than a delicious meal.

Soon enough, though, I got tired of eating the same bland foods over and over. I was hungry for a new way of cooking and eating that could help me live aligned with my values *and* excite my taste buds. I was also literally hungry. Smoothie bowls are not meals.

This hunger is what pushed me to become a better cook. A *much* better cook.

Once I could no longer rely on the usual suspects—mountains of cheese and sticks of butter (yes, plural *sticks*)—I went back to the fundamentals of good cooking that I had learned as a teenager. From there, I started exploring how to layer the most flavor into my recipes using plant-based ingredients and how to treat vegetables as the star. I learned that, with the help of a few flavor boosters, I could re-create my favorite foods using staples like chickpeas and red lentils.

It didn't take long for me to realize that I had stumbled upon a new way of cooking that was more creative and more satisfying than anything I had ever cooked before. It was like a hidden treasure chest of superstar foods had just been unlocked: I could make cashews as creamy as heavy cream, and cabbage could become buttery.

I was discovering the abundance of delicious food in the plant-based world and so many unique ways to cook plants that it made my head spin, and I knew I was only scratching the surface.

With these realizations, my purpose began to crystallize. I knew I wanted to use my growing arsenal of cooking skills to inspire others to eat more plants and fewer animals.

But I wanted to do it in a fun, realistic, and balanced way. I didn't want folks to feel bad if they didn't sneak six vegetables into their "mac and cheese." I wanted them to enjoy the nostalgia of a truly indulgent mac and cheese, while also teaching them how to get the most flavor out of a head of cauliflower and a can of beans.

The more I honed this flavor-forward approach, the more my audience grew. And the more my audience grew, the more challenges I noticed folks were having when they went vegan. They missed their favorite foods and felt restricted by a diet that told them "lentils are a great substitute for meat" without showing them how to make lentils taste remotely meaty. And they felt not only misunderstood by family members who mocked their "rabbit food" diets but also detached from the food cultures they had grown up with.

So I started to spend hours, then days, and then years researching and testing the best ways to veganize comfort foods: how to make the best fudgy brownies and the best fluffy pancakes, how to best mimic the texture of scrambled eggs and Bolognese and paneer, and how to deliver universally loved flavors while using everyday plant-based ingredients.

I'd tinker in the kitchen day after day, mixing lentils or beans or tofu with just the right blend of savory ingredients until these plants started to feel like truly satisfying alternatives to meat.

And as a first-generation Indian American who grew up in Small Town America, I could relate to how isolating it felt when others didn't understand or appreciate the food you ate. So I became passionate about delivering that simple sense of normalcy to my audience, that ability to bring a wow-worthy plant-based dish to a family holiday dinner or a potluck without anyone batting an eye.

Along my vegan journey, I found myself reconnecting with a part of my culture I had long buried: Indian food, and my mom's cooking in particular. By my late twenties, I had finally recovered from the aggressive climate of assimilation in the '90s, the trite but hurtful "Your house smells like curry" jokes. I was ready to not only explore but embrace Indian cuisine and its array of plant-friendly dishes.

I'd find myself calling my mom, saying things like, "How was your day today? Cool. So, what spices do you use in your dal?" Eventually, though, I didn't need to hide behind a pretext. I'd just text her, "What do you put in your chana masala that makes it taste better than mine?" only to receive a phone call thirty seconds later. "*Beta*, it would take me an hour to text this. Okay, so first, you have to use black tea . . ."

Of course, my mom never gave me any actual "recipes." Though she's been cooking for over four decades, she's never owned a set of measuring cups. She measures ginger by the length of her fingers and tomatoes with the palm of her hand. She eyeballs spices and even fiery chile peppers.

But from these informal cooking lessons, I developed an appreciation for intuitive cooking. I learned to cook by **sight** (*wait until the oil oozes out of the tomatoes when you're making a masala*, I remember her saying), by **smell** (*when the garlic starts to smell nice, it's time to add in the ground spices*), and by **instinct** (*don't ever trust a recipe that says to cook the onions for 2 minutes; you can't do anything to onions in 2 minutes*).

I didn't know it then, but my mom's approach to cooking began to spark the *why* and *how* for me. I started to ask, *Why* does cooking onions for 10 minutes instead of 2 minutes make the entire dish taste better? And *how* does adding lemon juice at the end make the food pop?

As a book-smart nerd with a lifelong passion for learning, I genuinely enjoyed geeking out on food science. But it also brought me closer to my mission as a content creator. Not only could I deliver to Rainbow Plant Life viewers and readers flavor-packed vegan recipes that would impress their loved ones, I could also equip them with a new approach to cooking, one that would enable them to whip up incredible meals using intuition and creativity.

Which is why, in my videos and blog posts, you won't find just a recipe with measurements. When you try my chickpea curry recipe, for instance, you will also learn *why* blooming whole spices makes a big difference and *how* to prevent ground spices from burning.

In many ways, this book is an extension of the work I do on YouTube, my blog, and social media, but in a different form. It's the distillation not only of everything I now know about cooking maximally flavorful vegan food that anyone—vegan or not—will enjoy, but of years of learning how to share that information with home cooks in a fun, approachable way.

The big-picture principles in this book, as well as the recipes, will help you master how to build big vegan flavor, how to balance and pair flavors so you can reliably cook really good food without a recipe, and how to re-create your favorite food textures using plants. The *why* and *how* peppered throughout this book will guide you on a Tuesday night as you whip up a clean-out-the-fridge meal and on a summer afternoon when you decide it's a good time to veganize your grandmother's famous blueberry pie recipe.

My goal in writing this book is to educate, energize, and excite cooks who are interested in eating more plants, from the plant curious to full-fledged vegans. And my hope is that this book will help you become more confident in the kitchen and feel empowered to cook the best possible vegan food. And maybe, just maybe, even fall in love with this creative, abundant way of cooking and living.

I still pinch myself that my job is to teach home cooks how to cook incredible vegan food. Thank you to everyone in the Rainbow Plant Life community who has helped me embrace my childhood passions in a way I couldn't have imagined was possible.

With my deepest love and gratitude,
Nisha

My Approach to Vegan Cooking

y main goal has always been to encourage as many people as possible to eat more plants and, as a result, fewer animals. I am overjoyed when a reader shares that my recipes helped them adopt a plant-based diet, but I also know that most folks who make one of my recipes won't go vegan. And that's okay.

Eating plant-based even once a week has a huge impact. If all Americans did "Meatless Monday" for just a year, it would save a billion and a half animals, at least a hundred billion gallons of water, and seventy million gallons of gas.

But convincing totally random people on the internet to eat less meat and dairy is really hard. And I get why.

For one thing, animal products are in nearly all our favorite foods, either obviously so or secretly lurking (why do so many crackers contain milk?). We've also been conditioned to revolve our meals around meat and to include a generous helping of dairy.

And then there's the widespread stereotype that vegan food is bland and boring. If I'm being honest, vegan food *can* be bland and boring. I've made recipes that taste like bird food and hippie commune food from the '70s. I've tried making the healthiest plant-based version of recipes, cutting out all the gluten, sugar, and oil (and as a result, all the flavor and fun).

It was only once I started approaching vegan cooking from a flavor-forward mindset that it became easier to get others on board.

Instead of asking, "How many vegetables can I fit onto this plate?" I started asking, "How can I build flavor at every step of the cooking process so that this vegetable tastes as delicious as possible?"

Once I put this philosophy into practice, my cooking shifted dramatically. I stopped making things like zoodles masquerading as pasta and instead focused on hyperflavorful dishes with global inspiration. My partner loved our meals so much that he switched to eating meat just once a week instead of at every meal. And the more I have embraced this big-flavor approach, the more my readers (both vegan and omnivore) have come back to my recipes to feed themselves and their families.

With each recipe I create, my goal is always this: make it as flavorful as possible.

You Can Be More Creative in the Kitchen with Plants

Plants offer endless possibilities for exciting your creativity and imagination, much more so than when you cook with animal-based ingredients. If you start with a pork roast or a chicken breast, for example, there are only so many methods you can safely use to prepare it before things start to get risky. The rest of the meal is about *well, what can I serve this hunk of animal flesh with?* The side dishes are an afterthought.

If you start with vegetables, though, you have so many more vantage points from which to jump-start the creative process. Let's take beets as an example.

1. You could start with **seasonality**. If it's early spring, your beets will be small and only mildly earthy, and the greens perfectly tender and delicate. If it's late summer or fall, your beets will be larger and earthier (see Joshua McFadden's excellent cookbook *Six Seasons* for more on this guiding principle). Knowing this will help guide your cooking.

2. Or consider whether you'd like to have the beets **raw or cooked**. This is almost never a question you can even ask when you're preparing animal foods in a home kitchen. If you're going for a light and crunchy salad, raw beets are perfection; for something heartier, cooked beets will satisfy.

3. Try approaching the beets from a **cooking technique** perspective: *Do I want to steam, roast, steam roast, grill, sauté, parboil then roast, braise, blanch, fry, or even salt roast the beets?* See? So many options!

4. Think about **flavors** you've enjoyed paired with beets before. Maybe you love them with walnuts or arugula; try the Creamy & Crunchy Beet Salad with Crispy Fennel Crumbs (page 377).

5. Consider the **role** you want the beets to play in your meal. For main dish status, think big: smoke them over a BBQ, mix them with beans or rice to form a burger patty, or roast, tear, and glaze them (see the Glazed Torn Beets with Pistachio Butter & Mint, page 395). To use them as a base, layer

cooked beets in a salad or thinly shave roasted beets to make a beet "carpaccio." Or show off their vibrant color by roasting and pureeing them into risottos, pasta sauces, or gnocchi dough. You can even jazz up your condiments and puree beets into hummus or tahini sauce.

So go ahead: Pamper your plants with a bold marinade (try the Pomegranate-Glazed Tofu on page 277 or Mushroom Shawarma on page 532), or brine them until perfectly tender (Miso Butter–Seared King Oyster "Scallops" on page 537). Braise your vegetables in wine ("Cream"-Braised Leeks with Crispy Bits on page 414) or in olive oil (Braised Carrots & Chickpeas with Dill Gremolata on page 419). Rub them lovingly with a freshly ground spice blend or homemade seasoning, or cook them down until they become unbelievably tender (Jammy Roasted Eggplant on page 339).

Sear your veggies until caramelized (Citrus-Braised Fennel with White Beans on page 398), or experiment with nontraditional cuts, like "steak cuts" for broccoli, cabbage, or cauliflower (page 421). And if you're feeling frisky, try deep-frying (Buttermilk Fried "Chicken" on page 524), bake them in salt (Hannah's Carrot Lox on page 431), or infuse them with smoky char.

Plants spark endless inspiration! Let's treat them like the kings and queens they are.

What You'll Find in This Cookbook

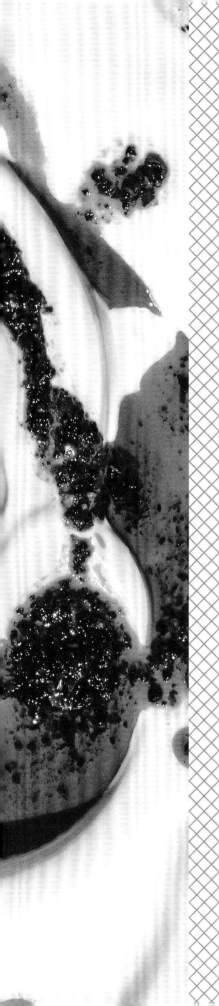

With this book, I hope to make flavor-forward vegan cooking easy and approachable for your everyday life, as well as to give you a collection of wow-worthy recipes you can rely on time and again for every occasion.

In part 1, you'll find techniques for building maximal flavor and achieving craveable food textures using plants, and practical tips for the modern home cook. My goal is to help you unlock the best that vegan food has to offer and also to help you feel like a badass in the kitchen so you don't have to always rely on a formal recipe (even if it eventually puts me out of a job!).

In parts 2 and 3, you'll find more than 150 globally inspired recipes, with a few comfort-food favorites remixed. In part 2, you'll find four chapters of what I call "building blocks," which are condiments, proteins, grains, and vegetables that you can mix and match during the week to make cooking breezy and genuinely delicious.

At the end of part 2, you'll find a guide on how to use these chapters to make meal planning fun and tasty.

In part 3, you'll find a whole host of exciting recipes for every occasion, from hearty salads to show-stopping main courses to weekend brunch eats. And at the very end, you'll find suggested menus for the fancy times in your life.

Throughout the book, you'll notice easy-to-customize charts and recipes remixed a few ways so you can personalize meals based on your favorite flavors and what you have on hand.

Along with each recipe, you'll also find lots of useful information, such as:

Ingredient Notes:

Notes specific to an ingredient used, including recommended varieties, substitutions, where to purchase it, and the optimal season for the star vegetable or fruit.

Tips:

Tips related to the cooking technique, recommended cookware, how to store leftovers, and so on.

Use It for Big Flavor:

How to use flavor boosters, sauces, and dressings to dial up the flavor in your meals.

Big-Flavor Meals:

Suggestions for how to turn lighter recipes into full meals or how to pair them.

Make Ahead:

What you can prep or make ahead of time.

Easy Variations:

Swaps you can make in a recipe to tailor it to your liking and based on what you have on hand.

Allergen Markers:

These markers indicate if a recipe is free of gluten (**GF**), tree nuts or peanuts (**NF**), and/or soy (**SF**), or if it has the option (**O**) of being so. For instance, a recipe that's gluten-free, soy-free, and has a nut-free option will say **GF, SF, NFO**. Where a substitute won't significantly alter the recipe, suggested substitutes are offered.

Maste

PART 1

Cook

ring

Vegan

ing

Back when I was a lawyer and trying to figure out how not to be a lawyer, I took one of those online career assessments that recommends a profession for you based on your interests, strengths, and skills. An hour later, the algorithm spat out, with 95 percent confidence, a recommendation I did not expect: I should become a teacher in the creative arts.

I sat there in disbelief. Was I supposed to teach children how to paint? I had no experience with or interest in painting, or in children (or in painting children, for that matter).

But, nearly a decade later, I have to admit that the assessment was accurate. Because these days, I make a living teaching people how to cook, a skill that arguably falls under the creative arts. And I *love* teaching.

Which is why the next four chapters are my favorite part of this book. I mean, the recipes that follow in parts 2 and 3 are also wonderful (in my humble opinion), but this part—part 1—is where you'll get more than just a collection of recipes.

I think of this section as an education in vegan cooking, but more lighthearted and without any pop quizzes. It's designed to help you become a better home cook so that you can ultimately cook intuitively without a recipe.

Everyone has that one friend who possesses the enviable skill of being able to comfortably whip up impressive meals in any kitchen, even with a full glass of wine in hand and even when the host has forgotten half of the grocery list. Read the next four chapters, and soon enough, *you* will be that friend.

Chapter 1 covers a few basic principles of good cooking that are particularly important when you don't add meat or dairy products into the equation. Incorporating these into your arsenal will enhance your ability to improvise in the kitchen.

Chapter 2 takes a deep dive into the flavor profiles that animate our favorite meals, from savory and sweet to spicy and tart. It's packed with ideas on how you can build big global flavors using plant-based ingredients and how you can draw out the most flavor from ordinary ingredients like beans and garlic.

Chapter 3 focuses on texture, and how to leverage certain techniques and ingredients to deliver the best food textures: creamy, crunchy and crispy, and chewy.

Chapter 4 features an array of practical cooking tips, from recommended vegan pantry staples and cookware to strategies for getting the most out of your produce.

I recommend reading part 1 from start to end, then returning to the concepts that pique your interest. Fellow nerds, take notes. Everyone else, just have fun with it and cook up incredible meals for your favorite people (and of course, for yourself).

1

The Basic Principles

This chapter outlines the principles of good cooking I've learned in the twenty years since I started my culinary journey, as well as from my constant trial and error in the Rainbow Plant Life kitchen.

These pillars are useful for any kind of cooking, but when you can't rely on a seared steak or a ton of parmesan as a culinary crutch, the fundamentals become all the more important. The techniques that are often overlooked or skipped in standard home cooking can make a world of difference when you're cooking plant-based, taking dishes from "It's good enough for vegan food" to "It's great, period."

Use the Best, Freshest Ingredients You Can Find and Afford

If you'd like to become a better cook without having to learn a single new skill, there's one thing you can do: shop at a farmers' market. The produce is locally grown and in season, which means it's fresher, sweeter, riper, and even more nutritious.

If you've ever eaten a supermarket beefsteak tomato in winter, you may rightfully think tomatoes are mealy, watery blobs with squishy yet firm insides. But a locally grown heirloom tomato in August? A tomato at the peak of its season is unbelievably sweet, juicy, even meaty, and melts in your mouth.

And using seasonal produce when possible and affordable makes a huge difference in vegan cooking in particular. After all, if your main dish is a broccoli steak, it better be a damn good broccoli.

Even if you don't have access to a farmers' market, shopping in season at the grocery store still pays off. Buy zucchini in January and it'll taste like watery cardboard; come July, though, you'll get sweet nuttiness.

Let chapter 9 (Big-Personality Salads) and chapter 10 (Vegetables Are the Main Event) inspire you. While most of the recipes in these chapters are tasty year-round, some are particularly magical during the ingredients' peak seasons. Try the Garlicky Asparagus & Beans with Lemon-Infused Olive Oil (page 379) in spring or the "Cream"-Braised Leeks with Crispy Bits (page 414) in winter.

You can check what's in season in your region by doing a simple Google search (e.g., "When is fennel in season in New York?") or use the website seasonalfoodguide.org.

Layer Flavors

Layering flavors is a vague phrase that reminds me of American sayings like *shooting the breeze* or *Monday-morning quarterback*. As the child of immigrants, I didn't learn any American phrases growing up, so I feel it is my duty to give a simple example of what "layering flavors" actually means, because in cooking, especially plant-based cooking, layering flavors is everything.

Consider a lentil ragù

To make this dish, the easiest option would be to toss your onions, garlic, tomato paste, herbs, salt and pepper, and lentils into a pot, cover them with veg broth, and simmer. While a one-step ragù sounds nice (so easy!), this will undoubtedly produce a one-note ragù that no one will want to eat.

Instead, start by heating up olive oil in a pot. Add the onions, season them with a pinch of salt, and cook until they are deeply browned.

> *Cooking the onions separately and seasoning them with salt draws out their water and enhances their innate sweetness; cooking them until well browned unleashes their natural umami. That's the first layer of flavor.*

Add the garlic, fresh herbs, and tomato paste and briefly sauté.

> *This releases the herbs' volatile oils and the garlic's aroma. It also coaxes out the umami and sweetness from the tomato paste. More layers of flavor.*

Next, deglaze the pan with some red wine and let it bubble for a few minutes.

> *This picks up those browned flavor nuggets from the bottom of the pan and releases them back into the ragù. It also enhances the tomatoes' acidity and the lentils' meaty earthiness. Even more flavor.*

Add the lentils, tomatoes, and broth and season with salt and pepper. Simmer away. When it's time to finish the ragù, add a spoonful of aged balsamic vinegar.

The tangy vinegar adds a subtle sweet zing, makes the lentils taste meatier, and rounds out all the previously developed flavors.

Last, season with salt and pepper to taste.

This final layer brings out the essence of each ingredient a little more.

When you build different layers of flavor before introducing the main ingredient (in this case, the lentils), you add much more complexity and interest to a dish.

DEGLAZING: A SECRET WEAPON

Whether you are braising a vegetable or building a soup or sauce base, deglazing is an easy technique to add rich flavor profiles in plant-based cooking.

Deglazing simply means adding a liquid—broth, wine, vinegar, citrus juice—to a hot pan, and then using the bubbling liquid to help you scrape up those pieces of food and browned bits stuck to the bottom of the pan. Once loosened, these flavor nuggets melt into the background of your dish, lending a more dynamic flavor.

The best tool to use is a flat-edged wooden spoon, along with arm muscle. You'll get more deglazing action (and flavor) if you are using a well-loved pan, especially cast iron, enameled cast iron, or stainless steel, as opposed to a shiny new nonstick pan. When deglazing with alcohol, cook until the liquid has almost evaporated and the smell of booze has dissipated.

Certain flavor compounds are alcohol soluble, so a splash of alcohol unleashes more of their flavor—that bit of wine or vodka releases flavor compounds hidden in tomatoes, for example. Cooking with wine also concentrates its natural acids and sugars, making it a more powerful source of tartness and subtle sweetness. But if you prefer not to cook with alcohol, check out the substitutes on page 59.

Choose the Right Salt, Season Often, and Taste as You Go

I don't own a saltshaker, but you will find several containers of salt scattered around my kitchen. Kosher salt sits near the stove ready to be used in almost everything, along with everyday sea salt. Tucked in a cabinet you'll find the pricier stuff: sustainably harvested Celtic

SINCE 1886

Diamond Crystal

Pure and Natural
KOSHER
SALT

THIS SALT DOES NOT SUPPLY IODIDE,
A NECESSARY NUTRIENT
NET WT 48 OZ (3 LB) 1.36 kg)

SELINA NATURALLY.

1976
CELTIC
SEA SALT.

JACOBSEN
SALT CO.

Maldon
EST 1882

Maldon
SMOKED
SEA SALT

PURE FLAKE SEA SALT

Netarts Bay, Oregon, USA

NET WT 4oz (113g)

This salt does not provide iodide, a necessary nutrient

BURLAP & BARREL
SINGLE ORIGIN SPICES

Kiln-Fired
BLACK
MINERAL
SALT

UTTAR PRADESH, INDIA

Seasonello®
From the island
of Sardegna, Italy

Fine iodized sea salt
This salt supplies iodine,
a necessary nutrient

For all your dishes

CABE

sea salt and large-flake sea salts from Maldon and Jacobsen. There's also smoked sea salt, used occasionally to draw out an ingredient's meatiness, and kala namak, which I use for its distinctive eggy flavor.

Why go through all that trouble just for salt, an ingredient that provides zero sustenance? Well, as many very famous actual chefs have noted before me, **salt is the one ingredient that makes food taste the most like food.**

Salt unlocks aromas and flavors that might otherwise lie dormant, and it can do this at various stages of the prep and cooking process.

Cut a slice of tomato and taste it plain. Then sprinkle it with sea salt and taste it again. Does the tomato taste sweeter? Brighter? Fruitier? More like a tomato should taste?

Types of salt

Diamond Crystal kosher salt is my go-to salt. It has a light, flaky, pinchable texture that gives you the most control over how much salt you add (try pinching table salt; it slips through your fingers). And it's about half as salty as table salt and some sea salts, tablespoon for tablespoon, giving you more control over how salty your dish tastes. It's also cheap and doesn't have the tinny aftertaste that table salt has.

HOW TO SUBSTITUTE DIFFERENT SALTS

- If a recipe calls for kosher salt and you're using sea salt or table salt, always use less salt to avoid a too-salty dish.

- When using **fine sea salt** or **Morton kosher salt**
  1 teaspoon DC kosher salt = ½ teaspoon + ⅛ teaspoon salt (½ heaping teaspoon)

- When using **table salt**
  1 teaspoon DC kosher salt = ½ teaspoon salt

I use **fine sea salt** in uncooked foods like salads, where its quality makes a difference, and desserts, where I want fine salt crystals to dissolve.

For finishing, I look to **flaky sea salt**, which adds a delicate salty crunch and makes virtually any food shine even more.

If you wait to salt your dish until right before you eat it, you're likely to end up with a dish that is either bland or too salty.

In contrast, if you season with a bit of salt during various stages of the cooking process, you'll get a well-seasoned dish with nuance and complexity. That's because salt enhances the flavor of other ingredients and makes them taste more like themselves (remember that tomato from page 33?).

So try to taste for salt at every opportunity you get. And by "taste for salt," what I really mean is "taste for *seasoning*." Is there enough salt to help the other flavors shine? To tame any bitterness? To balance sweetness or fieriness?

By the time you sit down to eat, the dish should be perfectly seasoned. Hence, no need for a saltshaker at the table (though I always welcome accompaniments like pickled vegetables, hot sauce, or yogurt).

A health note about salt: An overwhelming majority (75 to 90 percent!) of dietary sodium in the US comes from processed foods and dining out, not from cooking at home with salt. Also, if you are concerned about using non-iodized kosher salt, consider an iodine supplement or a multivitamin, try an iodized sea salt, and/ or add more seaweed to your diet (a few recipes in this book will help you do that).

Take a look at the Lemony Pasta with Sausage & Broccoli (page 502). You'll notice the steps instruct you to add salt (or a salty ingredient) five times while making this dish. The first instance is when you make the lemon vinaigrette. The second is the pasta water, which gets salted because those dense tendrils need to be flavored from within and because the pasta water is used to emulsify the sauce (and we want flavor in our sauce). Third, the broccoli stems and garlic get a pinch of salt to mellow their bitterness. Fourth, capers are added near the end for a salty bite. Finally, the dish is seasoned with a pinch of salt at the end to accentuate all the flavors.

The result is not a salty dish but a light yet indulgent pasta that is well balanced and well seasoned.

MORE TIPS FOR COOKING WITH SALT

When to season with more salt:

(1) the flavors of the ingredients aren't popping; (2) the flavor fades quickly after you take a bite; (3) a dish tastes too bitter; (4) you want to add complexity to sweetness; (5) you want to enhance the tart flavors in a dish.

How to avoid oversalting:

(1) Use Diamond Crystal kosher salt in most cooking. That's the salt I used in testing the recipes in this book (unless sea salt is specified). (2) Start slowly and season with a little bit of salt at various stages instead of adding a lot of salt at once, especially at the end.

Help, my food tastes too salty!

Salad: Add more unseasoned greens or veggies, or supplement with cooked grains.

Soup: Add water or plant milk, and finish with a drizzle of olive oil.

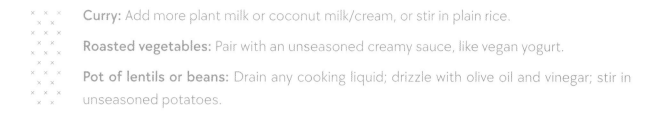

Curry: Add more plant milk or coconut milk/cream, or stir in plain rice.

Roasted vegetables: Pair with an unseasoned creamy sauce, like vegan yogurt.

Pot of lentils or beans: Drain any cooking liquid; drizzle with olive oil and vinegar; stir in unseasoned potatoes.

Remove Excess Water from Your Ingredients

Everyone agrees that watery food is not good food. But some plant foods are super watery, so taking the time to ensure your ingredients are not a soggy mess is even more important when cooking vegan.

The key is to extract the excess water. Generally, this not only improves the ingredient's texture but also concentrates its flavor.

In many of my **tofu** recipes, you'll see instructions to press or squeeze the tofu because if you want that elusive crispy texture and golden crust, you have to remove as much water as possible. With less water weighing it down, tofu can not only crisp up but also better absorb the flavors of the marinades, spices, and sauces it's cooked in.

In the smashed cucumber salad on page 365, you'll notice the **cucumbers** get salted first. This is because cukes are long blobs of water, and salting them expels some of it, making them crunchier vehicles for absorbing tasty sauces.

Same thing goes for **tomatoes**. If you're making a salsa, salting the tomatoes first not only makes it less watery but also makes the tomato meatier, with more tomato essence.

When you sauté **onions** in oil, you extract water, helping the onions brown more and intensifying the natural sugars, which makes the onions taste sweeter and more complex.

2

Maximizing Flavor

When I first went vegan, let's just say my cooking would not have been described as flavor-forward. Or even flavor-adjacent. Mostly because I was cooking by subtraction and simple substitution.

Subtract the chicken thighs. Replace with lentils.

Subtract the butter. Replace with olive oil.

Subtract the cheese and yogurt and cream and fish sauce and anchovies. Full stop.

But once I reframed vegan cooking as *distinct* and *unique*, not *less than*, my approach changed.

Instead of relying on meat and dairy to carry the day, I started finding ways to jazz up vegetables, grains, and legumes using flavor bombs I had never even considered, like pomegranate molasses to perk up a pot of beans and tahini to creamify lentils. I started devising little techniques to deliver the flavors I craved and loved—salty, sweet, savory, tart, spicy, herby, and fatty—in a plant-based way.

And as I began writing this book, I came to a realization. Whether I'm meticulously developing recipes in my office or just throwing together a weeknight dinner, I consult a cast of supporting characters to make plant-based staples—beans, lentils, tofu, grains, and vegetables—taste fresh and exciting.

The precise identity of these characters changes based on the lead actor. Is it fennel or oyster mushrooms? French green lentils or white beans? Considerations like flavor profile and seasonality shape the dish, but this cast of supporting characters is always present.

In this chapter, I'll walk you through these essential ingredients (without any additional acting analogies, I promise). We'll talk about what they are and how you can use them on their own or in combination with one another to cook vegan food that is big on flavor. But first, an example.

Take the Indonesian-inspired Sweet & Sour Tempeh Peanut Stir-Fry on page 480.

The first thing I think about is **salt**. Like any dish, it needs to be well seasoned. So I'll plan to layer in salt at several points.

But I also want to maximize the savoriness, particularly in recipes where meat is ordinarily used or its **umami** flavor would be appreciated, like a stir-fry. Tempeh is already a good source of umami, but I want to draw out this flavor even further, so I add soy sauce to give the dish a deeply savory backbone.

Since there is a fair amount of richness in this dish, I want to make sure the sauce pops and feels fresh. When I think about which sources of **acidity** can be added to achieve this, lime juice makes good sense, as this is a Southeast Asian stir-fry. Then I remember that tempeh is quite bitter, so I double down on the acidity and also add tamarind paste, a common ingredient in Indonesian cuisine.

Next, I might think about which seasonings I can fold in besides salt, such as complementary **aromatics, herbs, spices,** and **chiles.** Scallions, ginger, and garlic start off the stir-fry, creating a flavor base for the vegetables and tempeh to come. Lemongrass and makrut lime leaves are added for their fragrant aroma and to help regionally locate the dish, ground coriander for citrusy warmth, and sambal oelek plus Thai chiles for fiery heat.

At this stage, I figure that some **sweetness** might be needed to balance the spiciness and acidity that have been added, so I spoon a little brown sugar into the sauce. Once again, I remember that tempeh is bitter, so I sprinkle in a tad more sugar than if I were using, say, mild-flavored tofu.

Somewhere along the way, I also think about how I can best deliver the flavors and textures of the dish. Usually, **fat** is an important vehicle to unlocking this. Here, a **cooking fat,** such as grapeseed oil, will not only draw out the fat-soluble flavors in the aromatics and spices but also transform rubbery blocks of tempeh into crispy browned nuggets.

Sometimes, I look to a **finishing or supplementary fat** to help the other flavors and textures mingle better (the free wine at an awkward office mixer, if you will) or to simply soften out the intensity of bold ingredients. In this case, peanut butter and roasted peanuts simultaneously add rich body and mellow out some of the spiciness.

In the end, some tried-and-true key ingredients help me turn hard-to-love, bitter, and crumbly tempeh into a crispy, multilayered, and well-balanced stir-fry in a kind of magical alchemy.

Now let's look at each "flavor" category these ingredients represent more closely. (For a discussion on salt, flip back to page 31.)

Umami

In science speak, umami is simply glutamic acid, a.k.a. an amino acid or protein building block.

In practical terms, umami is that **rich, deeply savory flavor** that is almost meaty and brothy but sometimes also a tad sweet. Building over time, it lingers on the tongue a bit longer than other flavors, brings a full-bodied mouthfeel, and adds to the complexity of almost any dish. Sometimes it's subtle, allowing other flavors—sweet, spicy, salty, bitter—to dance in harmony.

Unfortunately, this powerful flavor is often absent in plant-based cooking, to the detriment of our overall eating experience. From a purely flavor perspective, many meals will simply taste better with a source (or two) of umami layered in. And from an experience perspective, if we're told we're eating "vegan taco meat," yet what we're eating has absolutely no meaty flavor, it will most likely dampen our enjoyment of the food.

So I've made it one of my missions to explore different ways to draw out these savory flavors we all crave and love so much.

As you read this list, you may notice that many sources of umami are from East Asian cooking. While these are certainly some of the most delicious cuisines on the planet, I hope this book will inspire you to use these ingredients and apply these techniques in all kinds of recipes.

Plant sources
of umami

Seaweeds

In 1908, Japanese chemist Kikunae Ikeda discovered the distinct taste of umami not by chomping on a piece of meat or cheese but by eating seaweed (kombu, to be precise). He identified glutamate—an amino acid that naturally occurs in the body and in many foods—as the compound that gives kombu its delicious savory taste.

There's a wide variety of seaweed you can incorporate into your diet, but kombu and nori pack in a hefty dose of umami. Bonus: Seaweed is high in protein, omega-3 fatty acids, vitamins, and minerals like iodine and iron.

TIPS FOR BUYING: Asian markets have the most options; well-stocked grocery stores sell a few options. You can also buy seaweed online.

USE IT FOR BIG FLAVOR: Add a sheet of kombu to Asian soups and curries, homemade veg broth, a pot of rice, or even a pot of beans (it helps with digestion). Add dulse flakes or crumble nori into faux tuna salad or ceviche, or in dishes that typically contain anchovies.

RECIPES TO TRY: For savory broths, try the Miso Butter–Seared King Oyster "Scallops" (page 537) or Malaysian Curry Noodle Soup (page 468). Or check out the super-savory Fancy Caesar Salad (page 362), which gets a double hit of nori.

Mushrooms

Virtually all shrooms contain some umami, but dried ones—particularly shiitakes—are bursting with it. Thanks to their naturally meaty texture and depth of flavor, shrooms make an excellent meat substitute (skip to chapter 12 to satisfy your cravings for shawarma, fried chicken, and more).

USE IT FOR BIG FLAVOR: Steep dried shiitakes in water, then use the stock to add depth to sauces, broths, or soups. Or blitz dried porcini mushrooms into a fairy dust powder: a spoon of porcini powder will give dishes like chilis, ragùs, and stews more savory oomph.

Tomatoes

The longer you cook tomatoes, the more concentrated their savory flavor becomes, so tomato paste, canned tomatoes, and sun-dried tomatoes are great sources of umami.

Tomatoes *(cont.)*	**USE IT FOR BIG FLAVOR:** Unleash the true potential of tomato paste by cooking it down for a few minutes until it's dark red and caramelized, usually in oil along with aromatics, before any liquid is added. Fold sun-dried tomatoes into pastas, cooked greens, tomato sauces, and condiments for a pleasant chewiness.

Fermented foods **Plant sources of umami**	While glutamates exist naturally in certain foods like seaweed, they can also develop through the powers of fermentation and time. For instance, once soybeans are fermented into soy sauce or miso, they pack a serious savory punch. *Note:* Many of these fermented foods can be quite salty, so start slowly if they're new to you. **NUTRITIONAL YEAST:** You may already be familiar with good ol' nooch if you have experience with vegan cooking. Once brewer's yeast is fermented and then deactivated, you're left with these kinda dusty golden flakes that don't taste like much on their own. But when incorporated into cooking, nooch adds a cheesy, nutty, salty . . . dare I say subtle chicken-esque flavor? **USE IT FOR BIG FLAVOR:** Use nooch in cheese recipes and egg substitutes like tofu scramble, fold it into savory sauces and pastas, and sprinkle it into anything that needs a savory, slightly cheesy boost. When making a béchamel, stir some in after adding the plant milk. **MISO:** A Japanese fermented paste made from soybeans, salt, and a mold called koji; it may also contain rice, barley, or other grains. It's intensely savory, salty, a little sweet, and a tad funky. White miso (e.g., sweet or shiro miso) is my go-to for adding savoriness without overwhelming the delicate flavors of plants. I use it in East Asian recipes but also in sauces and marinades, dressings and dips, and cheeses for a background richness and very subtle cheesiness. Darker misos (e.g., red or brown) are more pungent, saltier, and funkier. A little goes a long way, and they're best in boldly flavored dishes.

TIPS FOR BUYING: A good brand that's widely available is Miso Master (they also sell soy-free chickpea miso), but you'll find a huge variety at Japanese markets. You can store miso in the fridge for basically forever.

USE IT FOR BIG FLAVOR: Cream white miso with softened vegan butter and add to mashed potatoes or cauliflower, or smear on baked sweet potatoes. Fold into vegan cheeses, like Whipped Tofu Ricotta (page 206). Mix miso and tahini to creamify lentils, or combine miso and vegan mayo and let your creativity guide you (add lime juice, ginger, and agave; or minced shallots and garlic with lemon juice).

SOY SAUCE AND TAMARI: I reach for soy sauce when I want to add saltiness *plus* savoriness because it introduces a depth and boldness that salt alone can't bring. I use it for obvious choices like Thai curries and Chinese stir-fries, but also unexpected things like BBQ sauce.

Tamari is a Japanese soy sauce that's typically brewed without wheat, so it's a great choice for gluten-free folks (though you should always check labels to confirm it's free of wheat). Compared to soy sauce, it tends to be a tad less salty and richer in soy flavor, but for my recipes, you can use them interchangeably.

USE IT FOR BIG FLAVOR: Use in virtually any stir-fry, but also to finish a tofu scramble and in homemade BBQ sauce.

TIPS FOR BUYING: At Asian markets, you'll find "light" soy sauce (usually Chinese, sometimes Thai). *Light* refers to color, not sodium levels. These are actually saltier than standard supermarket soy sauces (e.g., Kikkoman or San-J). If using light soy sauce, use a smaller quantity to avoid oversalting.

TEMPEH: Unlike its more popular cousin, tofu, tempeh is a good source of umami thanks to fermentation. This also makes it easy to digest, even for those afflicted with soy troubles. The flavor is meaty, nutty, and a little mushroomy. Skip to chapter 6 for tips on how to make this often-unloved ingredient taste delicious.

Plant sources of umami

UMEBOSHI PASTE: Found in Japanese cuisine, umeboshi are pickled, fermented ume fruits (like a plum-apricot hybrid) that are wildly sour and salty.

Umeboshi paste is the puree of that fruit, and it packs a concentrated punch of tart, tangy, funky savoriness. It's a transformative ingredient and makes savory foods taste richer and multilayered. It's great in recipes that call for fish sauce and anchovies, and I like using it in broths, sauces, marinades, and dressings. Plus, when you briefly fry it, it smells like bacon, so there's that. A little goes a long way.

USE IT FOR BIG FLAVOR: Stir in a bit at the end when sautéing mushrooms or toasting almonds or walnuts in oil. See a recipe that calls for anchovies or fish sauce? Try a tiny bit of this instead.

UME PLUM VINEGAR: The brine leftover from pickling ume. It's like vinegar's much more pungent and complex cousin: sour and almost fruity with a subtle oceany flavor, and salty as hell.

TIPS FOR BUYING: The brand Eden Foods sells both the paste and the vinegar. You can also find them at Japanese and some pan-Asian markets, or online.

CHINESE BLACK VINEGAR: The most common variety in the US is Chinkiang black vinegar, made from fermented sticky rice and grains. It's full-bodied with complex flavors from fermentation: mildly sweet and sour, funky and savory, malty and woody. Bonus: It's inexpensive and lasts basically forever.

USE IT FOR BIG FLAVOR: Use a splash to finish noodles or smashed cucumber salads, add to stir-fry sauces and braised tofu, or mix with equal parts soy sauce for a dipping sauce.

MIRIN: A fermented rice wine that often brings a je ne sais quoi to Japanese dishes. It's sweet but not like sugar, a bit tangy but not like vinegar, salty but not like salt, with a deep funky flavor and rich body. I use it in glazes, sauces, and stir-fries.

GOCHUJANG: This Korean staple is a lustrous red paste made from fermented soybeans, chile flakes, salt, and sticky rice and adds excellent spicy-savory-sweet flavor to tofu and tempeh, marinades, and sauces. Look for gochujang sold in plastic tubs, not "gochujang sauces," which have been thinned out with sugar and vinegar.

USE IT FOR BIG FLAVOR: Stir a bit of gochujang into vegan mayo and yogurt to make the easiest yet best sandwich spread, rice bowl topper, or dip for fries.

AGED BALSAMIC VINEGAR: Traditional balsamic is made from grape must aged in barrels for at least twelve years or up to twenty-five years and can only be made in two regions of Italy (Italians take food labels seriously). It's *very* pricey. On the opposite end is three-dollar imitation balsamic vinegar, which is watered down and sour. Don't buy it.

WHAT I RECOMMEND: Somewhere in the middle are the products labeled "Balsamic Vinegar of Modena IGP," which have been aged but not for as long. You can find these in the ten- to forty-dollar range. My go-to brand is Giuseppe Giusti—their red bottle has been aged for twelve years and is sweet, tangy, and full-bodied with a syrupy consistency. For a more affordable but still high-quality option, I like the Whole Foods Aged Balsamic Vinegar of Modena (1.16 density).

USE IT FOR BIG FLAVOR: Finish lentil and bean dishes with a drizzle to brighten and enhance their meatiness. Drizzle over salads, roasted eggplant or zucchini, fruit, and vegan cheese plates.

PRESERVED LEMONS: You might think preserved lemons offer just acidity (lemons = acid), but they are also savory thanks to fermentation. Even just a spoonful of minced preserved lemon adds a unique, hard-to-place lemony depth of flavor to stews, dips, and salads like the Spicy, Crunchy Kale Salad with Preserved Lemon Vinaigrette (page 374). More ideas for how to use them can be found on page 157.

OLIVES: Olives cured in brine or salt are particularly rich in umami. Their buttery, salty meatiness is great in condiments, veggie dishes, and pastas.

Cooked alliums	When onions are slowly caramelized, their sugars and amino acids are heated until they eventually break down, leading to beautiful browning and the development of glutamate (a.k.a. umami).
	When garlic is roasted, it undergoes a similar process and brings that beloved sweet-savory flavor. Black garlic (essentially fermented garlic) is a particularly potent source of umami.

Vegetables	While mushrooms and tomatoes reign supreme, other vegetables—including asparagus, broccoli, green peas, cabbage, and corn—offer small doses of umami, especially when roasted or grilled.

Nuts	Toasted walnuts are an umami powerhouse, while roasted and especially smoked almonds also dabble in umami territory.
	USE IT FOR BIG FLAVOR: Fold crushed toasted walnuts into meat substitutes, like taco or burger meat. Blitz roasted and salted pistachios in a spice grinder for cheesy, savory nooch-esque vibes (pistachio dust, if you will).

Miscellaneous	**VEGAN BROTH BASES,** such as the vegan "chicken"- or "beef"-flavored ones from Orrington Farms or Better Than Bouillon, are like vegetable broth on umami steroids. They're quite processed and salty, so I don't use them often, but they're very effective if you want to dial up a stew, soup, or faux meat dish. When using these instead of vegetable broth in a recipe, go easy on the salt.
Plant sources of umami	**KALA NAMAK:** Also known as Indian black salt, this is a volcanic rock salt from the Himalayas that's kiln fired and used often in South Asian cooking. It's a concentrated source of complex umami and brings a pungent eggy flavor to vegan egg alternatives like tofu scramble and savory pancakes. Smells funky but tastes great.

Miscellaneous
(cont.)

VEGAN WORCESTERSHIRE SAUCE: No anchovies are needed to make this super-savory, salty, tangy, and slightly sweet and spicy condiment. It's great at enhancing meat-adjacent ingredients like mushrooms.

SMOKED SEA SALT: Sprinkle before serving to intensify the meatiness of Mushroom Bacon (page 433), corn on the cob, and caramelized onions, or use it in marinades (try Hannah's Carrot Lox on page 431).

LIQUID AMINOS: These are similar in flavor to soy sauce, with a salty, savory, and almost yeasty flavor. Made from soybeans that have been chemically broken down into amino acids, they're naturally gluten-free. These are different from *coconut* aminos, which are fairly sweet.

LIQUID SMOKE: Lends an intense smokiness reminiscent of meats cooked over a grill. Start slowly because it's easy to overdo.

Tangy, Tart, and Sour

The first time I tried making chili with actual whole chiles, I was on the brink of devastation. My first taste was quite bitter. Had I burned the chile peppers when I toasted them? Added too much cocoa powder? Determined to salvage my first adult chili, I put on my tinkering hat.

A little sugar, some salt, then some more salt. *Definitely better, but it's still missing something.*

A few squeezes of lime. *Ohhh, so that's what it was missing. But . . . it could use more.*

A couple more squeezes. *Better. But it still needs something else.*

I scoured my pantry, wondering whether red wine vinegar is acceptable in a Tex-Mex recipe. *Well, let's see.* A couple of dashes went in.

Aha! Now that's a good chili.

The combination of two sour ingredients—lime and vinegar—turned my chili around, doing so many things at once: they mellowed the natural bitterness of the chile peppers, enhanced the savoriness of the tomatoes, and brightened the whole dish.

Whenever a dish tastes underseasoned, you might assume it is missing salt. But if it tastes one-dimensional or flat, consider adding acid. Whether it's vinegar or a mustard of sorts, lemon or lime juice, yogurt or mayo, or a generous glass of wine (the cook needs a drink, too), acid can make a dish sing.

Essential as they are, though, acidic ingredients are never the star of the show (I love Dijon mustard, but a meal it does not make). As a result, they're typically underused, and their absence is felt most sharply in vegan cooking, where you can't just slap a ton of cheese on something to mask its underwhelming flavors.

But if you get to know them, these magical tangy and tart foods will transform your cooking.

Using acids to balance and enhance other flavors

Acidic ingredients can both (1) balance flavors through nuance and (2) enhance flavors by unlocking different flavor profiles that might otherwise lie dormant. If you've read *Salt Fat Acid Heat* by Samin Nosrat, you already knew that (and if you haven't read it, why haven't you??).

How to balance flavors with acid

BRIGHTEN AND LIGHTEN RICH DISHES. Acid slices through fatty ingredients, making them taste less flat and heavy. This is why a crisp Sauvignon Blanc is lovely in a velvety risotto and why I finish rich curries with lemon or lime juice and creamy dishes like "Cream"-Braised Leeks with Crispy Bits (page 414) with perky Dijon mustard.

When in doubt, finish a fatty dish with a splash of acid that has a complementary flavor.

TIPS FOR COOKING WITH LEMONS AND LIMES

- Stick to freshly squeezed juice. It's brighter and tastes better than the bottled stuff, which has additives and is often bitter.

- To get the most juice, roll the fruit back and forth on the counter using your palm until it becomes softer, then use a citrus squeezer or reamer.

- If it's practical, juice your citrus shortly before using it to get the freshest flavor.

- Need to swap limes for lemons? Use a bit less, as lime is more acidic.

MELLOW SPICY FLAVORS. This is why raita, an Indian yogurt condiment, is the perfect pairing for fiery curries. The next time a dish makes you sweat, instead of reaching for sugar, try a splash of vinegar, a squeeze of lemon or lime juice, or a dollop of vegan yogurt. Sour is usually a more nuanced solution than sweet (nobody wants a bowl of sweet chili).

BALANCE BITTERNESS. If you were a fellow AP Chemistry nerd in high school, you know that bitter foods are alkaline, the opposite of acidic. So adding some acid to a dish can balance any bitterness.

That's why I always pair my tahini sauces with citrus: the acidity mellows the subtle bitterness of sesame seeds, leaving you with a smooth, nutty flavor. And it's why I almost always coat naturally bitter tempeh in tart sauces (see the recipes on page 293).

How to enhance flavors with acid

ACCENT SWEETNESS. The marriage of sweet and sour is what makes lemon desserts so irresistible (get your fix with the Lemon Corn Cake with Lavender & Rosemary on page 561). And the classic pairing of coffee (acidic) with chocolate (sweet and bitter) is what amps up the chocolatey-ness in some of the best chocolate desserts.

BOOST SALTY, UMAMI FLAVORS. Think of how a splash of vinegar perks up a plate of salty French fries. This is the reason I like to deglaze lentil and bean dishes with wine: the acidity intensifies the earthy savoriness and makes these legumes taste meatier. Or try the umami blockbuster Miso Butter–Seared King Oyster "Scallops" (page 537), where the umami in mushrooms gets amped up with hyper-tart umeboshi plum vinegar.

MAKE SOUR FLAVORS MORE DYNAMIC. Mixing a few types of acids makes for more complex dishes. For instance, in the Mushroom Shawarma (page 532), tart but sweet pomegranate molasses plays with the mouth-puckering acidity of lemon juice to make an irresistible marinade.

Try the Creamy Chickpea Spinach Masala (page 483). Taste it just before adding the lime or lemon juice, then again afterward. Does it taste complete? More balanced? Dollop with vegan yogurt. Does it taste more refreshing?

Make the Radicchio Salad with Ranch & Smoky Seed Sprinkle (page 389). Taste a raw radicchio leaf—be prepared, it will be wildly bitter(!), but after you coat it in the acid-heavy (and salt-heavy) dressing, you end up with a bold yet well-balanced salad.

Try the Dark Chocolate Mousse (page 577). It should be sweet and quite rich. Now top it with the tart raspberry compote. Does it feel lighter? Do you taste new flavors in the chocolate?

Plant sources of acid

×

Turn the page for the ingredients I use
again and again to add tangy, tart, and
sour flavors, as well as ideas for how to
incorporate them into your own cooking.

Lemons and limes	Lemons work well with so many diverse cuisines, from Indian and North African to Italian and Greek. When cooking Latin American and Southeast Asian dishes, limes make more sense.

Don't skip the citrus zest

While citrus zest is not bracingly acidic, often when you're cooking with citrus juice, you can also use the zest to boost the flavor. The zest—which is home to the fruit's natural oils—gives you a purer citrus, mildly floral flavor with a concentrated zing. Try using lemon and lime zest, of course, but also orange, grapefruit, and Meyer lemon zest. You'll find citrus zest used liberally in this book in foods as diverse as cakes, tofu marinades, and salads.

Plant sources of acid

SIMPLE WAYS TO USE CITRUS ZEST

- Finish roasted vegetables with a squeeze of lemon juice *and* a sprinkle of zest.

- When making a vinaigrette, pasta sauce, or pan sauce with citrus juice, fold in the zest toward the end.

- Grate lemon zest on top of hot pasta or salads right before serving, or fold it into toasted bread crumbs.

- After toasting whole spices and chile flakes in olive oil, briefly toast lemon zest, then pour the infused oil over beans, lentils, or grains.

- Add citrus zest to lighten up creamy sauces and dressings, including vegan mayo.

- Any lemon (or lime) dessert will always be better with the zest, not just the juice.

- Use a vegetable peeler to get lemon peel strips, then lightly fry them in oil. This amps up the flavor even more (try this in the Lemon-Garlic Brussels Sprouts with Rosemary on page 334).

Try the Macerated Berries with Basil & Mint (page 549). Taste the berries before adding the orange zest, then again afterward. Can you name what the orange zest adds? (I can't, but I know that it tastes better.)

TIPS FOR COOKING WITH CITRUS ZEST

- Since you're eating the peel, wash whole citrus fruits in cold water, then dry them. If you can afford it, you may want to opt for organic.

- Always zest first, then slice the fruit in half and juice it (zesting a halved lemon is tricky). Try not to zest too far in advance because the zest will dry out.

- A Microplane is the best tool for zesting, as it removes just the aromatic peel and not the bitter white pith that lies below it. In contrast, regular graters peel deeper into the fruit.

- When baking with lemon zest, massage it into the sugar with your hands first. This releases the lemon's oils (and flavor).

Vinegars (of all kinds)

Plant sources of acid

I say "all kinds" because my pantry has met its vinegar capacity: at any given time, I have rice vinegar, balsamic vinegar (two kinds), red wine vinegar, apple cider vinegar, sherry vinegar, champagne vinegar (also two kinds), Chinese black vinegar, and distilled white vinegar. Some people collect stamps, I collect vinegar.

You certainly don't need all of these, and if I had to pick just three, it'd be a nice aged balsamic vinegar for its sweet-tangy syrupy quality, unseasoned rice vinegar for Asian cooking, and distilled white vinegar for all things pickling. If you let me pick a fourth, champagne vinegar for vinaigrettes.

USE IT FOR BIG FLAVOR: Toss salads with a drizzle of your best-quality balsamic, champagne, or red wine vinegar for a zingy pop. Finish a pot of beans or lentils with a splash of vinegar to perk them up. Mix a vinegar with fresh lemon juice for more complex-tasting vinaigrettes; use white wine or champagne vinegar for delicate vinaigrettes, red wine for punchier ones.

Pomegranate molasses

When pomegranate juice is cooked down, its sweetness shifts to the background and it becomes mouth-puckeringly tart, almost like a vinegar. Commonly used in Persian and Middle Eastern cooking, it's a high-impact ingredient with bright acidity and tangy sweetness that brings a depth of complexity and plenty of pizzazz.

USE IT FOR BIG FLAVOR: Add pomegranate molasses to tahini sauces (page 197) or yogurt sauces, and pair it with veg like eggplant, zucchini, cauliflower, and sweet potatoes. Drizzle in a few spoonfuls to add depth to stews or tomato sauces. And combine it with other acidic ingredients like lime or lemon, sumac, or mustard for layers of brightness (try the Pomegranate Molasses Vinaigrette on page 165).

TIPS FOR BUYING: You can find pomegranate molasses at Middle Eastern markets, specialty grocery stores, and online. Buy "pure" pomegranate molasses made with 100 percent pomegranate juice (no sugar added). My favorites are Al Wadi Pomegranate Molasses All Natural and Eat Well Pomegranate Molasses.

Wine (and beer)

I wish I liked beer enough to cook with it, but most beers are too bitter for me, and unlike with bitter *food*, I can't add a splash of vinegar to an IPA.

So, let's talk wine, shall we? Wine, especially a crisp white or lighter-bodied red, is a natural source of acidity. As I mentioned on page 31, when you deglaze a pan with wine, it fortifies the flavor of the wine, adding a more layered form of acidity with a slight sweetness. Skip the "cooking wines" and use wine you'd actually drink. It doesn't need to be expensive. A ten-dollar bottle works. Use high-acid white wines like Sauvignon Blanc or Riesling to slice through rich dairy-esque dishes, like "cream" sauces and risotto.

And watch out for wines that are not vegan. One of the saddest days of my life was learning that many wines are filtered using animal products like egg whites. Use barnivore.com to check whether your wine is vegan. Natural wines, which are typically unrefined and unfiltered, are usually vegan.

Plant sources of acid

Tomato products

Tomatoes are a good source of both umami and acidity, making them a versatile ingredient. When it's not tomato season, I opt for canned tomatoes or sweeter cherry tomatoes, and focus on cooked tomato dishes.

TIPS FOR BUYING: In a tomato-heavy recipe, use the best-quality canned tomatoes you can get. Bianco DiNapoli is my favorite (sweet yet tangy), followed by San Merican and Cento. When I make tomato-forward recipes, I prefer to use whole peeled tomatoes, which have more pure tomato flavor. I crush them with my hands, which gives me more control over the texture. In contrast, canned diced and crushed tomatoes have additives and vary in texture depending on the brand.

Pickled things

As I've gotten older, my palate has moved in a tangy, pickled direction. Sweet potatoes topped with sauerkraut and pickled chiles instead of marshmallows? Yes, please!

Use the following ingredients to add a tangy sharpness to virtually any savory food, to make umami-packed foods taste even better, or to brighten fiery-hot food.

If you prefer not to cook with alcohol, there are substitutions that will work.

To replace red wine, add:

· a smaller amount of red grape juice or pomegranate juice (no-sugar-added varieties)

· or a bit of red wine vinegar.

To replace white wine, add:

· a smaller amount of white grape juice (a no-sugar-added variety)

· or a bit of white wine vinegar.

When using vinegars, dilute them in veg broth or water, about 1 part vinegar to 3 parts broth. You'll get similar flavors, though not the same complexity you'd get from wine.

Or, if a recipe calls for vegetable broth in a later step, you can deglaze with broth. Depending on the other flavors, consider adding a splash of vinegar or lemon juice to the broth, and/or finish the dish with a bit of vinegar or lemon juice (and lemon zest, if appropriate).

Pickled things (*cont.*)

Plant sources of acid

PICKLED VEGETABLES: I love pickled vegetables so much that I've given you a smorgasbord of them starting on page 168.

PICKLED JALAPEÑOS: No time to pickle peppers yourself? Jarred pickled jalapeños offer a one-two punch of acidity and heat. Perfect for nacho-flavored vibes.

Try the Extremely Easy Queso Sauce (page 199) before adding the pickled jalapeños, then after. Do they make it tangier? Saltier? Cheesier?

SAUERKRAUT: Sauerkraut makes my gut happy, plus its tangy crispness works great in salads, sandwiches, tofu scrambles, and even as a topping for tacos, cold pizza, and dal. To get the gut health benefits, buy refrigerated sauerkraut that says "raw," "live," or "probiotics."

CAPERS: Capers are tiny but mighty gems that bring tang and salt. I love their briny, funky punch in salads, pastas, vinaigrettes (like the Buttery Caper–Pine Nut Dressing on page 174), herby condiments like Italian Basil & Parsley Salsa Verde (page 181), and faux tuna salads. They may be even better when fried (page 167). I reach for them when a recipe needs a salty tang but salt and lemon juice/vinegar alone don't quite do it.

USE IT FOR BIG FLAVOR: Don't skip the caper brine. A little will perk up vinaigrettes, yogurt sauces, vegan mayo, and super-creamy pastas. Or add a spoonful to your pickling brine.

PRESERVED LEMONS: Preserved lemons are a great source of both umami and bright lemony flavor. See more on page 157.

OLIVES: I add olives to condiments, hearty stews, and red sauces when I want a pungent, pickled bite and/or a meaty texture.

Castelvetrano olives are a great gateway olive—mild in flavor, with a firm, almost crisp texture and buttery mouthfeel; perfect in any of the recipes in this book. Cerignola olives are another good option for olive skeptics, with a

Pickled things (*cont.*)	tender bite and a mild, buttery flavor. Kalamata olives are quite salty, a little fruity, and smoky—great in anything Greek.
Vegan yogurt	You'll find I use vegan yogurt in a lot of recipes in this book, usually to add a tart contrast, creamy texture, or cooling element to savory foods. I have strong opinions on yogurt, most likely because I am Indian and grew up with a gallon-size vat of tangy homemade yogurt on every dinner (and often, breakfast) table. A good vegan yogurt should (1) be plain and unsweetened (I have absolutely zero use for strawberry-rhubarb yogurt); (2) have a tart, tangy flavor; and (3) have a creamy texture. My current favorites that fit these criteria: Culina, Cocojune, GT'S Cocoyo, and Kite Hill Greek yogurt (all coconut-based except for the latter, which is a thick almond yogurt).
Dijon mustard	I use it in dressings to add a slightly spicy sharpness and to awaken creamy dishes without adding a "mustardy" taste. **USE IT FOR BIG FLAVOR:** Vinaigrette on the thin side? Squeeze in a bit of Dijon. It clings to oil and naturally emulsifies the dressing. Plus, it adds great flavor.
Sumac	Tart and lemony but also fruity with notes of cranberry, sumac is a ray of sunshine used in Middle Eastern and Persian dishes. I use it to make Za'atar (page 179) and perk up hummus and Whipped Feta (page 209), and sprinkle it over roasted chickpeas, salads, cucumbers, and melons. **TIPS FOR BUYING:** Find it at Middle Eastern markets, well-stocked grocery stores, and online.
Tamarind	Tamarind is a podlike fruit with a tangy, sweet flavor used across many cuisines. I buy tamarind paste or concentrate for ease. It adds a sweet-sour brightness to stews and curries and a zingy pop when used as a finishing agent, like in my Mom's Tomato-Garlic Chutney (page 192).

Sweet

Years ago, my partner Max and I quit our law firm jobs and backpacked around the world. Along our "eat-pray-love" journey, we spent a month in Vietnam, where we slurped down noodle soups and brothy stews while sitting on roadside plastic chairs.

We loved the food so much that we signed up for several cooking classes. To my shock, almost every recipe we were taught used sugar. Sugar went into the sweet-and-sour nước chấm dipping sauce, which made sense, but also into our phở and bánh mì, the chile oil, even into the meat stews (I was decidedly not vegan back then).

Yet none of these foods tasted sweet. They were savory, a little salty, bright, and fresh.

The sugar, I learned, was there to balance and round out the flavors. It made the noodles and stews taste more savory, it played off the bracing acidity of lime juice, and it tamed the heat of chiles. It made each dish a harmonious balance of salty, spicy, bitter, sour, and sweet.

Before traveling through Southeast Asia, I had rarely used sugar in my savory cooking. When I returned home, though, I found myself tinkering with sweetness in the kitchen more often. I tried being more generous with the sriracha, adding a spoonful of sugar to marinara sauce, and fixing my too-tart vinaigrettes with a dash of maple syrup.

Not to be dramatic, but the difference sugar made in my cooking was, well, dramatic. It not only rounded out the flavors but also dialed up their intensity and brought out new tastes I hadn't even experienced before.

Used thoughtfully and in small amounts, sugar in its many forms can make a recipe more delicious. It makes spicy food more tolerable, rounds out mouth-puckering citrus, and tames naturally bitter vegetables.

And sweetness doesn't just balance contrasting flavors. It can also help salty and savory foods reach their star potential. This is why cornbread is the ultimate pairing for the fried "chicken" on page 524—it has that sweet-salty-umami combo that the human brain is wired to crave.

In fact, many cuisine-defining ingredients have some amount of sweetness. Japanese miso and mirin are subtly sweet. Chinese Shaoxing wine and black vinegar are a mix of sweet, sour, and umami. Korean gochujang is sweet, salty, spicy, and savory. In Middle Eastern cuisines, pomegranate molasses is part tangy and part sweet, as is aged balsamic vinegar in Italian cuisine.

TIPS FOR COOKING WITH SUGAR

- If a savory recipe calls for a small quantity of cane sugar, you can typically sub another sugar, like coconut sugar (or a liquid sweetener like maple syrup or agave).

- In baking, substitutes are more challenging, since sugar adds not just sweetness but also moisture, chewiness, and structure. You can try subbing raw turbinado sugar for cane sugar, though the texture won't be as smooth. You can also sub coconut sugar for brown sugar, though you will get less perfect results in baked goods that rely on brown sugar for moisture, as coconut sugar has a sandier texture. If a recipe calls for coconut sugar, you can always use brown sugar.

Plant sources of sweetness

✕

This section features my go-to
ingredients for adding sweetness
to both sweet and savory foods.

Sugars

Long ago, the sugar industry decided that consumers could tolerate only extremely uniform, white granulated sugar, and since sugar doesn't naturally exist in this form, they decided to refine and filter it . . . through charred animal bones. So unfortunately, a lot of commercially made sugar in the US is not vegan. Here are some good alternatives to conventional sugar:

ORGANIC CANE SUGAR: Luckily, organic cane sugar is vegan, since certified organic products cannot include animal bone char. Unrefined or raw sugars are vegan as well. You can find these options at almost any grocery store. The crystals of organic cane sugar are a tad larger and are off-white in color (the horror!), but they work great as a 1:1 sub for granulated white sugar. Zulka and Whole Foods Fair Trade cane sugar are good alternatives that are not organic but still vegan.

I use sugar in small quantities to balance other flavors in savory foods where a neutral-flavored sweetness is desired (and in larger quantities when baking).

ORGANIC BROWN SUGAR: As with cane sugar, I use organic brown sugar in small amounts in marinades and sauces to balance other flavors. In baking, I prefer it over cane sugar when I want a more robust flavor and slightly more moisture, which is often lacking in egg-free baked goods.

ORGANIC POWDERED SUGAR: Organic powdered sugar works just like regular powdered sugar in icings and frostings but is vegan.

COCONUT SUGAR: Since coconut sugar has a lower glycemic index (GI) than cane sugar and small amounts of minerals, it is a common choice for a more healthful sugar (it's still sugar, though). It has a nice caramelly flavor.

Pure maple syrup

Maple syrup is my favorite liquid sweetener. I don't eat sugar for its health benefits, but maple syrup does have antioxidants, minerals, and prebiotics, so there's that.

Pure maple syrup (*cont.*)

USE IT FOR BIG FLAVOR: Use small amounts of maple syrup to balance tart vinaigrettes and yogurt sauces, as well as tahini sauces. Add a bit when roasting winter squash or carrots to highlight their natural sweetness. Add to tofu and tempeh sauces, as the caramelizing sugars help the tofu and tempeh brown better.

Agave nectar

Agave is my other go-to liquid sweetener. I use it instead of maple syrup when (1) I want a neutral flavor (maple syrup is more robust), and/or (2) I want a more viscous texture.

Dark chocolate

I love using dark or bittersweet chocolate in my desserts. Cacao content-wise, I tend to choose chocolate that hovers in the 65% to 75% range. If you go lower, you may need to add less sugar, and vice versa.

TIPS FOR BUYING: Always read the label to ensure no milk solids are lurking in your dark chocolate (*note:* "cacao butter" is totally vegan; it's just the fat from cocoa beans). Some brands of chocolate are certified vegan; others are incidentally vegan. A Google search can tell you which brands sell vegan-friendly chocolate.

Fresh and dried fruits

Plant sources of sweetness

Sweetness need not always take the form of added sugar because the fruit (and vegetable) world abounds with natural sugar. And this doesn't apply to just breakfast.

For instance, in the Rainbow Veggie Slaw (page 390), the star ingredient is juicy mango, whose sweetness shines vis-à-vis the tangy, anise-forward Green Goddess Dressing (page 182). In the Swiss Chard & Carrot Slaw with Crispy Bread Crumbs (page 385), pureed golden raisins offer the perfect amount of sweetness to meet the earthy, bitter flavors of chard.

If you make a salad that tastes too vegetal or bitter, try adding a bit of fresh fruit—thinly sliced apples or pears, tangerine segments, sliced stone fruit, or pomegranate seeds, depending on the season.

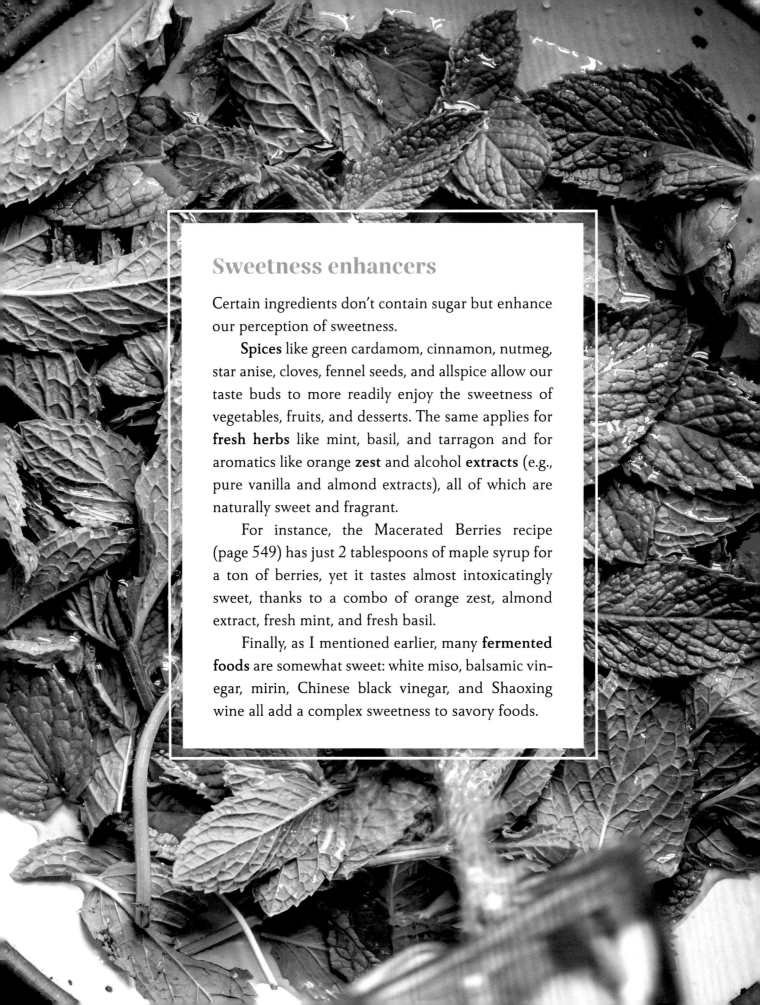

Sweetness enhancers

Certain ingredients don't contain sugar but enhance our perception of sweetness.

Spices like green cardamom, cinnamon, nutmeg, star anise, cloves, fennel seeds, and allspice allow our taste buds to more readily enjoy the sweetness of vegetables, fruits, and desserts. The same applies for **fresh herbs** like mint, basil, and tarragon and for aromatics like orange **zest** and alcohol **extracts** (e.g., pure vanilla and almond extracts), all of which are naturally sweet and fragrant.

For instance, the Macerated Berries recipe (page 549) has just 2 tablespoons of maple syrup for a ton of berries, yet it tastes almost intoxicatingly sweet, thanks to a combo of orange zest, almond extract, fresh mint, and fresh basil.

Finally, as I mentioned earlier, many **fermented foods** are somewhat sweet: white miso, balsamic vinegar, mirin, Chinese black vinegar, and Shaoxing wine all add a complex sweetness to savory foods.

Fresh and dried fruits (*cont.*)

And in the dessert realm, fruit has boundless potential, especially when you let seasonality guide you. In late summer, the Perfectly Sweet-yet-Tart Plum Galette (page 570) should definitely be on your menu. Come fall, you can swap in apples or make the Crispy Spiced Cobbler Cake with Pears (page 563). And when it's mango season, the Chai-Spiced Custard Tart with Mango (page 567) is my absolute favorite dessert.

Dates

The sticky chewiness of dates is spectacular, and they add supercharged sweetness. Their velvety body makes for incredible no-bake desserts that rival desserts made with eggs and dairy, like the Dark Chocolate Mousse with Raspberry Compote (page 577). I always use Medjool dates, which are much softer and blend more readily than smaller Deglet dates. You can roast dates in the oven to amp up their sweetness and chewiness even more (try them this way in Spice-Roasted Whole Carrots on page 329).

Vegetables

Some vegetables are naturally sweet (e.g., carrots). Others are not, but when cooked in certain ways, they do become sweet. Caramelized onions are the most obvious example, but even zucchini is subtly sweet when cooked down.

I like to let the seasons guide me as much as possible, as vegetables are sweetest when they are eaten seasonally. Think tomatoes and corn in summer, kabocha and butternut squash in fall, sweet potatoes and fennel in winter, beets and peas in spring.

USE IT FOR BIG FLAVOR: Pair sweet vegetables with contrasting tastes—salty, savory, bitter, sour, or spicy—for an explosion of flavors. Some examples: sweet corn with spicy garam masala and tart lime juice (Indian-Spiced Charred Corn Salad, page 383) or sweet heirloom tomatoes with a drizzle of umami-rich aged balsamic vinegar and flaky sea salt (page 361).

Plant sources of sweetness

Spicy, Herby, and Piquant

Spices, herbs, and chile peppers are true miracle ingredients that can transform your cooking, particularly plant-based cooking, where their impact is felt more dramatically. They infuse flavor, warmth, and dynamic energy into food, and my hope is that this section, along with the recipes in this book, will inspire you to fold these ingredients into your cooking more often.

Spices

I am blessed to have grown up in an Indian home where my mom effortlessly used spices in her daily cooking. I'm even more blessed that she has passed down some of her spice knowledge to me.

One evening, while I was writing this book, she invited me over to teach me her cilantro chutney recipe. There were no measuring spoons, let alone a digital scale, in sight.

"How much jeera [cumin] should I add?" I asked. She pinched her fingers together, then apart to show an imaginary amount that looked like a vast range to me. Mildly exasperated by my confusion, she grabbed a flatware teaspoon and said, "Like this much. One teaspoon." Her stainless steel dinner teaspoons most certainly do not hold the same quantity as standard measuring teaspoons, but I stopped trying to convince her of that years ago.

Measurements or no measurements, the chutney is always perfect. I can sense the cumin, but it isn't overwhelming. What I detect instead is that familiar and harmonious blend of grassy, spicy, and tart that my mom has been perfecting over decades.

"When you make tadka," she explained over the phone another afternoon, "you don't add all the spices at once. Mustard seeds always come first. Wait until they splatter."

"Splatter?!" I asked apprehensively.

"You know what I mean, *beta*. Wait until they sputter. Then, you add the cumin seeds. Add the curry leaves and dried chiles last so they don't burn."

"Do you add any other spices?" I asked. "Well, if you want to be a typical Indian," she said, emphasizing *typical* to suggest that I do not fall into this group, "you also add hing. Just a tiny bit. And make sure you hide it someplace so Max can't smell it."

But much of her spice wisdom is not something she can readily teach her overeager daughter.

One day at family brunch, when she made her beloved chai, redolent with spicy, sweet, and citrus flavors, I asked what spices she used. She rattled off seven different spices. When I asked her which spices are the most important, her eyes responded with, *What kind of question is that?*

I persisted. "Okay, but, like, if you had to pick just one, which spice would you say is the most essential in chai?"

"Fine . . . okay, green cardamom and ginger."

I pushed further, silently wondering why my mother isn't a walking encyclopedia of Indian cooking. "What would you say those spices add? Why are they the most important?"

"Just drink the chai, *beta*," she said. I grabbed the mug she'd made specially for me: oat milk, just a pinch of sugar. The cardamom is my favorite part.

×

While spices are intricately woven into the fabric of Indian food, they can electrify all kinds of cuisines and dishes.

Take the Mushroom Carnitas Tacos (page 540) as an example. A simple Mexican-inspired spice blend, along with the heat of the oven, transforms raw mushrooms into crispy, chewy packages brimming with smoky, spicy flavor.

Wherever you are on your spice journey, I hope that you'll find delight in the spices used in this book and be inspired to expand your spice cabinet.

Why you should toast your spices

The essence of a spice's flavor lives in its volatile oils. Heating a spice breaks down the flavor compounds in those oils, allowing the oils to recombine into new compounds.

So, toasting spices in a hot pan **adds complexity and introduces flavors that otherwise would be nonexistent.**

Heat also **intensifies a spice's potency**, making it taste bolder and more alive. Heat is what takes raw cumin seeds from slightly bitter and sharp to warm, nutty, and subtly citrusy.

Finally, toasting spices **masks bitterness** found in raw spices, which you may have discovered if you've ever made a chili and just plopped the raw spices into the cooking liquid. Instead, if you briefly toast the spices in the oil you use to cook the onions and other aromatics, you'll get a deeper, richer spiced flavor.

How to toast spices in oil (a.k.a. blooming spices)

Toasting or tempering spices in fat, such as hot oil or butter, is a hallmark technique of Indian cooking. (Depending on the region of India, this technique is called *tadka*, *vaghar*, *chhonk*, or *oggarane*.) But it can be used in so many other types of dishes, from Mediterranean lentil salads to East African stews to reimagined American desserts.

Most flavor compounds in spices are fat soluble, so toasting them in fat (as little as a couple of teaspoons of oil) brings those flavor and aroma compounds to the forefront. The hot oil extracts the essence of the spices, intensifies their flavor, and imparts that to the final dish. At the same time, the spices imbue the oil with their flavor. It's symbiotic magic.

You can bloom both whole spices (it makes the seeds delightfully crunchy) and ground spices (it makes them nutty and toasty). If you are using a mixture of both, add the ground spices last to avoid burning—they need just 30 to 60 seconds, sometimes less.

You can toast spices in oil just before serving a dish to make a finishing oil (e.g., a tadka). Other dishes benefit from toasting spices during the cooking process. For instance, in the Creamy Chickpea Spinach Masala with Tadka (page 483), you toast the cardamom, coriander, cumin, and cinnamon before adding the aromatics.

How to dry toast spices

While blooming spices in a fat will give you the biggest bang for your buck, you can also dry toast spices to release their flavor. You may want to dry toast spices in a few scenarios: You can grind toasted whole spices in lieu of using preground, either to add them later in the cooking process or to make your own spice blend (such as the Berbere Spice Blend on page 488). You can also *partially* grind toasted whole spices and retain some texture, which makes a nice coating for vegetables or tofu; or you can dry toast spices if limiting your oil intake.

Dry toasting is best with whole spices, as ground spices burn quickly (they need just 15 to 20 seconds).

To dry toast, place a skillet over medium heat and once hot, add your whole spices. Toast, shaking the pan or stirring frequently, until very fragrant and nutty and a bit darker in color, 1 to 3 minutes, depending on the type of spice and pan. Remove the spices from the pan (to prevent overcooking) and let cool. Easy!

When toasting spices that vary widely in size, add the larger ones first (e.g., star anise before cumin seeds).

How to incorporate spices into your cooking

TEMPER/BLOOM THEM. Again, I encourage you to add blooming spices to your repertoire, as it's an easy way to make your dishes more vibrant (and impress your friends, which is what cooking is really all about).

MAKE YOUR OWN SPICE BLENDS. These will likely be fresher than standard blends from the grocery store, and they're a fun way to experiment with flavor pairings. Start with simple

GRINDING SPICES

To grind whole spices, you need some tools. A **spice grinder** finely grinds them in mere seconds, and it is necessary if you want a superfine grind, especially for sturdy spices like cinnamon sticks. A **mortar and pestle** is a great alternative, as it gives you more control over the texture.

I recommend having at least one of these tools in your kitchen. You can also use a coffee grinder, but reserve it just for spices (otherwise, your coffee will taste like coriander).

If you don't have one of these tools or if you want to release the flavor of the spice but retain some texture, you can *partially* crush whole spices with the base of a small cast-iron skillet or a heavy mug, or by using a chef's knife to chop them. You can also place the spices in a resealable plastic bag and crush them with a rolling pin or mallet. Finally, don't grind spices while they are still hot, as the prized volatile aromas will disappear into thin air.

blends (for Indian or Middle Eastern dishes, for example, try turmeric mixed with toasted and ground whole cumin and coriander) and work your way up. When stored well, they will last for 6 months.

USE A SPICE RUB ON TOFU AND VEGETABLES. Rub spices into tofu slabs or big cuts of sturdy vegetables like cauliflower or carrots, then sear them in hot oil or roast in the oven. To add more texture, use coarsely ground whole spices.

JAZZ UP MARINADES AND CONDIMENTS. Mix a spice blend into olive oil or yogurt and use as a marinade for tofu, tempeh, or hearty vegetables like mushrooms, cabbage, or cauliflower. Or give simple condiments, like tahini or yogurt sauces, a twist with a few spices.

RECIPES TO TRY: Mushroom Shawarma (page 532), Turkish-Spiced Tahini Sauce (page 198).

FINISH WITH THEM. Some spices lend an extra zing if you add them just before serving. In North Indian dishes, for instance, garam masala and fenugreek leaves are stirred in as finishing spices for maximal flavor. To make certain Middle Eastern flatbreads, add za'atar just before baking or brush it on with oil before serving.

RECIPE TO TRY: Simple Flatbread (page 535).

Tips for buying spices

OPT FOR WHOLE SPICES WHEN IT MAKES SENSE. Whole spices have protective barriers that lock in their volatile oils, which is where all the flavor lives. Ground spices, in contrast, gradually lose some potency. That's not to say you can't make tasty meals with ground spices. You certainly can, and you'll find many such recipes in this book.

But whole spices make a world of difference. So if you're whipping up a special-occasion meal or looking to impress, using whole spices—whether you're grinding them to make your own spice blend or blooming them before adding your aromatics—is worth the extra five minutes. You get more complex flavors and freshness, and even some fun texture if you don't finely grind your spices.

CHECK THE DATE. Before buying a spice bottle at the supermarket, check the manufacture date. Ideally, that date won't be too far in the distant past; if it is, keep moving.

SKIP THE FAMILY SIZES, ESPECIALLY FOR GROUND SPICES. Unless it's a spice you use very regularly.

STORE SMARTLY AND KEEP CHECKING FOR FRESHNESS. Store spices in your pantry or spice cabinet, ideally in glass bottles, since plastic is porous and can let air in. Also be sure to keep them away from sunlight and heat (for example, don't store spices above your stove). Ground spices will stay fresh for about a year once you open them, while whole spices are good for two to three years (another great reason to cook with whole spices when you can). Spices don't go rancid per se, but they're also not like a bottle of fine wine: they do *not* get better with age. If you detect just a faint aroma or not much at all, it's time to restock.

SHOP SUSTAINABLY IF YOU CAN. I used to assume that the spices lining grocery shelves were mere prepackaged ingredients. But spices—like vegetables and fruits—are grown by actual human farmers working in fields, and these farmers depend on fair partnerships to make a living.

In general, brands with shorter supply chains are better for farmers *and* sell better-quality spices. My favorites are Burlap & Barrel and Diaspora Co. Both companies' spices are unique, complex, and wildly delicious (and more potent, so you can use less). They work directly with small farmers to equitably and sustainably harvest single-origin spices.

Good grocery store options include Frontier Co-op (fair trade–certified spices; many are organic) and Simply Organic. Both brands prioritize sustainable sourcing.

Herbs

The first time I recall feeling genuinely impressed with a salad was when I made one of Otto-lenghi's recipes. There was no lettuce, just a bed of fresh herbs, along with raw beets and a simple vinaigrette.

"This is a salad?!" asked my Manhattan-raised friend with a decidedly sophisticated palate. "My salads never taste this good." Neither did mine.

That salad taught me about the multifaceted powers of fresh herbs. They bring dimension and nuance, depth of flavor, pleasing aromas, and even layers of texture.

Cilantro, with its lemony and limey flavors, can perk up sweet, tart tomatoes in a pico de gallo while also cooling down the heat from the chiles. Rosemary, with its piney, camphor-y aroma, can make foods as diverse as potatoes and lemon cakes even more irresistible. In Vietnamese noodle dishes, handfuls of fresh mint, cilantro, and Thai basil add layers of flavors and sensations: citrus and anise, sweet and cooling (see page 473).

Herbs also help locate regional dishes. A curry finished with cilantro tastes decidedly more Indian, a tomato sauce with basil uniquely Italian, a potato salad with dill classically American.

If you're new to cooking with fresh herbs or you're wary about wasting them, this section has plenty of guidance on how to use and preserve them.

How to incorporate fresh herbs into your cooking

TIE A BOUQUET GARNI. A fancy French word for a bundle of herbs, typically sturdy herbs like rosemary, sage, thyme, oregano, and/or bay leaves. Use kitchen twine to tie up the herbs and submerge into soups or stews, braises, white or tomato sauces, or pots of beans/lentils for a woodsy depth of flavor. If you don't have kitchen twine, you can use unwaxed, unflavored dental floss or even a few long scallions. Bonus: It's easier than chopping up herbs and sautéing them first, and you get just as much flavor.

RECIPE TO TRY: A Really Good Pot of Saucy Beans (page 233).

SWAP SOME (OR ALL) OF THE LETTUCE IN YOUR SALAD. Eating a plant-based diet often means eating a fair amount of salad. Give your salads variety by adding handfuls of soft herbs—basil, cilantro, mint, parsley, dill, tarragon, chervil, chives—to salads, or replace the lettuce altogether with herbs. For added texture, keep small leaves whole, chop large leaves finely, and tear some with your hands.

RECIPES TO TRY: My Weekly Herby Green Salad (page 357), Shaved Carrot Salad with Pickled Shallots & Fresh Herbs (page 371).

MAKE AN HERBY CONDIMENT. When summer basil is gone, use parsley or cilantro to make pesto. Or give pesto a rest-o and try an Italian Basil & Parsley Salsa Verde (page 181) or a Middle Eastern spicy mint sauce (page 189).

USE IT FOR BIG FLAVOR: Have a handful of leftover herbs on their last legs? Toss them into sauces like cashew cream, tahini sauces, yogurt dips, or salad dressings, like Green Goddess Dressing (page 182). You can blend soft herbs directly into sauces; for tough herbs, sauté briefly in oil before using.

FINISH WITH FRESH HERBS. A smattering of fresh herbs brightens nearly any dish, especially rich ones, and brings unique aromas at the last minute. Finishing a Thai curry (page 489) with Thai basil perfumes it with sweet-spicy flavors, while chives add a grassy bite that awakens the indulgent Cheesy Herb Bread Pudding with Caramelized Leeks (page 459).

Substituting fresh herbs with dried herbs

In a pinch, dried herbs can get the job done in soups, stews, and other cooked dishes, though you'll be missing out on the same complexity of flavor (and freshness). Dried herbs are more concentrated, so use one-third to one-quarter the amount (1 tablespoon fresh rosemary ≈ 1 teaspoon dried rosemary).

Some dried herbs are useless (I'm looking at you, parsley and basil), so leave them at the grocery store. On the other hand, dried oregano is lovely with its pungent earthiness, and dried mint is great in Middle Eastern recipes.

When you can't find fresh curry leaves or makrut lime leaves, the dried versions do a good job of adding the distinctive flavors of South Asian and Southeast Asian cuisine, respectively. For these, the fresh leaves are actually more potent, so use roughly double the amount when using dried.

How to clean and store fresh herbs

Finding a sopping wet bag of cilantro in the back of your fridge is gross and sad, so here's how to avoid that situation.

When you get home from grocery shopping, unpack your herbs first. If they're tied up, remove the twist tie or rubber band so they can breathe. For soft herbs like dill, cilantro, and parsley, treat them like flowers and trim an inch (2.5 cm) from the stems.

Now it's time for the washing. I like to wash soft herbs in a large bowl filled with cold water, then dry them in a salad spinner. If you have the counter space and time, you can dry the herbs spread out on dish towels (arranging them in front of a fan will speed things up). While you let the herbs dry, put away the rest of your groceries.

Next comes the swaddle. Lovingly swaddle herbs in damp paper towels or a thin dish towel and stick them in a resealable bag, container, or salad clamshell in the crisper drawer. Most varieties should stay fresh for 2 weeks.

For bruise-prone basil, wash only once you're ready to use it and be gentle (no salad spinner). For basil with roots, trim the ends like you would with flowers, store it in a jar with just a little bit of water at room temperature (uncovered or loosely covered with a plastic bag), and change the water every day (otherwise, it starts to smell). For pre-clipped basil in a box, leave as is, but line the bottom and top of the box with a paper towel. For potted basil plants, keep the soil moist and store on a sunny windowsill.

How to upcycle fresh herbs

MAKE HERB CUBES. This is my favorite way to preserve sturdy herbs like rosemary, thyme, sage, and oregano. Chop them, add a teaspoon or tablespoon to ice cube molds, and pour enough olive oil to cover. Freeze the cubes; once frozen, transfer them to a resealable bag. Just plop the frozen cubes into a hot pan to start a pan sauce or pasta sauce or to gently fry vegetables or legumes.

For soft herbs, puree leftover herbs with enough water or olive oil until thick, and pour into ice cube molds and freeze. Add a cube or two to homemade broths, soups, or stews for herby flavor.

When fresh mint or basil is near its end, chop it up, add to an ice cube tray, cover with water, and freeze. Now you have fancy ice cubes for all your summer bevvies.

MAKE INFUSED OILS OR SYRUPS.

ROSEMARY-INFUSED OLIVE OIL. Add 2 large sprigs of rosemary to a small saucepan with ½ cup (112 g) olive oil and gently cook over medium heat for 5 minutes. Remove from the heat; once cool, transfer the sprigs and oil to a glass bottle, seal, and refrigerate for 3 to 4 weeks. Use to roast potatoes and sauté mushrooms; stir into lentil soups; or drizzle over pasta, pots of white beans (see page 233), or garlic-scraped bread.

HERB-INFUSED VINEGAR. To a sterilized and dry jar, add 2 sprigs of sturdy herbs like rosemary, thyme, or sage, or a few handfuls of soft herbs like basil, dill, or tarragon. Add a few strips of orange or lemon peel. Heat 1½ cups (360 ml) white or red wine vinegar (or distilled white vinegar) in a saucepan until very small bubbles form. Pour into the jar. Once cool, seal, and let infuse in the fridge for a minimum of 48 hours, ideally 2 weeks. Strain and use in vinaigrettes, marinades, and pan sauces.

HERB-INFUSED SIMPLE SYRUP. Mix equal parts sugar and water in a saucepan; add a few handfuls of herbs. Certain herbs like rosemary and thyme are strong, so start with a 1:4 ratio of herbs to water; for milder herbs like cilantro and basil, use a 1:1 ratio. Boil for 1 minute, then steep for 30 minutes. Once cool, strain and store the syrup in a sealed jar in the fridge for up to 1 month. Use in cocktails and mocktails, lemonades and iced teas, and fruity desserts.

Chile peppers

Now is as good a time as any to admit that I used to be a real babymouth. (And by that I mean I had the spice tolerance of a baby—so zero.) So much so that, when I was a child, my mom had to cook a separate batch of each recipe for me. So much so that mild salsa was my limit in college. MILD SALSA. IN COLLEGE.

By my midtwenties, I was tired of being an embarrassment to my spice-loving family. So, I started venturing very slowly into the world of chiles. I started with sriracha, then with jalapeños in my guacamole, until one day I found myself at the Whole Foods hot bar dousing my rice bowl in ghost pepper hot sauce. (*Oh no. I've gone too far. Make the burning stop!*)

As my babymouth life faded into the distance, I learned what I had been missing: how much oomph red pepper flakes sautéed in olive oil adds to pasta, how a dash of cayenne or a jalapeño can make a dessert taste sweeter and warmer, and how much better Mexican food is with hot salsa instead of mild. I also learned that you should never touch your eyes after cutting chile peppers, especially when you're on a coffee run at a fast-casual restaurant with a poor excuse for a bathroom sink.

These days, I relish cooking with new chiles, and I can even order a 7 out of 10 spice level at a Thai restaurant (even my dad, who eats habaneros for fun, admits that's spicy).

And that's because most of us can develop spice tolerances **over time**. If mild salsa girl can do it, you can do it. If you're wary of too much spice, start slowly with condiments: fruity hot sauces, chile sauces like harissa, or Chinese chili crisp (page 187). Then work your way up to cooking with crushed chiles and fresh chile peppers in small doses. Over time, you'll learn to love the uniquely delicious flavors, aromas, and sensations that heat brings.

Tips for cooking with chile peppers

SPICE TO YOUR TASTE. I like my food spicier than most Americans, so my recipes that call for chiles include tips on how to moderate the heat. When in doubt, go easy. You can usually add more heat later using hot sauce, chili crisp, pickled chile peppers, chile flakes, or some other spicy condiment. If you love spicy food, look for guidance to make a dish "*spicy!*" in the recipes.

IT'S ALL IN THE MEMBRANES. Most of the capsaicin—the stuff that makes chiles spicy—is found in the white membranes. The seeds have some heat, and the pepper itself has the least heat. I give the option to remove the membranes, though I personally leave them in.

TEST THE HEAT IN ADVANCE. Test how spicy a pepper is by rubbing a cut pepper on the back of your hand and licking it. Is that jalapeño a baby green bell pepper or more like a serrano?

HELP! MY DISH TURNED OUT TOO SPICY.

Reach for an **acidic** ingredient to make the food taste brighter and less fiery (e.g., a generous squeeze of lime for beans or chili). Add a dollop of **creamy, fatty stuff** (e.g., vegan yogurt for Indian food, vegan sour cream or avocado for things like tacos). **Sugar** can soften burning heat, but don't overdo it in savory foods. Or pair your food with a **plain starch** (bread or rice) to turn down the heat.

SAFETY FIRST. Wear food-safe gloves if you're new to working with chile peppers and/or finely dicing them. If not, after working with chile peppers, rub your hands with vegetable oil (capsaicin is fat soluble), then wash with water and a grease-cutting dish soap.

VENTILATE AND PROTECT. Before pureeing chiles or cooking them over high heat, open your windows. If you start coughing, it's the capsaicin irritating your lungs. Annoying but harmless. To prevent this, wrap a damp bandana or dish towel over your mouth and nose.

How to incorporate chiles into your cooking

INFUSE OIL. As mentioned above, capsaicin is fat soluble, so infusing hot oil with chile flakes not only makes for a flavorful oil but also enhances the heat and flavor of the chile flakes. I drizzle chile oil on yogurt, tofu, grains, pasta, and roasted cauliflower. Really, anything.

RECIPES TO TRY: Life-Changing Homemade Chili Crisp (page 187), Heirloom Tomato Salad with Ricotta & Chile Oil (page 361).

SPICE UP YOUR CONDIMENTS. Perk up a tahini sauce, like the Turkish-Spiced Tahini Sauce, which is flecked with Aleppo pepper (page 198), or chuck a green chile into Mint-Pistachio Pesto (page 178). Blend chipotle peppers in adobo sauce into vegan mayo or cashew creams (page 201). Blitz fresh peppers to make Indian chutneys or Middle Eastern hot sauces (like the Spicy Mint & Cilantro Sauce on page 189). Or sprinkle chile powder on yogurt dips for a cooling-heat contrast.

PICKLE PEPPERS. Spicy, tangy, salty, and a little sweet, pickled peppers are great for topping tacos, shawarma, pizza, sandwiches, and noodles. Try the pickled chile pepper recipes (see page 170) and experiment with flavorings.

GIVE THEM SOME CHAR. Charring chile peppers concentrates their flavor and adds smokiness (try the Avocado Crema on page 204). You can char peppers over an open gas flame, under the broiler, or in a cast-iron skillet.

MAKE A SPICE RUB. Rub hearty vegetables with chile flakes or powder (along with salt, pepper, and oil) and roast in the oven.

PAIR WITH AROMATICS (see page 89). If a recipe calls for ginger or garlic, sauté a diced fresh chile pepper at the same time to jolt your food awake. If you are using crushed chile flakes, add them after the aromatics and cook for about 30 seconds.

Chile pastes and sauces

Chile pastes and sauces are an easy way to add more kick to your cooking.

HARISSA: Harissa is a North African chile paste mixed with olive oil, spices, and garlic. It's smoky but a little fruity. I mix it into hummus, add it to sauces and marinades, and use it to take (vegan) shakshuka over the top (page 437).

ASIAN CHILI SAUCES AND PASTES: Huy Fong makes two excellent chili sauces: Vietnamese **chili-garlic sauce**, which is made with fresh chiles, vinegar, garlic, and salt; and Indonesian **sambal oelek**, which is similar but without garlic. I use these sauces in stir-fries, noodle dishes, and Korean BBQ sauce and swirl them into noodle soups.

Then there's also Korean **gochujang**, a sweet-salty-spicy powerhouse (see page 47), and **sriracha**, which needs no introduction. And finally, Southeast Asian **curry pastes**. You can make your own (the Malaysian curry paste on page 468 is not to be missed!) or buy a vegan-friendly Thai curry paste.

CHINESE CHILI CRISP: I reach for this when I want chile heat but also some saltiness, funk, and crunchiness. It instantly jazzes up simple meals, from noodles and frozen dumplings to cucumber salads and leftover pizza. See my Life-Changing Homemade Chili Crisp on page 187, but for store-bought, I like Lao Gan Ma, Momofuku, and Fly By Jing.

USE IT FOR BIG FLAVOR: Instead of using a neutral-flavored oil, opt for Chinese chili oil or the oil from chili crisp when cooking an East Asian or Southeast Asian stir-fry.

CALABRIAN CHILI PASTE: Made from hot Italian chiles packed in oil, this is simultaneously spicy, tangy, and oily. Drizzle it on pizza, pasta, tofu scramble, and even buttered toast.

USE IT FOR BIG FLAVOR: Use in place of red pepper flakes for more complex flavor and great mouthfeel, and stir into creamy condiments like vegan mayo, Whipped Tofu Ricotta (page 206), or Whipped Feta (page 209) for a kick.

Chile peppers

Crushed chile peppers

While I love the heat of standard Italian **red pepper flakes**, there's a whole world of other options to explore. I've listed the ones that are on heavy rotation in my kitchen. Most of these are less spicy than red pepper flakes, making them great gateway chile options.

ALEPPO PEPPER: Aleppo pepper is bright, fruity, tart, yet earthy, with a subtle tomatoey flavor and mild heat. I cook with it often but also sprinkle it as a finish. It's traditionally made from oily peppers grown in Aleppo, though due to the Syrian civil war, it's now typically made in Turkey or the US.

URFA BIBER: Dark burgundy Turkish chile flakes with a mild to moderate heat and deeply rich flavor—smoky, earthy, salty, and with undertones of raisin, coffee, and chocolate. I use Urfa biber in creamy spreads and dips like hummus or vegan yogurt sauces, as well as salad dressings, tofu scrambles, and hearty vegetables. You can find it and Aleppo pepper at Middle Eastern markets or online specialty spice shops.

GOCHUGARU: These Korean chile flakes are fairly sweet and fruity, a little earthy, and mellow in heat. I love gochugaru in marinades, dressings, chile oil or chili crisp, noodles, and even with avocado toast. Find a wide variety at Korean grocery stores, as well as a few options at Whole Foods.

CHIPOTLE CHILE FLAKES: Smoky with fruity chocolate undertones and a heat that builds. I use chipotle chile flakes/crushed chipotle chiles in lieu of red pepper flakes when I want a smoky heat and in Mexican-inspired recipes. You can find them at most grocery stores.

SICHUAN CHILE FLAKES: Made from whole Sichuan chile peppers that are fried in oil, then ground into flakes, these are toasty and a little nutty in flavor (and spicy). I use them in Chinese dishes, particularly in my Life-Changing Homemade Chili Crisp (page 187). Find them at Chinese grocery stores or online.

Crushed chile peppers *(cont.)*:

INDIAN RED CHILE POWDER: This powder is made entirely from dried chiles and comes in two variations: Kashmiri chile powder, which is mild in heat, and standard red chile powders often labeled *mirchi* or *lal mirch*, which have a similar heat level to cayenne pepper. You can find both varieties at South Asian grocers, or online.

Fresh and dried chile peppers

Fresh chile peppers are grassy, sharp, and mildly bitter. The more they age, the sweeter and fruitier they become. When a fresh chile pepper is dried, its flavors are concentrated, with the grassiness mellowing into earthy fruitiness.

POBLANO: These look like skinny dark green bell peppers and are *very* mild with a slightly smoky flavor. Best when charred on the stove or in the oven, as it makes them sweeter.

JALAPEÑO: Grassy and bright with moderate heat (occasionally, you'll get a super-spicy pepper that makes you sweat).

Chile peppers

FRESNO: Similar to jalapeño but bright red and has a tad more heat. In raw or quick-pickled applications, I prefer these over jalapeños for their fruitier flavor.

SERRANO: Skinny green peppers similar in flavor to jalapeños but several times spicier. This is my go-to green chile pepper, but if you want less heat, sub with a jalapeño.

THAI: These tiny fresh chile peppers pack in a lot of heat. My go-to for Southeast Asian and East Asian recipes.

CHIPOTLE IN ADOBO: Smoked, dried jalapeños that have been rehydrated and canned in tomato puree. They're smoky, spicy, and tangy, and add a velvety body when pureed. Babymouths, go easy on these spicy bad boys.

Aromatics

I didn't really understand what an aromatic was, or how important it could be, until I started observing my mom cook Indian food. I'd watch her chop pounds of onions, her eyes welling with tears. One day, I blurted out, "Stop cooking onions if they make you cry!" Her response was something like, "You nitwit. *This* is how I make the food taste good."

My mom chopped buckets of onions even though it burned her eyes, blitzed chile peppers even though it made her cough, and peeled and froze pounds of garlic and ginger because it was worth it. Frying these ingredients in hot oil before adding the legumes or vegetables imparted bold but well-rounded flavors into the food we ate each night.

From my informal cooking lessons with Mom, I learned that cooking aromatics in a fat source activates flavor compounds in the aromatics that would otherwise lie dormant. And that, in turn, adds this vague thing we call "depth of flavor" to each dish. By extension, I learned that a lot of bland food could be improved just by starting the recipe off with some sautéed aromatics, vegetables, and seasonings. This is what I call the *Aromatic Approach*.

The Aromatic Approach is a way of building flavors in all kinds of cooking, but it's especially important in plant-based cooking. So what if you can't brown a slab of meat? You can brown the heck out of onions. And carrots and fennel and tofu and tempeh.

Take the humble onion, for example. As you sauté an onion, its cells break down, releasing a mixture of sugars and proteins. When the sugars and amino acids eventually break down (the Maillard reaction), they release the essence of umami and introduce new flavor compounds. And when onions are cooked long and slow, their sugars eventually caramelize, yielding rich, sweet-savory flavors that make the result feel like an entirely different food than the pungent raw onions that made my mother cry.

Garlic also takes on new life when cooked. Raw, it's sharp and even spicy, but heating garlic causes its enzymes to break down and recombine. For instance, when sautéed in oil, garlic develops a more complex, robust savory flavor that makes its companion ingredients magically taste better. When roasted in the oven, its sugars break down and melt into buttery richness with a mild, sweet flavor.

×

The next time you make a soup or stew (for instance, the Ethiopian Red Lentil Stew with Spiced Butter on page 486), instead of briefly sautéing the onions, cook them until they are dark golden and almost jammy. This one change will lend your dish a deeper, subtly sweet flavor.

×

Aromatics by cuisine

The Aromatic Approach—cooking aromatics and vegetables in a fat source before adding other ingredients—is a long-standing technique common in nearly every culture.

Below you'll find some basic aromatic groupings by cuisine. Keep this list handy the next time you want to get creative in the kitchen, whether it's to whip up a Chinese stir-fry or an Italian bean stew.

French
onions + carrots + celery, cooked in vegan butter
Known as *mirepoix*.

German
carrots + leeks + celery root, cooked in neutral oil or vegan butter
Parsley, thyme, onion, or rutabaga may also be added. Known as *Suppengrün* ("soup greens").

Northern Italian
onions + carrots + celery, cooked in olive oil (occasionally vegan butter)
May be enhanced with garlic, fennel, parsley, rosemary, sage, or basil. Known as *soffritto*.

Southern Italian
garlic + tomatoes + basil, cooked in olive oil

Spanish and Latin
onions + tomatoes + garlic + bell peppers, cooked in olive oil
Known as *sofrito*, and variations abound across countries. Some add chile peppers; others cilantro or cumin seeds; others oregano.

Tip:
Season the aromatics early on with a bit of salt. This draws out the moisture from the vegetables and speeds up the cooking and browning process.

Creole and Cajun
onions + green bell pepper + celery, cooked in vegetable oil
Known as the Holy Trinity.

Jamaican
scallions + garlic + thyme, cooked in neutral oil or coconut oil
Scotch bonnet peppers and allspice are often added.

Chinese
scallions + garlic + ginger, cooked in neutral oil or peanut oil
These same aromatics may be used again later in the cooking process. Regional variations are plentiful; spicy Sichuan cuisine, for instance, adds chiles.

Indian
onions + garlic + ginger + chile peppers, cooked in neutral oil, mustard oil, or coconut oil
Ghee is often used as the fat source, but vegan butter works well. A variety of spices are typically added before and/or after the aromatics.

Thai
galangal (or ginger) + shallots + lemongrass, cooked in neutral oil or coconut oil
Makrut lime leaves may also be added, and Thai basil is often added at the end.

West Africa
onions + tomatoes + chile peppers, cooked in vegetable oil, red palm oil, or coconut oil
Variations abound across countries. Some add ginger; others herbs, seeds, and nuts.

Cooking Fats

Fat doesn't usually have a strong flavor on its own, but it's earned its right to be in this chapter because it plays a crucial role in allowing other flavors to sing.*

Fat is uniquely important in vegan cooking, which, by definition, does not contain high-fat meats and dairy. After all, if a meal consists entirely of fat-free steamed lentils and cauliflower, it will be 100 percent unappetizing (and maybe even inedible).

I know that some folks prefer to follow a low-fat or oil-free plant-based diet for heart-health reasons. I don't claim to be a nutritionist. **I speak only from the perspective of wanting to empower people to cook really excellent, maximally flavorful vegan food** (in the hope that, eventually, they will be inspired to eat more plants and fewer animals).

Why fat matters

FAT CARRIES, RELEASES, AND SUPERCHARGES FLAVOR. Many essential ingredients in a plant-based kitchen (e.g., garlic, cumin, red pepper flakes, bay leaves) have volatile flavor and aroma compounds that are largely fat soluble. This means a fat source can uniquely release the flavors and aromas trapped inside those ingredients. In other words, fat supercharges the flavor of aromatics, spices, chiles, and certain herbs, the cornerstones of big vegan flavor that we talked about earlier in this chapter.

For instance, when you sauté onions and garlic in olive oil, the fat in olive oil carries higher concentrations of these onion and garlic flavors to our tongues. In contrast, when they are sautéed in water (rather, steamed), the flavor compounds never get released.

Fat also extracts more flavor from ingredients in baking. When you fold vanilla and espresso into a brownie batter, the fat in the chocolate and butter or oil helps the batter better hold on to the vanilla and coffee flavors during baking.

FAT DRAMATICALLY ENHANCES TEXTURE. Fat is responsible for many of our favorite food textures: flaky, tender, crispy, crunchy, creamy, smooth, and crumbly. I talk about the role of fat in creating irresistible creamy textures in more detail on page 114.

In baking, again, fat enhances texture in several ways:

- When fat (e.g., vegan butter) coats flour, it weakens the gluten bonds, which yields a tender texture. This is why dinner rolls are more tender than nearly fat-free sourdough.

---

* A lot of what I've learned about cooking with fat comes from the greats like Samin Nosrat, Yotam Ottolenghi, Ina Garten, Harold McGee, and the folks at America's Test Kitchen.

- Liquid fats, such as oils, keep cakes moist, contributing a luxurious mouthfeel, even in cakes made without eggs and dairy.

- When vegan butter is creamed with sugar, it creates pockets of air that expand in the oven, giving your cakes and muffins a light, fluffy texture.

- Fat also aids in browning, which is why a cake made with vegan butter and full-fat oat milk has a more golden crust than one made with applesauce and thin almond milk.

FAT BRINGS A RICH MOUTHFEEL. Fat is the secret behind silky, creamy Thai curries and velvety Indian gravies. It's why a dollop of cashew cream or tahini will make any grain bowl better and why mashed potatoes almost melt in your mouth.

Fat can do this during the cooking process ("cooking fats") but also right before serving ("finishing fats"). Think of how a drizzle of olive oil swirled into a pureed soup adds great mouthfeel or how chunks of buttery avocado can make a salad almost indulgent.

FAT TAMES BITTERNESS. A creamy salad dressing transforms radicchio from unbearably bitter to delicious, while cocoa butter takes cacao from an inedible bitter seed to melt-in-your-mouth chocolate.

FAT CONCENTRATES, EVOKES, AND PRESERVES FLAVORS. The chemical structure of fat molecules allows them to concentrate flavors more easily (science!). For example, when spices are bloomed in oil, the hot oil extracts the essence of each spice, concentrates its flavor, and then imparts that intensified spice flavor to the final dish.

Fat also has the power to evoke flavors. A raw black mustard seed and a curry leaf do not taste like much. But after sizzling in hot oil, they immediately transport your palate to India.

When you infuse oils with herbs, spices, peppers, or aromatics (e.g., chile oil, garlic confit), the oil brings out and intensifies those flavors. The aromatics, in turn, impart their flavor to the oil. It's symbiosis (science again!).

FAT CAN IMPART ITS OWN FLAVOR. If the fat source has its own distinctive flavor, it lends that to the other ingredients (e.g., adding vegan butter to waffle batter = waffles that taste buttery). Or it can be used as a finishing ingredient that brings everything together (e.g., drizzling toasted sesame oil over a stir-fry).

FAT MAKES VEGETABLES CRAVEABLE. Fat does what every parent has been seeking for generations. Try feeding your kid steamed cauliflower and then olive oil–roasted cauliflower and see which one wins. In other words, **fat = flavor and texture**.

FAT IS ALSO A NECESSARY NUTRIENT. It enables our bodies to absorb fat-soluble vitamins and keeps us feeling full.

Am I encouraging you to go on a high-fat, high-sugar, fast-food-and-junk-food bender? Nope.

This is just a reminder that when you're cooking plant-based food and you want it to taste delicious—so delicious that, perhaps, you don't feel the need to order takeout or eat meat and dairy very often—fat is essential in at least one form.

 ## A NOTE ON COOKING WITH OIL

Occasionally, a recipe will give a range for cooking oil (e.g., 2 to 3 tablespoons avocado oil). The greater amount will typically yield the best results (for instance, crispier tofu or better browning on vegetables), but you will still get good results with the lower amount. Similarly, if a recipe calls for a generous glug of olive oil but you're limiting your oil intake, use a drizzle instead while understanding the recipe won't turn out exactly as intended.

Plant sources
of fat

Cooking fats

OLIVE OIL: Olive oil is my go-to oil. It's delicious and adds gorgeous mouthfeel, especially in uncooked applications. Plus, it's got those good monounsaturated fats that have helped folks in the Mediterranean live until they're one hundred (google the Blue Zones).

I keep several types on hand. First, my everyday extra-virgin olive oil, which I use for many things—sautéing or roasting vegetables, braises, sauces, pastas, vinaigrettes, and so on. I use California Olive Ranch, Terra Delyssa Organic, and ZOE, all of which have a good price-to-quality ratio. If I'm shallow frying or cooking a richly flavored dish where I won't taste the difference, I use a more inexpensive olive oil blend. Finally, there's the pricey extra-virgin olive oil I reserve for finishing: salads with minimalist dressings, dipping bread, drizzling over raw veg or dips. For this, I love Brightland and Olio Verde.

USE IT FOR BIG FLAVOR: Most soups—especially pureed or creamy soups—and dips can be improved with a drizzle of good olive oil right before serving. It adds rich flavor and butteriness (without the butter).

NEUTRAL-FLAVORED OILS: When I don't want the flavor of the oil to be prominent or I'm cooking Asian recipes, I opt for avocado, grapeseed, or sunflower oil. If a recipe calls for a "neutral-flavored oil," use one of these, or canola or vegetable oil. If you prefer olive oil, you can almost always make that swap, but stick to a mellow one that won't dominate other flavors.

TIP: Preheat your pan first, then add your cooking oil and allow the oil to heat up a bit before adding any ingredients. This is especially important when cooking in stainless steel and cast-iron pans to avoid sticking.

COCONUT OIL: I use unrefined coconut oil only when a coconut flavor is desired, such as in a Thai curry or a coconut cake. Refined coconut oil is more processed but has essentially the same nutritional profile, along with a neutral flavor, making it more versatile. Solid at room temperature, coconut oil is often a pretty good sub for butter in baking.

TIP: If a savory recipe calls for coconut oil, feel free to sub with your preferred neutral-flavored oil.

Plant sources of fat

TOASTED SESAME OIL: Toasted sesame oil has a rich, intensely nutty, roasty flavor I adore. It's not a workhorse cooking oil, though, as it can burn when cooked for too long. I use it in Asian-inspired vinaigrettes and marinades, as a final drizzle over stir-fries and noodles, and paired with salted edamame served over rice. Start slowly, because it's bold. The best one I've tried is from Ottogi.

VEGAN BUTTER: I use vegan butter in baking and in savory dishes where a buttery taste is desired, such as polenta or risotto. Earth Balance is widely available and works great (I prefer the buttery sticks to the tub; they also make a soy-free variety). Where the taste of the butter matters (e.g., when slathered on toast) or I want to mimic the browning capabilities of butter, I reach for Violife Plant Butter or Miyoko's cultured vegan butter.

USE IT FOR BIG FLAVOR: Stir a tablespoon of vegan butter in at the end when making Indian curries, dals, and vegetable dishes to add a touch of richness.

Supplementary or finishing fats

While oils and vegan butter are typically used as cooking fats, there are other fats we supplement or finish dishes with. Many of these—nuts, seeds, tahini, avocado, coconut milk, and other plant milks, as well as vegan yogurt, sour cream, and mayo—can be used to mimic the high-fat creamy textures of dairy, often in a more wholesome way. I talk about this more on page 104.

Balancing and Pairing Flavors

On our backpacking trip, Max and I found ourselves on an extended stay in Thailand, where we ate like kings and queens for just a few dollars a day. Many nights, overwhelmed by choice, we would visit three or four street vendors, each one a master in a singular craft.

Even when it was swelteringly hot and humid (pretty much always), we waited in a forty-five-minute line to get the best khao soi, a northern Thai curry noodle soup made with a rich coconut broth and topped with a nest of crispy fried noodles. Even during a torrential downpour, we crisscrossed the tarp-covered side streets and alleys of Bangkok in our flip-flops to find the best crispy Thai crepes.

Eating really excellent Thai food three times a day for a month taught me that the essence of good cooking is balance.

The fiery chile peppers used in nearly every Thai dish were always tempered by a pinch of sugar. Soy sauce was always awakened by tart lime juice or tamarind, then balanced with sugar or the creaminess of coconut milk. Herbs like Thai basil, lemongrass, and makrut lime leaves added a refreshing fragrance that sliced through even the richest dishes.

At the weekend-long cooking retreat we attended, every time a chef made a sauce, I watched them tinker with it over and over until it was the perfect blend of sour, sweet, bitter, salty, and spicy.

The result was that no dish we ate in Thailand felt too heavy or cloying, or too light and unsatisfying, or too one-note of anything.

Except that one time I pulled an Icarus and flew too close to the sun and ordered noodles that were "Thai spicy." They were definitely too spicy. I flapped my wings to the nearest 7-Eleven and spent the next hour shoving a loaf of white bread into my mouth.

Putting it all together

It's one thing to understand that mushrooms are a source of umami or that lemon juice adds an acidic taste. But it's the process of balancing these flavors, accentuating and fine-tuning them, and contrasting them with other flavors and aromas that makes a dish memorable.

Learning how to cook on the fly, how to intuitively balance flavors, how to pair complementary ingredients—all of this comes with experience. My hope is that with all the ingredients, principles, and recipes in this book, you will feel equipped and inspired to experiment in your kitchen and whip up vegan food that's big on flavor.

Contrasting flavor pairings

While these flavor pairings may seem like they're on opposite ends of the spectrum, they actually work in harmony.

SWEET AND SOUR. If your vinaigrette or tomato sauce is too sour, a tiny amount of sugar can fix it. On the other hand, lemon juice is a great way to add balance to certain desserts.

RECIPE TO TRY: The Vietnamese Rice Noodle Bowls with Crispy Tofu & Mushrooms (page 473) have an addictive sweet-and-sour sauce.

SWEET AND SALTY / UMAMI. The sodium ions in salt curb bitter flavor compounds, making any sweet flavors that are present seem stronger. That's why sea salt on a brownie is heaven—the salt amplifies the sugar by minimizing the bitterness of cacao. This is also why fermented foods like miso deliver a euphoric sweet-and-savory combo.

RECIPE TO TRY: Korean BBQ Tempeh (page 294).

SWEET AND SPICY. A spicy condiment or dish can almost always benefit from a touch of sweetness. I love adding sweet vegetables like winter squash, carrots, and sweet potatoes to spicy curries for this reason.

RECIPE TO TRY: Spicy Noodle Stir-Fry with Salt & Pepper Tofu (page 465)—a combo of brown sugar and chili sauce makes this stir-fry addictively good.

SWEET AND BITTER. Sweetness pairs very well with bitterness (it's the reason we add sugar to chocolate!). In savory foods, use sugar sparingly and rely more heavily on salt, acid, or fat to avoid a sweet dish.

RECIPE TO TRY: Chocolate-Covered Dates with Pistachio Butter (page 574; dark chocolate + dates = heaven).

SALTY AND BITTER. Remember, sodium ions in salt temper bitter flavors. When you're making a salad with bitter greens, go a little heavier on the salt.

RECIPE TO TRY: Radicchio Salad with Ranch & Smoky Seed Sprinkle (page 389)—taste the radicchio raw and then with the salty, umami-heavy dressing. It's like night and day.

SOUR AND BITTER. Acids also curb bitter flavor compounds, making them taste brighter. Kale and arugula salads are always better with lemon juice.

RECIPE TO TRY: Creamy & Crunchy Beet Salad with Crispy Fennel Crumbs (page 377)—notice how the tangy vinaigrette makes the arugula taste less bitter.

SOUR AND SALTY / UMAMI. Acids make salty and savory foods even more enjoyable. When serving something fried and salty, it's a good idea to add lemon or lime wedges on the side.

RECIPE TO TRY: The Buttermilk Fried "Chicken" (page 524)—the tangy vegan buttermilk enhances the umami in the mushrooms, while a squeeze of lemon intensifies the savory experience and freshens things up.

SOUR AND SPICY. Sour, tangy foods tend to make spicy foods taste less flaming hot. If you make something too spicy, try lemon or lime juice or vegan yogurt.

RECIPE TO TRY: Creamy Chickpea Spinach Masala with Tadka (page 483)—notice how the lime juice at the end slices through some of the heat.

Accenting similar flavors

While so much of the magic in cooking comes from balancing contrasting flavors, layering similar flavors can also produce delicious results.

Try layering two or three sources of **umami** for a powerhouse savory dish.

A FEW GOOD COMBOS:

tomatoes
(especially canned tomatoes)
+
olives

mushrooms
+
soy sauce
+
miso

ume plum vinegar
+
kombu

RECIPE TO TRY: Malaysian Curry Noodle Soup (page 468), featuring seaweed and soy sauce.

Combine two or three types of **acids** for more dynamic flavors, like mouth-puckering lime juice and milder rice vinegar in Southeast Asian recipes, or lemon juice and pomegranate molasses in Middle Eastern recipes.

RECIPE TO TRY: Spicy, Crunchy Kale Salad with Preserved Lemon Vinaigrette (page 374), which, in addition to the vinaigrette, features vinegar-pickled shallots and chile peppers.

Pair subtly **sweet** vegetables (e.g., winter squash, carrots, beets, fennel, sweet potatoes) with sweet-enhancing spices (e.g., cinnamon, nutmeg, green cardamom, and fennel seeds). And you can do the same with desserts but using fruits.

RECIPE TO TRY: Chai-Spiced Custard Tart with Mango (page 567).

3

Creating Irresistible Textures

Texture is often an afterthought in Western cuisine, particularly when it comes to plants. For the most part, a vegetable is a vegetable (excluding potatoes, which get the full range of treatment, from crunchy potato hash to crispy yet fluffy French fries to creamy mashed potatoes).

This is most unfortunate given that the texture of a dish often brings us just as much enjoyment as the flavor does, sometimes even more. When we crave ice cream, for instance, it's the creamy *texture* we're seeking, not the rocky road or Chunky Monkey flavor.

And at first glance, most of our beloved food textures come from animal proteins and fats. Like the *creamy* mouthfeel of a northern Italian polenta made with butter and cheese or the satisfying *crunch* of southern fried chicken.

But with a little creativity, we can absolutely achieve our most prized food textures— **creamy, crunchy, crispy, chewy**—using exclusively plant-based ingredients.

In this chapter and in the recipes that follow, we'll explore how you can re-create the same magic of your favorite food textures by combining certain plant-based ingredients with particular cooking techniques.

Creamy

When I was growing up, from Monday to Friday, my saint of a mother chauffeured my sister and me from school to every imaginable extracurricular activity, then came home and cooked a full Indian dinner.

But weekends were different. We'd sleep in late and Mom would make us her "American specialties": mac and cheese, mashed potatoes, or grilled cheese. In the evenings after work, my dad would occasionally take us out for ice cream.

None of these treats were gourmet. We got our ice cream scoops at Rite Aid, and Kraft was the only mac and cheese we knew. And none were very flavorful. But they were creamy. And that meant they were comforting.

Creamy foods are particularly comforting because, if you recall from page 93, fat is a great carrier of flavor, so flavors tend to cling to fat molecules. As a result, the taste of these creamy foods lingers on our tongues with each bite.

Yet most of our favorite creamy foods are drowning in dairy. Re-creating these satisfying creamy textures is one of the biggest challenges when cooking plant-based.

How do you create a decadent lasagna with a creamy interior when most store-bought vegan cheeses don't melt or ooze particularly well? How do you deliver the mouthfeel of a Caesar dressing or chocolate mousse without eggs, the silkiness of a tomato bisque without heavy cream? How do you remake the spinach artichoke dip from your childhood when most versions contain cream cheese, sour cream, mayo, *and* shredded cheese?

Over the last several years, I've devoted myself to exploring these questions. And over time, many of my signature creamy recipes—from classic American mac and cheese and spinach artichoke dip to indulgent Indian and Thai curries—have become "vegan gateway recipes," the recipes that have convinced countless omnivores that eating a vegan diet doesn't have to mean giving up your favorite comfort foods.

In this section, we'll dive into the diverse world of plant-based ingredients and cooking techniques that can help you achieve remarkably creamy textures in your home kitchen.

How to achieve creamy textures in vegan cooking

NUTS AND SEEDS: Raw nuts and seeds bring a surprisingly creamy texture and rich mouthfeel when they are first soaked in water and then blended.

Raw cashews are king, with their buttery smoothness and neutral taste. Cashew cream—raw cashews blended with water or plant milk until smooth—is vegan magic and can be tailored to your liking with tons of different flavors (see page 201). Cashews are also the secret behind some of the best vegan cheeses, including my Fermented Cashew Cheese (page 210).

I typically buy raw nuts. They're versatile, and freshly toasting them at home lends the best flavor. I do buy a few roasted versions—mostly almonds, peanuts, pistachios, and sesame seeds—for convenience (and sometimes, snacking).

How to soak nuts for nut creams

- Soaking your raw cashews (or other nuts)

    × **Traditional method:** Cover cashews with cool water in a bowl, cover, and soak for 8 hours, or overnight. Drain and rinse.

    × **Quick-soak methods:** (1) Add cashews to a saucepan, cover with water, and boil for 15 minutes. Drain and rinse. (2) If you have a high-powered blender and the recipe has a decent amount of liquid, you can cover the cashews in boiling water and soak for just 15 minutes.

- Cashew substitutes

    × If you are allergic to cashews, walnuts and blanched almonds will work in nut creams, but add 1 tablespoon of extra-virgin olive oil for better texture and flavor. Macadamia nuts have a great texture, but they are subtly sweet and generally better suited for desserts. If you have a nut allergy, sunflower seeds and hemp seeds can be used but are best with bold, spice-forward, or herby sauces, which help mask the distinctive taste of these seeds.

NUT AND SEED BUTTERS: Nut and seed butters add a dense creaminess and rich nutty flavor. I typically stick with almond or cashew butter, as the flavors are subtler than peanut butter. I buy roasted nut butters (for more flavor) in the smooth varieties (for versatility in cooking). You can make nut butters at home with a high-powered blender or food processor. Use the method on page 194.

USE IT TO BOOST TEXTURE: Add a few spoonfuls of nut butter to your next curry for extra creaminess and a subtle nutty taste.

TAHINI: Commonly used in Middle Eastern cooking, tahini is simply sesame seed paste. It's liquid gold and delectably creamy, and brings nutty indulgence to both savory and sweet foods. Check out page 196 for tips on how to pick a good tahini.

HOW TO USE: Use tahini to make hummus, of course, or drizzle it over lentils, beans, grain bowls, or roasted vegetables. Whipping tahini with lemon juice, water, and seasonings is the easiest way to make a lusciously creamy sauce you can pour on so many savory foods.

RECIPE TO TRY: Creamy Tahini Sauce, 3 Ways (page 197).

VEGETABLES: Certain vegetables—winter squash, sweet potatoes, cauliflower, eggplant, carrots, and celery root—get legit creamy when they are cooked down and then pureed. I say *certain* vegetables because if you try to "cream" celery, you will be disappointed. Celery is for juicing fads (and maybe salads), not for creaming.

USE IT TO BOOST TEXTURE: Roast these vegetables, then puree them in a food processor or blender. Use the puree in creamy sauces or pour into soups as a natural thickener. Puree winter squash or sweet potatoes with some plant milk, then fold into curries to add great body and a subtle sweetness to balance the heat.

RECIPE TO TRY: Cauliflower Steaks with Italian Basil & Parsley Salsa Verde (page 421), featuring cauliflower cream.

BEANS AND LENTILS: Soft, overcooked legumes might not sound exciting, but they pack a creamy punch.

USE IT TO BOOST TEXTURE: Puree cooked beans, then fold them into sauces or creams, or dips like hummus. Slightly overcooked beans or lentils are a great thickener for soups and stews. Red and yellow lentils get completely soft when cooked, adding a naturally thick texture to dals, curries, soups, and stews.

RECIPES TO TRY: My Favorite Dal Tadka (page 497), "Cream"-Braised Leeks with Crispy Bits (page 414).

GRAINS: Certain grains, when cooked in certain ways, can also become naturally creamy. Again, I say *certain* grains cooked in *certain* ways because quinoa cooked in water for 15 minutes will not make anything creamy.

USE IT TO BOOST TEXTURE: Make polenta (page 513), a naturally creamy grain, or risotto, which gets its luxe creaminess from the sticky starches in short-grain rice that break down during the low-and-slow cooking method. You can even use whole grains like farro and barley, which soften into creaminess when cooked using the risotto method.

RECIPES TO TRY: Rosemary Farrotto with Cheesy Pine Nuts (page 311), Creamy Baked Wild Rice with Carrots (page 317).

TOFU: This list is full of shockers. First vegetables, then beans, and now tofu? But it's true!

USE IT TO BOOST TEXTURE: Soft silken tofu is like jiggly Jell-O but creamier. Puree it for desserts like mousses and no-bake pie fillings, or use it to thicken smoothies or make salad dressings. You can also blend firmer varieties to add a creaminess to savory dishes, as in my Whipped Tofu Ricotta (page 206).

RECIPES TO TRY: Dark Chocolate Mousse with Raspberry Compote (page 577), All Hail Caesar Dressing (page 155).

AVOCADOS: Buttery and rich yet super nutrient-dense, a ripe avocado is a vegan's best friend.

Keep in mind that avocado has little flavor on its own. Always pair it with salt and an acid (e.g., lemon or lime juice or vinegar).

USE IT TO BOOST TEXTURE: Puree avocado to make a luxe sauce or dressing, like the Avocado Crema (page 204). Toss chunks of ripe avocado into a salad for that crisp-creamy contrast, or mix with lemon juice to massage a kale salad. Add to pesto and use less oil for a creamier spin.

Dairy substitutes

CANNED COCONUT MILK AND CREAM: These are the stars behind many curries and desserts that frequently prompt eaters to ask, "Are you *sure* this is vegan?" (Yes, yes, I am sure.)

TIPS FOR BUYING: Buy full-fat, unsweetened coconut milk in a can (not from the refrigerated section). The fewer ingredients, the better. If a dessert calls for coconut *cream*, you can either buy canned coconut cream, which has a higher ratio of coconut cream to liquid, or refrigerate a can of full-fat coconut milk for 24 hours so the cream separates from the liquid.

Note: If a savory recipe calls for coconut milk but you can't consume it, a relatively thin cashew cream is usually a good sub.

USE IT TO BOOST TEXTURE: In Southeast Asian and South Asian curries, to thicken pureed soups, to make creamy sauces and dressings, as the base for homemade yogurt, and in cream-esque fillings for desserts.

RECIPES TO TRY: Sticky Coconut Milk–Braised Tofu (page 278), Chai-Spiced Custard Tart with Mango (page 567).

PLANT-BASED MILKS: There's a huge variety of nondairy milks—or "alternative milk beverages," as the dairy industry insists we call them. It can be tricky figuring out which plant-based milks work best in cooking and baking. With that said, here are my opinionated thoughts from a flavor perspective.

Plain **full-fat oat milk** is my first choice for most savory and sweet applications. It's very creamy and fairly neutral in taste. Its sugar content helps baked goods brown better. Oatly and Califia are good, widely available options. Barista-style milks, sold in the shelf-stable section, are often the creamiest.

Many vegan recipes use **soy milk** in savory recipes, but I personally find soy's natural sweetness to be a bit off-putting. I prefer it in sweet recipes, for breakfasty things like granola, or when I need a protein boost.

Cashew milk is quite creamy and generally works well in both savory and sweet uses, though there's a significant variation in texture across brands. **"Drinking coconut milk,"** which comes in a carton, is a decent option in savory and sweet foods. I rarely use **almond milk**, which is quite thin and one of the least sustainable options.

RECIPES TO TRY: Rosemary Farrotto with Cheesy Pine Nuts (page 311), Cheesy Herb Bread Pudding with Caramelized Leeks (page 459).

DAIRY-ESQUE CONDIMENTS: Yogurt, mayo, and sour cream offer a one-two hit of acidity and creaminess. Luckily, there are some great vegan alternatives.

Vegan sour cream can take chili and tacos over the top and brings just the right amount of rich flavor to pancakes and waffles (page 446) and muffins and cakes (page 585). My favorite brands are Tofutti, Kite Hill, and Follow Your Heart.

SUBSTITUTING VEGAN SOUR CREAM: If you can't find vegan sour cream, modify the cashew cream on page 201 to use in savory recipes: use just enough water as needed to blend, add 1 teaspoon of distilled white vinegar and just 1 teaspoon of nutritional yeast, and omit the onion powder and fresh garlic, unless desired.

USE IT TO BOOST TEXTURE AND ADD BIG FLAVOR: Swap ½ cup (120 ml) of plant milk in a cake or muffin recipe with vegan sour cream for richer flavor and a more tender crumb.

I reach for **vegan mayo** in sandwiches and coleslaws and when I need a quick hit of tang and creaminess. My preferred brand, Follow Your Heart Original Vegenaise, is widely available.

Use **vegan yogurt** to make a creamy yogurt sauce (Yogurt Sauce, 3 Ways, page 213), and pair with roasted lentils or chickpeas or crunchy salads for a delightful creamy-crunchy contrast. Use in dips, use as a base for dragging roasted or grilled vegetables through, or blend into a soup at the end. My recommended brands are on page 61.

THICKENERS: Most thickeners—including cornstarch, arrowroot powder, potato starch, tapioca starch, agar agar, and all-purpose flour—are naturally vegan and can be used to creamify sauces, dressings, gravies, soups, stews, and desserts.

TIPS FOR USING PLANT-BASED THICKENERS

- When using arrowroot and cornstarch, start by making a slurry with cold water, stirring until smooth. Slowly pour the slurry into your hot or warm liquid, whisking well until thickened.

- Unlike cornstarch, arrowroot powder has no taste and also leaves food looking glossier. It does break down at higher temperatures, so add it toward the end of cooking (it thickens more quickly than cornstarch).

    RECIPE TO TRY: Tahini Custard (page 559).

Crunchy and Crispy*

> The appeal of crispy food appears, like our inalienable rights to life, liberty, and the pursuit of happiness, to be self-evident. Everybody seems to enjoy crispy food.
> —John S. Allen, *The Omnivorous Mind: Our Evolving Relationship with Food*

As I entered the first big writing phase of this book, I hunkered down at my computer and rarely left my office. My normally overstuffed fridge was barren (the irony!), so I ate a lot of

---

* A note on the terms *crispy* and *crunchy*: I am grouping the two together for efficiency's sake, though they are distinct. Puff pastry and potato chips are shatteringly airy and *crispy*. Granola and carrot chips are denser and *crunchy*. And then there's *crisp*, which is possibly, maybe, different. Romaine is crisp, but would you call it crispy?

snacks at my desk. One afternoon, I found, to my surprise, that I had eaten an entire 16-ounce bag of raw crinkle-cut carrots.

The flavor was cardboardy and I didn't even have a creamy dip, yet I ate an entire pound of carrots like an actual rabbit.

I suspect this happened only because I was enjoying the audible sound of crunching. Each time I ate a carrot, the rattling alerted my brain—*Hey, I'm doing a lot of crunchy chewing. This is kind of fun. Let's keep this rabbit party going.*

In his book *The Omnivorous Mind*, anthropologist John S. Allen argues that one of the reasons we flock to crispy and crunchy food is that we can hear it. It turns eating into a full sensory experience, making us think about the noisy food as we're eating it, which, in turn, makes eating less repetitive.

This makes sense when you think about how multisensory eating actually is. Much of our excitement at going to a fancy restaurant, for instance, is the visual appeal of the food (sight). Touch, too, plays a role, which is why using your hands to scoop up Indian masalas with a piece of roti is way more fun than eating them with a spoon. Eating crispy or crunchy foods adds in yet another sensation: sound. When you hear the food you're eating, it stimulates your brain more.

This is perhaps why it's impossible to eat just one potato chip (or if you're a fellow rabbit, just one carrot chip).

How to achieve crispy and crunchy textures in vegan cooking

Naturally crispy and crunchy foods

I am a big advocate of keeping several crunchy and crispy condiments in your pantry to make mealtime exciting. Pop over to the section starting on page 216 for inspiration.

TOASTED NUTS AND SEEDS: You'll find several nut and seed mixes in this book that'll elevate savory meals with an irresistible crunch.

And yes, toasting is required.

Toasting nuts and seeds releases their essential oils, allowing their true nutty essence to shine and giving you a deeper yet nuanced flavor and aroma. When using nuts and seeds for an accent, toasting them is a small but high-impact step: it costs nothing and can be done in 5 to 10 minutes. The reward? Bigger, roastier flavor and a firmer, crunchier texture. And who doesn't love a little crunch?

How to toast nuts and seeds

- You can toast nuts dry or with a bit of oil (oil adds a little more flavor and is essential if you want to add other seasonings, like spices and herbs).

- **Oven:** Spread the nuts or seeds out in a single layer on a sheet pan, or if using a smaller quantity, place them in a round or square baking pan (it's easier to shake the pan without them spilling out). Roast at 350°F (175°C) for 5 to 15 minutes, depending on the size and density of the nut or seed, shaking the pan halfway through. They're done when they smell aromatic and roasty.

- **Stovetop:** Heat up a skillet for a few minutes, typically over medium heat, but some nuts need medium-low heat (see the chart on page 115). Add the nuts or seeds and toss or shake fairly frequently to avoid burning. The goal is nuts or seeds that are lightly browned but not charred, with a nutty aroma.

- *Note:* I recommend the oven method for large nuts, as they toast more evenly; in contrast, on the stove, they burn in spots. Smaller nuts and seeds, such as pine nuts, sesame seeds, pepitas (shelled pumpkin seeds), and sunflower seeds work well with either method.

Try a raw walnut. If you're like me, you may not enjoy the flavor— they're bitter, waxy, and too earthy. Now toast some in the oven for 8 to 10 minutes. Are they still bitter? Or are they nutty, meaty, and even a little rich?

BREAD CRUMBS AND CROUTONS: Traditional store-bought bread crumbs are meh, but Japanese panko bread crumbs, which have a flaky, airy texture, are a magical ingredient. (Just check the label, as some brands add milk or eggs.) And while a classic crouton is always a welcome topper for a soup or salad, for extra punch, try the Nori Croutons on page 362.

USE IT TO BOOST TEXTURE AND ADD BIG FLAVOR: Toast panko in olive oil and salt to bring out its flavors and texture, and sprinkle it over pastas and soups for a salty and crunchy finish, cheesy baked dishes for textural contrast, or salads for a quick crispy topper. For more nutrition and pizzazz, toast panko alongside chopped nuts or seeds (see page 220). Use panko to bread vegetables or tofu, like the Crispy Sesame Baked Tofu on page 270, or as a crispy topping for a creamy casserole, like the braised leeks (page 414).

RAW VEGETABLES: Another reason we're attracted to crispy textures is that they're a reliable indicator that produce is fresh. Most of the salads in chapter 9 offer some level of crisp and/or crunchy textures, but here are even more ideas for using naturally crisp (crispy??) vegetables:

- **Fennel**, thinly sliced or shaved. Great in salads, especially with citrus (page 368).

- **Cucumbers**, smashed or chunked. Try the smashed cucumber salad on page 365.

- **Jicama**, sliced or matchsticked. Use in salads and slaws (especially good with lime juice, cilantro, and chile peppers).

- **Cabbage**, shredded finely. Great for slaws. Try the dilly one on page 529.

- **Kohlrabi**, spiralized or matchsticked. Use in salads with a creamy sauce or in a slaw with apples and shredded carrots.

- **Romaine or Little Gem lettuce**, chopped or sliced finely. In salads, obviously.

WHOLE SPICES: Coriander; mustard, cumin, and sesame seeds and dried curry and makrut lime leaves offer a lovely, if subtle, crunch when toasted or bloomed in oil.
RECIPE TO TRY: Cold Tofu with Coconut-Ginger-Lime Crisp (page 284).

FLAKY SEA SALT: Just a pinch or two of these crackly, crunchy flecks before serving will make most dishes taste better. Sprinkle on cooked vegetables, tomatoes, salads, bowls of beans, crunchy condiments, desserts, even avocado toast, and enter texture wonderland.

PICKLED VEGGIES: In addition to their bright acidic flavor, these add a nice crisp bite. You'll find a whole section of recipes starting on page 168.

FLOURS AND STARCHES: Flours and starches often aid in creating crispy or crunchy textures. Dredging vegetables or tofu in cornstarch, rice flour, all-purpose flour, or cornmeal makes for a lovely crispy coating, as in the Crunchy Spiced Tofu Nuggets (page 274) or Buttermilk Fried "Chicken" (page 524). And coating tofu in potato starch or arrowroot powder before baking or pan-frying gives it a delightful crunchy exterior.

Heat + fat = crispy and crunchy textures

As Harold McGee explains in *On Food and Cooking*, when fat is used to transfer heat to food (e.g., when eggplant is fried in oil), it helps it cook and brown more quickly. This unlocks new textures that would be impossible to achieve by cooking in water, and it also produces a richer flavor.

METHODS FOR TOASTING NUTS AND SEEDS

RAW NUT/SEED	OVEN (350°F/175°C) *(shake pan halfway through)*	STOVETOP *(preheat the pan for a few minutes)*
Almonds	10 minutes (15 minutes for deeply browned)	Medium or medium-low heat for 5 minutes, stirring frequently
Walnuts	8 to 10 minutes	Medium-low heat for 3 to 4 minutes, stirring frequently
Cashews	8 to 10 minutes	Not recommended
Pecans	5 to 7 minutes	Medium-low heat for 5 minutes, stirring frequently
Macadamia nuts	8 to 10 minutes	Not recommended
Pine nuts	6 to 8 minutes	Medium heat for 3 to 4 minutes, stirring frequently (preferred)
Pistachios	8 to 10 minutes	Medium heat for 3 to 4 minutes, stirring occasionally
Hazelnuts	10 to 15 minutes	Medium heat for 4 to 6 minutes, stirring occasionally
Sunflower seeds	8 to 10 minutes	Medium heat for 3 to 5 minutes, stirring frequently
Pepitas (shelled pumpkin seeds)	8 to 10 minutes	Medium heat for 3 to 5 minutes, stirring frequently
Sesame seeds	6 to 8 minutes	Medium heat for 2 to 4 minutes, stirring frequently

Heat plus fat is how squidgy mushrooms can get as crunchy as fried chicken (see page 524) and how dense potatoes can develop flaky, crispy bits (see page 407).

Some foods are naturally crispy or crunchy, but many others need to be cooked in a certain way to achieve these prized textures. Often, a chemical reaction is involved, such as the **Maillard reaction**—when the sugars and proteins in a food are heated and then take on new flavors and aromas—or **caramelization**, when the sugars in a food are heated and broken down, altering the flavor into something toastier, nuttier, and sweeter.

These reactions brown the surface of food, unlock new flavors, *and* contribute to crispy or crunchy textures. But they occur only at high temperatures and in dry heat (e.g., roasting, frying, searing, grilling, etc.), not in water. The highest temperature water can reach—212°F (100°C)—is not hot enough to jump-start these reactions, so no matter how hard you try, you'll never get crispy mushrooms by sautéing them in water.

Since fat heats up faster than water, it can transfer heat to food at higher temperatures. And that makes it uniquely able to unlock these new textures (and flavors) in many foods.

Potatoes + Fat + Heat: A classic winning combo. Bonus points if you steam or boil the potatoes, then roast or fry them: you'll get creamy, fluffy interiors yet crispy, flaky exteriors.

RECIPE TO TRY: Crispy Smashed Potatoes with Lots of Saucy Options (page 407).

Alliums + Fat + Heat: One of my favorite ways to boost flavor *and* texture is to shallow fry shallots, garlic, or leek tops. The crispy Fried Shallots (page 224) add a subtle crunch and mellow onion flavor to soups, salads, and veg plates. And fried dark green leek tops are not only a great way to reduce food waste but also downright delicious (see page 417).

USE IT TO BOOST TEXTURE AND ADD BIG FLAVOR: Gently fry thinly sliced garlic in warm olive oil and you'll get fantastically crunchy garlic chips (page 226). Add these to bowls of beans and lentils, pastas, and condiments like Life-Changing Homemade Chili Crisp (page 187).

Cruciferous Veggies + Fat + Heat: When you think of crispy foods, you probably don't think of the world's healthiest foods. But even cauliflower, broccoli, kale, cabbage, and Brussels sprouts can get a little crispy when cooked in a bit of fat at a high temperature.

RECIPE TO TRY: Lemon-Garlic Brussels Sprouts with Rosemary (page 334).

Legumes + Fat + Heat: Again, add a little oil and some high heat, and you can turn beans and lentils into addictively crunchy morsels. Get your crispy chickpea, bean, and lentil fix on pages 236, 240, and 253.

Chewy

After law school, I worked at a corporate law firm for two years. You were expected to be surgically glued to your BlackBerry, the mahogany walls were lined with enormous portraits of old white dudes, and no one used exclamation points in their emails. It was not my scene. But there was one thing I did like: the Snack Room.

Every afternoon, you could choose from either the least desirable fresh fruit (mealy Red Delicious apples) or big vats of candy, so I never left without a cupful of Sour Patch Kids. On occasion, though, the SPK stash had been drained, and I'd settle for the next best option: Swedish Fish.

I actually disliked the cough syrup–esque flavor of Swedish Fish. But the texture? I could spend an entire minute eating one candy, the repetitive chewing distracting me from the awfully boring memos I was writing.

And chewy food textures are often associated with exactly this: highly processed candy. Or worse, with overcooked meats.

But when done right, chewy foods are fantastic. They force you to spend more time with them. And the more you have to chew a food, the longer it sits on your palate, so the more it unfolds on your taste buds. All this time spent masticating contributes to a richer, more pleasurable eating experience. Luckily, there's a host of chewy food textures we can call upon in the plant world.

How to achieve chewy textures in vegan cooking

WHOLE GRAINS: Whole grains are delicious and nutritious, and my favorite grain of all, farro, is delightfully chewy. Wheat berries are even chewier. Barley, spelt, and even steel-cut oats also offer a nice chew. And while not a *whole* grain, pearl couscous brings a lovely bouncy chew.

RECIPES TO TRY: Rosemary Farrotto with Cheesy Pine Nuts (page 311), Customizable Grain Salad with Garlicky Spiced Oil & Fresh Herbs (page 305).

PASTA (AL DENTE): Soft pasta is what we serve babies and folks recovering from dental surgery. *Al dente* pasta, on the other hand, is chewy and feels like an adult meal. This is why my recipes typically say to cook pasta "until just al dente," or even a couple of minutes less than that when you're finishing the pasta in a pan sauce.

VEGAN MEAT SUBSTITUTES

TOFU: Tofu on its own is not chewy, but with a few techniques up your sleeve, it definitely can be.

First, **freezing tofu** changes its molecular composition, causing the water molecules inside it to expand. Once thawed, the tofu develops aerated, spongelike pockets. This has several benefits: (1) it extracts a lot of water, making the tofu chewier; (2) thanks to the more porous texture, the tofu can better absorb flavors from marinades and sauces; and (3) the tofu crisps up better when seared, fried, or baked.

I've tested several recipes using (1) refrigerated tofu and (2) previously frozen and thawed tofu, and the latter usually wins: it ends up more flavorful and has a pleasing chewy texture. It doesn't taste like meat, but the spongy pockets do mimic meat proteins and thus the chewiness of meat (in a less aggressive way). One caveat: Skip the thawed tofu when *deep-frying*, as the tofu will absorb too much oil.

Second, **briefly boiling tofu in generously salted water or soaking it in salted boiling water** also makes it spongier and chewier. Plus, the salt seasons the tofu from within, improving its flavor. See these techniques in the Thai Red Curry with Tofu (page 489) and Tofu 65 (page 477), respectively.

Third, **coating tofu with a starch**—potato starch, cornstarch, or arrowroot powder—before baking or frying will enhance its chewiness (and crispiness).

Alternatively, **braising tofu**, as in the Sticky Coconut Milk–Braised Tofu (page 278), makes it delightfully chewy yet tender.

TIPS FOR BUYING: Buy firm, extra-firm, and especially super-firm varieties for chewiness. Not all brands are created equally. My favorites are Wildwood, House Foods' organic line, Hodo Foods, and Nasoya.

RECIPE TO TRY: I Can't Believe It's Not Chicken (Super-Savory Grated Tofu) on page 281 (grated super-firm tofu = supremely chewy and meaty).

TEMPEH: Tempeh, made from fermented whole cooked soybeans, brings a subtle chewiness. Plus, it's a good source of umami, making it a great meat substitute. To learn how to make tempeh taste amazing, check out page 291.

JACKFRUIT: At first glance, jackfruit—a low-calorie tropical tree fruit—is an odd choice for a meat substitute. However, when shredded, it mimics the chewy texture of pulled pork or chicken remarkably well.

TIPS FOR BUYING: Look for "young" or "green" jackfruit canned in water or brine, not syrup. I prefer the cans from Trader Joe's, as they have only a modest amount of sodium.

USE IT TO BOOST TEXTURE: Use jackfruit as a "pulled" meat substitute for tacos or sandwiches, or in "chicken" noodle soup, curries, or enchiladas. Add it to chili or lettuce wraps, use in "crab" cakes, or batter and deep-fry it like chicken. When cooking jackfruit on the stove, sear it first in a hot pan to crisp it up before adding any liquid.

OTHER MEAT SUBSTITUTES

Then there are the more processed meat substitutes, which mirror the chewiness of animal-based meats extremely well. These include seitan (essentially wheat gluten), TVP (textured vegetable protein), and the ever-growing number of premade meat substitutes.

While I use these products pretty sparingly, here are my thoughts. For vegan sausage, I'm partial to Beyond Meat, which has the same chewy texture as classic sausage. I also like Field Roast sausages, which taste less meaty but have great chew. For "ground" meat, I think Impossible Foods' burger is best.

RECIPES TO TRY: Korean BBQ Jackfruit Sandwiches with Creamy Sesame Slaw (page 508), The Sexy Skillet Lasagna (page 519).

SUN-DRIED TOMATOES (OIL-PACKED): These chewy, umami-rich nuggets are great in pastas, condiments like the Italian Basil & Parsley Salsa Verde on page 181, and stews. Oil-packed ones have more flavor and a juicier texture than dry-packed ones, which need to be rehydrated.

DRIED FRUITS: Dried fruits offer a lovely chewiness in both savory and sweet recipes. A few pairings I enjoy that you may, too:

- **Dried cranberries and cherries** in Brussels sprouts or kale salads and wild rice salads.

- **Medjool dates** with roasted cauliflower, winter squash, or carrots; in Middle Eastern–ish rice or grain dishes; and in no-bake desserts.

- **Dried apricots** in Middle Eastern–inspired rice or grain dishes or tagines. I prefer Turkish apricots, which are plumper and chewier.

- **Golden raisins** in Indian- and Middle Eastern–inspired rice or grain dishes, as well as in tagines. They're delicious pickled (use the quick-pickle brine on page 168).

RECIPES TO TRY: Spice-Roasted Whole Carrots with dates (page 329), Pearl Couscous & Chickpea Salad with Preserved Lemon (page 323).

MUSHROOMS: When cooked right, mushrooms can be a great source of chewiness. I love them so much that I have included a mini chapter of shroom recipes in chapter 12.

BREADS: In particular, sourdough, focaccia, naan, and flatbreads offer exceptional chew. Many of my recipes include a serving suggestion for "a hunk of bread" because it's the lowest-stress and arguably most delicious way to round out a meal. I buy loaves from local bakeries and freeze what I can't eat in a few days.

RECIPE TO TRY: Simple Flatbread (page 535).

DON'T THROW AWAY THAT OLD BREAD! To revive stale bread, briefly run your bread under tap water (weird, right?!), trying not to get the cut side wet. Bake on a sheet pan in the oven at 300°F (150°C) until dry and crunchy on the outside, 6 to 12 minutes.

CORN TORTILLAS: I love the hefty chew of a corn tortilla. When you char tortillas over an open gas flame, they become wonderfully crisp-chewy.

EAST ASIAN AND SOUTHEAST ASIAN INGREDIENTS: Many ingredients in East Asian and Southeast Asian cuisine epitomize chewiness, like Korean and Japanese rice cakes. Even some of the more commonly available Asian foods—like chubby udon noodles, sticky rice, and all varieties of rice noodles—offer a nice chew.

RECIPE TO TRY: Malaysian Curry Noodle Soup (page 468). You get two kinds of chewiness: rice noodles and tofu puffs.

CERTAIN BAKED GOODS: Flax "eggs"—simply a mixture of flaxseed meal and water—are particularly helpful for developing chewiness in baked goods. And aquafaba—the liquid from a can of chickpeas—when whipped with sugar for several minutes makes for the best chewy yet fudgy vegan brownies.

TIPS FOR USING: To make 1 flax egg, mix 1 tablespoon flaxseed meal with 2½ tablespoons warm water; whisk well and rest for 15 minutes to gel. Aquafaba, when just lightly whipped until foamy, is an excellent egg substitute for a different reason: it adds a fluffy tenderness to cakes and muffins. Typically, you will use 3 tablespoons aquafaba to replace 1 egg.

RECIPES TO TRY: Soft & Chewy Ginger Cookies with Cardamom Sugar (page 553), Fudgy Skillet Brownies with Raspberry Swirl Ice Cream (page 580).

Pairing Textures

We expect certain foods to have a uniform texture—crunchy carrot chips, crisp apples, chewy raisins. But, as with flavor, often our greatest pleasure comes from eating dishes with textural contrast, as it gives us a varied sensory experience.

Think about the contrast in a Caesar salad with its addictive medley of crisp romaine, crunchy croutons, and creamy dressing. Or how we fight over the chewy cookie dough chunks tucked into a pint of soft ice cream. The differing physical sensations work in tandem to heighten our pleasure.

Contrasting textures also deliver a varied taste experience. Imagine a dish that features butternut squash two ways. First, half of the squash is peeled and cubed; roasted in oil, maple syrup, salt, and pepper; then pureed. The puree gets smeared on a serving plate. The other half of the squash is peeled and also roasted with the same ingredients, but this time it's sliced very thinly so it crisps up in the oven. These crispy slices are served on top of the creamy puree.

Both are made from the same ingredients, but because their textures are so distinct, they will release their tastes differently in our mouths.

Here's a sampling of some recipes that pair contrasting textures beautifully:

"Cream"-Braised Leeks with Crispy Bits (page 414)

creamy + crispy

The Fancy Caesar Salad (page 362)

creamy + crisp + crunchy + chewy

Mushroom Carnitas Tacos (page 540)

creamy + crispy + crisp + chewy

Glazed Torn Beets with Pistachio Butter & Mint (page 395)

creamy + chewy

Cheesy Herb Bread Pudding with Caramelized Leeks (page 459)

creamy + crunchy + chewy

Smashed Cucumbers with Yogurt-Tahini Sauce & Spicy "Honey" (page 365)

creamy + crunchy

Crispy Indian-ish Lentils with Rice & Yogurt (page 259)

creamy + crunchy + chewy

Rosemary Farrotto with Cheesy Pine Nuts (page 311)

creamy + chewy + crunchy

Indian-Spiced Charred Corn Salad (page 383)

crunchy + chewy

The next time you're whipping up a meal on the fly, try to remember that one of the best ways to turn a meh dish into a great one is to add textural variety. Fold buttery avocado chunks into a crisp salad, then pepper it with crunchy dukkah (page 62), and your salad will be infinitely better. Finish a velvety soup with toasted panko and your taste buds will squeal with delight at the creamy-crunchy contrast. If you're eager to get started, flip to chapter 5 and explore the many creamy and crispy/crunchy flavor boosters you can start adding to your rotation.

A QUICK HANDY GUIDE FOR COOKING ON THE FLY

1. Does the dish taste well seasoned?

If the flavors feel muted, try adding a pinch or two of salt.

2. Do any of the flavors feel dull or flat?

Consult the sources of acidity starting on page 54 and add a splash or squeeze of what you have on hand that makes the most sense flavorwise.

3. Do the flavors feel balanced overall? Or is one flavor dominating the others? Is there a particular flavor you wish you could taste more?

Consult page 100 to see what ingredients you have on hand that can tame any overpowering flavors and/or enhance any lackluster flavors.

4. What are the textures like?

If the dish feels too one-note creamy, is there something crunchy or crispy in your pantry you can add to jazz things up? If a soup is lacking in mouthfeel, try a drizzle of olive oil. If a salad feels too monotonous, fold in a few different textures, like creamy Whipped Tofu Ricotta (page 206), crisp fresh vegetables, crunchy toasted nuts, or chewy dried fruit.

Conquering Your Kitchen

As much as I'd love to continue waxing poetic about the *how* and the *why* of cooking, it's time to move on to some everyday tips that will also help you master vegan cooking.

Certain kitchen tools will make meal planning and weeknight cooking a breeze, and certain pantry ingredients will set you up for success when you're freestyling in the kitchen, so I've listed my go-to equipment and pantry staples in the following sections.

As you expand your arsenal of ingredients and up your vegetable intake, you may find yourself struggling to keep your ingredients fresh, so you'll also find techniques for the optimal storage of plant-based ingredients and getting the most out of your food.

Recommended Kitchenware

I rarely use specialty kitchen gadgets, but I do rely on a handful of essential tools to make plant-based cooking easier and more enjoyable. Some of these tools are absolute musts (e.g., good knives), while others aren't necessary per se but make cooking more efficient (e.g., citrus squeezer). If you have a restaurant supply store in your area, you can stock up on restaurant-quality equipment at a deep discount.

Blending and mixing

FOOD PROCESSOR: A food processor is essential for many high-impact condiments: vegan cheeses, nut mixes and butters, curry pastes, herb sauces, and more. You can also use the standard S-blade and pulse function to roughly chop veg, rice cauliflower, knead dough, and grind oats into "flour." And the slicing and shredding discs allow you to quickly slice or shred large amounts of veg. If you have the space, I recommend a model with a 12 cup (3 L) or greater capacity.

HIGH-POWERED BLENDER: Invaluable for truly smooth nut-based creams, sauces, and butters. I also use it to puree velvety soups and legumes into creamy concoctions. I opt for my Vitamix over the food processor when blending a lot of liquid or when I want a *super*smooth consistency. Having a small-capacity blender cup (e.g., 32 ounces or 1 L) is helpful if you regularly blend ingredients that don't contain very much liquid (e.g., curry paste, nut butters, or cashew creams).

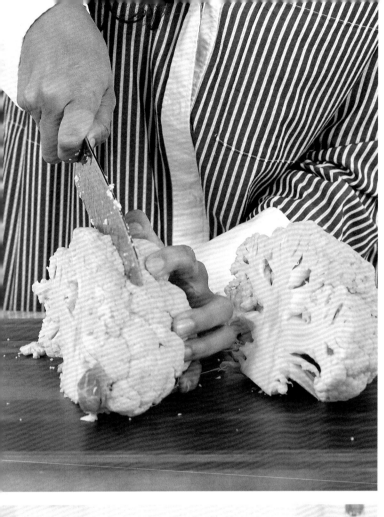

While high-powered blenders are expensive, they are very durable. I had the same Vitamix for twelve years before a Black Friday sale lured me into buying a new one. You can save money by purchasing a "refurbished" blender.

COOKING TIP: Blend a third or half of any soup, chili, stew, or gravy, then stir it back into the rest of the pot. It's a natural thickener (no nuts or cream needed)!

IMMERSION BLENDER: Nice when you don't want to break out the regular blender.

HANDHELD ELECTRIC MIXER: Necessary if you bake regularly.

Cooking pans

After dabbling in the trendy world of made-for-Instagram kitchenware, I've found that it's far more sensible to invest in—and slowly collect—high-quality pans that will last decades.

CAST-IRON PANS: Cast-iron pans are the Cabernet Sauvignon of the pots-and-pans crew: they age well, can last decades, and bring joy. Unlike nonstick pans, you can get them ripping hot, and they retain heat better, so you get sexy caramelized crusts and edges. Plus, they're versatile and can be used on the stovetop, in the oven, even in baking.

I recommend a medium (9- or 10-inch/23 or 25 cm) skillet and a deeper, large (12-inch/30 cm) skillet for versatility, though if you can spring for just one, pick the larger one. I prefer enameled cast iron, as it's easier to care for, but raw cast iron is also great (just avoid cooking acidic foods for long periods of time in it).

STAINLESS STEEL SKILLETS AND POTS: A stainless steel skillet and saucepan are solid everyday pans you can use for most things. Food does stick a bit more with these, but the flip side is you get great searing and gorgeously golden-brown exteriors. I prefer a 10-inch (25 cm) skillet for things like toasting nuts and frying garlic, and a deeper 12-inch (30 cm) sauté pan for more involved cooking. A medium (3-quart/2.8 L) saucepan is versatile for most tasks.

COOKING TIP: To prevent sticking in stainless steel cookware, preheat the pan for 2 to 3 minutes over medium or medium-high heat. To test if the pan is hot enough, add a few droplets of water to the pan. If the water evaporates or sizzles immediately, it's not hot enough. If the water beads up and starts gliding across the pan, the pan is ready. Now add your oil to briefly heat, followed by the food.

NONSTICK SKILLETS: Useful for foods that stick a lot, like tofu, tempeh, and pancakes. The best one I own is the Tramontina Professional Fry Pan, which tends to brown food better than most nonstick pans, but no nonstick pan will last forever. Once it starts to lose its coating, it's time for a new one. Use silicone or wooden spatulas with these. If you have just one size, a 12-inch (30 cm) pan will be most versatile.

ENAMELED DUTCH OVEN: An all-purpose pot with even heat circulation useful for stews, soups, curries, vegetable braises, pots of beans, and more. Also great for stove-to-oven cooking (these pans are heavy, though, so bend them knees). I recommend a 5- or 6-quart (5 or 6 L) model for most folks, but smaller options work if you cook for just one or two or have difficulty lifting heavy pots.

FLAT-BOTTOMED WOK: The best tool for high-heat, quick-cooking stir-fries, especially woks made from carbon steel. They're lightweight, so you can easily toss the wok and prevent the food from burning. Very helpful if you like to make East Asian and Southeast Asian dishes.

RIMMED SHEET PANS: I use large rimmed sheet pans (a.k.a. half sheet pans, 18 × 13 inches/45 × 33 cm in size) for many things: to roast vegetables, toast bread, make croutons, bake tofu, get nuts roasty. Choose aluminum pans, which conduct heat the best. And don't be tempted to toss your well-worn pans: they brown vegetables (and tofu and beans) better and quicker.

BAKING PANS: For baking enthusiasts, an 8-inch (20 cm) and/or 9-inch (23 cm) square pan and a 9 × 5-inch (23 × 13 cm) loaf pan are essential. Round 8- or 9-inch (20 or 23 cm) cake pans are nice too. For baked goods, use metal pans, as they bake more evenly than glass (something to do with physics).

ELECTRIC PRESSURE COOKER: If you like to batch cook beans/lentils/grains, this is invaluable. I'm partial to the Instant Pot because, well, my first cookbook is *The Vegan Instant Pot Cookbook*.

Cooking tools

SILICONE SPATULAS: There is no better way to scrape out *all* the batter from a bowl or food processor than a silicone spoonula. I keep several spatula styles on hand, including a turner that can be used to flip delicate items like tofu.

WOODEN SPOONS: A workhorse tool you can use in many ways. I also recommend a flat-edged wooden spoon for deglazing, to scrape up all the sticky browned bits from the bottom of the pot.

TONGS: Large metal tongs are very useful for flipping things when you're cooking over high heat and want to keep distance between your precious bodily flesh and the flame. Also they're great for tossing pasta to properly coat it in a sauce.

SMALL OFFSET SPATULA: Surprisingly useful for many things, including flipping delicate items like tofu, loosening baked goods from pans, and frosting cakes like a pro.

BALLOON WHISK: Stainless steel whisks are sturdiest, but use a silicone whisk in a nonstick pan.

SLOTTED SPOONS: Slotted spoons are the best tool to remove pasta, potatoes, or veggies from a pot when you want to keep the liquid. A spider is essential for deep-frying.

Prep tools

SHARP KNIVES: A sharp chef's knife or santoku knife and a paring knife are essential. A serrated bread knife and a utility knife (kind of a mini chef's knife) are great if you have room in your budget.

MANDOLINE: A mandoline is extremely useful when you need to thinly and evenly slice a vegetable or aromatic. It's also great for shaving raw vegetables into delicate wisps for salads. The OXO handheld mandoline slicer works with most foods and takes up very little drawer space. If you like your hands, always wear a cut-resistant glove while using a mandoline.

SPICE GRINDER AND/OR MORTAR AND PESTLE: For grinding whole spices (see page 74). An electric spice grinder can pulverize spices in seconds. A mortar and pestle is a nice alternative, especially if you want to retain some texture.

MICROPLANES AND GRATERS: Whenever a recipe calls for citrus zest, I use a Microplane, as it's the best way to get all the zest without the bitter white pith below. I also use it to grate nutmeg and to turn ginger and garlic into a pulp. If you want to retain more texture with your garlic and ginger, use a medium etched grater, which is faster than mincing by hand and easier to clean than a garlic press.

WOODEN CUTTING BOARD: I'm partial to my oversize Boos Block. It clocks in at 24 inches long, which means it has SO MUCH space for all the prep that needs prepping.

SALAD SPINNER: I use my salad spinner to efficiently wash salad greens, herbs, and berries, as well as to dry beans before baking. It's also useful for removing excess water from salted veggies, like cucumbers or eggplant.

COLANDERS AND SIEVES: Colanders are for draining the big things (pasta, beans, veggies); fine-mesh sieves for the smaller things (rice, sifting sugar or cocoa, straining sauces).

BENCH SCRAPER: I use a bench scraper to neatly scrape up my prepped ingredients from the cutting board and transfer them to the pan.

CITRUS SQUEEZER: This gets *all* the juice out of your lemons and limes and is quicker than juicing by hand.

Y-SHAPED PEELER: Peels quicker and smoother than a standard swivel peeler and makes for gorgeous vegetable ribbons.

MIXING BOWLS: A set of inexpensive nested mixing bowls in various sizes makes mise en place and baking much smoother. Always err on the side of choosing a bowl that looks too big. You need a surprising amount of empty space at the top of a bowl to properly mix a cake batter and dress a salad.

Precision tools

DIGITAL SCALE: Some folks think that a digital scale is overkill, but measuring by weight instead of by volume yields more accurate results, especially in baking. It's also faster and cleaner than using five different measuring cups. Plus, you don't have to deal with the impossible task of figuring out how to properly measure, say, 1 cup of whole mushrooms. If you prefer measuring cups, use dry measuring cups for dry ingredients (flours, sugars, etc.) and liquid measuring cups for liquids (oils, water, milks, syrups, etc.).

MEASURING SPOONS: Measuring spoons are a necessity because a flatware tablespoon does NOT equal a measuring tablespoon (Mom, are you reading?).

OVEN THERMOMETER: The oven in my second Brooklyn apartment was off by 100°F (37°C)! Once you know what temperature you're truly working with, you can adjust it accordingly. I swear by the ThermoWorks DOT thermometer, which attaches to the outside of your oven while a long metal probe reaches into your oven.

PAINTER'S TAPE: To label all the sauces and condiments you'll be making in this book. Write the name and date made.

KITCHEN TIMER: If your robot voice assistant always mangles your instructions, a good old-fashioned kitchen timer is key (or use the timer function on your oven or microwave).

For those new-ish to vegan cooking (or cooking in general), I've created some bonus video content to help you master techniques used throughout this book. These short videos cover everything from how to clean and tear mushrooms to how to grind whole spices. To watch the videos, visit **rainbowplantlife.com /mastery.**

A NOTE ON MEASUREMENTS

I typically measure ingredients *before* chopping. When an ingredient has been chopped and then measured afterward, the ingredient will say "¼ cup (40 g) chopped dried cranberries." On the other hand, "¼ cup (40 g) dried cranberries, chopped" means to measure ¼ cup/40 g of dried cranberries, then chop them.

The Vegan Flavor Pantry

Here is a list of the pantry ingredients I regularly use for big flavor. I've covered most of these in more detail in chapters 1 through 3. See page 264 for more info on tofu, page 232 for more on beans, and page 522 for more on mushrooms.

Salts (and Pepper)

○ Diamond Crystal kosher salt

○ Fine sea salt

○ Flaky or coarse sea salt (e.g., Maldon or Jacobsen)

○ Indian black salt (kala namak)

○ Freshly ground black pepper

Cooking Fats

○ Extra-virgin olive oil

○ Neutral-flavored oils, like grapeseed oil, avocado oil, canola oil, sunflower oil

○ Coconut oil (refined for a more neutral flavor; unrefined for a coconut flavor)

○ Vegan butter (sticks or blocks, not tubs or spreads)

Fatty Condiments

○ Nuts, especially cashews, almonds (raw and roasted), walnuts, pistachios (raw and roasted), and pine nuts

○ Seeds, including pepitas (shelled pumpkin seeds), sunflower seeds, white and black sesame seeds, hemp seeds, and flaxseed meal (for baking)

○ Tahini

○ Almond butter (roasted unsweetened)

○ Canned full-fat coconut milk

○ Creamy plant milks (e.g., oat, soy)

○ Olives

○ Toasted sesame oil

Savory Condiments

○ Soy sauce or tamari

○ White miso paste

○ Umeboshi paste

○ Nutritional yeast

○ Vegetable broth and/or bouillon

○ Dried shiitake and porcini mushrooms (and porcini mushroom powder)

○ Tomato paste (in a tube)

○ Canned whole peeled tomatoes and crushed tomatoes

○ Sun-dried tomatoes (oil-packed)

○ Seaweeds (e.g., nori, kombu)

Tangy Condiments

- ○ Lemons and limes
- ○ Distilled white vinegar
- ○ Unseasoned rice vinegar
- ○ Champagne vinegar and/or red wine vinegar
- ○ Apple cider vinegar
- ○ Aged balsamic vinegar
- ○ Pomegranate molasses (no sugar added)
- ○ White wine and red wine (vegan-friendly)
- ○ Dijon mustard
- ○ Capers
- ○ Tamarind paste/concentrate

Sweet Condiments

- ○ Pure maple syrup
- ○ Agave nectar
- ○ Organic cane sugar
- ○ Organic brown sugar
- ○ Coconut sugar
- ○ Medjool dates

Spices

- ○ Too many to list here! Flip to page 70 for inspiration.

Spicy Condiments

- ○ Spicy chile flakes (red pepper flakes, Sichuan chile flakes)
- ○ Mild chile flakes (Aleppo pepper, gochugaru)
- ○ Chili sauces and pastes (sambal oelek, chili-garlic sauce, gochujang, harissa, Calabrian chili paste)
- ○ Thai curry pastes (vegan-friendly)
- ○ Chipotle peppers in adobo

Protein Essentials

- ○ Canned and dried beans of all ilks, especially chickpeas and cannellini beans
- ○ Dried lentils
  - Red lentils
  - Split yellow lentils
  - French green lentils or black beluga lentils
  - Green or brown lentils

Grain Essentials

- ○ Long-grain white rice (e.g., jasmine and basmati)
- ○ Long-grain brown rice
- ○ Farro
- ○ Many kinds of noodles, especially ramen, udon, and thin rice noodles

Optimal food storage

×

The reality of food waste is hard to
ignore, with up to 40 percent of food
grown in the US ending up in landfills.
Here are a few tips and tricks for
getting the most out of the plant-based
food you bring into your home.

Nuts and seeds	There's nothing more disappointing than spending forty-seven dollars on a half cup of pine nuts only to realize they've gone rancid. Nuts and seeds can go bad quickly, so I prefer to freeze most of them, as they thaw almost immediately and don't take up valuable fridge real estate. If you use certain nuts or seeds regularly, you can store small quantities in your pantry. Nut flours, once opened, should be refrigerated or frozen.
Dried beans and lentils	These stay good for at least a year if kept in a cool, dry area away from sunlight. Store in an airtight container instead of the bags they came in for longer freshness. You can freeze cooked lentils or beans for up to 6 months.
Grains and flours	Store in airtight containers away from heat and light for maximal freshness and shelf life. Freeze the varieties you use infrequently.
Spices	See page 70.
Fresh herbs	See page 76. GET MORE OUT OF IT: Cilantro's and parsley's tender stems are edible and tasty. I use them unless specified. For more ideas on upcycling herbs, check out page 80.
Sturdy greens	Strip kale, collards, and chard from their stems and tear into pieces or slice thinly. Wash well, then dry in a salad spinner or on towels. Add to a large resealable bag lined with a few paper towels or thin dish towel; refrigerate for up to 10 days. GET MORE OUT OF IT · To make it more likely you'll actually eat the kale you bought, when you get home from the market, wash, strip, and finely shred the kale. Briefly

Sturdy greens *(cont.)*	massage with a little olive oil and/or lemon juice. Store in an airtight bag, perforated with holes, for up to 1 week.
	· Raw kale stems taste like horse roughage, but when briefly sautéed, they're excellent, as in the Garlicky Kale on page 333. Vibrant rainbow chard stems are begging to be pickled (use the quick-pickle brine on page 168).
Lettuces	When you get home, wrap lettuce heads in paper towels or a thin dish towel, then store in a resealable bag or salad clamshell; wash when ready to use. Whole heads are typically fresher than prepackaged ones.
	GET MORE OUT OF IT
	· To extend the life of prepackaged salad greens, soak in cold water for 10 minutes and dry well in a salad spinner or on towels.
	· Salad greens typically stay fresh longer when stored in plastic clamshell containers instead of plastic bags. Line the container with a paper towel or a thin dish towel, add your greens, and cover with another layer of towels. They should last for around 10 days.
	· Found sad, limp lettuce in the back of your crisper? Submerge the leaves in a bowl of ice water, refrigerate, and soak for 30 minutes (or longer if needed). Rinse with fresh water and dry well.
Root vegetables	Look for carrots and beets that have their green tops still attached—it usually means they've been picked more recently than their topless counterparts.
	Once you get home, remove those tops, as they strip moisture out of the veggies. Rinse the tops now or later, and store loosely wrapped in towel-lined bags for a few days. Store the vegetables in a sealed bag or container in the crisper (when stored loosely, they shrivel up).
	GET MORE OUT OF IT: When carrots, beets, radishes, or turnips are in season and their green tops look good, use them in pesto, gremolata, or other

Optimal food storage

Root vegetables *(cont.)*	herby condiments. Stir into a tofu scramble or soup, mix with mellow-flavored butter lettuce for a salad, use in homemade broth, or sauté with garlic.
Potatoes	Store in a cool, dark area, like your cupboards. Don't store with onions so that both vegetables stay fresh longer.
Onions and garlic	Store on the counter for a couple of weeks, uncovered and unbagged (generally, produce at room temperature needs to breathe).
Ginger	Fresh ginger stays good in the fridge for several weeks, even longer when frozen. Plus, frozen ginger is easier to grate and doesn't need to be thawed. Freeze in 1- or 2-inch (2.5 to 5 cm) chunks to conveniently use in recipes. PS: When using ginger in cooked applications like curries and soups, I don't bother peeling it because the skin is edible.
Tomatoes	For the love of all that is delicious, stop refrigerating tomatoes. It zaps their aroma and flavor. Looking at you, Mom and Dad! To extend their shelf life, store tomatoes stem side down.
Citrus	If you go through lemons frequently like I do, you can store them on the counter for 7 to 10 days. For longer storage, place in a tightly sealed bag or in a bowl of water and refrigerate for up to a month. For cut citrus, wrap it in food or plastic wrap and refrigerate for a few days. GET MORE OUT OF IT: Use citrus zest whenever you can! You can also zest or peel your citrus, place it on parchment paper, and freeze briefly; once frozen, transfer to an airtight bag for 1 to 2 months (the zest loses color but keeps most of its punch). You can freeze leftover citrus juice, but use only in recipes that require a small amount.

When you cook plant-based, you regularly end up with stray bits and bobs of asparagus stalks, onion ends, scallion tops, and less-than-perky carrots in the back of the crisper. Store these in a gallon-size (2 L) freezer-safe bag in your freezer. When it's full, make vegetable broth.

BROCCOLI AND CAULIFLOWER STALKS. Cruciferous vegetables might turn broth bitter, but there are many other things you can do with leftover stalks.

First, cook the broccoli stalks, because they're just as tasty as the florets. Sliced into coins, they brown well; chopped finely, they add crunch to stir-fries. You can also use a Y-shaped peeler to shave the stalks into paper-thin wisps for salads. Or pulse them in a food processor to make "broccoli rice" or "cauliflower rice."

POTATO AND BUTTERNUT SQUASH PEELS. Toss the peels with olive oil, salt, and seasonings; spread out on a sheet pan, and bake at 425°F (220°C) until browned and crispy, 15 to 25 minutes. Makes an oddly satisfying snack. Since potatoes are starchy, soak the peels in cold water for 15 to 30 minutes, then dry in a salad spinner before baking.

LEEK TOPS. Dark green leek tops are often discarded as "too tough," but they're edible! Just remove any wilted or browned tops, then cook them alongside the leek whites. Or take them to the next level and fry until crispy (check out page 417).

FENNEL FRONDS AND STALKS. The fronds are the frilly, wispy leaves attached to fennel stalks. They have a lovely anise flavor, and I always use them as a garnish when using fennel bulbs. Fold them into salads, pesto, or herby salsas, and use in place of dill or parsley. The stalks are tough, so chop them very finely if using raw, or freeze for soups and broth.

CELERY AND CAULIFLOWER LEAVES. Celery leaves are great in salads. Stir-fry cauliflower leaves.

Optimal food storage

Vegetable scraps (*cont.*)	**LEMONGRASS STALKS.** When making a curry or soup, cut the tough stalks and outer layers into manageable pieces (see page 472) and simmer in the liquid for extra flavor (discard before serving). To freeze leftover lemongrass, cut into 2-inch (5 cm) chunks and store in a freezer bag for several months.

GET MORE OUT OF IT: Make lemongrass tea with the inedible parts: smash down on the stalks to release the aroma, roughly chop, and add to a saucepan with water; chuck in some sliced ginger. Boil for 5 to 10 minutes; steep covered for 5 minutes; strain and sweeten to taste. |
| **Canned condiments** | **CHIPOTLE PEPPERS IN ADOBO.** Most recipes call for just one or two of these peppers, so transfer leftovers to a glass jar and refrigerate for 1 to 2 months. Or transfer one to two peppers along with 1 teaspoon or 1 tablespoon of the sauce to ice cube trays and freeze. Once frozen, store in a resealable bag. If adding the cubes to a hot liquid, no need to thaw.

TOMATO PASTE. I always recommend buying tomato paste in a tube instead of a can for both flavor and food waste reasons. Flavorwise, tube tomato paste has no tinny aftertaste and is preserved with salt instead of citric acid, so it has a brighter tomato flavor. Plus, you can also store an opened tube in your fridge for 6 weeks, compared to 6 days for an opened can. For longer storage, use the ice cube freezer technique from above. |
| **Jarred condiments** | I love using pickle juice and olive brine in condiments, like the Cheesy Crunchies on page 223, as well as in vinaigrettes and dressings for potato salad, pasta salad, and coleslaw. Olive brine is great in olive-heavy cuisines (e.g., Mediterranean and Middle Eastern) and is a fun addition to hummus, aioli, and marinara sauce. Caper brine is fantastic in pasta sauces and vinaigrettes, especially creamy ones that need some tang. If using an oil-preserved condiment, like sun-dried tomatoes or artichokes, save the flavored oil for vinaigrettes. |

Before You Begin

A few final thoughts to help you nail every recipe in this book (and all recipes for the rest of eternity).

Cook with all your senses

Be sure to taste as you go, but don't rely solely on your sense of taste. Use your sense of *touch* to pick out the best produce at the market and your sense of *hearing* to test whether the oil is hot enough (did the onions sizzle when they hit the pan?). Use your sense of *smell* to tell if the nuts are done toasting and *sight* to notice that your sauce is drying out and needs more broth.

Read through the recipe first

Making a recipe before you read it through is like trying to answer reading comprehension questions on the SAT before reading the prompt. If you take a couple of minutes to read the recipe and the headnote (which is packed with valuable information and the occasional charming anecdote), I promise it will save you time and stress later on.

A digital scale is your best friend

To make the recipes friendly for all, I have provided imperial and metric measurements. If you use the metric measurements with a digital scale, you will get the most precise results. If you're using measuring cups, don't pack an ingredient loosely or tightly unless specified.

Don't be afraid to adjust the heat

In my spare time, I imagine a world where everyone has the exact same stove and oven. It's a gas stove with the environmental footprint of an induction stove and has (at least) four burners whose temperature-control knobs always match the stated heat level. The oven is spacious and circulates heat evenly, and the broiler has various temperature settings.

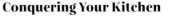

I've done my best to provide detailed instructions, but some recipes will work differently for you because we all have different stoves, ovens, and cookware. If the recipe says the onions should take 12 minutes to turn brown, but your onions have dark edges by the 7-minute mark, turn down the heat. A visual indicator is always superior to a precise time. If your oven runs hot, consider reducing the temperature by 25°F (5°C) and/or checking a few minutes earlier (and get an oven thermometer!). Speaking of ovens, open your oven door only when needed and close it as reasonably quickly as you can. Leaving the door open for just a few seconds can significantly drop the oven's internal temperature, increasing the cook time of your dishes.

Season and taste as you go

Remember, adding a little salt throughout the cooking process will make your food taste more balanced and more flavorful than if you just season it all at once. And if you're able to taste a recipe while it's still cooking, PLEASE take advantage of this opportunity. When you taste as you go, you have so much more control over how your meal ends up tasting.

Take shortcuts if you need to

If your budget allows it, buy precut veggies and prewashed salad greens. Or swap the grain in a recipe with frozen 3-minute rice if that's what the day calls for. And don't bother peeling ginger.

Don't be afraid to get your hands dirty

There's no tool that can do what the human hand can do. Your hands are the best way to gauge whether a lime is juicy, the best utensil for adding the right pinch of salt, and the best tool for dredging tofu. Using your hands brings you closer to your food and to yourself, elevating cooking from a practical activity to a form of engaged and intuitive mindfulness.

Also, cooking with your hands is just a lot of fun. And cooking should be fun.

The Build Block

ing
Recipes

I think of building blocks as categories of foods—veggies, proteins, grains, sauces, toppings, and so on—that you combine to make complete meals. Building blocks can often be prepped ahead of time, and they almost always pair beautifully with a variety of foods, making them great for weekly meal planning and prep.

The next four chapters are packed with building blocks that will allow you to create a huge variety of meals.

In chapter 5, you'll find condiments and flavor boosters. These supercharge everyday meals, from tacos to noodles to salads, with delicious flavor and tantalizing texture—and keeping a few on hand will inspire you to whip up creative meals without having to consult a formal recipe.

In chapter 6, you'll find the proteins. These are foundational components that are flavorful enough to be the star of your meal so you can pair them simply to make a complete meal (with leftover cooked grains, vegetables in the crisper, bread on the counter, pasta in the pantry, etc.).

Chapter 7 does the same thing but for grains. And chapter 8 has the everyday veggies that are super simple to make and can be mixed and matched with an almost limitless number of condiments, proteins, or grains.

There are a few ways you can use these chapters to make meal planning and weeknight meals low-maintenance but super high reward.

You can pick out a couple of condiments to make each week, then plan meals that revolve around them. For instance, if you have overgrown basil in summer, you might make the Lemon-Basil Cashew Cream (page 202) and Italian Basil & Parsley Salsa Verde (page 181) on Sunday, and then plan a few Italian-ish or Mediterranean-ish meals for that week.

Or flip through chapter 6 and pick out one or two proteins you'd like to make that week. If you have tofu to use up, maybe you choose the Pomegranate-Glazed Tofu (page 277) and Masala Baked Tofu (page 271), and put on a big pot of brown rice to serve with both of them.

And if you have no idea what pairs with what or the creative juices aren't flowing, flip to page 346, where you'll find sample meal planning menus. Each menu starts with a condiment from chapter 5 that you can meal prep, followed by three meal ideas you can build around this condiment and supplement with proteins, grains, and veggies.

5

Condiments & Flavor Boosters

A good condiment can take a basic bowl of rice and beans to new heights, bridge leftovers into an exciting lunch, and come to the rescue at 7 p.m. when you have no idea what to make for dinner. Basically, a good condiment can make an entire meal.

And having *a few* good condiments on hand gives you the gift of flexibility when meal planning. It gives you freedom to stray from your rigid grocery list and to instead pick up whatever produce looks good at the farmers' market or whichever plant-based proteins are on sale.

Perhaps the word *condiment* doesn't fully explain these culinary saviors. Everyone agrees that ketchup and mustard are condiments, but what about pesto? Toasted bread crumbs? Ricotta?

The term *flavor booster* is probably more accurate. These are little things, not full meals or even side dishes, but they can dial up the flavor in so many meals. They are often quick to make and have a decent shelf life and include dressings, vinaigrettes, and sauces, but also chutneys, pastes, and salsas.

Here, you'll find flavor boosters running the texture gamut from crunchy and crispy to creamy, the flavor gamut from savory to herby and cheesy, and the global gamut from East Asian to Mexican to Middle Eastern. You'll find easy-to-customize recipes and recipes with several flavor variations to suit your taste buds.

Many of these condiments can be used in multiple ways throughout the week.

For instance, use the Green Goddess Dressing to make the Rainbow Veggie Slaw (page 390) on Tuesday, then use leftovers to make a smashed chickpea sandwich on Thursday. If you still have leftovers, use it as a dip for crudités at Friday evening happy hour. Or if you make the Pomegranate Molasses Vinaigrette (page 165), use it to make the Pomegranate-Glazed Tofu (page 277) and drizzle the rest over roasted vegetables or warm salads.

Keep a handful of these condiments and flavor boosters in your pantry and fridge, and you'll never eat another boring meal again (a big promise, I know, but one I stand by).

A NOTE ON STORING SALAD DRESSINGS

Creamy salad dressings thicken as they rest in the fridge. If needed, loosen them with a spoonful or two of water, or depending on the ingredients, a splash of citrus juice or vinegar. For vinaigrettes, take them out of the fridge at least 10 minutes before using, as refrigerated oil may solidify. Dressings with a high ratio of acid will stay fresh for at least 1 week, often longer.

All Hail Caesar Dressing

Makes about 1½ cups (360 ml) | GFO, NF

Caesar dressing is the least vegan-friendly dressing, yet I wanted to develop a version that was as close to the real deal as possible because I like a challenge (I also love Caesar salad).

Silken tofu adds a surprisingly creamy body to this dressing, and a heavy-hitting combo of umeboshi paste, nori, nooch, and miso brings all the depth of savoriness you need. It's basically an umami delivery vehicle that's simultaneously salty, tangy, and garlicky.

Ingredient Notes: If you're not a fan of nori, omit it. If you have umeboshi paste (see page 46), it takes the dressing over the top. If not, increase the miso to 3 tablespoons. If vegan Worcestershire sauce is not available, use soy sauce or Bragg liquid aminos.

GF Option: Sub or omit the vegan Worcestershire sauce, unless you can find a vegan and GF one.

½ cup (120 g) **silken, soft, or firm tofu**

1 sheet (3 g) **roasted nori** (optional; see Ingredient Notes)

1½ teaspoons **lemon zest**

3 tablespoons freshly squeezed **lemon juice**

3 tablespoons **extra-virgin olive oil**

¾ teaspoon **onion powder**

1½ to 2 teaspoons **Dijon mustard**

1½ tablespoon **capers** + 1½ tablespoons **caper brine**

1½ tablespoons **nutritional yeast**

2 tablespoons **white miso paste**

1 teaspoon **umeboshi paste** (see Ingredient Notes)

1 tablespoon **vegan Worcestershire sauce** (see Ingredient Notes)

¼ teaspoon **fine sea salt**, plus more to taste

Freshly ground **black pepper**

1. Drain the tofu. For silken tofu, measure it out, then drain any liquid that has accumulated.

2. Using tongs, hold the nori a few inches above a low flame on a gas stove. Flip every 3 to 4 seconds until it shrinks a bit, about 20 seconds. Crumple it with your hands, then tear into little strips. If you don't have a gas stove, you can either skip the toasting or place the nori on a sheet pan 6 inches (15 cm) underneath the broiler (use a low or medium setting if you have it) and keep a watchful eye.

3. In a high-powered blender, combine the drained tofu, lemon zest and juice, 3 tablespoons of water, the olive oil, onion powder, 1½ teaspoons of the mustard, the capers and brine, nutritional yeast, miso, umeboshi paste, and Worcestershire sauce. Blend on medium speed until smooth, stopping to scrape down the sides several times. Season with the salt and pepper, then add the nori and pulse just until it's incorporated but not dissolved. Season to taste, adding more salt, pepper, or mustard as desired. You can also use a food processor to make the dressing. Just puree the tofu first, then add everything else.

4. Store in the fridge in a jar for a week.

Preserved Lemons

Makes 1 big jar of lemons | GF, SF, NF

Preserved lemons are fresh lemons that have been pickled or fermented in lots of salt and their own juices. Simple enough, but it's a transformative ingredient that delivers layers of savory saltiness with bright complexity and a supremely lemony flavor.

Ingredient Notes: If Meyer lemons are not available, use the smallest lemons you can find. Avoid thick-skinned lemons, as they don't soften fully. You'll be eating the peel, so use organic lemons as desired. If your lemons are very small, buy a couple extra.

Tip: You need a 32- to 36-ounce (1 L) glass jar, or a smaller jar if you are halving the recipe. I like to use one with a rubber gasket to prevent corrosion.

Use It for Big Flavor

× Add to North African tagines or hearty stews for a contrasting brightness and zing.

× Blend the peel and/or pulp into vinaigrettes. Or finely mince the peel and sprinkle on salads (especially good with fresh mint).

× Brighten up grains, like the Pearl Couscous & Chickpea Salad (page 323), and lentils, like the Spiced Lentil Salad with Fresh Herbs (page 257).

× Add to any lemon pasta or use to flavor roasted vegetables.

× Make an herby condiment or salad dressing, like Preserved Lemon Salsa (page 184) or Preserved Lemon Vinaigrette (page 164).

× Mix with creamy condiments like vegan mayo, yogurt, or hummus. For every ½ cup (112 g) of mayo, use 1 to 1½ tablespoons chopped peel; use as a sandwich or burger spread or for potato or macaroni salad.

× Mash into avocado with your favorite seasonings for upgraded avocado toast.

8 to 12 **Meyer lemons** (see Ingredient Notes)

Lots of **kosher salt**

Optional Flavorings

½ teaspoon **black peppercorns**

1 **cinnamon stick**, whole or broken into a few pieces

1 to 2 teaspoons **fennel seeds**

1 to 2 teaspoons **coriander seeds**

3 to 4 **whole cloves**

1. Wash a 32- to 36-ounce (1 L) canning jar (and the lid) with warm, soapy water and dry well.

2. Rinse and scrub the lemons. Set aside 1 or 2 lemons. Cover the bottom of your jar with 1 to 2 tablespoons of kosher salt.

3. For the remaining lemons, cut off a thin slice from both ends of each lemon so they have a flat bottom and top. Stand each lemon up and slice it in half lengthwise, cutting almost all the way through but keeping the lemon attached at the base. Turn the lemon 90 degrees and slice lengthwise again, as if quartering into wedges, but again, not all the way through.

recipe continues

4. Gently pry the lemons open but do not detach the segments. Fill each crevice with a generous amount of salt (a generous tablespoon). Don't skimp on the salt, as it prevents bad bacteria from thriving. Seal up the lemons to close.

5. Add a few salt-stuffed lemons to the jar and press down with a muddler, tongs, a pestle, or a sturdy spoon so they release their juices and you can make room for more lemons. Pack the jar as tightly as you can with the lemons, pressing down to cover the lemons with their own juices.

6. Add any optional flavorings at this point.

7. If the juices do not cover the lemons or flavorings, squeeze the juice from the reserved lemons on top. Cover the lemons and any flavorings with 2 tablespoons kosher salt.

   Note: If the lemons aren't submerged, use a fermentation weight, a small resealable plastic bag filled with water, or a clean, heavy stone to weigh them down. You can remove the weight after 1 week. This is necessary to prevent air from entering, which causes mold to develop.

8. Seal the jar and let rest at cool room temperature, such as in your pantry, until the lemon rinds are very soft, at least 3 weeks. During the first 2 weeks, gently shake the jar every day, turning it upside down.

9. Once the lemons are fermented, transfer the sealed jar to the fridge and start using them! You can use the entire lemon, but the great flavor is concentrated in the peel (you can smash the flesh into dressings or sauces, or chuck it into a stew). If desired, rinse the lemon peel before slicing or mincing to make it less salty. Preserved lemons will stay good in a sealed jar in the fridge for at least 6 months.

Outrageously Good Red Sauce (but Not Marinara)

Makes 3½ cups (28 ounces/800 g) | GF, SF, NF

When I originally set out to make a marinara, I read everything I could find on making an "authentic" Italian marinara. My first attempts were *fine*, but Rao's marinara sauce was better and it took 2 minutes to buy instead of 2 hours to make.

It was only once I ditched my attachment to making "authentic" marinara that I came up with an outrageously good red sauce. My culinary assistant, Hannah, served it to a couple from Italy, and between the two of them, they devoured the entire pound of pasta and said it was the only American dish that reminded them of pasta back home. And to my relief, they never even asked, *But is this a true marinara??*

Ingredient Notes: Canned tomatoes are the star here, so use the best-quality ones you can find. My favorites are Bianco DiNapoli, San Merican, and Cento. Depending on the sweetness of the tomatoes, you may need a splash of red wine vinegar and/or sugar at the end. For maximal flavor, don't skip the red wine.

Tips: If you prefer a very saucy pasta, use 12 to 14 ounces (340 to 400 g) of pasta instead of 16 ounces (455 g). Cook the pasta in salted water until al dente and reserve a bit of the pasta water to help bring the pasta and sauce together. To make it heartier, toss in some browned vegan sausage at the end. If you have Cheesy Crunchies on hand (page 223), they make an excellent topping.

Use It for Big Flavor: This is my favorite sauce with any pasta, and it's also delicious on homemade pizza, polenta (page 513), or in lasagna (the Sexy Skillet Lasagna on page 519 is not to be missed).

¼ cup (56 g) **extra-virgin olive oil**

1 very large **yellow onion** (about 12 ounces/340 g), finely diced

Kosher salt and freshly ground **black pepper**

8 **garlic cloves**, minced

¼ to ½ teaspoon **red pepper flakes** (¼ teaspoon for mild)

1 teaspoon **dried oregano**

1 tablespoon chopped **fresh rosemary**

3 tablespoons **tomato paste** (preferably from a tube)

½ cup (120 ml) **dry red wine**, such as Pinot Noir, Syrah, Chianti, or Sangiovese

1 (28-ounce/800 g) can **whole peeled tomatoes**, crushed with your hands

2 **bay leaves**

½ cup (8 g) **fresh basil** leaves, slivered

1 small handful **fresh flat-leaf parsley** leaves and tender stems, chopped

Red wine vinegar and/or **organic cane sugar**, as needed (see Ingredient Notes)

recipe and ingredients continue

For Serving (optional)

12 to 16 ounces (340 to 455 g) cooked **egg-free pasta**, such as linguine, penne rigate, rigatoni, cavatappi, or fusilli (see Tips), pasta water reserved

1. In a large, deep sauté pan or Dutch oven, heat the olive oil over medium to medium-high heat. Once shimmering, add the onions and ¼ teaspoon salt and sauté until the onions are golden brown, 10 to 13 minutes. Stir only occasionally so the onions can get some color. If they brown quickly or stick to the pan too much, reduce the heat a touch and add a splash of water to deglaze the pan.

2. Reduce the heat to medium. Add the garlic, pepper flakes, oregano, and rosemary. Cook for 90 seconds, stirring frequently to prevent burning. If the pan looks dry, add a splash of water and deglaze.

3. Push the aromatics to the edges of the pan. Add the tomato paste to the center and cook, stirring almost constantly, until it darkens in color, 2 to 3 minutes. Reduce the heat as needed to prevent burning.

4. Pour in the wine and deglaze, scraping up any browned bits. Simmer rapidly until the liquid has mostly evaporated and the smell of booze has worn off, 3 to 4 minutes.

5. Add the crushed tomatoes, bay leaves, 1 teaspoon salt, and lots of black pepper. Cook at a rapid simmer, stirring and smashing the tomatoes occasionally until they are broken down and the sauce thickens, about 15 minutes.

6. Add the basil and parsley and simmer for 2 to 3 minutes. Season with salt and black pepper to taste. Add a splash of vinegar or a pinch of sugar, as needed. Remove the bay leaves.

7. If serving with pasta, transfer the hot cooked pasta to the sauce and use tongs and some elbow grease to toss well, adding pasta water as needed to bring everything together.

8. Store leftover sauce in the fridge for up to 1 week or freeze for several months.

Herby Shallot–Garlic Confit

Makes about 4 cups (960 g) | GF, SF, NF

Meltingly sweet, buttery, and rich, this confit is what dreams are made of.

Tips: This recipe requires a lot of olive oil, so I use the most affordable jug at the store. Avoid wider saucepans, as you'll need to use a lot more oil.

Use It for Big Flavor: Spread vegan ricotta (page 206), vegan cream cheese, or hummus on toast, then schmear confit on top, or use as a sandwich topping or spread. Use the confit to top pizzas and flatbreads; stir into a pot of lentils; spoon over blanched green beans, broccoli, or asparagus; or blend some of the shallots and garlic into hummus. The oil is great in pastas, pasta salads, and grain salads, as well as in vinaigrettes, dips, and spreads; or use it to roast vegetables or chickpeas, or to fry tofu.

Safety Note! To minimize the risk of food-borne botulism, garlic stored in oil must always be chilled, not kept at room temperature. Please read the storage instructions below carefully!

1½ pounds (680 g) small or medium **shallots**, peeled, trimmed, and halved (small shallots can be left whole)

12 fat **garlic cloves**, peeled and left whole

2 cups (430 g) **extra-virgin olive oil** (see Tips), plus more as needed

8 to 10 **thyme** sprigs

1 **rosemary** sprig

2 **bay leaves**

½ to 1 teaspoon **red pepper flakes** (1 teaspoon for *spicy!*)

1½ teaspoons **kosher salt**

Freshly ground **black pepper**

1. Preheat the oven to 400°F (205°C). In a small or medium Dutch oven, or other small ovenproof saucepan or baking dish (see Tips), combine the shallots, garlic, and olive oil.

2. Using kitchen twine, make an herb bundle (bouquet garni) out of the thyme, rosemary, and bay leaves and add it to the pan (if you don't have twine, just add the herbs whole). Add the pepper flakes, salt, and a good amount of black pepper. Add more oil as needed to fully submerge the shallots (they'll dry out if not covered). Cover with the pan's lid or tightly with foil.

3. Bake for 1 hour, until the shallots are falling apart and very tender and the garlic is golden and soft.

4. Transfer the shallots, garlic, and oil to a large glass jar with a tight-sealing lid, discarding the herbs. Let cool slightly for 10 to 15 minutes, then seal tightly and refrigerate. **Never store at room temperature!** Always use a clean spoon to serve (grab a new spoon if it comes into contact with other food). Store in the fridge for a few weeks (or freeze up to 3 months).

Preserved Lemon Vinaigrette

Makes ¾ cup (180 g) | GF, SF, NF

An upgrade on classic lemon vinaigrette featuring bright and savory preserved lemons. Don't have preserved lemons on hand? Sub with the zest of 1 large or 2 small lemons.

¼ cup (60 ml) freshly squeezed **lemon juice**

1 teaspoon **pure maple syrup**, plus more to taste

1 tablespoon minced **preserved lemon peel** (page 157; or the zest from 1 large or 2 small lemons)

1 **garlic clove**, grated or finely minced

1 small **shallot**, minced

¼ cup (56 g) **extra-virgin olive oil**

2 tablespoons finely chopped **fresh mint** leaves (optional but recommended)

¼ to ½ teaspoon **fine sea salt** (depends on the saltiness of the preserved lemons)

Freshly ground **black pepper**

1. In a bowl, whisk together the lemon juice, maple syrup, preserved lemon peel, garlic, and shallot. Stream in the olive oil, whisking as you go. Stir in the mint and season with ¼ teaspoon of the salt and several cracks of pepper. Or add all the ingredients to a jar with a lid and shake vigorously until emulsified.

2. Taste, adding more maple syrup or salt as needed. Store leftovers in a sealed jar in the fridge for up to 2 weeks.

Pomegranate Molasses Vinaigrette

Makes ¾ heaping cup (215 g) | GF, SF, NF

A delightfully tart, slightly sweet, and herbaceous vinaigrette with Middle Eastern flavors.

Ingredient Note: You can buy pomegranate molasses at Middle Eastern markets, well-stocked grocery stores, and online. Look for ones made with 100 percent pomegranate juice and nothing else. My favorites are Al Wadi Pomegranate Molasses All Natural and Eat Well Pomegranate Molasses.

Use It for Big Flavor: Use as a sauce to drizzle over roasted veggies like the sweet potatoes, carrots, butternut squash, or eggplant in chapter 8, as well as on baked tofu (page 269), shawarma (page 532), and falafel, or a simple bowl of white beans. Mix with vegan yogurt and dollop over grain bowls and rice or smashed potatoes (page 407), or mix with vegan mayo as a sandwich spread. For salads, thin out with a bit of water and pour over crisp lettuces.

3 **garlic cloves**, chopped

⅓ cup (5 g) **fresh mint** leaves

¼ cup (4 g) **fresh flat-leaf parsley** leaves and tender stems

2½ tablespoons **pure pomegranate molasses** (see Ingredient Note)

1 tablespoon chopped **preserved lemon peel** (page 157)

2 teaspoons **Dijon mustard**

1 tablespoon + 1 teaspoon **sumac**

¼ teaspoon **ground cardamom**

½ teaspoon **ground cumin**

2 teaspoons **pure maple syrup** or **agave nectar**

¼ teaspoon **fine sea salt**, plus more to taste

1 teaspoon **Aleppo pepper**, plus more to taste

⅓ cup (75 g) **extra-virgin olive oil**

1. In a food processor, add the garlic, mint, and parsley. Blend briefly to chop everything up. Add the pomegranate molasses, preserved lemon peel, mustard, sumac, cardamom, cumin, maple syrup, salt, and Aleppo pepper. Blend until the mixture starts to come together.

2. With the motor running, stream in the olive oil, stopping to scrape down the sides as you go. For a more classic vinaigrette consistency, add 2 tablespoons water and blend again. Add more water as needed until you reach your desired consistency. If you prefer a thick consistency, omit the water or use just a splash. Taste, adding salt or Aleppo pepper as needed. Store leftovers in the fridge for up to 2 weeks, thinning out with a splash of water as needed.

Grapefruit–Shallot Vinaigrette

Makes ¾ scant cup (165 g) | GF, SF, NF

Zingy, tart, slightly sweet, and earthy. A touch of maple syrup tones down grapefruit's natural bitterness.

Use It for Big Flavor: Serve over a salad made with mild greens (e.g., romaine, Little Gem, Bibb lettuce, mesclun, baby spinach) or sturdier greens like Swiss chard or beet greens. Or pair with thinly sliced fennel (page 368), thinly shaved beets, or any kind of citrus-avocado salad.

1 small-to-medium **shallot**, finely minced (about ¼ cup/30 g)

2 tablespoons **champagne vinegar** or **red wine vinegar**, plus more to taste

2 teaspoons **grapefruit zest**, ideally from a pink or red grapefruit

1½ tablespoons freshly squeezed **grapefruit juice**

1½ teaspoons **Dijon mustard**, plus more to taste

1½ teaspoons minced **fresh thyme** leaves (optional)

1 teaspoon **pure maple syrup**

⅓ cup (75 g) **extra-virgin olive oil**

¼ teaspoon **fine sea salt**, plus more to taste

Freshly ground **black pepper**

In a small bowl, combine the shallots and vinegar and macerate for 10 minutes to mellow. Then, add the grapefruit zest and juice, mustard, thyme (if using), and maple syrup. Slowly whisk in the olive oil until well combined. Season with the salt and several cracks of pepper. Taste, adding more salt, vinegar, or mustard as needed to balance the grapefruit. Or add all the ingredients to a jar with a lid and shake vigorously until emulsified. Store leftovers in the fridge for up to 1 week.

Fried Capers

Makes ¼ heaping cup (20 g) | GF, SF, NF

I love the briny, salty tang that capers offer. When you briefly fry them, you get all of that with less pungency and a magical crispy, almost airy, crunch.

Use It for Big Flavor: Use as a topping for pasta salad, potato salad, creamy soups, avocado toast, or hot pasta, like the Pasta & Chickpeas with Fried Capers & Tomato-Shallot Butter on page 501. Add to nearly any salad with the All Hail Caesar Dressing (page 155) or Throwback Ranch Dressing (page 203), or a summer heirloom tomato salad. If you're making Hannah's Carrot Lox (page 431) to serve with bagels, these are a super-fun topping.

¼ cup (40 g) drained **capers**

1½ tablespoons **arrowroot powder** or **cornstarch**

3 tablespoons **extra-virgin olive oil**

1. Add the capers to a few paper towels and gently roll to remove as much liquid as possible. In a small bowl, toss them with the arrowroot powder to coat. Transfer to a fine-mesh sieve and shake off some excess starch but not too much. Line a plate with paper towels.

2. Heat a medium skillet over medium-high heat for 2 minutes. Add the oil and heat for 30 seconds. Add the capers and fry, shaking the pan and flipping from time to time, until crispy, about 4 minutes. Scoop the capers out onto the lined plate to drain and further crisp up. These are crispiest on day one, but leftovers can be stored at room temperature in a container lined with several paper towels for up to 1 week.

Quick-Pickled Vegetables

Fills one 32-ounce (950 ml) jar | GF, SF, NF

Quick-pickled vegetables add a one-two punch of acidity and saltiness. I reach for them when a meal feels flat or like it's missing something and salt or lemon juice alone won't do the trick.

They take minutes to prepare and can be ready to enjoy in as little as 8 hours. And they're easy to customize with flavors. Keep one or three of these in your fridge to spruce up all kinds of meals: salads, grain bowls, tofu scrambles, lentil salads, tacos, sandwiches, and more.

Tips: For larger cuts or sturdy vegetables like fennel or cauliflower, a wide-mouth jar works best. For vegetables that need to be sliced as thinly as possible, a mandoline is ideal.

Use It for Big Flavor

× Top tacos and dal with pickled onions

× Add pickled carrots in an Asian tofu or tempeh rice bowl

× Include pickled cauliflower with a mezze hummus platter (or pair with anything fried)

× Top avocado toast with pickled radishes

× Add pickled chile peppers to pizza or kale salads

Veggies, Aromatics, Spices, and Herbs

Choose from the chart on page 170

Brine (enough for a 1-quart/1 L jar)

½ cup + 2 tablespoons (150 ml) **distilled white vinegar**

2 tablespoons **organic cane sugar**

1 tablespoon + 1 teaspoon **kosher salt**

1. Wash a quart jar or two pint jars, along with the lid(s) and sealing ring(s), with warm, soapy water and dry well. Rinse the vegetables and any aromatics, herbs, or spices.

2. Slice your chosen vegetable(s) according to the chart.

3. Add the aromatics, spices, and herbs to your jar. Pack the vegetables in as tightly as you can without smushing them, making sure there is ½ to 1 inch (1 to 2.5 cm) of space from the rim of the jar to the top of the vegetables.

4. In a small saucepan, bring the vinegar, 1¼ cups (300 ml) of water, the sugar, and salt to a boil, whisking to dissolve the sugar and salt. Remove from the heat.

5. Over the sink, pour the hot brine over everything in the jar and submerge, pressing down on the vegetables with the end of a spoon if needed.

6. Gently tap the jar(s) against the counter a few times to remove all the air bubbles. Top with more brine if necessary and seal the jar(s).

7. Let cool to room temperature before refrigerating. Taste after 8 hours, but try to wait 48 hours to allow the flavors to fully develop. Store in the fridge for 3 to 4 weeks.

recipe continues

VEGETABLE	BASIC FLAVORINGS	ADDITIONAL FLAVORING OPTIONS OR NOTES
2 medium-large **red onions**, sliced as thinly as possible	• ½ to 1 teaspoon red pepper flakes (or mild chile flakes, such as Aleppo pepper) • 1 teaspoon black peppercorns	2 teaspoons brown or yellow mustard seeds
3 to 4 medium **red or golden beets**, peeled and sliced as thinly as possible	• 1½ teaspoons fennel seeds • 1 teaspoon caraway seeds • 3 smashed garlic cloves • 1 tablespoon chopped fresh dill • 2 long strips orange peel, squeezed with your fingers	
½ small **red cabbage**, sliced as thinly as possible	• 4 smashed garlic cloves • 1 teaspoon black peppercorns • 1 teaspoon caraway seeds • 1 tablespoon chopped fresh dill	
1 pound (455 g) **skinny carrots**, peeled and thinly sliced on a diagonal or cut into matchsticks	• 2 small dried red chile peppers, cracked for more heat • 1 teaspoon coriander seeds • ½ teaspoon cumin seeds • 1-inch (2.5 cm) piece fresh ginger, peeled and sliced • 4 smashed garlic cloves	When sliced ¼ inch (0.5 cm) thick, the carrots retain a noticeable crunch; more thinly sliced carrots get fairly soft, with a slight crunch. I like using a variety of thicknesses for texture diversity.
1 pound (455 g) **Kirby or Persian cucumbers**, sliced (but not too thinly) or cut into spears	• 1½ to 2 tablespoons chopped fresh dill • 1 to 2 pinches red pepper flakes (or mild chile flakes) • 2 smashed garlic cloves • 1 small serrano pepper, thinly sliced (for *spicy!*)	• 2 strips lemon peel, squeezed with your fingers • ½ teaspoon brown or yellow mustard seeds
2 medium **fennel bulbs**, sliced as thinly as possible	• 1 to 1½ teaspoons fennel seeds • 2 long strips orange peel, squeezed with your fingers • 2 smashed garlic cloves	4 thyme sprigs
4 cups (360 g) bite-size **cauliflower florets**	• 4 smashed garlic cloves • 2 teaspoons black peppercorns • 1 to 2 serrano peppers (for *spicy!*) • 2 tablespoons freshly squeezed lime juice	• Stir the lime juice into the hot brine after step 4. • Push the florets down into the jar to get them to fit.
2 bunches **radishes**, thinly sliced	• 1 teaspoon fennel seeds • 1 teaspoon black peppercorns • 1 teaspoon chopped fresh dill • 2 long strips orange peel, squeezed with your fingers	1 to 2 pinches red pepper flakes
15 to 20 moderately hot small **chiles** (jalapeños, serranos, or Fresnos) or 6 to 10 large **mild peppers**, such as banana peppers	• 6 smashed garlic cloves • 1 teaspoon brown or yellow mustard seeds or celery seeds (optional)	• Option A: Thinly slice peppers into rounds. This is quicker but yields very spicy peppers. • Option B: Slice peppers vertically in half, then scrape out the membranes and seeds. Pickle them halved or slice into half-moons.

Citrus–Date Vinaigrette

Makes 1 heaping cup (275 g) | GF, SF, NF

Medjool dates add sweetness and a velvety body, making this a surprisingly creamy vinaigrette. Orange and lemon zest add citrusy notes that are warmed up by a touch of cumin and coriander.

Use It for Big Flavor: Serve this tangy-sweet dressing with any salad, especially greens that are spicy, peppery, or earthy (e.g., arugula, endive, Swiss chard). It's also perfect with beets (page 377), grain salads, and a couscous or freekeh salad.

4 **Medjool dates**

¼ cup + 2 tablespoons (84 g) **extra-virgin olive oil**

2 teaspoons **lemon zest**

⅓ cup (80 ml) freshly squeezed **lemon juice** (about 2 medium lemons)

1 to 2 teaspoons **orange zest**

2 tablespoons freshly squeezed **orange juice**

2 teaspoons **Dijon mustard** or **whole-grain mustard**, plus more to taste

1 teaspoon **ground cumin**

1 teaspoon **sweet or hot paprika** (or use smoked paprika for a subtle smoky flavor)

½ teaspoon **ground coriander**

½ to ¾ teaspoon **fine sea salt**

Freshly ground **black pepper**

1. If your dates aren't very soft, cover them with warm water for 10 minutes. Drain and pat dry. Remove the pits and chop or tear the dates.

2. In a high-powered blender or food processor, add the dates, olive oil, lemon zest and juice, 1 teaspoon of the orange zest, the orange juice, mustard, cumin, paprika, coriander, ½ teaspoon of the salt, and pepper to taste. Blend until smooth, stopping to scrape down the sides as you go. If serving now, continue to step 3. If not, add the water to thin when ready to serve.

3. With the motor running, drizzle in 1 tablespoon of water at a time until you reach your desired consistency. Season to taste, adding more mustard for tang, the additional teaspoon orange zest for floral sweetness, or ¼ teaspoon salt as needed. Refrigerate leftovers in a sealed jar for up to 2 weeks. It thickens as it rests, so thin it out with lemon juice and water.

Tomato-Shallot Butter

Makes about 2½ cups (580 g) | GF, SFO, NF

This is more of a sauce than a "butter," but once you taste this rich, buttery concoction with sweet roasted tomatoes and shallots, you'll understand the name.

Ingredient Notes: If fresh tomatoes are not in season, you can substitute a 28-ounce (800 g) can of good-quality whole peeled San Marzano tomatoes. If soy-free, use a soy-free vegan butter or sub olive oil for the butter.

Use It for Big Flavor: This is an excellent pasta sauce (use in Pasta & Chickpeas with Fried Capers & Tomato-Shallot Butter on page 501). Dollop it on roasted potatoes (page 407) or cauliflower (page 421), or use as a pizza sauce. Or toast bread in olive oil, rub raw garlic across it, and schmear this on top. Like an Italian version of pan con tomate (but better??).

2 pints **cherry or grape tomatoes** (20 to 22 ounces/560 to 625 g)

8 **garlic cloves**, peeled but left whole

5 to 6 large **shallots** (11 to 12 ounces/about 325 g), peeled and halved

6 to 8 **thyme** sprigs

3 tablespoons **extra-virgin olive oil**

1¾ teaspoons **kosher salt**, plus more to taste

Freshly ground **black pepper**

½ cup (8 g) **fresh basil** leaves

3 tablespoons **vegan butter**, melted (see Ingredient Notes)

1 to 2 teaspoons freshly squeezed **lemon juice**

1. Preheat the oven to 450°F (230°C). In a 13 × 9-inch (3 L) baking dish, combine the tomatoes, garlic, shallots, thyme, olive oil, salt, and a generous amount of pepper. Toss to combine.

2. Roast for 27 to 30 minutes, until the tomatoes are wrinkly, blistered in spots, and bursting. Strip the leaves from the thyme, discarding the stems.

3. Transfer the vegetables, including any juices, to a blender or food processor and blend until pureed. Add the basil, butter, and 1 teaspoon of the lemon juice. Blend again until thick and relatively smooth. Season to taste. I usually add an additional ½ teaspoon kosher salt, a bit of pepper, and the remaining 1 teaspoon of lemon juice. Store leftovers in the fridge for up to 1 week.

Buttery Caper–Pine Nut Dressing

Makes 1 heaping cup (260 g) │ GF, SF

Pine nuts make this dressing remarkably creamy and add toasty, nutty flavors. Golden raisins and shallots add sweetness, capers make it zingy, and lemon adds the perfect tang.

Use It for Big Flavor: Drizzle over sturdy greens like Swiss chard (page 385) or beet greens, or pair with slightly bitter or peppery greens like arugula. Spoon over roasted broccoli, cauliflower, or eggplant, toss with blanched green beans, or dress fingerling potatoes with it for a spin on potato salad.

1 medium-large **lemon**

¼ cup (40 g) **golden raisins** (if not available, use Thompson/brown raisins)

1 small **shallot**, minced

1 **garlic clove**, minced

2 ounces (57 g) **pine nuts** (½ scant cup)

2 tablespoons **capers**, drained

¼ cup (56 g) **extra-virgin olive oil**

¼ teaspoon **fine sea salt**, plus more to taste

¼ teaspoon **red pepper flakes** (or ½ teaspoon Aleppo pepper)

Freshly ground **black pepper**

1. Zest the lemon, reserving half of the zest for any salad you're making. Juice the lemon; you should have about 3 tablespoons juice.

2. In a small bowl, combine the raisins, shallots, garlic, and lemon juice. Macerate for 20 to 30 minutes, stirring a couple of times, until the raisins are slightly plump and the shallots and garlic have softened.

3. Meanwhile, heat a skillet over medium heat for a few minutes. Add the pine nuts and shake the pan frequently until golden brown, 3 to 4 minutes. Let cool.

4. Transfer the macerated raisin mixture to a food processor. Add the toasted pine nuts, capers, and remaining lemon zest. Blend until you have a paste, stopping to scrape down the sides as you go. With the motor running, stream in the olive oil until the mixture is emulsified.

5. Season with the salt, pepper flakes, and a few cracks of black pepper. Add 2 tablespoons of water and blend until pourable but still thick. Taste, adding more salt as needed. If you have time, chill the dressing for the best flavor. Store in a jar in the fridge for up to 10 days.

Korean BBQ Sauce

Makes 1 heaping cup (280 g) | GFO, NF

While I like classic BBQ sauce, I *love* Korean BBQ sauce. Gochujang, a fermented Korean red chile paste, adds incredible depth of flavor and a lustrous texture. It makes a BBQ sauce that is slightly sweet, tangy, spicy, and bursting with umami.

Ingredient Notes: Asian or Korean pears are in season from August through winter and can be found at Asian supermarkets and well-stocked stores; if you can't find them, use Bosc pears or Fuji apples.

In a pinch, substitute rice vinegar for mirin and add a tad more sugar.

You can find gochujang at Asian markets and well-stocked grocery stores.

Tip: For a thicker consistency, mix together 1 tablespoon arrowroot powder and 3 tablespoons cold water and add to the BBQ sauce after step 2; whisk frequently for 1 minute, then immediately remove from the heat.

Use It for Big Flavor: This makes a great sauce or marinade for vegan meat substitutes, like jackfruit (page 508) or tempeh and tofu (page 294), or with hearty veg like oyster mushrooms or cauliflower.

GF Option: Look for GF gochujang (e.g., Sempio, Chung Jung One) and use tamari instead of soy sauce.

¼ cup (68 ml) **reduced-sodium soy sauce** or **tamari**

¾ cup (110 g) unpeeled, chopped **Asian pear** (see Ingredient Notes)

1 tablespoon **rice vinegar**

1 tablespoon **mirin** (see Ingredient Notes)

1 tablespoon **gochujang** (see Ingredient Notes)

¼ cup (40 g) **organic brown sugar** (or coconut sugar)

1 tablespoon **toasted sesame oil**

1½ teaspoons **chili-garlic sauce** or **sambal oelek** (use less for a milder version)

1 **scallion**, roughly chopped

2 **garlic cloves**, roughly chopped

1-inch (2.5 cm) piece **fresh ginger**, grated or chopped

¼ teaspoon freshly ground **black pepper**

1. In a blender or food processor, combine the soy sauce, ¼ cup (60 ml) of water, the pear, vinegar, mirin, gochujang, brown sugar, sesame oil, chili-garlic sauce, scallion, garlic, ginger, and pepper. Blend on medium speed until smooth.

2. Pour the sauce into a small saucepan and bring to a boil. Reduce to a simmer and cook, whisking occasionally, until thick enough to coat the back of a spoon, 8 to 10 minutes. Let cool.

3. Store in a sealed jar in the fridge for up to 3 weeks. It also freezes well.

Spicy "Honey" with Candied Jalapeños

Makes about ½ cup (165 g) | GF, SF, NF

An intoxicatingly delicious sweet-and-spicy combo, this nectar is like a vegan version of hot honey but with candied jalapeños. It's quite sweet, so a little goes a long way.

Use It for Big Flavor: Drizzle over naturally bitter vegetables like Brussels sprouts or on crunchy salads, especially those with a creamy element, like the Smashed Cucumbers with Yogurt-Tahini Sauce & Spicy "Honey" (page 365). Spread Whipped Feta (page 209) or Whipped Tofu Ricotta (page 206) on sourdough, top with Jammy Roasted Eggplant (page 339) or Jammy Zucchini (page 330), and drizzle with a little nectar for a great open-faced sandwich. Add to a vinaigrette for a spicy-sweet kick, drizzle over ice cream or cornbread (page 528), or use it to make a spicy margarita.

½ cup (165 g) **agave nectar**

3 **jalapeño peppers**, sliced

1. In a small saucepan over medium heat, combine the agave and jalapeños. Heat until the mixture just starts to bubble, then gently simmer for 2 minutes, stirring to submerge the jalapeños.

2. Remove from the heat and let infuse for 10 minutes. Once cool, store in a sealed jar in the fridge for up to 1 month.

Mint-Pistachio Pesto

Makes 1 heaping cup (260 g) | GF, SF

While it's probably frowned upon to say this in Italy, I think of pesto more as a formula than as a single recipe. Hence this mint pesto, which is subtly tart and sweet, buttery, lemony, and a little spicy.

Ingredient Note: If you are using unroasted pistachios, see page 115 for tips for roasting. You can also use walnuts instead of pistachios.

Use It for Big Flavor: This pesto is great with most roasted vegetables. Spoon on bread or pita for sandwiches; drizzle over grain bowls or couscous or a chickpea salad. Pair with crackers, crudités, olives, and soft vegan cheeses for a sharing platter. Or toss with orzo, vegan feta, and preserved lemons (page 157) for a summer pasta salad.

½ cup (65 g) **shelled roasted pistachios** (see Ingredient Note)

2 heaping cups (32 g) **fresh mint** leaves

1½ loosely packed cups (22 g) **fresh cilantro** leaves and tender stems

2 large **garlic cloves**, roughly chopped

1 small **serrano pepper** (optional), membranes and seeds removed and roughly chopped (leave some in for *spicy!*)

1 medium **lemon**, zested

2 tablespoons freshly squeezed **lemon juice**

1 to 2 tablespoons **pure pomegranate molasses**

½ teaspoon **Aleppo pepper** (optional; omit for less heat)

⅓ cup (75 g) **extra-virgin olive oil**, plus more as needed

Kosher salt or **fine sea salt**

1. In a food processor, blend the nuts until almost ground. Add the mint, cilantro, garlic, and serrano (if using) and blend again until a paste forms. Add the lemon zest and juice, 1 tablespoon of the pomegranate molasses, and the Aleppo pepper (if using) and blend until it starts to come together. Scrape the pesto into the center near the blades.

2. With the motor running, stream in the olive oil. Stop and scrape down the sides as you go, streaming in more as needed until you have a relatively smooth texture. Add 2 tablespoons of water and blend again. This makes for a spreadable consistency; for a pourable consistency, add 1 to 2 tablespoons more water.

3. Season to taste with salt. For more tanginess, add more pomegranate molasses (I like to add the remaining 1 tablespoon). Store in a sealed jar in the fridge for 5 to 7 days or freeze for up to 6 months.

Za'atar

Makes about 7 tablespoons (40 g) | GF, SF, NF

Za'atar is an herb grown in the Levant, but it also refers to its namesake condiment. Variations abound across the Middle East, though it usually features woodsy herbs like za'atar, thyme, oregano, and/or marjoram, along with sesame seeds, sumac, and salt. It's a low-effort, high-reward condiment with salty, tangy, earthy flavors that I use often.

Tip: If a recipe calls for za'atar and you don't have time to make it, store-bought za'atar is totally fine. The best one I've tried is from Z&Z, a Palestinian family-owned business.

Use It for Big Flavor: Sprinkle over hummus or yogurt sauces, as well as on salads, especially those with tomatoes, watermelon, or cucumbers; or use on cooked vegetables, especially eggplant and zucchini. Dunk bread in olive oil, then coat it in za'atar, or bloom za'atar in oil, then serve with bread. Sprinkle it over tofu scramble (page 439) or avocado toast, or stir into citrus vinaigrettes or tofu/tempeh marinades.

2 tablespoons **white sesame seeds**

2 tablespoons minced **fresh thyme** leaves or 2 teaspoons **dried thyme**

2 tablespoons **dried oregano**

2 tablespoons **ground sumac**

½ heaping teaspoon **flaky sea salt**

Heat a medium skillet over medium heat. After a minute or two, add the sesame seeds. Toss occasionally until lightly golden, 3 to 4 minutes. Transfer to a small bowl to stop the cooking and let cool slightly. Add the thyme, oregano, sumac, and salt and mix well to combine. Store leftovers in a sealed jar for up to 1 month. If you used fresh thyme, store in the fridge; if you used dried thyme, store in the pantry.

**Spicy Mint &
Cilantro Sauce,**
PAGE 189

**Italian Basil & Parsley
Salsa Verde**

Italian Basil & Parsley Salsa Verde

Makes about 1 cup (230 g) | GF, SF, NF

Italian salsa verde is like a zingy, bolder, nut-free pesto. In my version, sun-dried tomatoes add incredible umami and mouthfeel in lieu of anchovies, capers add salty tang, raw garlic adds a bite, and lemon zest brightens it all up.

Use It for Big Flavor: Spread over focaccia for sandwiches, or mix with vegan mayo as a spread. Spoon over tofu scramble (page 439), grilled asparagus, or a summer tomato salad. Try the Cauliflower Steaks with Italian Basil & Parsley Salsa Verde (page 421) or with Crispy Smashed Potatoes with Lots of Saucy Options (page 407), or use with crostini. Mix into a pot of beans or lentils, drizzle over pizza or flatbread, or stir into braised leafy greens.

2 cups (28 g) **fresh flat-leaf parsley** leaves (tender stems okay)

2 loosely packed cups (60 g) **fresh basil** leaves

1 ounce (28 g) **oil-packed sun-dried tomatoes** (about 5)

1½ tablespoons **capers**, drained

2 **garlic cloves**, roughly chopped

1 medium **lemon**, zested

½ teaspoon **red pepper flakes**

½ teaspoon **fine sea salt**, plus more to taste

Freshly ground **black pepper**

⅓ cup (75 g) **extra-virgin olive oil**, plus more as needed

1 tablespoon freshly squeezed **lemon juice**, plus more to taste

1. In a food processor, combine the parsley and basil. Pulse about five times to break down. Add the sun-dried tomatoes, capers, and garlic and pulse 10 to 12 times, until everything is minced. Scrape into a medium bowl. Add the lemon zest, pepper flakes, salt, and several cracks of black pepper. Stream in the olive oil, whisking as you go. For a thinner, saucier consistency, add more oil.

2. When ready to serve, add the lemon juice. Taste for seasoning (I usually add a pinch or two of salt) and add more lemon juice as needed. Transfer leftovers to a jar, seal, and store in the fridge for up to 1 week (the basil may darken, but it'll still taste good). Leftovers are best served at room temperature.

Green Goddess Dressing

Makes 1½ heaping cups (375 g) | GF, SF, NF

This herb-heavy dressing is naturally very fresh, but it's the anise notes from the tarragon that make it special. The creaminess comes from protein-packed hemp seeds, so it's also good for you. In a pinch, use just two or three herbs, but don't use more than 2 tablespoons of tarragon.

Use It for Big Flavor: Pour over salads of sturdy lettuces or shredded veggie salads (page 390). Douse cold macaroni or potatoes with it, pour it over a grain bowl, or use as a dip for crudités. My personal fave: Mix with vegan mayo and coat smashed chickpeas; scoop onto toasted bread and top with pickled onions (see page 168) for a killer sandwich.

1 cup (130 g) **hemp seeds or hearts**

⅓ cup (80 ml) freshly squeezed **lemon juice** (about 2 medium lemons), plus more to taste

2 tablespoons **extra-virgin olive oil**

¼ cup (4 g) **fresh dill** leaves

¼ cup (4 g) **fresh basil** leaves

½ cup (6 g) **fresh flat-leaf parsley** leaves (or more basil)

2 tablespoons **fresh tarragon** leaves

2 tablespoons chopped **chives** (or chopped scallions, white and light green parts only)

3 **garlic cloves**, roughly chopped

½ teaspoon **fine sea salt**, plus more to taste

¼ teaspoon freshly ground **black pepper**, plus more to taste

1. In a high-powered blender or food processor, add the hemp seeds, lemon juice, and ½ cup (120 ml) of water and blend on medium, gradually increasing the speed, until the mixture comes together. Add the olive oil, dill, basil, parsley, tarragon, chives, garlic, salt, and pepper and blend until smooth and creamy, stopping to scrape down the sides as needed. If it's too thick, add a spoonful or two of water. Taste, adding more salt, pepper, or lemon juice as needed. You can serve the dressing now, but I refrigerate it so it thickens more.

2. Store leftovers in the fridge for 5 to 6 days. After a few days, add a squeeze of lemon juice and drizzle of olive oil to revive the flavors and a splash of water if it's too thick.

Mojo Sauce

Makes about 1½ cups (360 g) | GF, SF, NF

After watching the movie *Chef* starring Jon Favreau, I wanted to open my own food truck. When I learned how demanding it was, I settled on the next best thing: making a version of the movie's popular mojo sauce.

Mojo is a spicy citrus, herb, and olive oil sauce, often used as a marinade or dip, with many variations in the Caribbean and Latin America. In Cuba, sour orange juice is used, but since sour oranges aren't readily available here, I use a mix of bracingly sour lime juice plus orange juice.

Initially, the sauce will be very spicy, but it mellows out after resting and once it's cooked.

Use It for Big Flavor: Spoon over a simple burrito bowl with rice and black beans or over scrambled tofu (page 439) or scrambled chickpeas (page 455). Drizzle over roasted cauliflower, crispy smashed potatoes (page 407), or fried plantains. Use as a tofu or tempeh marinade (page 294), mix into vegan mayo or cream cheese for a sandwich spread, or toss with cooked jackfruit for tacos.

1 scant cup (14 g) **fresh cilantro** leaves and tender stems

8 **garlic cloves**

2 teaspoons **orange zest**

½ cup (120 ml) freshly squeezed **orange juice** (1 extra-large or 2 medium oranges)

⅓ cup (80 ml) freshly squeezed **lime juice** (about 3 limes)

1 to 2 medium **Fresno (or jalapeño) peppers**, roughly chopped (membranes and seeds removed for mild heat)

3 **oregano** sprigs, leaves roughly chopped

¼ cup + 2 tablespoons (84 g) **extra-virgin olive oil**

1½ teaspoons **ground cumin**

1½ teaspoons **kosher salt** (or ¾ teaspoon fine sea salt), plus more to taste

Freshly ground **black pepper**

In a blender or food processor, combine the cilantro, garlic, orange zest and juice, lime juice, Fresno pepper, oregano, olive oil, cumin, salt, and a generous amount of black pepper. Blend until the herbs and garlic are finely chopped and the sauce comes together, stopping to scrape down the sides as you go. Store in a lidded jar in the fridge for 1 to 2 weeks.

Preserved Lemon Salsa

Makes 1 cup (230 g) | GF, SF, NF

This is a citrusy, summery "salsa" I like to make when I see preserved lemons in my fridge and think, "What else can I do with you gals?"

Use It for Big Flavor: Add to brighten savory foods, like A Really Good Pot of Saucy Beans (page 233), tofu scramble (page 439), or Crispy Smashed Potatoes with Lots of Saucy Options (page 407). Add a couple of spoonfuls to bowl meals and grain salads. Mix with vegan mayo and Dijon mustard and use as a sauce for potato, pasta, or green bean salad. Stir into thick vegan yogurt as a cooling, tangy dip for crudités.

1 small whole **lemon**, plus more freshly squeezed **lemon juice** (or champagne vinegar or white wine vinegar) as needed

2 tablespoons minced **preserved lemon peel** (page 157), plus more to taste

½ cup (8 g) **fresh cilantro** leaves and tender stems, finely chopped

½ cup (8 g) **fresh mint** leaves, finely chopped

¼ cup (4 g) **fresh flat-leaf parsley** leaves and tender stems, finely chopped (or more cilantro)

1 small **shallot**, minced

1 small **jalapeño pepper**, finely chopped (use half for moderate heat; omit membranes and seeds for mild heat)

½ small **cucumber**, finely chopped (4 to 5 ounces/120 to 150 g)

1 tablespoon **capers**, drained and roughly chopped

1 tablespoon + 1 teaspoon **extra-virgin olive oil**

⅛ teaspoon **fine sea salt**, plus more to taste

⅛ teaspoon ground **white pepper** or freshly ground **black pepper**, plus more to taste

1. Use a paring knife to peel the whole lemon, removing the white pith. Cut the lemon into quarters, remove any seeds and fibrous membranes, and chop each quarter finely. Transfer to a medium bowl, along with any juice.

2. Add the preserved lemon peel, cilantro, mint, parsley, shallots, jalapeño, cucumber, and capers to the bowl. Toss to combine. Taste, adding more preserved lemon peel as desired.

3. Add the olive oil, salt, and white pepper and mix again. Taste, adding more salt and pepper or lemon juice as needed (if you don't have extra lemon juice, add a splash of champagne vinegar or white wine vinegar). Store leftovers in the fridge for up to 1 week.

Life-Changing Homemade Chili Crisp

Makes 2½ cups (600 g) | GF, NFO

Chinese chili crisp is a cult favorite for good reason, and I happily buy the options available in stores. But I'm also not exaggerating when I say this homemade version literally changed my life. It opened new parts of my taste buds I didn't know existed. And it delivers literally everything you want in a high-impact condiment: it's salty, savory, spicy, subtly sweet, garlicky, oniony, and crunchy.

Ingredient Notes: Chili crisp is traditionally made with Sichuan chile flakes, which are toasty and vibrantly red. If you don't have them, red pepper flakes, which have a slightly different taste, work fine. For milder heat, use a greater ratio of gochugaru. Porcini mushroom powder adds a powerful savoriness here. You can buy it online, or simply blitz dried porcini mushrooms into a fine dust using a food processor or spice grinder.

Tips: Always store chili crisp in the fridge, never at room temperature, and use a clean spoon to serve; it should stay good for 2 to 3 months. If you want all crunch and minimal oil, use a fine-mesh sieve when serving to strain the oil back into the jar, then sprinkle the crunchy stuff over your food. Use the oil in stir-fries, vinaigrettes, and sauces.

Use It for Big Flavor: Spoon over rice or noodles and toss in edamame or tofu for a quick dinner. Pair with tofu scramble (page 439), frozen dumplings, steamed broccoli, smashed cucumber salads, avocado toast, or phở (or any noodle soup). It's also magnificent in a grilled cheese (page 516) and a great accompaniment for the savory pancakes on page 443.

NF Option: Replace the peanuts with roasted salted soybeans.

1½ cups (320 g) **neutral-flavored oil** of choice

12 **garlic cloves**, thinly sliced (ideally on a mandoline for evenness)

3 **whole star anise**

2 (3-inch/7.5 cm) **cinnamon sticks**

2 **bay leaves**

2-inch (5 cm) piece **fresh ginger**, peeled and sliced into very thin matchsticks

⅓ cup (45 g) **dried onion granules/dried minced onion** (coarse granules, not onion powder)

¼ cup (25 g) **Sichuan chile flakes** or **red pepper flakes** (see Ingredient Notes)

¼ cup (27 g) **gochugaru** (Korean chile flakes; see Ingredient Notes)

3 tablespoons (24 g) **white sesame seeds**

¼ cup (35 g) **salted dry-roasted peanuts**, chopped

1 tablespoon **porcini mushroom powder** (see Ingredient Notes)

1 tablespoon + 1 teaspoon **organic cane sugar**, plus more as needed

1 teaspoon ground **white pepper**

1 tablespoon **tamari** or **soy sauce** (use tamari to keep GF)

recipe and ingredients continue

For Finishing

2 tablespoons **white miso paste**, softened at room temperature

2 teaspoons **umeboshi paste** (or an additional 1 tablespoon white miso)

1 tablespoon **toasted sesame oil**

Kosher salt

1. In a medium saucepan, combine the oil, garlic, star anise, cinnamon sticks, and bay leaves. Bring to a simmer over medium heat. Reduce the heat to low to maintain a gentle simmer (move to the smallest burner if needed). Swirl the pot occasionally and cook until the garlic is golden and crisp but not browned, 13 to 18 minutes (keep a close eye on it after 10 minutes).

2. Meanwhile, in a medium bowl, combine the ginger, onion granules, Sichuan chile flakes, gochugaru, sesame seeds, peanuts, mushroom powder, sugar, and white pepper. Stir well, then add the tamari. Set a fine-mesh sieve on top of the bowl.

3. When the garlic oil is done, strain it through the sieve, allowing the hot oil to drain onto the aromatics (it should sizzle). Stir well to distribute the oil. Let cool for 10 minutes, leaving the spices and garlic in the sieve (this helps the garlic crisp up).

4. When cool, whisk the miso, umeboshi paste, and sesame oil into the oil mixture. Stir the garlic into the oil mixture but discard the spices. Stir well and taste, adding salt or more sugar to taste. Transfer to a 32-ounce (1 L) jar or a few small jars and refrigerate for up to 3 months.

Spicy Mint & Cilantro Sauce

Makes ¾ scant cup (170 g) | GF, SF, NF

This is one of my go-to sauces for a super-quick burst of flavor. It's inspired by zhoug, the Yemeni green sauce made from fresh green chiles, cilantro, olive oil, garlic, and warming spices. I swap pickled jalapeños for the fresh chiles to keep things lightning fast and for added tang.

Use It for Big Flavor: Drizzle over falafel and Mushroom Shawarma (page 532) or crispy smashed potatoes (page 407). Spoon over tofu scramble (page 439) or Scrambled Shakshuka (page 437), avocado toast, or roasted veg, especially eggplant (page 339). Stir into vegan yogurt and pair with Middle Eastern or Indian dishes, spoon over hummus for a spicy kick, or stir into softened vegan butter and brush onto grilled corn.

1 cup (16 g) **fresh mint** leaves

1 cup (16 g) **fresh cilantro** leaves and tender stems (or flat-leaf parsley)

⅓ cup (50 g) **pickled jalapeños** + ⅓ cup (80 ml) **brine** (store-bought or homemade, page 168)

2 **garlic cloves**, roughly chopped

1 teaspoon **ground cumin**

½ teaspoon **ground coriander**

½ teaspoon **ground cardamom**

½ teaspoon **organic cane sugar**

2 tablespoons **extra-virgin olive oil**

Kosher salt and freshly ground **black pepper**, as needed

1. In a food processor, combine the mint, cilantro, pickled jalapeños and brine, garlic, cumin, coriander, cardamom, and sugar. Pulse several times, then blend until somewhat smooth, stopping to scrape down the sides as needed.

2. Add the olive oil to a glass jar, then add the herb mixture and mix together. Season to taste with salt and pepper as needed. Seal and store in the fridge for up to 2 weeks.

Quick Miso–Chile Hot Sauce

Makes 1 scant cup (225 g) | GF, NF

While there's no shortage of good hot sauces on the market, this is my absolute favorite and it's ridiculously easy to make: it's spicy, a little sweet, tart but not too acidic, and has a great velvety body. I've skipped the fermentation process to keep things quick, but miso adds a developed savory flavor.

Tips: This is a *spicy!* hot sauce, though the heat mellows a bit after the sauce rests in the fridge for a few days. If you want moderate heat, remove the membranes from about half the peppers (wear food-safe gloves for this). Be sure to refrigerate this hot sauce—it's not shelf stable.

Use It for Big Flavor: Use in most recipes that could use hot sauce, particularly tacos, avocado toast, rice bowls, tofu scramble (page 439), breakfast burritos, and savory pancakes (page 443).

6 to 7 ounces (about 200 g) **Fresno (or jalapeño) peppers**, stemmed (see Tips)

4 **garlic cloves**, peeled

1 heaping teaspoon **kosher salt**

½ cup (120 ml) **apple cider vinegar**

2 tablespoons **organic cane sugar**

1 tablespoon **white miso paste**

1 tablespoon **extra-virgin olive oil**

1. Wash a glass jar and its lid with warm, soapy water and dry well.

2. In a food processor or blender, add the peppers and garlic. Pulse several times until finely chopped. Transfer to a small or medium saucepan and add the salt, vinegar, and sugar. Bring to a simmer and simmer gently for 5 minutes.

3. Remove from the heat and transfer the mixture back to your food processor or blender. Once cool, add the miso. Start blending, stopping to scrape down the sides as you go. With the motor running, stream in the olive oil and blend until pureed.

4. Fit a fine-mesh sieve over your jar and strain the hot sauce, pushing down on the chiles with a spoon to extract as much liquid as possible. Discard the solids, or if you don't mind a chunkier hot sauce, skip the straining step. If you want to be fancy, you can then transfer the hot sauce to a hot sauce bottle or two.

5. Seal and store in the fridge for up to 1 month (see Tips).

Mom's Tomato-Garlic Chutney

Makes about 4 cups (1 L) | GF, SF, NF

My mom is a prolific chutney maker, so it was hard to pick just one of her chutneys, but this one is really excellent and versatile.

Tomato chutney is often served with South Indian breakfast foods, like dosa or idli, but it's wonderful with many dishes (see Use It for Big Flavor). Here, the chutney gets taken over the top with a tadka, a tempered spiced oil that lies at the heart of Indian cooking (see page 72 for more details). For the best flavor, make a fresh batch of tadka right before serving the chutney.

Ingredient Notes: Use 2 peppers for *spicy!* If you prefer mild heat, stick with 1 pepper and remove the membranes and seeds.

Tamarind paste is sold at well-stocked grocery stores, South Asian and Latin grocers, and online. Start with 2 tablespoons and add more as needed.

White urad dal adds a unique nutty aroma and flavor but is optional; find it at South Asian grocers or online.

Fresh curry leaves can be found at Indian grocers. While fresh curry leaves have the most flavor, you can also buy the dried version online. For fresh leaves, rinse and pat very dry with a towel, then rub gently to release more aroma; when adding fresh leaves to the tadka, cover the pot as soon as you add them, as their moisture will make the oil bubble up.

Tips: When it isn't tomato season, use 3 tablespoons of tamarind and add more salt to season. Or use a 28-ounce (800 g) can of whole peeled tomatoes.

Feel free to halve the recipe, but the chutney stays good in the fridge for up to 2 weeks, or several months in the freezer.

Use It for Big Flavor: Pair with the Crispy & Savory Moong Dal Pancakes (page 443). Spoon over the Crispy Indian-ish Lentils with Rice & Yogurt (page 259) or Masala Baked Tofu (page 271), or use in lieu of ketchup in sandwiches and burgers.

2 to 3 tablespoons **grapeseed oil** or **neutral-flavored oil** of choice

10 large **garlic cloves** (55 g), smashed

1 to 2 **serrano peppers**, quartered (see Ingredient Notes)

5 cups chopped **Roma or plum tomatoes** (about 10 tomatoes, or 2 pounds/910 g)

1½ cups chopped **red onion** (about 1 medium onion, or 7 ounces/200 g)

½ teaspoon **fine sea salt**, plus more to taste

2 to 3 tablespoons **tamarind paste or concentrate** (see Ingredient Notes and Tips)

Tadka

1 tablespoon **grapeseed oil** or **neutral-flavored oil** of choice

1 teaspoon **black or brown mustard seeds**

2 teaspoons **white urad dal** (optional; see Ingredient Notes)

5 **fresh curry leaves** (or 10 dried; see Ingredient Notes)

1. Heat a 12-inch (30 cm) skillet over medium-high heat. Add enough of the oil to cover the bottom. Once the oil is hot, add the garlic and serrano. Fry until the garlic starts to turn golden, 1 to 2 minutes, stirring frequently.

2. Add the tomatoes and onions. Cook, stirring occasionally, until the tomato liquid has completely evaporated and the tomatoes are broken down, soft, and tender, 17 to 20 minutes.

3. Remove from the heat and let cool slightly, then transfer to a blender and blend until smooth. Add the salt and 2 tablespoons of the tamarind. Blend again. Taste, adding more salt or tamarind as desired (see Tips).

4. **Just before serving, make the tadka** (see tips below). Heat the oil in a small skillet or saucepan over medium-high heat. When the oil is hot, add the mustard seeds. As soon as they just start to sputter, add the urad dal (if using). Once the urad dal starts turning golden brown, add the curry leaves (cover the pan immediately if using fresh curry leaves to avoid splatter). Cook briefly until the leaves change color and crackle. Immediately remove from the heat.

5. Pour the tadka only over the amount of chutney you plan to serve.

TIPS FOR MAKING TADKA

• Keep all your spices in a masala dabba, the quintessential Indian spice tin. The dabba holds seven small containers, each with its own tiny spoon: fill them up with your seven most commonly used spices. Use the large lid to keep the dabba covered to preserve the spices' freshness. A masala dabba also makes cooking easier (no need to dig spoons into seven individual spice bottles or bags) and more intuitive (e.g., add a half spoon more of chile powder if you like things spicy). If you don't have one, just measure the spices separately in pinch bowls so you can work quickly.

• Heat a few spoonfuls of oil in your smallest skillet or saucepan over medium or medium-high heat. The smaller the pan, the more efficiently the spices will cook. You can also purchase a specialty tadka pan at Indian grocers or online for ten dollars or less.

• Start by toasting whole spices, as they take longer to toast. Larger spices like cinnamon sticks and cardamom pods should be added first. Certain spices like mustard seeds take longer to toast than others (e.g., cumin seeds and curry leaves). Ground spices need just 15 to 30 seconds.

• Keep shaking the pan or stir frequently to prevent the spices from burning.

• Make the tadka right before serving for maximal flavor and immediately pour it onto your dish.

Pistachio Butter

Makes 1⅓ cups (340 g) │ GF, SF

Homemade pistachio butter is nutty, buttery, and impossibly good. Feel free to use this same method with roasted almonds, cashews, macadamia nuts, or peanuts.

Ingredient Notes: I buy raw pistachios and roast them at home, but pre-roasted pistachios also work. Lightly salted pistachios are fine, too, but if you use them, omit the salt or add just a pinch. However, "regular" salted pistachios are too salty here. Shell-on pistachios are cheaper, but it takes time to shell them, so I leave the trade-off up to you.

Tips: A food processor works great and is relatively quick, but if you want a super smooth texture, use a high-powered blender; if your blender cup is large (e.g., 64 ounces /2 L), you'll need at least 4 cups (18 ounces/520 g) of pistachios to get the motor moving smoothly.

Use It for Big Flavor: Stuff into Medjool dates for the ultimate easy sweet treat (page 574). Spread on toast and top with berries or sliced apples. Use as a filling for sweet crepes, or as the base for plating roasted beets (page 395), cauliflower, or winter squash. Blend into a latte or smoothie for a creamy treat.

3 cups (13.5 ounces/390 g) **raw, unsalted shelled pistachios** (see Ingredient Notes)

½ heaping teaspoon **fine sea salt**, plus more if needed (see Ingredient Notes)

1. **For raw pistachios:** Roast at 350°F (175°C) until lightly browned and fragrant, 8 to 10 minutes. Let cool slightly before blending.

2. **Blender option:** Add the pistachios to a high-powered blender. Start on low speed, then work your way up to high, using a tamper or a spatula to push down the nuts as the blender churns. As the machine heats up, take breaks to avoid overheating. Once the nuts look like almond flour, use a spoon to get underneath the blades to loosen any stuck pistachio butter or dump it out into a bowl, then add it back to the blender. Keep blending. The mixture will turn into a paste, then eventually into a thick but liquidy nut butter. Once you reach this stage, add the salt and blend again until super smooth and somewhat pourable. Taste, adding more salt as needed. This process will take 10 to 20 minutes, depending on your blender strength and age.

3. **Food processor option:** Add the pistachios to a food processor. Blend, stopping to scrape down the sides and bottom every minute. If your machine heats up, take breaks. After a few minutes, the pistachios will form a ball, but just keep going and the machine will break it up. Keep blending until it's smooth, creamy, and the consistency of a thick nut butter. Add the salt and blend to incorporate. This process should take 6 to 10 minutes.

4. Store the pistachio butter in a sealed jar in the fridge for up to 1 month.

An Ode to Tahini

I find the question "What's your favorite food?" unanswerable. It depends on my mood, the occasion, the season, and the company.

But ask me "What's your favorite ingredient?" and the answer is simpler. It's probably tahini. It's liquid gold, and I use it in some form multiple times a week.

Tahini has long been used in Middle Eastern cuisines, and it's a versatile ingredient that has the power to mimic the creamy consistency and gorgeously rich mouthfeel of dairy-based foods (without the heaviness). And since it's simply sesame seed paste, it's also high in protein, iron, calcium, and plant compounds that help reduce cholesterol.

Tahini can be drizzled plain on countless savory foods—shawarma and falafel of course, but also roasted or braised vegetables, salads, and any number of vegan bowls. And it can often be used interchangeably with almond or cashew butter to avoid nut allergies.

And when tahini is blended with a source of acidity and ice water, it becomes wildly creamy, almost fluffy, and truly indulgent. This is the base for the tahini sauces that follow.

It is important to find a good-quality tahini. It should be creamy and smooth in texture, nutty, and just slightly earthy in taste. And don't skimp on the citrus, as the acidity mellows out the subtly bitter sesame flavor.

My favorite tahini brands are Soom Foods (single-origin sesame seeds) and Seed + Mill (small batch): they have a smooth, homogenous texture that requires very little stirring and a buttery, nutty taste, so even a plain drizzle is delicious. A few more budget-friendly options I like are Beirut Tahini Sesame Paste, Ziyad, Baron's, and the Whole Foods 365 brand.

Creamy Tahini Sauce, 3 Ways

Each makes 1¼ cups (300 g) | GF, SF, NF

All of these sauces are creamy and buttery smooth with a slightly nutty flavor and bright tanginess. Store them in a jar in the fridge for up to 1 week (leftovers can also be frozen).

Tip: Tahini sauces thicken a bit after resting. When using leftovers or as a salad dressing, thin with water.

Lemon Tahini Sauce

This is a true all-purpose sauce.

Use It for Big Flavor: Drizzle it over warm bowls of veggies and lentils or grains and beans, over take-out shawarma to make it even better, or massage it into a kale salad. Very good with blanched green beans and asparagus and roasted veg like winter squash, cauliflower, and broccoli. For a spicy kick, replace the maple syrup with Spicy "Honey" with Candied Jalapeños (page 176).

¼ cup (60 ml) freshly squeezed **lemon juice**

½ cup (112 g) well-stirred **tahini**

¾ teaspoon **kosher salt**, plus more to taste

¼ teaspoon **ground cumin**

Freshly ground **black pepper**

2 **garlic cloves**, grated or crushed with a press

2 teaspoons **pure maple syrup**

6 to 8 tablespoons **ice water** (90 to 120 ml), plus more as needed

In a medium bowl, whisk together the lemon juice, tahini, salt, cumin, pepper to taste, garlic, and maple syrup. Add the ice water a tablespoon at a time, whisking as you go. It will get stiff at first but eventually will become creamy yet pourable. Taste for seasonings, adding more salt as desired.

Pomegranate Tahini Sauce

Addictively tart and tangy thanks to pomegranate molasses, with a hint of spice.

Use It for Big Flavor: Use as a dipping sauce for sweet potato fries or Charred Sweet Potato Wedges (page 345). Try with the Buttery Charred Cabbage in Spiced Tomatoes with Tahini (page 401), mushrooms, or roasted potatoes (page 407).

¼ cup (60 ml) freshly squeezed **lemon juice**

½ cup (112 g) well-stirred **tahini**

¾ teaspoon **kosher salt**, plus more to taste

¼ teaspoon **ground cardamom**

¼ teaspoon **ground coriander**

3 **garlic cloves**, grated or crushed with a press, plus more to taste

1½ tablespoons **pure pomegranate molasses**, plus more to taste

4 to 6 tablespoons (60 to 90 ml) **ice water**, plus more as needed

In a medium bowl, whisk together the lemon juice, tahini, salt, cardamom, coriander, garlic, and pomegranate molasses. Add the water a

recipe continues

tablespoon at a time, whisking as you go. The mixture will get stiff at first but eventually will become creamy yet pourable. Taste for seasonings, adding a pinch more salt, a bit more molasses for additional tang, or more garlic for sharpness.

Turkish-Spiced Tahini Sauce

This sauce is full of warmth and heat.

Use It for Big Flavor: Pair with falafel, drizzle on the Jammy Roasted Eggplant (page 339) or Jammy Zucchini (page 330), or spoon into pita pockets along with chickpeas, tomatoes, cucumbers, and salad greens.

1 teaspoon **coriander seeds**

1 teaspoon **cumin seeds**

1 teaspoon **fennel seeds**

1½ teaspoons **Aleppo pepper** or **Urfa biber**

3 to 4 tablespoons (45 to 60 ml) freshly squeezed **lemon juice**

½ cup (112 g) well-stirred **tahini**

¼ teaspoon **kosher salt**, plus more to taste

½ teaspoon **pure maple syrup**, **agave nectar**, or **organic cane sugar**

2 **garlic cloves**, grated or crushed with a press

1 tablespoon **sumac**

1 teaspoon **dried mint**

6 to 8 tablespoons (90 to 120 ml) **ice water**, plus more as needed

1. Heat a small skillet over medium-low heat. Add the coriander, cumin, and fennel seeds. Toast for 1 to 2 minutes, swirling or shaking the pan frequently. Add the Aleppo pepper and toast for 2 minutes, swirling frequently. Remove from the heat and let cool.

2. Add the cooled spices to a mortar and pestle or electric spice grinder. Grind coarsely so that some texture is remaining. Or if you prefer a completely smooth sauce, you can grind them finely as well.

3. In a medium bowl, whisk together 3 tablespoons of the lemon juice, the tahini, salt, maple syrup, garlic, sumac, mint, and the ground spice mixture. Add the water a tablespoon at a time, whisking as you go. The mixture will get stiff at first but eventually will become creamy yet pourable. Taste for seasonings, adding up to 1 additional tablespoon of lemon juice or more salt as desired.

Extremely Easy Queso Sauce

Makes 2 cups (480 g) (serves 8 to 10) | GF, SF

I call this a "vegan gateway recipe" because so many nonvegan folks have had their *aha!* moments after making this queso. It's "I can't believe it's not butter," but for cheese.

Use It for Big Flavor: You can serve this warm or at room temperature, and in all kinds of Mexican-inspired dishes. Spread onto large tortillas for quesadillas or burritos, drizzle over tacos and burrito bowls, or use in enchiladas. Spoon warm over a bed of nachos, or serve warm as a dip with chips and salsa.

1 cup (140 g) **raw cashews**, soaked or quick soaked, drained, and rinsed (see page 106)

½ cup (115 g) **unsweetened coconut yogurt**

½ cup (about 120 g) your favorite store-bought **salsa** (use hot salsa for a *spicy!* queso; mild salsa for a milder queso)

1 teaspoon **ground cumin**

½ teaspoon **chili powder**

½ teaspoon **smoked paprika**

Freshly ground **black pepper**

2 tablespoons **nutritional yeast**, plus more to taste

2 tablespoons **pickled jalapeños**, plus more to taste + 2 tablespoons **pickled jalapeño brine**

Kosher salt or **fine sea salt**

Plain **plant-based milk of choice**, for loosening (as needed)

1. In a high-powered blender, add the soaked and drained cashews, yogurt, salsa, 2 tablespoons of water, the cumin, chili powder, paprika, lots of pepper, nutritional yeast, and pickled jalapeños and brine. Blend until thick, creamy, and smooth, stopping to scrape down the sides as you go. Taste for seasonings, adding salt or more pickled jalapeños or nutritional yeast as desired.

2. If you want to serve the queso warm, gently heat in a small saucepan over low heat, stirring occasionally, for 8 minutes. If the queso seems thick, add a splash of plant milk or water to loosen. Store leftovers in an airtight container in the fridge for up to 1 week (or freeze for a few months; thaw in the fridge, then blend again, adding a splash of plant milk or water as needed).

Cashew Cream, Many Ways

Makes about 1 cup (260 g) | GF, SF

Cashew cream is a blank-canvas condiment that will rescue your weeknight dinners. It can be a substitute for creamy dairy things like sour cream or cream itself, but you can also use it as a dressing or a sauce. You can mix it up by adding herbs, spices, citrus, aromatic-infused oils, and even preserved lemons (lots of tasty ideas are in the chart that follows).

Ingredient Notes: Raw cashews are a must. When soaked, they swell up, which creates that super-lush creamy texture (roasted cashews don't do the same).

If you're allergic to cashews, you can sub raw walnuts or blanched almonds with *decent* results. Blanched almonds must be soaked longer, ideally for 24 hours. Since neither is as rich as cashews, add a tablespoon or two of extra-virgin olive oil when blending.

Tip: A high-powered blender yields the smoothest cashew cream. If you don't have one, use a food processor (it will take 4 to 5 minutes).

Use It for Big Flavor: Pour over grain bowls and roasted, grilled, or blanched vegetables. Stir into risotto or pureed soups, drizzle over tacos or burrito bowls, or use as a sandwich spread. Use as a dip for fries or roasted potatoes, drizzle over baked or fried tofu, or use to thicken curries in lieu of coconut milk.

1 cup (140 g) **raw cashews**, soaked or quick soaked, drained, and rinsed (see page 106 and Ingredient Notes)

2 tablespoons freshly squeezed **lemon juice**, plus more to taste

2 **garlic cloves**, roughly chopped

2 tablespoons **nutritional yeast**, plus more to taste (optional, for cheesiness/savoriness)

½ teaspoon **onion powder** (optional)

½ teaspoon **fine sea salt**, plus more to taste

Freshly ground **black pepper**

1. In a high-powered blender or food processor, add the soaked and drained cashews, ½ cup (120 ml) of water, the lemon juice, garlic, nutritional yeast (if using), onion powder (if using), salt, and several cracks of pepper. Blend until creamy and thick and all cashew bits have been pulverized, stopping to scrape down the sides as you go, 2 to 3 minutes (see Tip).

2. If it's too thick for your liking, add up to ¼ cup (60 ml) more water. Taste and adjust for seasonings, adding more salt, nutritional yeast for cheesy/umami flavors, and lemon juice for acidity.

recipe continues

3. Store in a sealed jar in the fridge for up to 1 week. Or freeze for a few months; thaw and blend again, adding a splash of plant milk or water as needed.

Cashew Cream—Flavor Variations

FLAVOR VARIATION	ADDITIONAL INGREDIENTS	INGREDIENTS TO OMIT + OTHER NOTES
Lemon-Basil	• 1 cup (16 g) fresh basil leaves • 1 medium lemon, zested (optional) • 3 tablespoons freshly squeezed lemon juice	Use the lower range of water, only ½ cup (120 ml).
Sriracha-Ginger	• 1 to 1½ tablespoons sriracha • 1 teaspoon agave nectar or pure maple syrup • 2 to 3 tablespoons freshly squeezed lime juice • 1 tablespoon peeled and grated fresh ginger	Omit the lemon juice and onion powder.
Dill-Caper	• ½ cup (8 g) fresh dill, tough stems removed • 1 tablespoon capers, drained • 1 teaspoon Dijon mustard (optional)	
Cilantro-Lime	• 2 to 3 tablespoons freshly squeezed lime juice • ¾ to 1 cup (9 to 12 g) fresh cilantro leaves • 1 to 2 jalapeño peppers, roughly chopped • ¼ teaspoon smoked paprika • ½ teaspoon ground cumin	Omit the lemon juice and onion powder.
Preserved Lemon	2 tablespoons chopped preserved lemon peel (page 157)	Omit the onion powder and salt. Start with 1 tablespoon lemon juice; add more as needed. Add salt only to taste.

Throwback Ranch Dressing

Makes ¾ cup (175 g) | GF, SFO, NF

This creamy, slightly tangy ranch dressing has a fantastic garlicky, oniony, dilly bite and will evoke all your childhood nostalgia in the best way possible.

Ingredient Note: Vegan mayo brands vary in thickness, so if the dressing feels thin, add an extra tablespoon; my favorite brand is Follow Your Heart Original Vegenaise but they also sell a soy-free variety.

Tip: If the dressing is too sharp, stir in a tablespoon of plain vegan yogurt.

Use It for Big Flavor: Pour over wedge salads or any crunchy salad, as well as on pasta or potato salads. Use as a dip for crudités, vegan "wings," or pizza; spoon over Crispy Smashed Potatoes (page 407) or use in lieu of ketchup on veggie burgers.

1 tablespoon plain **plant-based milk** of choice

¼ teaspoon **apple cider vinegar**

½ cup (112 g) **vegan mayo** (use soy-free mayo as needed; see Ingredient Note)

1 tablespoon freshly squeezed **lemon juice**, plus more to taste

1 large or 2 small **garlic cloves**, grated or finely minced

½ teaspoon **Dijon mustard**

½ teaspoon **onion powder**

1½ teaspoons **nutritional yeast**

¼ scant teaspoon **fine sea salt**, plus more to taste

2 tablespoons finely minced **fresh chives** or **scallions**

2 teaspoons chopped **fresh dill**

Freshly ground **black pepper**

1. In a small bowl, combine the milk and vinegar. Set aside until it curdles slightly, 5 to 10 minutes. This is your vegan buttermilk.

2. In a medium bowl, combine the mayo, lemon juice, garlic, mustard, onion powder, nutritional yeast, salt, chives, dill, and several cracks of pepper. Pour in the buttermilk and whisk until well combined. Taste for seasonings, adding more salt or pepper as desired or more lemon juice for acidity. I usually add a teaspoon of lemon juice and a pinch of salt. Chill the dressing for the best flavor. Store leftovers in the fridge for up to 1 week.

Crema, 2 Ways

Mexican crema is similar to sour cream but tangier, a little salty, and a bit thinner. Neither of these is a true crema, but they are both extremely delicious.

Use It for Big Flavor: Pair with tacos, burrito bowls, nachos, quesadillas, or enchiladas. Or simply use as "*the* sauce" to bring everything together, including a simple bowl of rice and beans. Drizzle over roasted cauliflower, baked tofu, or Crispy Smashed Potatoes with Lots of Saucy Options (page 407).

Avocado Crema

Makes 1½ to 2 cups (420 g) | GF, SF, NF

Tangy, limey, and spicy.

Ingredient Note: For mild heat, use 1 jalapeño and remove the membranes and seeds; for *spicy!*, use 2 jalapeños.

Avocado oil or **neutral-flavored oil** of choice

1 **poblano pepper**, quartered lengthwise and seeded

1 to 2 **jalapeño peppers**, whole with stem on (see Ingredient Note)

2 medium **avocados**, pits removed but reserved

⅓ cup (75 g) good-quality **unsweetened coconut yogurt**, plus more to taste (see page 61 for recommended brands)

3 **garlic cloves**, roughly chopped, plus more to taste

4 to 5 tablespoons (60 to 75 ml) freshly squeezed **lime juice**

1 cup (16 g) **fresh cilantro** leaves and tender stems

¾ teaspoon **ground cumin**

¾ teaspoon **fine sea salt**, plus more to taste

Freshly ground **black pepper**

1. Heat a cast-iron skillet over medium heat with just a thin coating of oil. Once warm, add the poblano and jalapeño peppers. Cook, turning occasionally, until charred all over, about 7 minutes for the jalapeño and 7 to 10 minutes for the poblano. Remove from the heat and let cool a bit. Remove the jalapeño stem(s).

2. Transfer the charred peppers to a blender or food processor and add the avocado, yogurt, garlic, 4 tablespoons of the lime juice, the cilantro, cumin, salt, and a generous amount of black pepper. Blend until smooth and creamy, stopping to scrape down the sides as you go, or use your blender's tamper. Taste for seasonings, adding more yogurt, garlic, salt, and pepper as needed. Add the additional 1 tablespoon lime juice for more tang, if desired. Store leftovers in an airtight container, put the reserved avocado pits in the middle, and refrigerate for 4 to 5 days (my thanks to Edgar Castrejón, author of *Provecho*, for this storage tip).

Chipotle Crema

Makes 1½ cups (360 g) | GF, SF

Smoky, tart, and slightly sweet. Cashews make the best crema, but if you are allergic, sub with 1 cup (130 g) hemp seeds. You can halve the recipe, but you'll need a small-capacity blender.

¼ cup + 2 tablespoons (90 ml) **aquafaba** (the liquid from a can of chickpeas)

1 heaping teaspoon **kosher salt**, plus more to taste

1 cup (140 g) **raw cashews**, soaked or quick soaked, drained, and rinsed (see page 106)

3 tablespoons freshly squeezed **lemon juice**, plus more to taste

3 tablespoons freshly squeezed **lime juice**, plus more to taste

4 **garlic cloves**, plus more to taste

4 **chipotle peppers in adobo** + 2 teaspoons of the **adobo sauce** (for mild heat, use 2 peppers)

½ teaspoon **smoked paprika**

1 teaspoon **pure maple syrup**, **agave nectar**, or **Spicy "Honey" with Candied Jalapeños** (page 176)

In a high-powered blender or food processor, add the aquafaba, ⅔ cup (160 ml) of water, and the salt. Blend on medium or high speed until everything is combined and a bit foamy, 10 to 15 seconds. Add the soaked and drained cashews, lemon and lime juices, garlic, chipotles and adobo sauce, paprika, and maple syrup. Blend on high speed until creamy, 2 to 4 minutes, stopping to scrape down the sides as you go. Taste for seasonings, adding more salt, garlic, or lemon/lime juice as needed. Store leftovers in the fridge for up to 1 week.

Whipped Tofu Ricotta

Makes 2 to 2½ cups (450 to 550 g) | GF, NF

With the same luxe creaminess and savory notes of ricotta, my signature tofu ricotta works smashingly well in any recipe that calls for ricotta. For a slightly thinner texture, use firm tofu.

Use It for Big Flavor: Perfect in any and all stuffed pastas, like lasagna (page 519). It's also great as a sandwich spread or spread onto pizza dough. Dollop leftovers onto grain bowls or salads for a creamy element.

Easy Variation: For a spicy version, stir in a few teaspoons of Calabrian chili paste.

1 (14-ounce/400 g) block **extra-firm tofu**

4 to 6 tablespoons (20 to 30 g) **nutritional yeast**

2 **garlic cloves**, roughly chopped

2 tablespoons **white miso paste**

¾ teaspoon **onion powder**

1 to 1½ teaspoons **kosher salt**

Freshly ground **black pepper**

1½ tablespoons **extra-virgin olive oil**

1 medium **lemon**, zested

2 to 3 tablespoons freshly squeezed **lemon juice**

1. Drain the tofu and dab away the excess water with a clean dish towel.

2. Crumble the tofu into a food processor. Add 4 tablespoons of the nutritional yeast, the garlic, miso, onion powder, 1 teaspoon of the salt, a generous amount of pepper, the olive oil, and lemon zest and 2 tablespoons of the lemon juice. Blend until creamy and smooth.

3. Taste for salt, acidity, and cheesiness. As needed, add the remaining ½ teaspoon salt, 1 tablespoon lemon juice, and/or 1 to 2 tablespoons nutritional yeast. The ricotta will stay good in the fridge for up to 1 week (it can also be frozen for up to 2 months; defrost in the fridge and whip again before using).

Whipped Feta

Makes 1¼ cups (300 g) | GF, SFO, NFO

I couldn't find even one edible vegan cheese when I went vegan in 2016, but now vegans can enjoy whipped "feta" just as much as everyone else. This is creamy, tangy, and salty deliciousness.

Ingredient Notes: For vegan feta, I recommend Violife or Trader Joe's brand, both of which are free of nuts and soy; for the cream cheese, I like Tofutti (nut-free) best, as well as Kite Hill (soy-free) and Oatly (nut- and soy-free).

Use It for Big Flavor: Spread on bagels and top with vegan lox (page 431), or spread on sliced sourdough for open-faced sandwiches. Use as a bed for the Garlicky Kale (page 333), Quick Roasted Cauliflower (page 342), or Spice-Roasted Whole Carrots (page 329); add Crunchy Roasted Chickpeas (page 236) to make it a meal. Serve as a dip and dust with Za'atar (page 179), chile flakes, soft herbs, and olive oil; serve with pita chips or grilled bread.

Easy Variation: For a spicy version, stir in a spoonful of Calabrian chili paste.

4 ounces (115 g) **vegan feta** (about 1 cup crumbled; see Ingredient Notes)

6 ounces (170 g) **vegan cream cheese** (about 1 cup; see Ingredient Notes)

1 **garlic clove**

1 medium-large **lemon**, zested

1 tablespoon freshly squeezed **lemon juice**, plus more to taste

1 tablespoon **extra-virgin olive oil**

¼ teaspoon **fine sea salt**, plus more to taste

Freshly ground **black pepper**

1. Drain the feta and add it to a food processor. Blend until it turns into tiny crumbs.

2. Add the cream cheese, garlic, lemon zest and juice, olive oil, salt, and several cracks of pepper. Puree until smooth and airy, stopping to scrape down the sides as needed. Taste, adding more lemon juice or salt as desired. You can serve the whipped feta now, but it will thicken more if it rests in the fridge for at least 30 minutes. Store in a jar or container in the fridge for up to 1 week.

Fermented Cashew Cheese

Serves 16 | GF, SF

Cashew "cheese" is already tasty, but when you ferment it, it tastes much more like actual cheese since most cheese is a fermented dairy product. And this "cheese" is the best dang vegan cheese I've tried over the years.

Don't let the word *fermentation* scare you either. All you need is a warm place, a day or two, seven ingredients, and 15 minutes of hands-on work. The result is homemade cheese logs that are (1) sliceable and spreadable (similar to the texture of goat cheese) and (2) cheesier tasting than almost any store-bought alternative.

Ingredient Note: Any plain vegan yogurt works, as long as it says "live active cultures" or "probiotics."

Tips: You need a warm but not hot place to ferment the cheese. I use my oven with the light bulb on (but don't place the jar too close to the bulb or it will overheat); leave a sign on the oven door so no one turns it on. Or use your kitchen counter or pantry.

The warmer the temperature, the less time it needs. With the oven, 16 hours is usually sufficient. If you are fermenting the cheese on the counter and your kitchen isn't very warm, ferment it for 48 hours.

Use It for Big Flavor: Make the best grilled cheese of your life (page 516), or slather on toasted bread and top with sea salt–flecked heirloom tomatoes. Use on a sandwich instead of mayo or on a bagel instead of cream cheese. Make it the star of a cheese board with crackers, olives, and fruit. Spread onto flatbread and add your favorite toppings and bake in the oven for a quick "pizza." Or just serve with crackers or spread onto crostini.

Safety Note! To minimize the risk of food-borne botulism, don't use fresh garlic; use only garlic powder.

1½ cups (200 g) **raw cashews**, soaked or quick soaked, drained, and rinsed (see page 106)

3 tablespoons **unsweetened vegan yogurt** (see Ingredient Note)

1 tablespoon freshly squeezed **lemon juice**

¼ cup (60 ml) **warm water**

⅓ cup (64 g) **refined coconut oil** (unrefined adds a coconutty taste)

½ cup (40 g) **nutritional yeast**

¾ teaspoon **garlic powder** (see Safety Note!)

¾ teaspoon **onion powder**

1¼ teaspoons **fine sea salt**

Optional Flavor Mix-Ins (for 1 cheese log)

4 **sun-dried tomatoes**, chopped + ½ teaspoon **dried oregano or basil**

¼ cup (40 g) **dried cranberries**, chopped + 1 tablespoon finely chopped **fresh dill**

2 large **Medjool dates**, finely chopped + ¼ cup (30 g) **walnuts** or **pistachios**, very finely chopped

12 to 14 **green olives**, minced + ½ to 1 teaspoon **dried oregano**

A few teaspoons (or more) of **everything bagel seasoning**

recipe continues

1. Wash a glass jar (and airtight lid) with warm, soapy water and dry well.

2. In a high-powered blender, add the soaked and drained cashews, yogurt, lemon juice, the warm water, and the oil. Blend on medium or high speed, stopping to scrape down the sides as you go, until relatively smooth and creamy. Add the nutritional yeast, garlic powder, onion powder, and salt and blend again until completely smooth.

3. Pour the mixture into the jar and seal tightly. Leave in a warm place to ferment for a minimum of 16 hours, or up to 48 hours (see Tips).

4. Once the cheese has fermented, give it a stir. You'll know it's fermented if it has some aeration (depending on the yogurt culture, it may have a little or a lot). Refrigerate the jar for at least 4 hours to firm.

5. Once solidified, spoon half the cheese onto a sheet of plastic wrap. Roll up the cheese in the wrap and use your hands and the plastic wrap to mold the cheese into a log shape. Repeat with the remaining cheese to make a second log (you can use parchment paper, but plastic wrap makes it easier to manipulate the shape).

6. If you are using flavor mix-ins, mix them together in a small bowl. Spread the toppings out on a plate, roll the cheese log(s) in the toppings, and wrap the logs in a new sheet of plastic.

7. Refrigerate the cheese logs for at least 2 hours to set. Store leftover cheese wrapped in plastic wrap in the fridge for 2 to 3 weeks (if using parchment paper, place the logs in an airtight container to prevent drying out). With toppings, the cheese logs have a shorter shelf life, depending on the freshness of the toppings.

Yogurt Sauce, 3 Ways

GF, SF, NF

I'm not a big yogurt-with-fruit for breakfast person, but I do rely heavily on yogurt sauces for savory dishes, and so you'll find them used liberally throughout this book. When mixed with lemon or lime juice and a few spices, yogurt sauces become transformative in savory food, adding a creamy texture, a cooling element, and bright, tangy flavor. Plus, they're quick to make, versatile, and can usually be made a few days ahead of time.

Ingredient Note: For a great yogurt sauce, you need a great vegan yogurt, ideally one that's tart in flavor and thick and creamy in texture. You can find my recommended vegan yogurt brands on page 61.

Mint Yogurt Sauce

Serves 2 to 4

A well-balanced yogurt sauce that's a little tart, a little spicy, and super quick to make.

Use It for Big Flavor: Spoon over Indian-inspired or Middle Eastern recipes, like dal (page 497) or chickpea salads (page 243), as well as fresh salads with heirloom tomatoes, thinly shaved kohlrabi, or celery. Use as a base for roasted beets or carrots (page 329).

½ cup (115 g) good-quality **unsweetened coconut yogurt** (or a thick Greek-style vegan yogurt; see Ingredient Note)

1 to 2 teaspoons freshly squeezed **lime juice** (or lemon juice)

1 small **garlic clove**, grated or crushed with a press

½ inch (1 to 1.5 cm) piece **fresh ginger**, peeled and grated or minced

¼ teaspoon **red pepper flakes**

¼ cup (4 g) **fresh mint** leaves, roughly chopped

¼ teaspoon **fine sea salt**, plus more to taste

In a medium bowl, mix together the yogurt, 1 teaspoon of the lime juice, the garlic, ginger, pepper flakes, mint, and salt. Taste, adding more salt and 1 additional teaspoon of lime juice as needed (will depend on the flavor of your yogurt). Serve immediately or let rest in the fridge for 30 minutes to marinate. Store leftovers in a sealed jar in the fridge for 3 or 4 days.

Yogurt Sauce with Chile Oil

Serves 4 to 6

A 5-minute chile oil infuses yogurt with a little heat, richness, and lots of flavor. Using Aleppo pepper or Urfa biber adds slightly smoky, earthy, and fruity notes with mild to moderate heat, but you can sub with 2 to 3 teaspoons of red pepper flakes.

Use It for Big Flavor: Spoon over scrambled chickpeas (page 455) or scrambled tofu (page 439),

recipe continues

Condiments & Flavor Boosters 213

use as a creamy base for dragging vegetables through, or serve as a dip for flatbread or pita. Pair with crunchy salads for a little richness.

2 tablespoons + 2 teaspoons **Aleppo pepper** or **Urfa biber** (or a mix of both)

4½ tablespoons (63 g) **extra-virgin olive oil**

¾ cup (170 g) good-quality **unsweetened coconut yogurt** (or a thick Greek-style vegan yogurt; see Ingredient Note)

2 **garlic cloves**, grated or finely minced

1 to 1½ tablespoons freshly squeezed **lemon juice**

½ teaspoon **dried mint** (optional)

Fine sea salt and freshly ground **black pepper**

1. In a small saucepan, heat the Aleppo pepper and olive oil over low heat. Once the mixture reaches a very gentle simmer (you're looking for tiny, slow bubbles), simmer for 5 minutes. Remove from the heat and pour into a bowl to stop the cooking.

2. In a medium bowl, stir together the yogurt, garlic, 1 tablespoon of the lemon juice, the mint (if using), ¼ heaping teaspoon salt, and a few cracks of black pepper. Taste, adding more salt and an additional ½ tablespoon of lemon juice as desired.

3. Just before using, drizzle some of the chile oil over the yogurt sauce. Reserve the rest of the chile oil for another use: store in a sterilized jar at room temperature for 1 to 2 months, or refrigerate if the jar isn't sterilized. Store leftover yogurt sauce in a jar in the fridge for 4 or 5 days.

Yogurt–Tahini Sauce

Serves 4 to 6

Adding my favorite ingredient, tahini, to yogurt makes for an extra creamy yogurt sauce with nutty notes.

Use It for Big Flavor: Spoon over shawarma (page 532), falafel, or other Middle Eastern recipes. Use as a creamy base to plate salads (page 365), roasted vegetables (especially eggplant), or as a dip for crudités.

¾ cup (170 g) good-quality **unsweetened coconut yogurt** (or a thick Greek-style vegan yogurt; see Ingredient Note)

3 to 4 tablespoons well-stirred **tahini**

1½ tablespoons freshly squeezed **lemon juice**, plus more as needed

1 large or 2 small **garlic cloves**, grated or finely minced

1 teaspoon **Aleppo pepper** (or ¼ teaspoon red pepper flakes)

¼ teaspoon **fine sea salt**, plus more to taste

Freshly ground **black pepper**

Optional Additions

½ teaspoon **dried mint** (for a touch of sweet earthiness)

1½ teaspoons **sumac** (for extra tanginess and subtle sweet fruity flavors)

¼ teaspoon **ground cardamom** (for a hint of herbal, sweet warmth)

In a medium bowl, whisk together the yogurt, 3 tablespoons of the tahini, the lemon juice, garlic, Aleppo pepper, and any optional additions until relatively smooth. Season with the salt and crack in some black pepper. Taste, adding more as needed. If your yogurt isn't tangy, add more lemon juice. For more richness, add the remaining 1 tablespoon tahini. Store in a jar in the fridge for 4 or 5 days.

Smoky Seed Sprinkle

Makes ¾ scant cup (100 g) │ GF, SF, NF

A versatile and nutrient-rich crunchy condiment. Feel free to double the recipe (just use a larger skillet).

Use It for Big Flavor: Add to your salads or bowl meals for crunch and a little smoky heat, especially Mexican-inspired meals, like the Saucy Black Beans in Sofrito (page 250) and Baked Tofu & Kale in Tomato-Chipotle Sauce (page 287). Pair with Roasted Butternut Wedges (page 337) and Chipotle or Avocado Crema (page 204) for a chewy-creamy-crunchy combo.

1 tablespoon **extra-virgin olive oil** (if using a nonstick pan, use 1½ to 2 teaspoons)

½ cup (70 g) **pepitas** (shelled pumpkin seeds) and/or **sunflower seeds**

1 tablespoon **white sesame seeds**

1 tablespoon **coriander seeds**

¼ to ½ teaspoon **red pepper flakes** (depending on spice preference)

1 teaspoon **smoked paprika**

½ teaspoon **flaky sea salt**

1. Line a plate with parchment paper. Heat a medium skillet over medium heat. Once warm but not hot, add the olive oil, pepitas, sesame seeds, coriander seeds, pepper flakes, paprika, and salt. Stir almost continuously until golden and the seeds are popping, 2 to 3 minutes.

2. Transfer to the plate and spread out with a spoon, ensuring the spices evenly coat the pepitas. Let cool, then use the parchment to funnel the mixture into a jar. Seal and store in a cool, dry place for 3 to 4 weeks.

Smoky Seed Sprinkle

Savory Walnut Crunch,
PAGE 220

Hazelnut Dukkah,
PAGE 219

Fried Shallots,
PAGE 224

Hazelnut Dukkah

Makes 1½ cups (170 g) | GF, SF, NFO

Dukkah—a spiced Egyptian nut and seed condiment that comes in many variations—is one of my favorite all-purpose seasonings. It takes 10 minutes to make, stays fresh for several months, and makes so many meals so much better.

Use It for Big Flavor: Stir into dips for flavor and crunch—hummus, baba ghanoush, beet dip, or any of the yogurt or tahini sauces in this chapter. Sprinkle over salads and whole grains, as well as grilled or roasted veg and pureed soups. Or mix with extra-virgin olive oil and serve as a dip for bread.

Easy Variation: For a zesty flavor profile, add 1 to 2 teaspoons sumac in step 5.

NF Option: Omit the hazelnuts and use a total of ¾ cup (105 g) pepitas and sunflower seeds.

½ cup (70 g) **raw hazelnuts**

Pick two and use ¼ cup (35 g) total:

   Raw almonds, shelled pistachios, **walnuts**, **sunflower seeds**, and/or **pepitas** (shelled pumpkin seeds)

2 tablespoons **coriander seeds**

1 tablespoon **cumin seeds**

1½ teaspoons **fennel seeds**

¼ cup (32 g) **white sesame seeds**

1 teaspoon **flaky sea salt**, plus more to taste

1 teaspoon **sweet or hot paprika**

1 teaspoon **Aleppo pepper** (or ¼ teaspoon red pepper flakes), plus more to taste

½ teaspoon freshly ground **black pepper**, plus more to taste

1. Coarsely chop the hazelnuts and any other nuts; keep seeds whole.

2. Heat a medium or large skillet over medium heat. Add the hazelnuts and nuts or seeds of your choice. Toast until lightly toasted and browned, shaking the pan occasionally to prevent burning, 3 to 5 minutes. Remove from the heat and transfer to a food processor.

3. Return the pan to medium heat. Add the coriander, cumin, fennel, and sesame seeds. Toast until very fragrant, shaking the pan occasionally, about 2 minutes. Remove from the heat to prevent burning.

4. Pulse the nut mixture several times in quick bursts until the nuts start to break down. Add the toasted spices and pulse again in quick bursts until you have a crunchy mixture, but do not overpulse or blend—you want a crunchy mix, not a fine powder.

5. Pour the nut-seed mixture into a jar or container. Add the salt, paprika, Aleppo pepper, and black pepper. Stir to combine. Taste for seasonings and add more salt, black pepper, or Aleppo pepper as desired. Once cooled, seal the jar or container. Store in a cool, dry place for 2 to 3 months.

Savory Walnut Crunch

Makes 2½ cups (270 g) | GFO, SF, NFO

A fun and breezy all-purpose crispy condiment that's a little indulgent and a little wholesome. This recipe makes a big batch, but it has a long shelf life and is very versatile.

Use It for Big Flavor: Sprinkle on salads, grain bowls, or any roasted or grilled veg for a crunchy element; use as a topper for soups; or stir into pasta for a crispy-chewy contrast. It is particularly good over the Pasta & Chickpeas with Fried Capers & Tomato-Shallot Butter (page 501) or a grain bowl with Saucy Glazed Pan-Fried Tempeh (page 293).

Easy Variations: Swap almonds or cashews for the walnuts, or replace the pepitas with sunflower seeds.

GF Option: Use gluten-free panko. It's not as flaky but works decently.

NF Option: Use a mix of pepitas, sesame seeds, and sunflower seeds instead of walnuts.

2 tablespoons **extra-virgin olive oil**

¾ cup **raw walnuts** (84 g), finely chopped (can pulse in a food processor)

½ cup (70 g) **pepitas** (shelled pumpkin seeds)

1¼ cups (100 g) **panko bread crumbs**

⅛ teaspoon **ground turmeric**

1 heaping teaspoon **flaky sea salt**

1 to 2 teaspoons **Aleppo pepper** (or ¼ to ½ teaspoon red pepper flakes; user lower range for mild heat)

Freshly ground **black pepper**

1. Heat a 12-inch (30 cm) skillet over medium heat. After a minute or two, add the olive oil, walnuts, and pepitas. Cook for 2 minutes, stirring frequently to prevent burning.

2. Add the panko, turmeric, salt, Aleppo pepper, and black pepper to taste. Stir the panko into the oil and stir very frequently to avoid burning. Cook until the panko is golden brown, about 3 minutes. Transfer to a plate and let cool. Store in a sealed jar or airtight container in a cool, dry place for about 1 month.

Cheesy Crunchies

Makes 1½ heaping cups (170 g) | GF, SF

They might not look like much, but these clustery nuggets have the deep cheesy richness of parmesan but with a crunchy, crumbly texture. Please don't sleep on them!

Ingredient Notes: If you have access to an olive bar, get your olives there for the best flavor and texture (though jarred olives also work well). If you can't find Castelvetrano olives, use another green olive, such as Lucques, Cerignola, or Manzanilla.

For the Tangy Stuff, if using option 2, taste your olive brine first; if it's not very tangy, use just 1 tablespoon of it and 2 tablespoons vinegar.

Use It for Big Flavor: Shower these over your meals for a savory, cheesy flavor explosion. They're particularly good in salads and pastas where you expect a salty, cheesy bite (e.g., The Fancy Caesar Salad, page 362). Use it as a crunchy topper for creamy soups, sprinkle over virtually any bowl meal, or enjoy as a snack.

½ cup (70 g) **raw cashews**

½ cup (70 g) **pine nuts**

½ cup (40 g) **nutritional yeast**

¾ teaspoon **fine sea salt**

¼ cup (35 g) pitted **Castelvetrano olives** (8 to 10 olives), minced (see Ingredient Notes)

3 tablespoons Tangy Stuff (see Ingredient Notes)

- **Option 1:** 3 tablespoons **unsweetened pickle juice**, such as the juice from kosher pickles

- **Option 2:** 1½ tablespoons **distilled white vinegar** + 1½ tablespoons **olive brine**

1. Arrange a rack in the middle of the oven. Preheat the oven to 325°F (165°C). Line a rimmed sheet pan with parchment paper (for easy cleanup).

2. In a high-powered blender or food processor, add the cashews. Pulse repeatedly in 1-second bursts until they're in small pieces (don't blend). Add the pine nuts, nutritional yeast, and salt. Pulse repeatedly until you have a fine, crumbly texture (again, don't blend). Transfer to a medium or large bowl.

3. Add the olives to the pulsed nut mixture. Stir in your tangy stuff, tossing gently with your hands or a fork until well incorporated. The mixture will be wet, almost like a paste.

4. Use your hands to crumble it onto the prepared pan, spreading it out as evenly as possible. Bake for 10 minutes, then stir and break up any large clumps with a spatula (clumps the size of a blueberry are okay). Rotate the pan by 180 degrees and bake for another 10 minutes, until dry, crunchy, and golden brown. If not yet golden and dry, bake for 5 to 10 more minutes.

5. Let cool in the pan for 20 to 30 minutes to dry out completely. Store in an airtight jar in the pantry for a few months.

Fried Shallots

Makes 1 cup (50 g), plus 6 to 7 tablespoons (80 g) of shallot oil | GF, NF, SF

Slightly crisp and a little chewy with a ridiculously delicious sweet and savory oniony flavor, these make the perfect topper for so many foods.

Tips: Using a mandoline for slicing ensures the shallots are uniform in thickness and will brown evenly. If your mandoline slices thinner than ⅛ inch (0.3 cm), the shallots may brown faster. Either a medium saucepan or skillet works fine, but the shallots tend to cook a bit more evenly in a saucepan.

Use It for Big Flavor: A great topping for Asian noodle soups and salads (like the Malaysian Curry Noodle Soup on page 468 or Vietnamese Rice Noodle Bowls with Crispy Tofu & Mushrooms on page 473), silky pureed soups, and any crunchy salad in chapter 9, as well as roasted or blanched veggies, lentil salads, dals, tacos, and pastas. Use leftover shallot oil in stir-fries, vinaigrettes, and noodles, or to fry more shallots.

2 extra-large or 4 medium **shallots**, very thinly sliced (about 1½ cups/160 g sliced shallots; see Tips)

½ cup (112 g) **avocado oil** or **neutral-flavored oil** of choice

1 tablespoon chopped **fresh rosemary or sage** (optional)

Kosher salt or **fine sea salt**

1. Cover a cutting board with paper towels and set a fine-mesh sieve over a medium bowl. Add the shallots and oil to a medium saucepan or skillet and turn the heat to high (adding the shallots to cold oil helps them cook more evenly). The shallots will start to form small bubbles, then more rapid bubbles. Let bubble rapidly for 1 minute.

2. Reduce the heat to medium-low. Cook, stirring occasionally with tongs or a wooden spoon to break up the shallots, until they are golden brown, 15 to 20 minutes. Keep in mind that the shallots won't change much in color during the first 75 percent of the cooking time but will quickly turn from light golden to dark brown in just a few minutes. If using the fresh rosemary or sage, add it during the last 3 to 4 minutes of cooking and cook until the shallots are deeply golden brown.

3. Strain the oil through the sieve and into the bowl. Transfer the fried shallots to the paper towels and spread them out to help them crisp up. Sprinkle with a few pinches of salt while still warm. Let cool completely.

4. Store the shallot oil in a sealed jar in the fridge for 1 to 2 weeks. Fried shallots are best on the day they are made but stay good for up to 2 weeks if stored in an airtight jar or container at room temperature.

Crispy Spiced Garlic

Serves 6 to 8 | GF, NF, SF

When gently fried, thinly sliced garlic takes on a crunchy, chip-like form, making it the perfect addition to, well, almost anything.

Use It for Big Flavor: Instantly liven up a pot of lentils or beans by showering it with fried garlic. Use as a garlicky garnish for creamy dips or soups as well as noodles and stir-fries. Scatter over roasted vegetables or mashed potatoes, or omit the spices and use in pastas or spoon over pizza.

1 teaspoon **cumin seeds**

1 teaspoon **coriander seeds**

2½ tablespoons **avocado oil** or **extra-virgin olive oil**

8 **garlic cloves**, thinly sliced (slice as uniformly as possible for even cooking)

Flaky sea salt

1. Lightly crush the cumin and coriander seeds in a mortar with a pestle or add to a spice grinder and pulse once or twice. For alternative methods, see page 74.

2. Set a fine-mesh sieve over a small bowl.

3. Add the oil and garlic to a small or medium skillet and turn the heat to medium (adding the garlic to cold oil helps the slices cook more evenly). Shake the pan often and use a spatula to separate the slices. Cook gently until the garlic is just turning golden around the edges, 3 to 4 minutes. Add the crushed spices and cook for 1 minute. If the garlic starts to brown, remove the pan from the heat or lower the heat.

4. Pour the spiced oil into the sieve to strain it. Sprinkle the mixture with a bit of flaky sea salt. Save the oil for another recipe.

Indian Peanut Crunchies

Makes about 1 cup (140 g) | GF, SF

Salty, garlicky, and deeply spiced, these peanut crunchies bring warm heat, pungent flavors, and delightful crunch to anything that needs a little Indian flair.

Ingredient Note: You can use cashews in this recipe if you have a peanut allergy.

Use It for Big Flavor: Use to top any kind of Indian chaat (snack) to add a crunchy element. Serve with Mint Yogurt Sauce (page 213) over Crispy Smashed Potatoes (page 407) or Quick Roasted Cauliflower (page 342). Or use to jazz up a simple bowl of rice, lentils, and yogurt.

½ cup (70 g) **unsalted peanuts** (raw or dry roasted)

1 tablespoon **cumin seeds**

1½ teaspoons **coriander seeds**

1½ teaspoons **black or brown mustard seeds**

1½ tablespoons **neutral-flavored oil**

1½ teaspoons **white sesame seeds**

4 fat **garlic cloves**, thinly sliced

½-inch (1 to 1.5 cm) piece **fresh ginger**, peeled and cut into matchsticks

½ **serrano pepper**, diced

1½ teaspoons **ground turmeric**

Kosher salt and freshly ground **black pepper**

1. Heat a skillet over medium heat. Once hot, add the peanuts and toast until fragrant, 3 to 5 minutes, shaking the pan occasionally. Transfer the peanuts to a cutting board and mince. Add the peanuts to a medium bowl. Reserve the skillet for step 3 (no need to wash).

2. Roughly crush the cumin, coriander, and mustard seeds in a mortar with a pestle or add to a spice grinder and pulse twice. For alternative methods, see page 74.

3. Add the oil to the skillet and heat over medium heat. Once the oil is warm, add the roughly crushed spices and sesame seeds. Toast, tossing occasionally, until fragrant and the sesame seeds are starting to turn golden, about 90 seconds. Add the garlic, ginger, serrano, turmeric, and a few cracks of pepper. Stir frequently for 60 to 90 seconds, then transfer to the bowl with the peanuts and stir to combine.

4. Taste and season with about ½ teaspoon salt and several more cracks of pepper. Once cool, store in a sealed jar in the fridge for 1 to 2 weeks.

Crispy Fennel-Spiced Crumbs

Makes about 1 cup (120 g) | GFO, SF

Another fresh and fun "panko meets nuts and seeds" mix that will jazz up countless salads and grain bowls.

Use It for Big Flavor: Use as a crunchy topper for all kinds of salads, especially those that pair nicely with fennel seeds (think beets, fresh fennel, kohlrabi, or citrus salads). Spoon over cooked white beans, creamy vegetable soups, or roasted cabbage or carrots (page 329).

GF Option: Use gluten-free panko. It's not as flaky but works decently.

1 tablespoon **extra-virgin olive oil**

¼ cup (35 g) **raw almonds or hazelnuts**, roughly chopped

¼ cup (35 g) **pepitas** (shelled pumpkin seeds)

½ cup (40 g) **panko bread crumbs**

2 teaspoons **coriander seeds**

2 teaspoons **fennel seeds**

½ teaspoon **flaky sea salt**

Heat a large skillet over medium heat. Once warm but not hot, add the oil and nuts. Cook, stirring frequently, until the nuts start to brown, 3 to 4 minutes. Add the pepitas, panko, coriander and fennel seeds, and salt. Stir, almost continuously, until the panko is golden brown, 1½ to 3 minutes. Transfer to a plate, spread out, and let cool. Store in a sealed jar or airtight container in a cool, dry place for about 1 month.

Classic Torn Croutons

Serves 4 | SF, NF

Tearing the bread by hand is not only more fun than slicing it into perfect cubes, it also makes for better-textured croutons.

Ingredient Note: You want day-old (or two-day-old) bread so the croutons can get crunchy. If you don't have day-old bread, a sourdough baguette works fine.

Use It for Big Flavor: Add to salads, obviously! But also creamy soups for that perfect textural contrast. Grain bowl feeling a little sad? Add a little carby crunch to it.

5 to 6 ounces (140 to 170 g) **day-old sourdough, Italian bread**, or **country bread** (see Ingredient Note)

1½ tablespoons **extra-virgin olive oil**

¼ teaspoon **fine sea salt**

1. Preheat the oven to 375°F (190°C). Tear the bread into bite-size pieces (about ¾ to 1 inch, or 2 cm) and place on a rimmed sheet pan. Drizzle with the olive oil, sprinkle with the salt, and toss well with your hands. Spread out into an even layer.

2. Bake for 8 minutes. Use a spatula to flip the croutons or shake the pan back and forth several times. Continue to bake until toasted, golden brown, and crunchy with a little chew in some spots, 3 to 5 more minutes. Let cool slightly before using. Store in a container or resealable plastic bag on the counter for up to 1 week.

6

Easy-to-Swap Proteins

Legumes—beans, lentils, tofu, tempeh—are great wholesome replacements for meat as a protein source. And keeping these staples on hand is key to rescuing busy weeknight dinners.

But more often than not, these legumes make their way into dinners in, shall we say . . . an *uninspired* way? Beans straight from the can are tossed into salads, plain lentils are scooped onto grain bowls, and soft, squidgy tofu is added to Meatless Monday stir-fries. Rarely are these foods given the special treatment they deserve.

So that's what this chapter is all about. **Glorifying the legume in all its forms.**

While you'll find legumes in nearly every chapter (save desserts; I prefer my brownies without beans, thank you), the recipes here are designed to be *the star* of your meal. They're flavorful enough that they can be paired simply—with a bowl of grains, a salad, roasted veg, or a hunk of bread—and each recipe offers ideas for turning it into a main course.

THE MAGIC OF BEANS

Beans are **nutrition superstars**: rich in fiber, protein, vitamins, and minerals that promote heart and metabolic health. They're also **inexpensive**, arguably the cheapest protein at any grocery store. And they're **versatile**: there's a huge variety of them, and they can be used in so many types of dishes and cuisines.

Beans can be creamy and luxurious, saucy and sexy, hearty and meaty, or even crunchy.

How to Boost the Flavor of Beans

- **Beans cooked from scratch** will taste more flavorful and richer. But slow living is not always practical, so you'll also find recipes here made using good ol' canned beans.

- If you do cook beans from scratch, a few tips:

  1. **Toss those dusty old beans.** They'll take forever to cook and taste meh.

  2. **Season your cooking water with aromatics**—a halved onion or carrot, bay leaves, dried chiles, whole spices, a bouquet garni; even better, sauté aromatics in oil first, then add your beans and water.

  3. **Beans like salt.** It's a myth that adding salt prevents beans from softening.

- **Finish beans with fat, acid, and freshness.** Finishing a pot of beans with a glug or two of olive oil adds the richness beans typically need. And a splash of vinegar or lemon juice can perk up beans, as can a handful of chopped fresh herbs.

A Really Good Pot of Saucy Beans

Serves 10 to 12 | GF, SF, NF

As much as I rely on canned beans in everyday cooking, when I'm eating beans plain, they must be cooked from scratch. Cooking them fresh envelops them in a silky broth, making them rich, creamy, and maximally flavorful.

Soaking beans in a salty solution produces more tender, evenly cooked beans, while baking soda speeds up the cook time a bit. Cooking them in the oven instead of on the stove makes them slightly creamier and is more hands-off. A bundle of herbs infuses the beans with a woodsy depth of flavor, two garlic heads add supercharged savoriness, and finishing with olive oil adds a velvety mouthfeel.

Tips: I always soak my dried beans overnight, as it aids with digestion and yields fewer split skins, but if you don't have the time, try a 30-minute soak. If you're using unsoaked beans, they will take longer to cook, at least 1½ hours. For extra flavor, replace some of the water with veg broth.

Big-Flavor Meals: So many options! Here are some of my favorites:

× Beans + Herby Shallot-Garlic Confit (page 163) piled high on crusty bread

× Beans on crusty bread + tomatoes flecked with sea salt + dukkah (page 219) or Savory Walnut Crunch (page 220)

× Beans + Italian Basil & Parsley Salsa Verde (page 181) + cooked farro

× Beans + Preserved Lemon Salsa (page 184) + cooked freekeh or pearl couscous

× Beans + any vegetable in chapter 8 or 10 + your favorite grain

For Soaking

1 pound (455 g) **dried white beans**, such as great northern, cannellini, or navy beans

1½ tablespoons **kosher salt**

2 teaspoons **baking soda**

For Cooking

Extra-virgin olive oil

1 large **yellow onion**, diced

1 teaspoon **kosher salt**, plus more to taste

Freshly ground **black pepper**

1 large or 2 small **rosemary** sprigs (or a few thyme sprigs)

1 large or 2 small **sage** sprigs

2 **bay leaves**

2 medium heads **garlic**

recipe continues

1. **Soak the beans.** Place the beans in a large bowl with plenty of cold water (about 8 cups/5 L). Add the salt and baking soda. Cover and soak for 8 to 12 hours, or overnight. Drain and rinse well.

2. Preheat the oven to 350°F (175°C).

3. **Cook the beans.** In a Dutch oven or large ovenproof soup pot, heat 2 teaspoons olive oil over medium-high heat. Add the onions and cook, stirring occasionally, until golden, 5 to 7 minutes. Add 6 cups (1.5 L) of water, the beans, salt, and lots of pepper. Using kitchen twine, make an herb bundle (bouquet garni) out of the rosemary, sage, and bay leaves and nestle it into the pan.

4. Partially cover the pan and bring to a boil. If a lot of foam surfaces, skim with a metal spoon. Once it comes to a boil, set a timer for 10 minutes.

5. Meanwhile, peel the loose papery outer skins from the garlic but leave the heads intact. Slice off about ¼ inch (0.5 cm) from the top of each head to expose the cloves (as if you were roasting whole garlic).

6. Once the beans have boiled for 10 minutes, turn off the heat and add the garlic heads. Pour a glug of olive oil on top of the garlic and beans. Cover the pan, transfer to the oven, and bake until the beans are tender, about 1 hour (if using small beans, like navy beans, check around 45 minutes).

7. Discard the bouquet garni. Squeeze the garlic cloves out of their skins and into the beans, stirring well. Season with salt to taste (be pretty generous—I use 2 to 3 teaspoons kosher salt). For richness, stir in another glug of olive oil.

8. Transfer the cooled beans to a storage container with their cooking liquid. They'll stay good in the fridge for up to 5 days, or you can freeze for up to 6 months.

Crunchy Roasted Chickpeas, 3 Ways

Each serves 3 | GF, SF, NF

Few foods are as versatile as roasted chickpeas. Wholesome afternoon snack? Check. Workout fuel that's not a chalky protein shake? Check. Shelf-stable travel snack that won't get confiscated by the TSA? Check. Crunchy topper for all kinds of foods? Check.

TIPS FOR CRUNCHY CHICKPEAS

× Dry the chickpeas. You can either (1) drain and rinse them, shake in a colander, spread out on a dish towel, and very gently rub; or (2) add them in batches to a salad spinner and gently spin, as I learned from the cookbook *Cool Beans* by Joe Yonan. If any skins loosen during this process, discard them so they don't burn.

× Keep it hot and simple. Roast chickpeas naked (with just oil, salt, and pepper), then toss with any bloomed spices afterward. Adding spices during roasting makes the chickpeas less crunchy.

× Double up! These are addictive and versatile. To double the recipes here, use two pans—one in the top third of the oven and one on the bottom rack—and switch them at the halfway mark.

× Let them breathe. While roasted chickpeas are crunchiest on the day you make them, they will stay good for 4 to 5 days. Store in a container with the lid slightly ajar at room temperature.

× Revive them. Transfer roasted chickpeas to a sheet pan and toss with about ¼ teaspoon oil; bake at 300°F (150°C) until hot and crisp, 7 to 8 minutes.

Classic Roasted Chickpeas

Simple but so so good! These pair well with almost every savory food.

Big-Flavor Meals: Use as a crunchy protein in a salad or grain bowl on Monday, scatter them over roasted root or cruciferous vegetables (especially alongside a creamy dip) on Tuesday, then use as crunchy soup toppers on Wednesday.

1 (15-ounce/425 g) can **chickpeas**, drained, rinsed, and dried well (see Tips)

2 teaspoons **extra-virgin olive oil**

¾ teaspoon **kosher salt**

Freshly ground **black pepper**

Arrange a rack in the top third of the oven. Preheat the oven to 425°F (220°C). Transfer the chickpeas to a rimmed sheet pan and toss with the oil, salt, and several cracks of pepper. Spread out in an even layer. Bake for 20 minutes, then shake the pan. Return to the oven and bake until crispy, golden all over, and browned in spots, another 5 to 10 minutes (well-worn pans will take less time).

recipe continues

Tandoori Roasted Chickpeas

Chickpeas with a delicious Indian-ish kick.

Big-Flavor Meals: Stuff into a baked sweet potato or scatter over rice, and drizzle with the Spicy Mint & Cilantro Sauce (page 189).

1 (15-ounce/425 g) can **chickpeas**, drained, rinsed, and dried well (see Tips on page 236)

1 tablespoon + 2 teaspoons **grapeseed oil**, **extra-virgin olive oil**, or any **neutral-flavored oil**

1 teaspoon **kosher salt**, plus more for finishing

Tandoori Spice Blend

½ teaspoon **ground cumin**

½ teaspoon **ground coriander**

½ teaspoon **sweet or hot paprika**

½ teaspoon **ground turmeric**

½ teaspoon **ground ginger**

¼ teaspoon **ground cinnamon**

¼ teaspoon **ground cardamom**

¼ teaspoon freshly ground **black pepper**

⅛ teaspoon **cayenne pepper** or **Indian red chile powder** (optional)

1. Follow the instructions for Classic Roasted Chickpeas (page 236) using 1 tablespoon oil and 1 teaspoon salt, then transfer the roasted chickpeas to a medium bowl.

2. Make the tandoori spice blend: While the chickpeas are roasting, in a small bowl, stir together the cumin, coriander, paprika, turmeric, ginger, cinnamon, cardamom, black pepper, and cayenne (if using).

3. When the chickpeas are almost done, in a small skillet, heat the remaining 2 teaspoons oil over medium-low heat. Once warm, add the spices and cook until aromatic, about 30 seconds, stirring frequently to prevent burning. Remove from the heat.

4. Stir the spiced oil before using, as the spices tend to settle. Pour on top of the roasted chickpeas, tossing well with a spoonula or your hands until there are no clumps. Sprinkle with a bit of salt and let cool for 5 minutes to crisp up.

BBQ Roasted Chickpeas

Classic BBQ flavors meet chickpeas!

Big-Flavor Meals: For an easy salad, serve over a bed of romaine with veggies from your crisper, drizzle with BBQ sauce, and dress with Throwback Ranch Dressing (page 203) or Green Goddess Dressing (page 182).

1 (15-ounce/425 g) can **chickpeas**, drained, rinsed, and dried well (see Tips on page 236)

1 tablespoon + 2 teaspoons **grapeseed oil**, **extra-virgin olive oil**, or any **neutral-flavored oil**

1 teaspoon **kosher salt**, plus more for finishing

BBQ Spice Blend

½ teaspoon **sweet or hot paprika**

½ teaspoon freshly ground **black pepper**

½ teaspoon **smoked paprika**

½ teaspoon **chili powder**

½ teaspoon **onion powder**

½ teaspoon **garlic powder**

⅛ teaspoon **cayenne pepper** (optional, for *spicy!*)

1 teaspoon **pure maple syrup**

1. **Make the BBQ spice blend.** In a small bowl, stir together the sweet or hot paprika, black pepper, smoked paprika, chili powder, onion powder, garlic powder, and cayenne (if using).

2. Follow steps 1 through 3 for the Tandoori Roasted Chickpeas (page 238), but use the BBQ spice blend.

3. Stir the maple syrup into the spiced oil, then immediately spoon it over the roasted chickpeas. Toss well with a spoonula or your hands until there are no clumps. Sprinkle with a bit of salt if desired and let cool for 5 minutes to crisp up.

Wildly Crunchy Cornmeal Beans

Serves 4 to 6 | GFO, SF, NF

These beans have the perfect texture-flavor combination: they get magically crunchy when coated in cornmeal and baked, *and* they soak up tons of flavor from spices and fresh herbs. Easy to make, they'll quickly become a weeknight staple. Use the chart for flavor inspiration. Feel free to use your favorite spice blend, but if it already has salt, use slightly less salt in step 2.

Big-Flavor Meals: Add to any salad, grain bowl, or rice bowl. My go-to is to serve them alongside a creamy condiment and a simply prepared vegetable. My personal faves include:

× Shawarma beans + Creamy Tahini Sauce (page 197) + Jammy Roasted Eggplant (page 339)

× Everyday beans + Whipped Tofu Ricotta (page 206) + Jammy Zucchini (page 330)

× Tandoori beans + Mint Yogurt Sauce (page 213) + Quick Roasted Cauliflower (page 342)

GF Option: Use gluten-free all-purpose flour and bake for an extra 10 minutes.

2 (15-ounce/425 g) cans **cannellini beans**, drained and rinsed

2 teaspoons **kosher salt** (if using fine sea salt, use 1 heaping teaspoon), plus more to taste

Freshly ground **black pepper**

3 tablespoons **medium-grind cornmeal**

2 tablespoons **all-purpose flour**

Spice Blend of choice (see chart)

3 tablespoons **extra-virgin olive oil**

Fresh Herb Blend of choice (see chart)

1. Arrange a rack in either the top third of the oven or on the bottommost shelf. Preheat the oven to 425°F (220°C). Gently dry the beans in a salad spinner or transfer to a large dish towel and gently roll back and forth. The beans should be moist, not wet or dry.

2. In a large bowl, combine the beans with the salt, several cracks of pepper, the cornmeal, flour, and spice blend of choice. Toss gently with a silicone spatula. Add the oil and fresh herb blend (if applicable) and toss gently. Transfer to a sheet pan, ideally a well-worn pan, shaking the pan back and forth to evenly spread the beans out with minimal overlap (it's okay if some beans are stuck together).

3. Bake without tossing until crunchy and golden brown, about 25 minutes (35 minutes if your pan is not well worn). For a saltier bite, add a pinch of salt while the beans are still warm.

4. Transfer cooled leftovers to an airtight container and refrigerate for up to 5 days. To revive, heat in a hot skillet with a bit of oil, stirring occasionally, until crisp.

Wildly Crunchy Cornmeal Beans—Flavor Variations

SPICE BLENDS	FRESH HERB BLENDS
Everyday Blend • 1 teaspoon garlic powder • ½ teaspoon onion powder • ¼ teaspoon red pepper flakes	3 tablespoons chopped fresh rosemary, thyme, and/or sage
1 tablespoon Shawarma Seasoning (page 532 or store-bought)	3 tablespoons chopped fresh rosemary, thyme, and/or oregano
1 tablespoon Tandoori Spice Blend (page 238 or store-bought)	No herbs
1 tablespoon BBQ Spice Blend (page 239 or store-bought)	1 to 2 tablespoons chopped fresh rosemary
1 tablespoon Berbere Spice Blend (page 488 or store-bought)	No herbs

Marinated Chickpeas

Serves 6 as a side, 3 as a main | GF, SF, NF

A low-effort but tasty protein to keep in your fridge during the week. Chickpeas are cooked in warm spices, then mixed with olive oil, lemon juice, and onions and garlic that have been macerated in champagne vinegar for a punchy, bright tang.

Tips: You can make this dish with canned chickpeas. Heat the olive oil in a skillet over medium heat. Toast the whole spices until aromatic and a few shades darker. Pour the spiced oil over two 15-ounce (425 g) cans of drained and rinsed chickpeas. Follow steps 4 through 6.

Big-Flavor Meals: Fold in salad greens, shredded carrots, and avocado or vegan feta for a main-course salad. Or serve with any cooked grains and crisp veggie in your fridge; finish with a Crispy & Crunchy Thing from chapter 5 (pages 216–29). These are also delicious with the Smashed Cucumbers with Yogurt-Tahini Sauce & Spicy "Honey" (page 365) or Buttery Charred Cabbage in Spiced Tomatoes with Tahini (page 401), and they make a great mezze platter with hummus, pickled veg, olives, and crostini.

Chickpeas

8 ounces (227 g) **dried chickpeas** (about 1 cup + 2 tablespoons)

Kosher salt and freshly ground **black pepper**

1 teaspoon **cumin seeds**

1 teaspoon **coriander seeds**

2 **bay leaves**

Salad

½ small **red onion**, finely diced

3 **garlic cloves**, grated or finely minced

3 tablespoons **champagne vinegar** (or white wine vinegar or red wine vinegar)

Kosher salt and freshly ground **black pepper**

1 medium **lemon**, zested

2 tablespoons freshly squeezed **lemon juice**, plus more to taste

¼ cup (56 g) **extra-virgin olive oil**

2 teaspoons **Aleppo pepper** (or ½ teaspoon red pepper flakes), or less for mild heat

1 cup (12 g) **fresh flat-leaf parsley** leaves, chopped (can sub cilantro or dill)

1. **Make the chickpeas.** In a large bowl, cover the chickpeas with cold water by about 2 inches. Add 2 teaspoons salt and stir to dissolve. Cover and soak for 8 to 12 hours, or overnight. Drain and rinse well.

recipe continues

2. Roughly grind the cumin and coriander seeds in a mortar with a pestle or add to a spice grinder and pulse just once or twice. For alternative methods, see page 74.

3. In a large saucepan, combine the soaked chickpeas, 6 cups (1.4 L) of water, 1 teaspoon salt, lots of pepper, the bay leaves, and cumin and coriander mixture. Bring to a boil over medium-high heat. Reduce the heat, cover, and cook at a rapid simmer for 40 to 45 minutes. The chickpeas should be tender but not soft or mushy. Drain but don't rinse them; discard the bay leaves. Transfer the chickpeas, including any spices, to a large bowl.

4. **Make the salad.** In a small bowl, combine the onions, garlic, vinegar, and a pinch of salt. Stir well to combine. Macerate for 10 minutes (or longer), stirring once or twice to evenly coat the onions.

5. Toss the chickpeas with the macerated onion mixture, the lemon zest and juice, olive oil, Aleppo pepper, and parsley. Season with ½ to ¾ teaspoon salt, black pepper to taste, and more lemon juice as needed.

6. Serve warm now, or for deeper flavor, let marinate in the fridge for 2 hours or overnight. Before serving, let sit at room temperature for 10 minutes. If the oil has solidified in the fridge, let the salad come to room temperature first. Store leftovers for up to 5 days.

Marinated White Beans & Fennel with Spiced Za'atar Oil

Serves 6 as a side, 3 as a main | GF, SF, NFO

This dish makes beans the star of a meal *and* does the most with highly underrated fennel, using the fennel bulb, fennel fronds, *and* fennel seeds. Za'atar, fennel seeds, and coriander are bloomed in olive oil, then poured over white beans, infusing each bite with Middle Eastern flavors, warm citrus spice, and a little crunch. Lemon, capers, and olives bring bright and salty notes, which are mellowed by the sweet anise flavors of fresh fennel.

Ingredient Note: I prefer a mild olive like Castelvetrano. If your olives are saltier or bolder, use fewer olives (and a bit less salt).

Big-Flavor Meals: This is quite hearty on its own, but you can bulk it up with avocado and serve with bread or Za'atar Pita (page 455); toss in hemp seeds for extra protein. Fold in salad greens like arugula or watercress and cooked farro or brown rice for a satisfying grain bowl.

Easy Variation: Substitute chickpeas for the white beans.

NF Option: Make the nut-free alternative to the Hazelnut Dukkah (see page 219) or sub the dukkah with toasted pepitas (shelled pumpkin seeds).

2 (15-ounce/425 g) cans **cannellini beans**, drained and rinsed (or 3 cups/500 g cooked white beans)

6 **garlic cloves**, grated or finely minced

1 medium **lemon**, zested and juiced

1 teaspoon **coriander seeds**

⅓ cup (75 g) **extra-virgin olive oil**

1 teaspoon **fennel seeds**

1 tablespoon **Za'atar** (page 179 or store-bought)

2 teaspoons **Aleppo pepper** or **Urfa biber**

¼ teaspoon **ground turmeric**

1 medium **fennel bulb**, ideally one with fronds

2 tablespoons **capers** + 1 tablespoon **caper brine**, plus more brine as needed

½ to ¾ cup (70 to 100 g) pitted **green olives**, such as Castelvetrano olives, halved or chopped (see Ingredient Note)

⅓ cup (5 g) **fresh dill** (tough stems removed), chopped (optional; can just use more fennel fronds if desired)

Kosher salt and freshly ground **black pepper**

⅓ cup (40 g) **Hazelnut Dukkah** (page 219)

recipe continues

1. In a large serving bowl, place the beans. In a small bowl, combine the garlic and lemon zest. Use the back of a large knife or a sturdy mug to roughly crush the coriander seeds. You can also use a mortar and pestle or blitz once in a spice grinder.

2. In a medium or large skillet, heat the olive oil over medium heat. Add the fennel seeds, crushed coriander, and za'atar and cook until toasty and nutty, 1 to 2 minutes. Add the Aleppo pepper and turmeric and cook for 30 to 60 seconds, stirring frequently. Remove from the heat and pour this spiced oil over the garlic and lemon zest. Allow to sizzle for 20 to 30 seconds, then stir.

3. Pour the warm oil over the beans and toss to combine. Stir 1 tablespoon of the lemon juice into the beans. Let rest at room temperature for at least 15 minutes or up to 1 hour.

4. Meanwhile, prep the fennel. Trim the stalks (you can freeze them for broth). Strip off the fronds and roughly chop a handful. For the bulb, slice in half lengthwise and remove the tough outer layer after cutting off the bottom core. Thinly slice the bulb crosswise using a mandoline or sharp knife.

5. To the beans, add the sliced fennel, another tablespoon of lemon juice, the capers and brine, olives, fennel fronds, dill (if using), lots of pepper, and ¾ teaspoon salt (use less if your olives are very salty). Toss to combine. Taste, adding more caper brine or lemon juice for tanginess.

6. Just before serving, add the dukkah and toss again. Season to taste with salt and pepper. Store leftovers in the fridge for 4 to 5 days.

Edamame Salad with Chili Crisp

Serves 3 to 4 | GF, NFO

If you have chili crisp in your fridge, this recipe is a fantastic way to infuse a simple protein with spicy, garlicky flavors and nutty crunch in less than 10 minutes.

Big-Flavor Meals: Serve with rice or noodles and a simple cucumber salad. Or stir-fry broccoli or bok choy with leftover cooked rice and serve alongside this salad.

NF Option: Make the nut-free alternative to the Life-Changing Homemade Chili Crisp (see page 187).

1 (12-ounce/340 g) bag frozen **shelled edamame**

1 teaspoon **kosher salt**

Flaky sea salt

3 tablespoons **Life-Changing Homemade Chili Crisp** (page 187), plus more to taste

2 **scallions**, thinly sliced on a bias

1 big handful **fresh cilantro** leaves and tender stems, chopped

1 tablespoon **champagne vinegar**, plus more to taste

1 scant teaspoon **agave nectar**, plus more to taste

1. Bring a medium saucepan of water to a boil. Add the edamame and kosher salt. Once it returns to a boil, boil for 2 minutes. Drain and shake well to get rid of excess water.

2. Transfer the warm edamame to a large bowl and sprinkle with several pinches of flaky salt. Add the chili crisp and toss to coat. Add the scallions, cilantro, vinegar, and agave. Toss to coat and season to taste, adding more chili crisp for savory-spicy flavor, vinegar for tang, agave for sweetness, or flaky salt as needed. Store leftovers in the fridge for up to 3 days.

Saucy Black Beans in Sofrito

Serves 4 to 6 | GF, SF, NF

For years, I had a love-hate relationship with black beans. I'd love them at Mexican restaurants, where they were creamy and redolent with spices. But at home, those canned black beans sitting in my bowl of rice were dry and flavorless. Luckily, you can turn canned black beans into restaurant-style beans with a few steps.

First, cook the beans *with* their starchy canning liquid (it's just the liquid the beans were cooked in): it lends a saucy, creamy consistency you usually only get with freshly cooked beans. Second, add the beans to a sofrito—a mixture of aromatics, spices, chiles, and vegetables that forms the base of many Latin American and Caribbean meals. It provides a depth of flavor you typically only get from slow-simmered beans. Use a serrano pepper instead of a jalapeño if you'd like more heat.

Tips: You can make this dish with dried beans. Cover 8 ounces (227 g) of black beans with 2 inches (5 cm) of water and add 1 teaspoon baking soda; soak overnight, then drain and rinse. Add a few sprigs of fresh oregano and a bay leaf to the cooking water and cook until tender, at least 1 hour; scoop out and discard 2 cups (480 ml) liquid. Make the sofrito and add it to the cooked beans along with 1 teaspoon kosher salt. Simmer rapidly until thickened and saucy, 15 to 20 minutes.

Big-Flavor Meals: Serve over rice for an elevated rice and beans meal. Spoon into tortillas and top with avocado and pickled onions (see page 168). Or serve with tofu scramble (page 439) for a hearty breakfast.

Sofrito

1 pound (455 g) ripe but firm **tomatoes**

2 tablespoons **avocado oil** or **extra-virgin olive oil**

1 small **yellow or red onion**, diced

Kosher salt and freshly ground **black pepper**

3 **garlic cloves**, chopped

1 **jalapeño or serrano pepper**, diced

6 **oregano** sprigs, leaves stripped from stems

½ teaspoon **chipotle chile flakes** (use 1 teaspoon for *spicy!*)

Black Beans

2 (15-ounce/425 g) cans **black beans**, undrained

A few splashes of **vegetable broth** (or water), as needed

Extra-virgin olive oil

1 tablespoon freshly squeezed **lime juice**, plus more to taste

1 cup (16 g) **fresh cilantro** leaves and tender stems, roughly chopped

recipe continues

1. In a food processor, add the tomatoes and pulse until very finely minced but not fully pureed. (Or grate them on the large holes of a box grater.)

2. **Make the sofrito.** In a large sauté pan, heat the oil over medium heat. Once shimmering, add the onions with a pinch of salt and cook, stirring occasionally, until softened and golden but not browned, 5 to 7 minutes. Add the garlic and jalapeño and cook for another 2 minutes, stirring frequently. Add the tomatoes, oregano, and chipotle flakes. Adjust the heat to maintain a rapid simmer and cook until the tomatoes release their liquid and soften completely and most of the liquid has evaporated, 10 to 15 minutes. Season with salt (about 1 teaspoon) and pepper to taste.

3. **Make the beans.** Add the beans and their canning liquid to the sofrito. Cook at a rapid simmer until the liquid has reduced a bit and is saucy, 15 minutes. For a looser texture, add a splash or two of vegetable broth.

4. To finish, add a couple of glugs of olive oil and the lime juice. Season with salt and pepper to taste and more lime juice as desired. Stir in the cilantro and remove from the heat. Store leftovers in the fridge for up to 5 days.

Crispy Lentils

Serves 3 to 4 | GF, SF, NF

Just like chickpeas and other beans, lentils can go from soft to delightfully crunchy when mixed with some fat and the dry heat of an oven.

Tip: Green lentils usually broil the quickest and typically need just 6 minutes under the broiler.

Use It for Big Flavor: Use in all kinds of salads and grain bowls, or anytime you want a crispy or crunchy protein-packed topper (these are excellent over creamy soups).

¾ cup (150 g) **green, brown, or French green lentils**

Kosher salt and freshly ground **black pepper**

1½ tablespoons **grapeseed oil** or **neutral-flavored high-heat oil** of choice

1. Bring a medium saucepan of water to a boil. Add the lentils and 2 teaspoons salt. Reduce the heat and simmer until the lentils are al dente (tender but with a bite), 10 to 12 minutes (17 to 20 minutes for French green lentils); they should not be soft. Drain and shake to get rid of excess water.

2. Transfer the lentils to a large dish towel to dry. I like to gently run my hands through the lentils so they dry more quickly.

3. Meanwhile, arrange a rack on the second shelf below the broiler. Preheat the broiler on high for about 5 minutes. Transfer the lentils to a rimmed sheet pan, toss with the oil, sprinkle with a pinch or two of salt and pepper, and shake the pan back and forth to spread the lentils out into an even layer, using your hands to smooth out any clumps.

4. Broil the lentils for 4 minutes. Toss with a spatula or shake the pan back and forth to evenly redistribute them. Broil for another 2 minutes and shake the pan again. If they're nicely crispy, they're done. If they're starting to crisp up, broil for 1 minute, then check and broil in 1-minute increments as needed. If they haven't started to crisp up yet, broil for 2 minutes, then check. Store cooled leftovers in an airtight container in the fridge for 4 to 5 days (they stay crunchy!).

An Ode to Lentils

When I was in third grade, my parents built a walk-in pantry. My mom installed a second fridge and lined the pantry shelves with empty glass jars. These weren't artisanal glass jars with wooden lids that sell for thirty dollars a pop. They were two-gallon glass jugs painted with sunflowers that were designed for lemonade. She filled these lemonade jars with a rainbow assortment of lentils, each jar labeled with a handwritten note in Gujarati.

When I'd hang around the kitchen, she'd often ask me to grab a particular jar, reminding me not to drop it. (You drop one important thing as a child, and you're forever reminded of it!) I'd examine the shelves, trying to guess which jug it might be based on how the name of the lentil sounded, unable to read the Gujarati characters on the notes. Very occasionally, I'd guess correctly. Then she'd start sorting through the lentils to make dal. And it was always a different-ish dal.

That's the beauty of lentils. They're so versatile. Even though my mom made dal often, she varied the taste and texture, along with the spices and aromatics, based on the lentil variety. And for special occasion dinners, she'd transform humble lentils into steamed rice-and-lentil cakes (idli or dhokla), fritters (pakoda or vada), savory vegetable cakes (handvo), lentil stew with dumplings (dal dhokli), and crispy crepes (dosa).

Common Varieties of Lentils

Brown and green. These get soft when cooked, making them good in soups/stews and pureed applications, but less great in salads.

French green (Puy). Smaller in size, with an emerald color, these hold their shape well and are my go-to for salads and sides.

Black beluga. These also hold their shape well, so they're another great option for salads and sides. They have a bold, earthy flavor.

Red. The perfect easy-to-find choice for dals and curries because they break down and become creamy when cooked. At Indian grocers, you'll find split red lentils (a.k.a. masoor dal), which cook a bit more quickly.

Yellow. Mostly sold as split lentils and labeled *moong dal* at Indian grocers; some well-stocked supermarkets also sell them.

How to Cook a Basic Pot of Lentils

1. Bring a saucepan of water to a boil and salt generously. Add the lentils and cook at a decent simmer until they reach your desired consistency, then drain. Basically, it's like cooking pasta, but not at a boil. For a salad, cook lentils until just al dente; if adding to a soup, cook until soft; and if pureeing, cook until very soft.

2. Use this method for green, brown, French green, and beluga lentils; green and brown lentils typically take 10 to 15 minutes, while French green and beluga lentils typically take about 20 minutes. For red and yellow lentils, cook them directly in soups, curries, dals, or stews.

How to Boost the Flavor of Lentils

When cooking a pot of lentils, add a few of these to the water:

- Shallot or small onion, halved
- Garlic cloves, smashed or halved
- Whole peppercorns
- Carrots or celery, roughly chopped
- Bay leaves
- Lightly crushed whole spices, such as cumin, coriander, or fennel seeds
- Bouquet garni of fresh herbs, such as thyme, oregano, rosemary, sage, or parsley
- Vegan bouillon cube or powder

And consider finishing your lentils with any of the following:

- Soft fresh herbs, such as cilantro, dill, mint, or parsley
- Pickled vegetables (page 168)
- Vinegar or citrus juice
- Crispy & Crunchy Things (starting on page 216)
- Flaky sea salt
- Something fatty (tahini, olive oil, avocado, or Creamy Things starting on page 194)

Spiced Lentil Salad with Fresh Herbs

Serves 4 | GF, SF, NFO

I haven't worked in an office since 2019 (thank the goddesses), but if I still did, this would be one of my go-to office lunches. It's filling, so you're less tempted to eat cookies at your desk, and it's also fun thanks to a spiced garlic oil, fresh herbs, and crunchy surprises, so you have something to look forward to. To make it heartier, fold in avocado and serve with bread.

Easy Variations: Add 1 teaspoon lightly crushed coriander and fennel seeds to the garlic oil. Swap the pomegranate molasses and lemon juice with 2 tablespoons balsamic or champagne vinegar. Fold in a handful of soft salad greens (add a squeeze of lemon juice, a drizzle of olive oil, and a pinch of salt, as needed) or serve with Charred Sweet Potato Wedges (page 345).

NF Option: Select the Smoky Seed Sprinkle or Fried Shallots from the Crunchy Things, or omit entirely.

1 cup (200 g) **French green lentils** (or black beluga lentils)

1 large **shallot** or small **onion**, quartered

1 **bay leaf**

Kosher salt and freshly ground **black pepper**

½ cup (8 g) **fresh basil** leaves, slivered (or mint or dill, chopped)

1 cup (16 g) **fresh flat-leaf parsley** (or cilantro) leaves, finely chopped

1½ to 2 tablespoons **pure pomegranate molasses**, plus more to taste

1 tablespoon freshly squeezed **lemon juice**, plus more to taste

2 to 3 tablespoons **Crunchy Things** (optional):
- Hazelnut Dukkah (page 219)
- Smoky Seed Sprinkle (page 216)
- Savory Walnut Crunch (page 220)
- Fried Shallots (page 224)

Flaky sea salt (optional)

Garlic Oil

2½ tablespoons **extra-virgin olive oil**

4 **garlic cloves**, thinly sliced

1 medium **lemon**, zested

¼ to ½ teaspoon **red pepper flakes** (or 1 teaspoon Aleppo pepper)

recipe continuess

1. **Cook the lentils.** Bring a medium saucepan of water to a boil. Add the lentils, shallot, bay leaf, 1 tablespoon salt, and several cracks of black pepper. Reduce the heat and simmer until the lentils are al dente (tender but with a bite), 17 to 20 minutes. Drain, discard the shallot and bay leaf, and shake the colander to get rid of excess water.

2. **Meanwhile, make the garlic oil.** Add the oil and garlic to a small saucepan or frying pan and turn the heat to medium (adding the garlic to cold oil helps it cook more evenly). Shake the pan often and use a spatula to separate the individual garlic slices. Cook until just starting to turn golden, 3 to 5 minutes. If the garlic starts to brown, take the pan off the heat or lower the heat. Add the lemon zest and pepper flakes and cook, swirling frequently, for 30 seconds. Remove from the heat and pour into a bowl to stop the cooking.

3. Transfer the lentils to a serving bowl and season with ½ teaspoon kosher salt. Pour the garlic oil on top, add the basil, parsley, pomegranate molasses, and lemon juice, and toss well to combine. Taste, adding more salt, black pepper, pomegranate molasses, or lemon juice as needed.

4. If desired, sprinkle crunchy things on the salad before serving. Otherwise, sprinkle with a pinch of flaky salt. Store leftovers in the fridge for up to 5 days.

Crispy Indian-ish Lentils with Rice & Yogurt

Serves 3 to 4 | GF, SF, NF

Even if you think you're "not a lentil person," this recipe, with its bold flavors and fun textures, will change your mind. Super-crispy broiled lentils are tossed in a hyperflavorful mixture of frizzled shallots, fried garlic and ginger, and punchy Indian spices, then drizzled with a cooling yogurt sauce. Served over a bed of rice, this dish hits all the texture notes: crunchy, creamy, and chewy.

Big-Flavor Meals: Serve alongside Quick Roasted Cauliflower (page 342) or an Indian kachumber salad: chopped tomato, cucumber, and red onion tossed with lemon juice, cilantro, cayenne pepper, and salt.

¾ cup (150 g) **brown, green, or French green lentils**

Kosher salt and freshly ground **black pepper**

1 cup (190 g) uncooked or 3 cups (425 g) cooked long-grain **white rice**

1 teaspoon **black or brown mustard seeds**

1 teaspoon **cumin seeds**

1 teaspoon **coriander seeds**

3 tablespoons **neutral-flavored high-heat oil** of choice

1 medium **shallot**, very thinly sliced into rounds (⅛-inch/0.3 cm slices)

4 **garlic cloves**, thinly sliced

1½-inch (3.75 cm) piece **fresh ginger**, peeled and sliced into matchsticks

1 small **serrano pepper**, thinly sliced into rounds (remove membranes and seeds for mild heat)

½ teaspoon **ground turmeric**

Flaky sea salt

Yogurt Sauce

½ cup (115 g) good-quality **unsweetened coconut yogurt** (see page 61 for recommended brands)

2 to 3 teaspoons freshly squeezed **lemon juice**

¼ teaspoon **organic cane sugar**

recipe and ingredients continue

½ teaspoon **ground cumin**

Kosher salt and freshly ground **black pepper**

For Finishing

¾ cup (12 g) **fresh cilantro** leaves and tender stems, chopped

1 tablespoon freshly squeezed **lemon juice**

1. Bring a medium saucepan of water to a boil. Add the lentils and 2 teaspoons kosher salt. Reduce the heat and simmer until the lentils are al dente (tender but with a bite), 10 to 12 minutes (17 to 20 minutes for French green lentils); they should not be soft. Drain and shake to get rid of excess water.

2. Transfer the lentils to a large dish towel to dry. I like to gently run my hands through the lentils so they dry more quickly.

3. Meanwhile, cook the rice using your preferred method, or get out your leftover cooked rice.

4. Lightly crush the mustard, cumin, and coriander seeds in a mortar with a pestle or add to a spice grinder and pulse just once or twice. For alternative methods, see page 74.

5. Place a fine-mesh strainer over a small or medium bowl and line a large plate with paper towels. Heat the oil in a medium or large skillet over medium heat. Once shimmering, add the shallots along with a pinch of salt. Cook, stirring occasionally and separating the shallot slices, until the edges are just turning golden, 3 to 4 minutes. Add the crushed spices, the garlic, ginger,

serrano, and turmeric and cook, stirring frequently, until the garlic is golden and very aromatic, 2 to 3 minutes. Remove from the heat and pour the mixture into the strainer; you'll use the oil that drains into the bowl to broil the lentils. Transfer the aromatics to the towel-lined plate and sprinkle with a pinch or two of flaky salt.

6. **While the lentils dry, make the yogurt sauce.** (This can also be made 1 to 2 days in advance.) In a small or medium bowl, mix together the yogurt, lemon juice, sugar, and cumin. Season to taste with kosher salt and black pepper.

7. Arrange a rack on the second shelf below the broiler. Preheat the broiler on high for about 5 minutes. Transfer the lentils to a rimmed sheet pan, toss with the reserved oil from step 5, sprinkle with a pinch or two of kosher salt and black pepper, and shake the pan back and forth to spread the lentils out into an even layer, using your hands to smooth out any clumps.

8. Broil the lentils for 4 minutes. Toss with a spatula or shake the pan back and forth to evenly redistribute them. Broil for 2 minutes and shake the pan again. If they're nicely crispy, they're done. If they're starting to crisp up, broil for 1 minute, then check and broil in 1-minute increments as needed. If they haven't started to crisp up yet, broil for 2 minutes, then check.

9. Transfer the crispy lentils to a serving bowl and toss with the reserved fried aromatics, cilantro, and lemon juice. Season to taste with flaky salt. Serve the lentils on top of rice and drizzle yogurt sauce on top.

Creamy Tahini Lentils with Crispy Spiced Garlic

Serves 6 to 8 | GF, SF, NF

In this Middle Eastern–inspired bowl, a lemony tahini sauce adds creamy indulgence to lentils, and crispy garlic chips and crunchy whole spices bring a lovely contrasting texture. A drizzle of tangy-sweet balsamic adds a zingy finish.

Ingredient Note: This dish is best with French green lentils (or black beluga lentils). Regular green or brown lentils work in a pinch but get a little mushy.

Tip: You can make the Lemon Tahini Sauce 3 to 4 days in advance, or make it while the lentils cook. The Crispy Spiced Garlic is best when fresh, so make it while the lentils cook.

Big-Flavor Meals: Serve with warm pita or crusty bread, or alongside lightly dressed greens and cooked grains. These lentils are also great with the Spice-Roasted Whole Carrots (page 329) or Quick Roasted Cauliflower (page 342).

Easy Variations: Swap the parsley with cilantro or dill. Finish with dukkah (page 219) for extra crunch.

1 tablespoon **extra-virgin olive oil**

1 large **sweet onion** (or yellow onion), diced

Kosher salt and freshly ground **black pepper**

4 cups (960 ml) **low-sodium vegetable broth**

12 ounces (340 g) **French green lentils** (about 1¾ cups; see Ingredient Note)

About ¾ cup (180 g) **Lemon Tahini Sauce** (page 197) or **Pomegranate Tahini Sauce** (page 197)

2 to 3 teaspoons **aged balsamic vinegar**

Crispy Spiced Garlic (page 226)

1 cup (12 g) **fresh flat-leaf parsley** leaves, chopped

1. In a large, deep sauté pan, heat the olive oil over medium heat. Once shimmering, add the onions and a pinch of salt and cook, stirring occasionally, until the onions are starting to get some color, 5 to 7 minutes. Add the broth and lentils and bring to a boil. Reduce the heat and cook at a rapid simmer until most of the liquid has been absorbed and the lentils are tender but still al dente, 27 to 32 minutes. Remove from the heat.

2. If you made the tahini sauce in advance, mix in some water to thin it before using. Stir ½ cup (120 g) of the sauce and 2 teaspoons of the balsamic vinegar into the cooked lentils. Season with salt (1 to 1½ teaspoons) and pepper. Taste for seasonings, adding more vinegar as desired.

3. When ready to serve, spoon some of the reserved tahini sauce on top of the lentils (if storing leftovers, keep some tahini sauce separate). Top the lentils with the crispy spiced garlic and parsley.

An Ode to Tofu

Tofu is an incredibly versatile workhorse in a plant-based kitchen. While it's often shamed for being flavorless, its neutral flavor base is actually part of its magic. It is adaptable to any cuisine, from East Asian stir-fries (page 465) to Middle Eastern marinades (page 277) to Mexican sauces (page 287). And you can use it in desserts, breakfast dishes, and so much more.

It's also nutrient dense. One 3-ounce (85 g) serving of extra-firm tofu is just 80 calories but has 8 grams of protein, 2 grams of fiber, 10 percent of your daily value of calcium, and 8 percent of your daily value of iron, along with a range of B vitamins and zinc.

So why isn't tofu universally loved? My theory is that most folks just don't know how to cook with it. A few simple tricks make all the difference, which I'll explain later in this section.

Here are the varieties of tofu I always have on hand:

Silken. Silken tofu is creamy, almost pudding-like. When served cold, it melts in your mouth (Cold Tofu with Coconut-Ginger-Lime Crisp, page 284). It can also make shockingly creamy dressings (All Hail Caesar Dressing, page 155) and indulgent no-bake desserts (Dark Chocolate Mousse with Raspberry Compote, page 577).

Firm. The consistency of firm tofu is perfect for mimicking the texture of scrambled eggs (it also has slightly more protein but none of the cholesterol!). When fried, it develops a magical crunchy crust but retains a soft and chewy interior (Tofu 65, page 477).

Extra-firm. Extra-firm tofu makes a great meat substitute, especially when previously frozen. It can be stir-fried, deep-fried, or grilled. It can be torn into chunks and pan-fried, or coated in starch and baked to become delightfully crispy.

Super-firm. Also sold as "high-protein" tofu, this variety has the least amount of water. As a result it's quite dense, which offers two benefits: it doesn't require pressing, and it can achieve a pretty convincing meat-like texture (as in I Can't Believe It's Not Chicken, page 281).

How to Boost the Flavor of Tofu

1. **Get rid of excess water.** Tofu is watery, so most varieties need to be pressed or squeezed to remove excess water so it can absorb other flavors and take on a better texture.

   - **The pressing method.** Drain the tofu. If cutting tofu into cubes or tearing into chunks, cut the tofu lengthwise into four slabs. If cutting tofu into squares or rectangles, follow the instructions on page 267. Cover the tofu with a thin dish towel and weight it down with a heavy cookbook, topped with a skillet or a few cans of beans. Press for 15 minutes, changing the towel once during this time if possible. If you have a tofu press, press the tofu whole and adjust the screws every 5 to 10 minutes.

     Tip: Pressing smaller cuts of tofu, like these slabs, gets water out more efficiently than pressing the entire block.

   - **The squeezing method.** Holding the tofu over the sink, use your palms to gently squeeze out as much water as you can without breaking the tofu, squeezing in sections (I wrap the tofu in a thin dish towel because it gets cold). On a cutting board, gently press down on the tofu with a towel to remove more water. If the tofu still feels watery, use the pressing method above for 5 to 10 minutes. After slicing the tofu according to the recipe, gently press down on the slices with a towel.

     Note: Squeezing works best with previously frozen and thawed tofu; for regular refrigerated tofu, stick with pressing.

2. **Freeze it:** Cooking with tofu that has been frozen and thawed creates chewier and crispier textures *and* allows the tofu to absorb more flavors. Whenever I buy tofu, I get an extra block or two, freeze it, and set a reminder to thaw it. That way, I can have previously frozen tofu on hand at all times.

   - **Preferred method (best texture):** Remove the tofu from the package and add it to an airtight container or freezer-safe bag. You can add the water from the package or discard it.
   - **Quicker method:** Chuck the unopened block of packaged tofu straight into the freezer.
   - If you are freezing multiple blocks of tofu directly in their packages or in freezer bags, don't stack them on top of each other (they won't freeze evenly).
   - Each block needs 10 hours to freeze fully. When it's time to thaw, you can:
     - **Thaw in the fridge.** It takes 1 to 2 days. Again, don't stack them on top of each other.
     - Thaw on a sheet pan on your counter for a few hours. Metals like aluminum absorb ambient heat and transfer it to food, leading to quicker thawing. Science!
     - Thaw in the microwave. If you're short on time, run the tofu under warm water until you can slide it out of its package. Place the tofu in a shallow bowl and microwave on high in 1- or 2-minute intervals until thawed, squeezing in between rounds to see if it's still frozen in the middle (takes 8 to 12 minutes).
   - Once thawed, squeeze or press the tofu as described on page 265 to remove excess water.

Basic Cuts of Tofu

	TYPE OF TOFU	COOKING METHOD	INSTRUCTIONS
Tofu Cubes	Extra-firm or firm	Baking, pan-frying, or deep-frying	• Slice the tofu vertically into four slabs. Press the slabs for 15 minutes. For thawed tofu, use the squeezing method and press for 10 minutes. • Slice each slab in half lengthwise, so you have eight slabs. • Chop the tofu into ¼- to 1-inch (0.5 to 2.5 cm) cubes, depending on the recipe.
Tofu Squares	Extra-firm or firm	Pan-frying, stir-frying, baking, or deep-frying	• For thawed tofu, squeeze the block with your hands first. • Slice the tofu in half vertically. Then flip one slab around and cut crosswise into squares about ⅓ inch (0.75 cm) thick. • Gently press down on the squares with a towel to remove water; repeat a few times with a dry towel.
Tofu Slabs	Extra-firm or firm	Pan-frying	• For thawed tofu, squeeze the block with your hands first. • Starting on the shorter side of the tofu block, slice the tofu crosswise into ⅓-inch (0.75 cm) slices. You should get about 12 slabs from a 14-ounce (400 g) block. • Gently press down on the slabs with a towel to remove water; repeat a few times with a dry towel.
Tofu Nuggets	Extra-firm or firm (ideally, previously frozen and thawed, unless deep-frying)	Pan-frying, stir-frying, baking, or deep-frying	• For thawed tofu, use the squeezing method and press for 5 to 10 minutes. • For regular tofu, press for 15 to 20 minutes. • Tear the tofu into bite-size chunks. Gently press down with towels to remove more water.
Grated Tofu	Extra-firm or super-firm	Pan-frying	• Gently squeeze the tofu (super-firm) or press for 5 to 10 minutes (extra-firm). • Use the large holes of a box grater to grate the whole block of tofu. It will look a bit like shredded mozzarella. If any small pieces break off, slice those thinly.

Basic Pan-Fried Tofu

Serves 3 | GF, NF

You will find many recipes for tofu in this chapter (and in several other chapters). But sometimes you don't need a "recipe." Sometimes you just need some simply seasoned, crispy tofu to go with Tuesday night's dinner.

Tip: For an extra-crispy coating, in a large bowl, gently coat the tofu with 1 teaspoon kosher salt, some black pepper, and 3 tablespoons cornstarch (and omit sprinkling with additional salt while cooking/serving).

1 (14-ounce/400 g) block **extra-firm tofu** (optional: previously frozen and thawed)

2 to 3 tablespoons **extra-virgin olive oil**, **avocado oil**, or **oil of choice** (3 tablespoons for extra crispy)

Kosher salt

1. Select one of the cuts of tofu from the chart on page 267 and follow the prep instructions.

2. In a 12-inch (30 cm) nonstick skillet, heat the olive oil over medium-high heat. Once shimmering, carefully add the tofu to the pan and move it around in the oil to coat it evenly. Sprinkle the top side with a couple of pinches of salt. Cook until the bottom is golden brown (the exact time depends on the cut and size). Use an angled silicone spatula or offset spatula to flip the tofu, then cook until golden brown on the second side. Transfer the tofu to a paper towel–lined plate to drain and sprinkle with a pinch or two of salt.

Basic Baked Tofu

Serves 3 to 4 | GF, NF

This is my go-to recipe for a simple baked tofu that can be used as a protein topper for nearly any recipe: grain bowls, curries, noodles, salads, you name it.

Ingredient Note: The tofu is best coated with potato starch; cornstarch can leave a chalky aftertaste with baked tofu. Arrowroot powder also works well. If using potato starch, separate the pieces as much as possible, as they can stick together.

Tips: You can press and cube the tofu up to 5 days in advance, then store in a container in the fridge. This will cut down your prep time on the day of cooking to 2 minutes. For baked tofu, don't press the tofu for more than 15 minutes, as it can then dry out too much in the oven.

1 (14-ounce/400 g) block **extra-firm tofu**

1½ tablespoons **extra virgin olive oil**, **avocado oil**, or **oil of choice**

1 teaspoon **kosher salt**

Freshly ground **black pepper**

2 tablespoons **potato starch** or **arrowroot powder** (see Ingredient Note)

1. Preheat the oven to 425°F (220°C). Line a rimmed sheet pan with parchment paper.

2. Follow the instructions for preparing tofu cubes on page 267, cutting the tofu into ½- to ¾-inch (1.5 to 2 cm) cubes; ½-inch cubes get crispier, but ¾-inch cubes feel more substantial, so take your pick.

3. In a large bowl, toss the tofu with the olive oil, salt, and pepper to taste. Add the potato starch and, as gently as possible, toss with your hands to avoid crushing the tofu.

4. Arrange the tofu on the prepared pan in a single layer, spreading out the pieces so they don't touch. Bake for 15 minutes. Flip the tofu with a spatula. Bake for 15 more minutes, until golden and crispy.

Crispy Baked Tofu, 2 Ways

Serves 3 to 4

Both of these recipes offer deceptively simple ways to turn tofu into addictively crispy morsels.

Ingredient Note: The tofu is best coated with potato starch or arrowroot powder; cornstarch can leave a chalky aftertaste with baked tofu. If using potato starch, separate the tofu pieces as much as possible, as they can stick together.

Tip: Leftover tofu can be briefly reheated in a skillet with a touch of oil until warmed through and crisp.

Crispy Sesame Baked Tofu

GFO, NF

Savory and nutty goodness.

Big-Flavor Meals: Use these in a noodle bowl (see the Vietnamese Rice Noodle Bowls with Crispy Tofu & Mushrooms, page 473) or serve with noodles or rice dressed with Life-Changing Homemade Chili Crisp (page 187) and shredded carrots tossed with lime juice. Use leftovers in lettuce wraps, or roll in rice paper for summer rolls.

1 (14-ounce/400 g) block **extra-firm tofu**, preferably previously frozen and thawed (see page 266)

1 tablespoon **neutral-flavored oil** of choice

2 teaspoons **toasted sesame oil**

1 tablespoon **tamari** or **soy sauce** (use tamari for GF)

1 tablespoon **pure maple syrup**

¼ teaspoon **kosher salt**

1 tablespoon **potato starch** or **arrowroot powder**

1½ tablespoons **panko bread crumbs** (use gluten-free panko for GF)

1 tablespoon **roasted black (or white) sesame seeds**

1. Arrange a rack in the bottom of the oven. Preheat the oven to 425°F (220°C). Line a rimmed sheet pan with parchment paper.

2. Follow the instructions for preparing tofu cubes on page 267, cutting the tofu into ½- to ¾-inch (1.5 to 2 cm) cubes (½-inch/1.5 cm cubes get crispier).

3. In a large bowl, add the tofu, oil, sesame oil, tamari, maple syrup, and salt (use a bit more salt if you are not using thawed tofu). Toss gently to combine. Add the potato starch, panko, and sesame seeds. As gently as possible, toss with your hands to avoid crushing the tofu.

4. Arrange the tofu on the prepared pan in a single layer, coating the tofu with any loose breading and spreading out the pieces so they don't touch. Bake for 15 minutes. Flip the tofu with a spatula. Rotate the pan by 180 degrees and bake for 12 to 15 more minutes, until browned and crispy (if using ½-inch/1.5 cm cubes, they need just 20 minutes total).

Masala Baked Tofu

GF, NF

Warm, earthy, and slightly spicy.

Big-Flavor Meals: Pair with Buttery Brown Rice with Warm Spices (page 309) or any grain of choice and drizzle with Spicy Mint & Cilantro Sauce (page 189) or Mint-Pistachio Pesto (page 178). Add leftovers to a wrap, topped with a yogurt sauce (page 213), chopped cucumbers and tomatoes, and shredded cabbage.

1 (14-ounce/400 g) block **extra-firm tofu**

1 teaspoon **ground cumin**

½ teaspoon **garam masala**

¼ teaspoon **cayenne pepper** (optional, for *spicy!*)

1 tablespoon **nutritional yeast**

1 teaspoon **kosher salt**

Freshly ground **black pepper**

1½ tablespoons **grapeseed oil** or other **neutral-flavored oil**

1 tablespoon **potato starch** or **arrowroot powder**

1. Preheat the oven to 425°F (220°C). Line a rimmed sheet pan with parchment paper.

2. Follow the instructions for preparing tofu cubes on page 267, cutting the tofu into ¼- to ¾-inch (0.5 to 2 cm) cubes (¼-inch/0.5 cm cubes will be extra crispy).

3. In a small bowl, mix together the cumin, garam masala, cayenne (if using), nutritional yeast, salt, and black pepper to taste.

4. In a large bowl, toss the tofu with the spice mix and oil. Add the potato starch and, as gently as possible, toss with your hands to avoid crushing the tofu.

5. Arrange the tofu on the prepared pan in a single layer, spreading out the pieces so they don't touch. Bake for 15 minutes. Flip the tofu with a spatula. Bake for 15 more minutes, until golden and crispy.

**Crispy
Sesame
Baked Tofu**

PAGE 270

Crunchy Spiced Tofu Nuggets

Serves 4 | GF, NF

These tofu nuggets are deceptively crunchy and chewy, easy to throw together, and regularly make their way into my weeknight dinners. Previously frozen tofu is torn into chunks, then coated in vegan buttermilk and breaded in a mixture of cornmeal, arrowroot powder, and warming spices before being pan-fried in olive oil until perfectly browned and crispy. These are a delicious addition to virtually any grain bowl or salad.

Tips: You can use a bit less oil in step 6, but the nuggets won't get as crispy. If you don't have a large skillet, cook in two batches to avoid steaming the tofu. Leftovers can be briefly reheated in a skillet until warmed through and crisp.

1 (14-ounce/400 g) block **extra-firm tofu**, previously frozen and thawed (see page 266)

⅓ cup (80 ml) plain **plant-based milk** of choice

1 teaspoon **apple cider vinegar**

Spice Blend

¼ teaspoon **ground turmeric**

½ teaspoon **ground cumin**

½ teaspoon **ground coriander**

½ teaspoon **garlic powder**

1 teaspoon **sweet or hot paprika**

⅛ to ¼ teaspoon **red pepper flakes** (⅛ teaspoon for very mild heat)

1 heaping teaspoon **kosher salt**

Freshly ground **black pepper**

¼ cup (38 g) **medium-grind cornmeal**

2 tablespoons **arrowroot powder** or **potato starch**

3 tablespoons **extra-virgin olive oil**, **avocado oil**, or **oil of choice** (see Tips)

1. Slice the tofu into four slabs, gently squeeze each slab with your hands to remove excess water, then press the tofu for 10 to 20 minutes (see page 265).

2. In a glass, whisk together the milk and vinegar. Set aside until it curdles slightly, 5 to 10 minutes. This is your vegan buttermilk.

3. **Make the spice blend.** In a small or medium bowl, stir together the turmeric, cumin, coriander, garlic powder, paprika, pepper flakes, salt, a generous amount of black pepper, the cornmeal, and arrowroot powder.

4. Once the tofu has been pressed, use your palms to squeeze out any more water from each slab. You want the tofu to feel fairly dry. Gently tear the tofu into pretty small chunks, about ½-inch (1 to 1.5 cm) pieces. Some smaller pieces will break off; that's okay—they get super crispy.

5. In a medium or large bowl, gently coat the tofu with the buttermilk using a silicone spatula. Pour half of the spice mixture on top, toss gently to coat, then add the rest and toss again until the tofu is well coated.

6. In a 12-inch (30 cm) or larger nonstick skillet, heat the olive oil over medium-high heat. Once shimmering, add the tofu pieces. Move them around to coat them in the oil, then spread them out in a single layer as much as you can. Cook undisturbed for 3 to 4 minutes. Use a wide spatula to flip and toss every 2 minutes until nicely browned all over, a total of 12 to 14 minutes. Some tofu pieces may stick together, but they'll be easy to separate later. Turn off the heat and transfer the tofu to a plate. Let rest for 5 minutes to further crisp up, then enjoy.

Pomegranate-Glazed Tofu

Serves 3 to 4 | GF, NF

Baked tofu is tossed in a uniquely delicious tart-yet-sweet vinaigrette, making it saucy and glistening without detracting from its crispiness. When pomegranate molasses is heated, its natural sugars caramelize on the tofu, giving you delightfully sticky bits.

Tip: The vinaigrette stays good in the fridge for at least 1 week, but if you want to use all of it, double the tofu. In step 3, toss the tofu in two batches; bake on two sheet pans; and toss the tofu and vinaigrette in two batches in step 5.

Big-Flavor Meals: Serve with the Customizable Grain Salad with Garlicky Spiced Oil & Fresh Herbs (page 305) or Buttery Brown Rice with Warm Spices (page 309). Round it out with the Spiced-Roasted Whole Carrots (page 329), Quick Roasted Cauliflower (page 342), Jammy Zucchini (page 330), or a green salad.

1 (14-ounce/400 g) block **extra-firm tofu**, previously frozen and thawed for a crispier, chewier texture (see page 266)

1 tablespoon **extra-virgin olive oil**

1 tablespoon **arrowroot powder** or **potato starch**, plus more as needed

¾ teaspoon **kosher salt**

½ recipe (about 6 tablespoons/90 g) **Pomegranate Molasses Vinaigrette** (page 165; see Tip)

1. Preheat the oven to 425°F (220°C). Line a rimmed sheet pan with parchment paper.

2. Follow the instructions for preparing the tofu cubes on page 267, cutting the tofu into ¾-inch (2 cm) cubes.

3. In a large bowl, using your hands, gently toss the tofu with the olive oil, arrowroot powder, and salt. If the tofu isn't fully covered by the starch, add a bit more.

4. Arrange the tofu on the prepared pan in a single layer. If using potato starch, space the pieces out as much as possible to prevent sticking. Bake for 15 minutes. Flip the tofu with a spatula. Bake for 15 more minutes, until golden and crisp.

5. Heat a large skillet over medium heat until warm. Add the pomegranate molasses vinaigrette and the baked tofu. Stir to coat and cook until the tofu is saucy, 1 to 2 minutes.

Sticky Coconut Milk–Braised Tofu

Serves 3 to 4 | GFO, NF

As much as I love crispy tofu, I may love this braised tofu even more. Here, squares of tofu are pan-fried until golden and crispy, then braised in a Thai-inspired blend of coconut milk, soy sauce, lemongrass, and spices. Frying the tofu first makes the perfect porous surface for the deeply savory and slightly sweet braising liquid to seep into, creating that spongy and chewy yet tender texture found in Chinese restaurant tofu dishes.

Tip: To serve a crowd, double the tofu and braising liquid. Fry the tofu in two batches; after frying the first batch, start simmering the liquid in a 3-quart (2.8 L) saucepan, then follow the recipe as written.

Big-Flavor Meals: Serve over a bed of jasmine white rice or brown rice, along with blanched or stir-fried green beans, bok choy, or broccolini.

1 (14-ounce/400 g) block **extra-firm tofu**, drained

Kosher salt

3 tablespoons **neutral-flavored oil** of choice

Braising Liquid

1 tablespoon **coriander seeds**

1 (13.5-ounce/400 ml) can **full-fat coconut milk**

½ cup (140 g) **soy sauce** or **tamari** (use tamari for GF)

¼ cup (84 g) **agave nectar** (or organic brown sugar or cane sugar)

2 **lemongrass** stalks, minced (see page 472 for prep tips)

1-inch (2.5 cm) piece **fresh ginger**, thinly sliced (peel on okay)

4 large **garlic cloves**, smashed

1 to 3 **Thai chiles** (or 1 serrano pepper), stemmed and sliced in half vertically (use 3 chiles for *spicy!*; omit for mild heat)

¼ teaspoon **ground white pepper**

1 (2-inch) **cinnamon stick**

For Serving

Cooked **white or brown rice**

Roasted black or white sesame seeds

1 handful chopped **cilantro** or **Thai basil** (optional)

recipe continues

1. Wrap the tofu in a thin dish towel or a few paper towels and press for 10 to 15 minutes (see page 265).

2. Slice the tofu in half vertically, then flip each slab around and slice crosswise into squares about ½-inch (1 to 1.5 cm) thick. Arrange the tofu in a single layer on a cutting board. Gently press down on the squares with a towel to release more water. Sprinkle the tofu with a couple of pinches of salt. Line a large plate with a few paper towels.

3. Heat a 12-inch (30 cm) nonstick skillet over medium-high heat for 2 minutes, then add the oil and heat for 30 seconds. Carefully add the tofu, arranging it in a single layer. Move the tofu around in the oil to evenly coat it and cook until golden brown on the bottom, 5 to 7 minutes. Use a thin spatula to flip and cook until the other side is also golden brown, 4 to 5 minutes.

4. **While the tofu cooks, make the braising liquid.** Use the back of a large knife or a sturdy mug to roughly crush the coriander seeds. Or you can use a mortar and pestle or pulse once in a spice grinder.

5. In a medium (2-quart/2 L) heavy-bottomed saucepan, combine the coconut milk, soy sauce, agave, lemongrass, ginger, garlic, chiles (if using), roughly crushed coriander, white pepper, and cinnamon. Bring to a boil, stirring occasionally, then reduce the heat and simmer for 7 to 8 minutes. It should be very flavorful and quite salty.

6. Add the fried tofu to the braising liquid and stir to coat. A few pieces of tofu will peek up above the liquid, but that's okay. Simmer gently, stirring occasionally, until the tofu is almost wrinkly and the liquid has thickened into a sauce that sticks to the tofu, about 35 minutes.

7. Remove from the heat and let cool briefly; discard the cinnamon stick. Serve over rice, pour a little braising liquid on top of the rice (not a lot, as it's quite potent), and garnish with sesame seeds and herbs.

I Can't Believe It's Not Chicken
(Super-Savory Grated Tofu)

Serves 4 | GFO, NF

Grating super-firm tofu is one of my favorite party tricks in the kitchen. It makes tofu not only quicker to prepare (no pressing required!) but also deceptively meaty. Here, the grated tofu is pan-fried until golden, then coated in an addictively good, flavor-rich sauce featuring some of my favorite pan-Asian condiments: fruity yet smoky gochugaru, nutty toasted sesame oil, plus umami-rich Chinese black vinegar and soy sauce.

The result is delightfully crispy, chewy, and super-savory tofu that is shockingly meaty. It's been described by friends as "spicy ground chicken," "larb-esque," and "I can't believe it's not chicken." It's delicious for dinner but also makes a regular appearance at my breakfast table.

Ingredient Notes: Super-firm tofu or "high-protein" tofu makes for a very convincing meat substitute, but if you don't have it, use extra-firm tofu and press for 10 minutes; grate the tofu, then dab with towels to remove water. Don't have gochugaru? Sub with 1 to 1½ teaspoons of Sichuan chile flakes or sriracha.

Big-Flavor Meals: Serve with rice and stir-fried or steamed green beans or broccoli for a quick yet delicious meal. For a fun appetizer, spoon into lettuce cups with chopped rice noodles and drizzle with the nước chấm–inspired sauce on page 473.

Make Ahead: You can grate the tofu and prep the aromatics the night before.

GF Option: Most Chinese black vinegar is fermented with grains. Substitute 2 parts rice vinegar to 1 part aged balsamic vinegar. Use tamari instead of soy sauce.

1 to 1½ cups (190 to 285 g) uncooked or 3 to 4½ cups (425 to 650 g) cooked **brown or white rice**

1 (10- to 12-ounce/280 to 340 g) block **super-firm tofu** (see Ingredient Notes)

1½ tablespoons **neutral-flavored oil** of choice

4 **scallions**, sliced on a bias (reserve dark green tops for garnish)

1 to 2 **Thai chiles** (or 1 small serrano pepper), thinly sliced (optional, for *spicy!*)

3 **garlic cloves**, thinly sliced

1 tablespoon **roasted black or white sesame seeds**

Sauce

3 tablespoons **tamari** or **soy sauce**

1 tablespoon **Chinese black vinegar**

1 teaspoon **organic cane sugar**, **pure maple syrup**, or **agave nectar**

1 tablespoon **gochugaru** (Korean chile flakes)

1 tablespoon **toasted sesame oil**

For Serving

1 handful **cilantro** leaves and tender stems, roughly chopped

recipe continues

1. Start by cooking the rice using your preferred method, or get out your leftover cooked rice.

2. Wrap the tofu in a thin dish towel and gently squeeze with your palms to remove some water but don't squish it. Using the large holes of a box grater, grate the tofu. If small pieces break off, slice them very thinly.

3. In a large nonstick skillet, heat the oil over medium-high heat. After a minute or two, add the scallions, chiles (if using), and garlic. Cook, stirring frequently, until the garlic is slightly golden and the scallions are softened, about 2 minutes.

4. Add the grated tofu to the pan and toss to coat it in the oil. Cook undisturbed for 2 minutes, then stir. Cook, stirring every 2 minutes, until the tofu is golden brown in some spots, a total of 10 to 14 minutes.

5. **Meanwhile, make the sauce.** In a small bowl, whisk together the tamari, vinegar, sugar, gochugaru, and sesame oil until well combined.

6. Pour the sauce into the pan—it will bubble rapidly—and stir with a silicone spatula to evenly coat the tofu. Cook for 1 minute. Remove from the heat and sprinkle with the sesame seeds.

7. Serve over cooked rice and top with the reserved scallion tops and cilantro. Store leftovers in an airtight container in the fridge for 4 to 5 days.

Cold Tofu with Coconut–Ginger–Lime Crisp

Serves 2 as a main, 4 to 6 as a side or starter | GFO, NF

This dish pairs the creamy, custard-like consistency of silken tofu with a mega-flavorful sauce and crispy fried aromatics like makrut lime leaves, ginger, and coconut flakes.

It takes just **15 minutes** to make, and the hardest part is (literally) getting the tofu out of its package. It's inspired by East Asian cold tofu dishes like Japanese hiyayakko but is certainly not authentic and is very much a "fusion" dish featuring fun, zingy, tropical-esque flavors. Serve as a starter or side dish, or as a main dish for two over rice.

Ingredient Notes: Silken tofu is sold in both shelf-stable aseptic packages and in the refrigerated section with block tofu (I prefer the latter). If you see varying degrees of firmness, choose silken (soft) or silken (firm) tofu. You can find Chinese black vinegar and dried makrut lime leaves at pan-Asian markets or online; if you can't get the latter, just omit them. If you don't mind big crunchy pieces, leave the lime leaves whole (otherwise, crumble them).

Tip: To open silken tofu, invert the package and use scissors to snip off a tiny piece of each of the four corners to create some air. Now slice open the wrapper using scissors or a knife. Invert the tofu over a plate with a lip or shallow bowl and gently wiggle the tofu onto the plate.

GF Option: Most Chinese black vinegar is fermented with grains. Substitute 2 parts rice vinegar to 1 part aged balsamic vinegar. Use tamari instead of soy sauce.

1 (12- to 16-ounce/340 to 450 g) block **silken soft tofu**, refrigerated (see Tip)

Kosher salt

1 tablespoon **soy sauce** or **tamari**

1 scant tablespoon **agave nectar**

1 scant tablespoon **Chinese black vinegar** (see Ingredient Notes)

Coconut-Ginger-Lime Crisp

2 tablespoons **neutral-flavored oil** of choice

1-inch (2.5 cm) piece **fresh ginger**, peeled and julienned

2 **Thai chiles** (or 1 serrano or Fresno pepper), sliced into rounds (optional, for *spicy!*; remove membranes and seeds for less heat)

3 **garlic cloves**, thinly sliced

2 **scallions**, sliced on a bias (reserve dark green tops for garnish)

½ cup (25 g) unsweetened **coconut flakes/chips** (the fat kind, not skinny shreds)

8 to 10 **dried makrut lime leaves**, crumbled or left whole (see Ingredient Notes)

2 teaspoons **roasted black and/or white sesame seeds**

recipe continues

1. Place the tofu on a plate with a lip or in a shallow bowl and gently tip the plate to drain any excess water. Sprinkle with a pinch of salt.

2. In a small bowl, whisk together the soy sauce, agave, and vinegar.

3. **Make the crisp.** In a small or medium skillet, heat the oil over medium heat. Add the ginger and chiles (if using) and cook, stirring occasionally, for 1 minute. Add the garlic, white and light green parts of the scallions, and coconut and cook, stirring occasionally, until the coconut is golden but not browned, 3 to 5 minutes. Add the lime leaves and cook for 1 minute. Remove from the heat and pour the mixture over the tofu.

4. Pour the soy sauce mixture on top of and around the tofu. Garnish with reserved scallion greens and sesame seeds. Serve immediately.

Baked Tofu & Kale in Tomato–Chipotle Sauce

Serves 3 to 4 | GF, NF

Chewy, crispy baked tofu is coated in a tangy and smoky Mexican-inspired sauce seasoned with warm spices, chipotle peppers, aromatics, and tomatoes. And the kale makes it a complete meal.

Ingredient Note: Use 1 chipotle pepper for moderate heat, or use 2 for *spicy!*

Big-Flavor Meals: Serve simply over brown rice, or scoop into corn tortillas with avocado or guacamole (if you have pickled onions or vegan sour cream, they're excellent here).

1 (14-ounce/400 g) block **extra-firm tofu**

1½ tablespoons **avocado oil** or other **neutral-flavored oil**

Kosher salt and freshly ground **black pepper**

2 tablespoons **potato starch** or **arrowroot powder**

1 to 1½ cups (190 to 285 g) uncooked or 3 to 4½ cups (425 to 650 g) cooked long-grain **brown or white rice**

Tomato-Chipotle Sauce

1 medium or large **sweet onion**, very roughly chopped

1 small **green bell pepper**, very roughly chopped

8 ounces (227 g) **tomatoes** (about 2 medium tomatoes), very roughly chopped

4 **garlic cloves**, roughly chopped

1½ tablespoons **avocado oil** or other **neutral-flavored oil**

1 teaspoon **cumin seeds** (or ¾ scant teaspoon ground cumin)

Kosher salt and freshly ground **black pepper**

¼ teaspoon **ground coriander**

1 teaspoon dried **Mexican oregano** (regular oregano is fine)

1 medium **lime**, zested and juiced

1 (8-ounce/227 g) can **tomato sauce**

1 to 2 **chipotle peppers in adobo sauce**, roughly chopped + 1 tablespoon **adobo sauce** (see Ingredient Note)

recipe and ingredients continue

3 cups (70 g) thinly sliced or shredded **lacinato kale**

¾ cup (12 g) **fresh cilantro** leaves and tender stems, chopped

Quick-pickled onions (page 168) and **vegan sour cream** (optional but recommended; can sub with avocado)

1. Preheat the oven to 425°F (220°C). Line a rimmed sheet pan with parchment paper.

2. Follow the instructions for preparing tofu cubes on page 267, cutting the tofu into ½- to ¾-inch (1.5 to 2 cm) cubes.

3. In a large bowl, gently toss the tofu with the oil, ½ teaspoon salt, and pepper to taste using a silicone spatula or your hands. Add the potato starch and, as gently as possible, toss with your hands.

4. Arrange the tofu on the prepared pan in a single layer. If using potato starch, space the pieces out as much as possible to prevent sticking. Bake for 15 minutes. Flip the tofu with a spatula. Bake for 15 more minutes, until lightly golden and crispy.

5. Meanwhile, cook the rice using your preferred method, or get out your leftover cooked rice.

6. **Make the sauce.** In a food processor, add the onions, bell pepper, tomatoes, and garlic. Pulse a few times until finely minced but not pureed.

7. In a large sauté pan, heat the oil over medium-high heat. Add the cumin seeds and cook until very fragrant, about 1 minute (if using ground cumin, add it in the next step with the coriander). Add the tomato mixture with its liquid and a pinch of salt. Cook, stirring occasionally, until the vegetables are lightly browned and completely softened and the liquid has evaporated, 10 to 13 minutes.

8. Add the coriander, oregano, 1½ teaspoons lime zest, and 1 tablespoon lime juice to the pan and cook for 30 to 60 seconds. Add the tomato sauce, chipotle pepper, and adobo sauce and season with 1 teaspoon salt and several cracks of black pepper. Simmer, stirring occasionally, until thickened, about 3 minutes.

9. Add the baked tofu and toss to coat. Add the kale and cilantro and cook until the kale is wilted, 3 to 4 minutes. Season to taste with salt, black pepper, and additional lime juice. Serve over rice with pickled onions and/or sour cream (if using).

thinly
sliced

crumbled

matchsticks

An Ode to Tempeh

There's a lot to love about tempeh. Its nutritional profile is wild (18 g protein, 6 g fiber, 10 percent of your daily value of iron in a 3-ounce serving). It's a gut-healthy fermented food. And it's naturally rich in umami, with a meaty depth.

But it can also be bitter, dry, and crumbly. Or, as one of my YouTube subscribers put it, "It's like an earthier bird seed version of tofu."

Yet once I developed a few tricks, I had a revelation: tempeh can actually be really good!

How to Boost the Flavor of Tempeh

Instead of slicing it into thicker cuts like cubes or triangles, **slice tempeh very thinly or crumble it finely.** This makes tempeh crispy, not dry, and gives it more surface area to absorb tasty sauces.

Pan-fry or stir-fry tempeh in oil to retain moisture. In contrast, when you bake tempeh, it tends to eat up marinades, leaving you with a dry texture and muted flavor.

For the most flavor, coat tempeh in a sauce that's fairly acidic and salty and a tad sweet. These flavors mask tempeh's bitterness. You can also steam tempeh for 10 minutes before cooking if you're very sensitive to bitter flavors.

My Go-To Methods for Preparing Tempeh

- Thinly sliced (for Saucy Glazed Pan-Fried Tempeh, 2 Ways, page 293)

- Crumbled (for taco "meat," chili, or stir-fries)

- Matchsticks (for stir-fries, like the Sweet & Sour Tempeh Peanut Stir-Fry, page 480)

Thinly Sliced Tempeh

Starting on the shorter end of the block, slice tempeh into ½-inch-thick (1.5 cm) strips. Place each strip on its side and slice in half lengthwise to make it thinner.

Crumbled Tempeh

Use your hands to crumble the tempeh finely. Or grate it on the large holes of a box grater. The smaller the pieces, the crispier it gets.

Matchstick Tempeh

Cut the tempeh crosswise into very thin slices, almost as thinly as you can. Stack several slices on top of each other and cut crosswise into tiny slivers.

20-Minute Tempeh Nuggets

Use in stir-fries, tacos, or rice bowls.

1. Follow the instructions above for crumbled tempeh or matchstick tempeh.

2. In a 12-inch (30 cm) nonstick skillet, heat ¼ cup (56 g) neutral-flavored, high-heat oil over medium-high heat until the oil is just smoking.

3. Add the tempeh and season with a couple of pinches of salt. Cook undisturbed for 2 minutes, then flip and cook, stirring every 1½ to 2 minutes, until mostly golden brown and slightly crisp, 12 to 14 minutes total. Transfer to a paper towel–lined surface to blot excess oil and season with a few pinches of salt.

4. **Optional:** Return the tempeh to the pan and pour in **about ½ cup (120 ml) of your favorite tangy-salty-sweet sauce.*** Toss and simmer until the tempeh is well coated, 2 to 3 minutes.

*Some good sauce options:

Either of the two sauces that follow on page 294

Pomegranate Molasses Vinaigrette (page 165)

Preserved Lemon Vinaigrette (page 164)

Spicy Mint & Cilantro Sauce (page 189)

Saucy Glazed Pan-Fried Tempeh, 2 Ways

Serves 3

This is my favorite method for making tempeh on weeknights—and even self-declared tempeh haters enjoy it. If I haven't yet convinced you of tempeh's wonders, you can also use these sauces with the Basic Baked Tofu on page 269.

Tips: Stick to tempeh varieties labeled "original" ("three-grain" varieties get too crunchy). If you're very sensitive to bitter food, steam the tempeh for 10 minutes before pan-frying.

Big-Flavor Meals

Bowl style

× Spiced Mojo tempeh + brown rice + black or pinto beans + Roasted Butternut Wedges (page 337) + leftover Mojo Sauce (page 183)

× Korean BBQ tempeh + rice or noodles + pickled carrots or radishes (page 168) + sliced cucumbers

Sandwiches or wraps

× Spiced Mojo tempeh + either of the cremas on page 204 + crunchy lettuce + radishes

× Korean BBQ tempeh + vegan mayo mixed with gochujang + scallions + cilantro + shaved carrots and cucumber

Pan-Fried Tempeh

GF, NF

1 (8-ounce/227 g) block **tempeh**

2 tablespoons **neutral-flavored oil** of choice

1. Slice the tempeh thinly according to the instructions on page 291. Line a plate with paper towels.

2. In a 12-inch (30 cm) nonstick skillet, heat 1½ tablespoons of the oil over medium heat. Once shimmering, add the tempeh slices in a single layer (if your pan is smaller, cook in two batches). Cook, moving the pieces to coat them in the oil evenly, until golden brown and crisp on the bottom, 3 to 4 minutes. Using a pastry brush, brush the top side of each tempeh slice with the remaining ½ tablespoon oil (or spray with cooking spray). This ensures the second side gets golden brown, not charred. Now flip each piece and cook until browned on the other side, 2 to 3 minutes. Transfer the tempeh to the paper towel–lined plate to absorb excess oil.

recipe continues

Spiced Mojo Flavor

GF, NF

Tempeh feels meaty yet fresh and bright thanks to the zingy, garlicky mojo sauce.

½ cup (120 g) **Mojo Sauce** (page 183; if using Basic Baked Tofu, use ⅓ cup/80 g)

¾ teaspoon **chili powder**

½ heaping teaspoon **onion powder**

½ teaspoon **ground coriander**

½ teaspoon **sweet or hot paprika**

1 teaspoon **cornstarch**

Pan-Fried Tempeh (or Basic Baked Tofu, page 269)

1 small handful **cilantro** leaves and tender stems, chopped

Squeeze of fresh **lime juice** (optional)

1. In a small bowl, stir together the Mojo Sauce, chili powder, onion powder, coriander, paprika, and cornstarch until well combined.

2. In a large skillet, warm the spiced sauce over medium-low heat, stirring with a silicone spatula, until thickened, 2 to 4 minutes. Add the tempeh and cook until the sauce coats the tempeh well, 1 to 3 minutes.

3. Garnish with cilantro and a squeeze of lime, if desired.

Korean BBQ Flavor

GFO, NF

Sweet, tangy, spicy, and savory, this tempeh is a little reminiscent of Korean BBQ takeout.

GF Option: Make the gluten-free alternative to the Korean BBQ Sauce (see page 175).

⅓ cup (100 g) **Korean BBQ Sauce** (page 175)

Pan-Fried Tempeh (or Basic Baked Tofu, page 269)

2 **scallions,** thinly sliced

1 small handful **cilantro** leaves and tender stems, chopped

2 teaspoons **roasted sesame seeds**

1. Heat a large skillet over medium-low heat. Once warm, pour in the Korean BBQ Sauce and cook, stirring with a silicone spatula, until gently simmering, about 3 minutes. Add the tempeh and cook until the sauce coats the tempeh well, 1 to 3 minutes.

2. Garnish with scallions, cilantro, and sesame seeds.

Variation 4
PAGE 298

✕

Crunchy Protein & Grain Bowls

✕

Variation 10
PAGE 298

Variation 1
PAGE 298

Variation 8
PAGE 298

Crunchy Protein

	Crunchy Protein	Condiment	Grain
1	Crispy Sesame Baked Tofu (page 270)	Life-Changing Homemade Chili Crisp (page 187)	Brown or jasmine rice
2	BBQ Roasted Chickpeas (page 239)	Throwback Ranch Dressing (page 203)	Quinoa
3	Masala Baked Tofu (page 271)	Mint Yogurt Sauce (page 213) or Spicy Mint & Cilantro Sauce (page 189)	Basmati rice
4	Wildly Crunchy Cornmeal Beans (page 240)	Yogurt-Tahini Sauce (page 215)	Farro or wheat berries
5	Basic Baked Tofu (page 269)	Avocado Crema (page 204)	Wild rice
6	Classic Roasted Chickpeas (page 236)	Italian Basil & Parsley Salsa Verde (page 181)	Farro or wheat berries
7	20-Minute Tempeh Nuggets (page 292)	Chipotle Crema (page 205)	Brown rice
8	Crunchy Spiced Tofu Nuggets (page 274)	Green Goddess Dressing (page 182)	Millet
9	Crispy Lentils (page 253)	Lemon Tahini Sauce (page 197)	Brown rice or quinoa
10	Tandoori Roasted Chickpeas (page 238)	Spicy Mint & Cilantro Sauce (page 189)	Basmati rice

& Grain Bowls —

Veggie	Jazzy Extras
Carrot ribbons or sautéed snap peas or green beans	Roasted sesame seeds and scallions
Romaine or Little Gem lettuce and cherry tomatoes	Crushed tortilla chips and charred corn kernels
Sliced cucumbers and tomatoes	Dry-roasted peanuts and fresh mint or cilantro
Lightly dressed salad greens	Sliced green olives and parsley
Charred Sweet Potato Wedges (page 345)	Quick-pickled onions or chiles (page 168)
Cherry tomatoes and shaved fennel	Toasted pine nuts
Roasted Butternut Wedges (page 337)	Smoky Seed Sprinkle (page 216) and quick-pickled onions (page 168)
Romaine or Little Gem lettuce	Toasted pepitas (shelled pumpkin seeds) and fresh dill or basil
Spice-Roasted Whole Carrots (page 329)	Preserved Lemons (page 157), pistachios, and dried apricots
Sliced cucumbers and tomatoes	Avocado and fresh cilantro or mint

7

The
Grains

Grains can be so much more than a simple side of rice. From brown rice and farro to freekeh, millet, and more, grains offer delicious diversity, versatility, and wholesomeness. They are also full of delightful textures: chewy, nutty, and even bouncy.

Like the recipes in the previous chapter, the recipes here are flavorful enough that they can be paired simply—add your favorite store-bought or homemade protein and a vegetable, and dinner is set. Or check out the **Big-Flavor Meals** notes for inspiration on how to take a few extra steps to turn one of these grain-forward recipes into a standout entrée.

How to Boost the Flavor of Grains

TOAST FOR DEEPER FLAVOR. To draw out a grain's flavor, toast it in a dry skillet over medium-high heat for a few minutes until it smells nutty and the grains are slightly darker. For even more flavor, toast in a bit of olive oil and aromatics (e.g., spices, chile flakes, garlic, shallots), as in the Buttery Brown Rice with Warm Spices (page 309), or in a bit of wine, as in the Rosemary Farrotto with Cheesy Pine Nuts (page 311).

ADD AROMATICS. As with lentils and beans, you can infuse flavor into your grains by adding aromatics to the cooking water. Think halved garlic or shallots, celery or carrot bits, bay leaves, a bouquet garni, or cracked whole spices.

COOK IN VEGETABLE BROTH. You can amp up the flavor of most grains by cooking them in vegetable broth instead of water. Or you can try 50 percent water, 50 percent broth.

Basic Cooking Methods for Your (My) Favorite Grains

Use this list when you need to cook a simple pot of grains. Note: These are the grains *I personally like to cook* (for instance, you will not find buckwheat here because I hate the taste—sorry!).

BARLEY: Toast 1 cup (195 g) pearl barley in a dry medium saucepan for a few minutes, stirring often. Add 3 cups (720 ml) of water, season with salt, and bring to a boil. Cover and simmer until the water is absorbed and the barley is tender and a bit chewy, 25 to 30 minutes. For hulled barley, soak for at least 3 hours and cook for 40 to 60 minutes.

BROWN RICE, LONG-GRAIN

Standard: Rinse 1 cup (190 g) rice until the water runs clear. In a medium saucepan, add 1¾ cups (420 ml) of water, the rice, and a drizzle of olive oil (optional). Bring to a boil, then reduce the heat, cover, and simmer until the water is absorbed and the rice is tender but a little toothsome, 40 to 45 minutes. Remove from the heat and steam, covered, for 10 minutes. Fluff with a fork and season with salt to taste.

    Pilaf-style: Mix 1 cup (190 g) rinsed rice with 1¾ cups (420 ml) of water or broth with seasonings of choice in a medium Dutch oven or ovenproof saucepan. Bake at 375°F (190°C) for 40 minutes. Steam, covered, for 10 minutes. Fluff with a fork and season with salt to taste.

FARRO: Bring 2½ cups (600 ml) of water to a boil in a medium saucepan. Season with salt (and aromatics of choice). Add 1 cup (190 g) farro. Simmer until al dente (tender yet chewy), 15 to 20 minutes for pearled farro; 20 to 30 minutes for semi-pearled farro. Drain and spread out on a sheet pan to dry.

FREEKEH: Rinse and drain 1 cup (160 g) freekeh. Toast freekeh in a dry medium saucepan for a few minutes, stirring often (optional). Add 2 cups (480 ml) of water, season with salt, and bring to a boil. Reduce the heat, cover, and simmer until the water is absorbed and tender, 20 to 25 minutes. Remove from the heat and steam, covered, for 10 minutes.

MILLET: In a medium saucepan, heat 2 teaspoons olive oil over medium heat. Toast 1 cup (195 g) millet for 3 to 5 minutes, until golden brown and it crackles a bit. Pour in 3 cups (720 ml) of water and season with salt. Bring to a boil, then reduce the heat to low, cover, and simmer for 20 to 25 minutes without stirring. Remove from the heat and steam, covered, for 10 minutes. Fluff with a fork. Transfer to a sheet pan and spread out; sprinkle with a few pinches of salt. Cool for 10 minutes. Serve immediately, as leftovers get clumpy.

PEARL COUSCOUS: In a medium saucepan, heat a touch of olive oil over medium heat. Toast 1 cup (150 g) pearl couscous until golden, 4 to 5 minutes. Add 1¼ cups (300 ml) of water and ¼ teaspoon fine sea salt, then bring to a boil. Reduce the heat, cover, and simmer until the liquid is absorbed and the couscous is just tender, 9 to 10 minutes. Set aside to cool slightly but not too long to prevent it from clumping.

QUINOA: Rinse and drain 1 cup (180 g) quinoa. In a medium saucepan, bring 1¼ cups (300 ml) of water to a boil, then add the quinoa and a pinch of salt. Reduce the heat to low, cover, and cook until the liquid has evaporated and the quinoa is tender (the germ should have separated from the seed), about 12 minutes. Fluff with a fork, then spread out on a sheet pan to dry.

WHEAT BERRIES: Bring 4 cups (1 L) of water to a boil in a medium saucepan. Add 1 cup (190 g) rinsed wheat berries and season with salt. Simmer uncovered until tender but chewy, 30 to 35 minutes for soft wheat berries; at least 60 minutes for hard berries. Drain well.

WHITE RICE, LONG-GRAIN (E.G., JASMINE OR BASMATI): Rinse 1 cup (190 g) rice until the water runs clear. In a medium saucepan, add 1½ cups (360 ml) of water, the rice, ¼ teaspoon kosher salt, and a drizzle of extra-virgin olive oil (optional). Bring to a boil, then reduce the heat, cover, and simmer until the water is absorbed and the rice is tender, 7 to 12 minutes. Remove from the heat and steam, covered, for 10 minutes. Fluff with a fork.

WILD RICE
Standard: Add 1 cup (175 g) wild rice to a medium saucepan, cover with several inches of water, and season with 1 teaspoon kosher salt. Bring to a boil, then reduce the heat to a rapid simmer and cook, uncovered, until tender and most grains have split, 45 to 50 minutes. Drain well, then fluff with a fork. If you have time, spread the rice out on a sheet pan to dry.
Baked: See Creamy Baked Wild Rice with Carrots on page 317.

Using Grains for Meal Planning

Cook a big batch of one grain, or a normal-size batch each of two grains, and store in the fridge for 5 to 6 days to use during the week. Use in grain bowls or to make a quick breakfast porridge; to bulk up soups, stews, and salads; or paired with any protein in chapter 6. When reheating grains, add a splash of water to loosen them up.

You can also freeze grains for longer storage. I like to freeze them in single-serve portions in labeled freezer-safe bags so they thaw quickly in the fridge. You can also add them frozen directly to a stew or soup.

Customizable Grain Salad with Garlicky Spiced Oil & Fresh Herbs

Serves 8 as a side | GFO, SF, NFO

Cooking farro in a bath of fresh orange juice and plenty of salt infuses each morsel with citrus flavor and a subtle sweetness that's later enhanced by dates. A spiced oil adds warm, garlicky flavor and crunchy garlic chips, while fresh herbs add bright dimension and pistachios a buttery nuttiness. A must-make for all your summer picnics, potlucks, and al fresco lunches.

Ingredient Notes: Most supermarket farro is pearled or semi-pearled, which means the bran or part of the bran has been removed. Whole farro takes at least 40 minutes to cook (soak it overnight). For wheat berries, use 5½ to 6 cups (1.3 to 1.4 L) of water and cook until tender but chewy (soft wheat berries may take just 30 minutes; hard wheat berries, 60 to 90 minutes).

Big-Flavor Meals: Toss in salad greens and ripe avocado, vegan feta, or roasted oyster mushrooms. Serve alongside Masala Baked Tofu (page 271) or crispy chickpeas or lentils (pages 236 and 253).

Easy Variations: You can use virtually any grain if you adjust the cook times (wheat berries are particularly fabulous here). Swap the dates for dried apricots, or for a juicy bite, add tangerines. You can use just one or two of the herbs or add in a few cups of arugula or some chopped cukes.

GF and NF Option: Use brown rice, quinoa, or millet instead of farro; swap toasted pepitas (shelled pumpkin seeds) for the pistachios.

Farro

¾ cup (180 ml) freshly squeezed **orange juice** (2 to 3 medium oranges)

1½ cups (285 g) **farro** (see Ingredient Notes)

2 **bay leaves**

1 large **shallot**, halved

1 tablespoon **kosher salt**

Freshly ground **black pepper**

Spiced Garlic Oil

3 tablespoons **extra-virgin olive oil**

6 **garlic cloves**, thinly sliced

1½ teaspoons **cumin seeds**

1½ teaspoons **coriander seeds**

Salad

1 medium **lemon**, zested and juiced

Kosher salt or **fine sea salt** and freshly ground **black pepper**

½ cup (6 g) **fresh flat-leaf parsley** leaves, roughly chopped

15 to 20 **fresh basil** leaves, slivered

recipe and ingredients continue

1 handful **fresh mint** leaves, slivered or torn by hand

4 large **Medjool dates**, finely chopped

¼ cup (35 g) **shelled roasted pistachios** (or almonds or walnuts), chopped (optional)

1. **Make the farro.** In a medium saucepan, bring the orange juice and 3 cups (720 ml) of water to a boil. Add the farro, bay leaves, shallot, salt, and several cracks of black pepper. Reduce to a simmer and cook until al dente (tender yet chewy), 15 to 20 minutes for pearled farro; 20 to 30 minutes for semi-pearled farro.

2. Drain the farro, then transfer it to a sheet pan, discarding the aromatics. Spread out and let dry for 15 to 20 minutes to prevent mushiness. Transfer to a large serving bowl.

3. **Meanwhile, make the spiced garlic oil.** In a small skillet over medium heat, heat the olive oil. Once it is warm but not hot, add the garlic and cook for 1 to 2 minutes, swirling the pan. Add the cumin and coriander seeds and swirl the skillet or stir frequently until the mixture is fragrant and the garlic is golden, about 1 minute. Do not let it brown. Immediately remove from the heat.

4. **Assemble the salad.** Pour the spiced oil mixture over the farro. Add the lemon zest and 2 tablespoons lemon juice and season with a bit of salt and pepper. Add the fresh herbs and toss to combine. Taste for seasonings, adding more lemon juice, salt, or pepper as needed.

5. Add the dates and toss gently. Before serving, scatter the nuts on top of the salad.

Buttery Brown Rice with Warm Spices

Serves 4 to 6 | GF, SF, NF

While I love brown rice, I know some folks think that it tastes like dirt. And to all of these people I say—this brown rice is buttery, tender, and flavor-forward (and not at all like dirt). Toasting the rice in sautéed aromatics and a Middle Eastern–inspired spice blend infuses it with warming flavors and a surprisingly rich mouthfeel, and finishing with lemon and mint adds a refreshing contrast to the heat of the spices. Baking the rice instead of simmering it on the stove keeps this mostly hands-off and makes for more evenly cooked brown rice.

Tips: Wait to add salt until the rice is done cooking, as it can prevent brown rice from cooking all the way through. When reheating leftovers, you may want to add a splash of water to keep the rice tender.

Big-Flavor Meals: Serve with steamed broccoli and Masala Baked Tofu (page 271); finish with Mint-Pistachio Pesto (page 178) or Spicy Mint & Cilantro Sauce (page 189). Or stir chickpeas and chopped greens into warmed rice. You can also use this as a bed for Maple-Roasted Squash & Chickpeas with Mint-Pistachio Pesto (page 404).

Easy Variations: Feel free to vary the spices, or use 1 heaping tablespoon of your favorite spice blend, like the shawarma blend on page 532 or the tandoori blend on page 238.

1 cup (190 g) uncooked long-grain **brown rice**, such as brown basmati rice

1 tablespoon **extra-virgin olive oil**

1 tablespoon **vegan butter** (or more olive oil)

1 small **yellow onion**, finely diced

3 **garlic cloves**, minced

1 teaspoon **ground cumin**

¾ teaspoon **ground coriander**

½ teaspoon **sweet or hot paprika**

½ teaspoon **ground turmeric**

¼ teaspoon **ground cinnamon**

¼ teaspoon **ground cloves**

⅛ teaspoon **cayenne pepper** (¼ teaspoon for more heat)

1½ to 2 teaspoons **kosher salt**

½ to 1 tablespoon freshly squeezed **lemon juice**

¾ cup (12 g) **fresh cilantro** leaves and tender stems, chopped

½ cup (8 g) **fresh mint** leaves, chopped

recipe continues

1. Arrange a rack in the middle of the oven. Preheat the oven to 375°F (190°C).

2. Rinse the rice a few times until the water runs clear. Place it in a medium bowl, cover it with warm water, and soak while you prep the other ingredients (15 to 20 minutes). When ready to use, drain the rice in a fine-mesh strainer.

3. In a medium saucepan, heat the oil and butter over medium heat. Add the onions and cook until softened and golden, 4 to 6 minutes. Add the garlic and cook for 1 minute, stirring frequently. Add the cumin, coriander, paprika, turmeric, cinnamon, cloves, and cayenne and toss to coat the spices in the onions for 1 minute. If the mixture starts to dry out, add a splash of water.

4. Add the drained rice and stir constantly to coat each grain with oil for 60 to 90 seconds. Add 1¾ cups (420 ml) of water and bring the mixture to a boil. Cover the pan with the lid and transfer to the oven. Bake for 40 minutes, or until the rice is tender and the water has been absorbed.

5. Remove from the oven and uncover the pan. Drape a clean dish towel on top of the pan and place the lid back on. Steam for 10 minutes. When you first take the pan out of the oven, some rice may appear stuck to the bottom of the pot, but after you steam it, the grains will loosen.

6. Fluff the rice with a fork. Season with 1½ teaspoons of the salt, ½ tablespoon of the lemon juice, and the cilantro. Taste, adding more salt or lemon juice as needed. To prevent the mint from blackening, fold it in just before serving.

Rosemary Farrotto with Cheesy Pine Nuts

Serves 4 to 6 | SF, NFO

I love risotto, but it's not something I can eat every day. Farro risotto, however, is. It's creamy like risotto made with arborio rice, but it's more wholesome and has an irresistible chewy, nutty bite—the best of both worlds. To unleash its true creamy potential and dramatically cut down on cook time, I soak the farro overnight, then roughly chop it to soften the grains. Full-fat oat milk and olive oil bring a buttery mouthfeel without any actual butter, and nutritional yeast adds a rich cheesiness.

Bonus: Unlike classic risotto, which quickly gets gummy, this version reheats well after several days (if needed, add a splash of broth while reheating on the stove).

Ingredient Note: Use a crisp white wine such as Sauvignon Blanc, Riesling, Pinot Gris, or Pinot Grigio. Wine enthusiasts, seek out underrated whites like Albariño, Verdicchio, or Soave.

Big-Flavor Meals: Serve with the Wildly Crunchy Cornmeal Beans (page 240), Citrus-Braised Fennel with White Beans (page 398), Marinated White Beans & Fennel with Spiced Za'atar Oil (page 245), or Cauliflower Steaks with Italian Basil & Parsley Salsa Verde (page 421). Or top with seared oyster or maitake mushrooms and vegan sausage.

Rosemary Farrotto

1½ cups (285 g) **farro** (pearled or semi-pearled)

2½ cups (600 ml) **low-sodium vegetable broth**

5 tablespoons (75 g) **extra-virgin olive oil**, plus more as needed

3 medium **shallots**, minced

Kosher salt and freshly ground **black pepper**

6 **garlic cloves**, minced

1½ tablespoons finely chopped **fresh rosemary**

½ cup (120 ml) **dry white wine** (see Ingredient Note)

¼ cup + 2 tablespoons (90 ml) **full-fat oat milk**

¼ cup (20 g) **nutritional yeast**

Cheesy Pine Nuts (optional)

⅓ cup (50 g) **pine nuts** (or walnuts)

½ cup (6 g) **fresh flat-leaf parsley** leaves, finely chopped

3 tablespoons **nutritional yeast**

1 fat **garlic clove**, grated or finely minced

recipe and ingredients continue

Pinch of **red pepper flakes** (optional)

¼ heaping teaspoon **flaky sea salt**

1. **Start the farrotto.** Place the farro in a large bowl, cover with cold water, and cover the bowl. Soak for 8 hours or overnight.

2. Drain the farro and pat dry. Transfer to a cutting board and run a chef's knife through it to roughly chop the grains (keep some whole).

3. **Make the cheesy pine nuts (if using).** Heat a small skillet over medium heat for a few minutes. Add the pine nuts and shake the pan occasionally, until golden brown, 3 to 4 minutes (if using walnuts, toast on medium-low heat for 3 to 5 minutes, then finely chop). Transfer to a small bowl and allow to cool. Stir in the parsley, nutritional yeast, garlic, pepper flakes (if using), and flaky salt. Set aside.

4. In a medium saucepan, heat the broth over medium-high heat until it comes to a rapid simmer. Lower the heat to maintain a gentle simmer.

5. In a large, deep sauté pan or Dutch oven, heat 3 tablespoons of the olive oil over medium heat. Once it is warm but not hot, add the shallots and season with a pinch of kosher salt. Cook, stirring frequently, until just softened, 4 to 5 minutes. Add the garlic and rosemary and cook for 1 minute, stirring frequently to prevent browning.

6. Add the farro, coating each grain in the oil, and cook until the farro starts to crackle, 1 to 2 minutes. If the mixture starts to stick, add a splash more oil. Pour in the wine and scrape up any browned bits. Simmer until mostly evaporated, about 5 minutes. Give it a sniff and make sure the smell of booze has worn off.

7. Ladle in 1 cup (240 ml, about two soup ladles) of the warm broth and stir frequently but not constantly, about every 30 seconds. Once the farro is mostly dry, add the next round of broth, 1 cup (240 ml) at a time. Continue this process and adjust the heat as needed to maintain a rapid simmer, until the farrotto is creamy and tender but still retains a chewy bite, about 15 minutes total. You may reach your desired texture before all the broth is used up.

8. In a small bowl, combine the oat milk and the remaining 2 tablespoons oil. When the farrotto is done, pour in this milk mixture and the nutritional yeast. Cook until thickened and creamy, 1 to 2 minutes. Season with kosher salt and black pepper to taste (I add about ½ teaspoon kosher salt if making the topping; use a bit more salt if omitting it).

9. Serve the farrotto in bowls, sprinkle the cheesy pine nuts on top of each bowl (if using), and drizzle with a little more olive oil.

Crispy Quinoa Salad with Savory Herbed Almonds

Serves 3 to 4 as a main, 8 as a side | GF, SF, NFO

I wish I loved quinoa because it's really good for you, but we don't get to choose the taste buds we're born with. The one exception I make is for *toasted* quinoa. It's crispy, a little chewy, and actually very fun. And when you toss it with a deeply savory, herby nut mix, you have the base for an amazing, texture-rich salad. Toasting the almonds in umeboshi paste makes them savory beyond your wildest dreams, while rosemary infuses a deep woodsy aroma into the salad. You can make this heartier by folding in chunks of avocado.

Ingredient Note: Umeboshi paste is an umami powerhouse and is worth seeking out. Find it at East Asian markets, online, or in well-stocked stores like Whole Foods. In a pinch, you can substitute 1 tablespoon white miso. Let the miso come to room temperature before adding it to the hot pan.

Tips: Make a double batch of the herbed almonds, and shower them on grain salads, green salads, and pureed soups.

NF Option: Use pepitas (shelled pumpkin seeds) instead of almonds; don't chop them and cook until toasty.

1 cup (180 g) uncooked **quinoa**, rinsed and drained

Kosher salt and freshly ground **black pepper**

1 tablespoon **extra-virgin olive oil**

Salad

1 (15-ounce/425 g) can **chickpeas**, drained and rinsed

1 medium **lemon**, juiced

1 teaspoon **extra-virgin olive oil**

Kosher salt and freshly ground **black pepper**

2 cups (33 g) **arugula**, **watercress**, or **salad green** of choice

1 cup (12 g) **fresh flat-leaf parsley** leaves, roughly chopped

Savory Herbed Almonds

½ cup (70 g) **raw almonds**, roughly chopped (a couple of pieces per almond)

3 tablespoons **extra-virgin olive oil**

2 teaspoons **umeboshi paste** (see Ingredient Note)

1 tablespoon finely chopped **fresh rosemary**

1 medium **lemon**, zested and juiced

1 to 2 teaspoons **Aleppo pepper** or **Urfa biber** (1 teaspoon for mild heat)

1 fat **garlic clove**, grated or finely minced

recipe continues

1. In a small or medium saucepan, bring 1¼ cups (300 ml) of water to a boil, then add the quinoa and a pinch of salt. Stir to combine. Reduce the heat to low, cover, and cook until the liquid has evaporated and the quinoa is tender, about 12 minutes. Fluff with a fork. Transfer the quinoa to a large sheet pan and spread it out in an even layer. Allow to cool slightly.

2. **Start the salad.** In a medium bowl, toss the chickpeas with the lemon juice, 1 teaspoon olive oil, ½ teaspoon salt, and several cracks of pepper. Set aside.

3. **Make the almonds.** In a small or medium saucepan, heat the almonds and 3 tablespoons olive oil over medium heat. Stir occasionally, until the almonds are a few shades darker but not totally browned, 5 to 6 minutes. Add the umeboshi paste and rosemary and cook, stirring frequently, for 1 minute. Add the lemon zest and Aleppo pepper and stir frequently for 30 seconds. Turn off the heat, add the garlic, and pour the mixture into a small bowl to stop the cooking process.

4. **Toast the quinoa.** Arrange an oven rack directly underneath the broiler and preheat the broiler to medium for about 5 minutes (see Note below). Toss the quinoa with the 1 tablespoon olive oil and season with a few pinches of salt and black pepper. Broil for 4 minutes, then stir the quinoa and rotate the pan by 180 degrees. Broil for 3 to 4 more minutes, or until some grains are golden brown and the quinoa is crispy.

   Note: If your broiler doesn't have a medium setting, arrange a rack on the second shelf and preheat to high. Broil the quinoa for 5 minutes, then stir it and rotate the pan by 180 degrees. Broil for 3 to 4 minutes, toss again, and broil for 3 to 4 more minutes if needed.

5. **Assemble the salad.** Transfer the quinoa to a large serving bowl. Add the arugula and chickpeas. Spoon the almond mixture on top, including any oil. Toss very well to coat all the quinoa in the oil. Add 1½ tablespoons lemon juice to the quinoa, along with the parsley, and toss again. Taste, adding additional lemon juice as needed, and season with salt and black pepper to taste. For leftovers, allow the salad to come to room temperature and add a squeeze of lemon juice and a pinch of salt if needed.

Creamy Baked Wild Rice with Carrots

Serves 4 to 6 as a side | GF, SF, NF

Wild rice is earthy and smoky, but slow baking it in coconut milk and a bit of maple syrup softens its intensity and makes it truly indulgent. Braising carrots with the rice makes them fall-apart silky and buttery, accenting the sweet notes of this dish. The finished dish has the creaminess of a rice pudding with plenty of chew and the perfect savory-and-sweet balance.

While wild rice has a long cook time, this is a pretty hands-off dish, making it a good option for weeknights when you can get an early start.

Tip: Don't soak the rice for longer than 3 hours, as the grains start to burst open. If you don't have time to soak the rice, rinse it well and cook for 65 to 75 minutes.

Easy Variations: Sub finely chopped butternut or kabocha squash for the carrots. Sear sliced cremini or oyster mushrooms before adding the garlic. Stir in finely chopped tender greens after baking.

1 cup (175 g) uncooked **wild rice** or **wild rice blend**

2 tablespoons **avocado oil**, **olive oil**, or **neutral-flavored oil** of choice

1 medium **yellow onion**, diced

Kosher salt and freshly ground **black pepper**

4 **garlic cloves**, finely chopped

1-inch (2.5 cm) piece **fresh ginger**, grated or minced

¾ teaspoon **red pepper flakes**

¼ teaspoon **ground turmeric**

2 tablespoons **pure maple syrup**

2 cups (480 ml) **vegetable broth**

1 cup (240 ml) **full-fat coconut milk**, well stirred

4 to 5 medium **carrots**, sliced on a bias (about ¼ inch/ 0.5 cm thick)

1 (15-ounce/425 g) can **white beans** or **chickpeas** (optional), drained and rinsed

¾ cup (12 g) **fresh cilantro** leaves and tender stems, chopped

1 medium **lime**, zested

1 tablespoon freshly squeezed **lime juice**, plus more to taste

recipe continues

1. Rinse the rice under running water for about 30 seconds, then drain. Add the rice to a medium bowl, cover with warm water, and soak for 2 to 3 hours, then drain (see Tip).

2. Arrange a rack in the middle of the oven. Preheat the oven to 400°F (205°C).

3. In a small or medium Dutch oven or oven-safe deep sauté pan, heat the oil over medium heat. Add the onions, season with a pinch of salt, and cook for 3 to 4 minutes, stirring occasionally, until just starting to soften. Add the garlic, ginger, pepper flakes, turmeric, ½ teaspoon salt, and 1 tablespoon of the maple syrup. Cook until the mixture is a bit sticky, 2 minutes.

4. Add the rice and stir to coat all the grains in the oil, cooking for 1 to 2 minutes. Pour in the broth and coconut milk, scraping up any browned bits. Add the carrots, the remaining 1 tablespoon maple syrup, and the beans or chickpeas (if using). Bring to a boil. Turn off the heat, cover the pan, transfer to the oven, and bake for 50 to 65 minutes, until the rice is chewy but tender and cooked through, not crunchy (wild rice blends should need only 50 minutes; see Tip).

5. Let rest, covered, for 5 minutes, then stir in the cilantro, lime zest, and lime juice. Season with salt and black pepper as needed and add more lime juice to taste.

Lemongrass Ginger Rice

Serves 4 | GF, NFO

I am not a "rice person." I know. My Indian family members and Asian friends also think I'm weird for it.

The exception is this lemongrass rice, which fuses Chinese, Japanese, and Thai flavors into a lighter, more herbaceous version of fried rice. Cooking the rice in green tea, a surprising source of umami, infuses it with savoriness, while lemongrass adds its delicate yet ornate aroma and lime adds bright, zesty notes. Ginger adds sweet warmth, and peanuts bring the perfect contrasting crunch to the tender rice.

The first time I made this, I ate the entire batch in one day, periodically exclaiming to no one but myself, *But I don't even like rice that much! I guess I do?*

Ingredient Notes: Don't have loose-leaf green tea? Use 2 or 3 plain Japanese green tea bags (no blueberry green tea!). Or skip the tea, and cook the rice in 1½ cups (360 ml) of water. If you are using a white rice other than jasmine, it may need a few minutes longer. If you have Life-Changing Homemade Chili Crisp (page 187), omit the sliced chile and top with chili crisp when serving. The peanuts are fabulous here, so don't skip them unless you are allergic.

Tip: For instructions on how to mince lemongrass, see page 472.

Big-Flavor Meals: Pair with store-bought tofu puffs, or make the Crispy Sesame Baked Tofu (page 270); round out with steamed or stir-fried broccolini, bok choy, or green beans.

2 tablespoons Japanese (or Chinese) **green tea leaves**, such as sencha (see Ingredient Notes)

1½ cups (360 ml) **boiling water**

1 cup (190 g) uncooked **white jasmine rice** (see Ingredient Notes)

Kosher salt

1 teaspoon + 1½ tablespoons **grapeseed oil** or **neutral-flavored oil** of choice

4 **lemongrass** stalks, minced (1½ to 2 tablespoons; see Tip)

2½ tablespoons grated or minced **fresh ginger**

6 **garlic cloves**, minced

3 **scallions**, thinly sliced (reserve dark green tops for garnish)

1 **Thai chile**, thinly sliced (omit for mild heat; see Ingredient Notes)

2 teaspoons **tamari** or **soy sauce** (use tamari to keep GF)

1 medium **lime**, zested

1½ tablespoons freshly squeezed **lime juice**

½ cup (8 g) **fresh cilantro** leaves and tender stems, chopped

⅓ cup (47 g) **unsalted dry-roasted peanuts**, roughly chopped (omit if nut-free)

recipe continues

1. Add the tea leaves to a bowl and cover with the boiling water. Cover with a plate and steep for 5 to 6 minutes.

2. Place the rice in a large bowl and run under cold tap water. While the water is running, agitate the rice with your hands for 1 minute. Drain in a fine-mesh sieve and transfer the rice to a medium saucepan. Fit the sieve on top of the pan. Pour the hot steeped tea into the sieve, so the tea goes into the rice; push the tea leaves against the sieve to squeeze out all the water; discard the tea leaves. Stir ¼ teaspoon salt and 1 teaspoon of the oil into the rice. Bring to a boil, then reduce the heat to a simmer, cover, and cook until the liquid is absorbed and the rice is tender (you may want to uncover the pan once or twice to ensure it's at a simmer, but don't stir), 7 to 8 minutes. Remove from the heat, uncover the pan, drape a clean dish towel on top of the pan, and place the lid back on. Steam for 10 minutes, then fluff the rice with a fork.

3. In a small bowl, combine the lemongrass with the ginger, garlic, white and light green parts of the scallions, and chile (if using).

4. Heat a small or medium skillet over medium-high heat for a few minutes. Add the remaining 1½ tablespoons oil and, once hot, add the lemongrass mixture. Stir frequently and cook until the mixture is very fragrant, 2 minutes. Remove from the heat.

5. Uncover the rice and add the lemongrass mixture. Season with ¼ teaspoon salt and toss well to coat the rice. Add the tamari, lime zest, and lime juice and toss again. Before serving, garnish with cilantro, peanuts, and the reserved scallion greens.

Pearl Couscous & Chickpea Salad with Preserved Lemon

Serves 8 as a side, 4 as a main | GFO, SF, NFO

When I have served this salad at dinner parties or al fresco lunches, a few guests have shyly said on more than one occasion, *"Ohhh, no offense, but I don't love couscous . . ."* Yet minutes later, there they were—eating not just one spoonful to be polite, but an entire bowlful.

To be fair, pearl couscous is not regular couscous. It's delightfully bouncy and chewy, and toasting it first brings out its slightly nutty flavor. When you add fragrant fresh herbs, buttery pistachios, and salty preserved lemons, it's easy to convert any couscous cynic. Another plus: If you keep preserved lemons in your fridge (as I insist you do), this dish comes together very quickly.

Easy Variations: Substitute cooked lentils or white beans for the chickpeas, cucumbers or shaved fennel for the bell pepper, more cilantro for the parsley, walnuts or pepitas for the pistachios, or dates for the apricots.

GF Option: Cook 1 cup (190 g) long-grain brown rice or 1 cup (195 g) millet instead of couscous.

NF Option: Use pepitas (shelled pumpkin seeds) instead of pistachios.

3 tablespoons **extra-virgin olive oil**, plus more as needed

1 cup (150 g) uncooked **pearl couscous**

¾ teaspoon **fine sea salt**, plus more to taste

2½ tablespoons finely chopped **preserved lemon peel** (page 157)

2 tablespoons freshly squeezed **lemon juice**

½ to 1 teaspoon **Aleppo pepper** (use 1 teaspoon for *spicy!*) or ¼ teaspoon **red pepper flakes**, plus more to taste

1 (15-ounce/425 g) can **chickpeas**, drained and rinsed

1 medium **red, orange, or yellow bell pepper**, diced (not a green pepper, please!)

¾ cup (12 g) **fresh cilantro** leaves and tender stems, chopped

¾ cup (12 g) **fresh flat-leaf parsley** leaves and tender stems, chopped

¼ cup (4 g) **fresh mint** leaves, chopped

⅓ cup (43 g) **shelled pistachios**, roughly chopped

6 to 8 **dried apricots** (preferably Turkish), chopped

recipe continues

1. In a medium saucepan, heat a touch of olive oil over medium heat. Add the couscous and toast, stirring frequently, until golden, 4 to 5 minutes. Add 1¼ cups (300 ml) of water and ¼ teaspoon of the salt. Increase the heat and bring to a boil. Reduce the heat and simmer, covered, until the liquid is absorbed and the couscous is just tender, 9 to 10 minutes. Set aside to cool slightly, but don't let it sit too long before dressing, as it will start to get clumpy.

2. Meanwhile, in a small bowl, combine the preserved lemon peel, the 3 tablespoons olive oil, and the lemon juice. Season with ½ teaspoon salt and the Aleppo pepper.

3. Transfer the cooked couscous to a serving bowl. Add the chickpeas, bell pepper, cilantro, parsley, mint, pistachios, and apricots. Drizzle with the lemon dressing and toss to combine. Season with salt to taste and an additional pinch or two of Aleppo pepper, if desired. Serve warm or at room temperature.

The Everyday Veggies

Once you've got your proteins, grains, and condiments sorted, it's so easy to whip up nearly any meal using whatever fresh produce you have on hand. In this short chapter, you'll find quick yet delicious vegetable staples I turn to on busy weeknights.

These recipes are intentionally simple to maximize their versatility: you can pair them with all kinds of meals and cuisines. And each recipe offers recommended pairings to jump-start your creativity.

See chapter 10 for dinners where veggies are the "main event." (I love those meals too!)

Spice-Roasted Whole Carrots

Serves 4 | GF, SF, NF

Roasting carrots at high heat concentrates their natural sweetness and gives them a nice caramelized exterior and slight char. While optional, roasting Medjool dates alongside the carrots creates layers of sweet flavor and amplifies the dates' sweet chewiness.

Ingredient Note: This method works best with skinny carrots, but if yours aren't skinny, slice the fatter top halves in half vertically (keep the thinner bottoms whole).

Big-Flavor Meals

× Dollop with Mint-Pistachio Pesto (page 178) and serve with the Customizable Grain Salad with Garlicky Spiced Oil & Fresh Herbs (page 305).

× Serve over Mint Yogurt Sauce (page 213) and garnish with Indian Peanut Crunchies (page 227); serve with Masala Baked Tofu (page 271) or Tandoori Roasted Chickpeas (page 238) for a complete meal.

× For a lighter meal, spoon Turkish-Spiced Tahini Sauce (page 198) on top and sprinkle with Hazelnut Dukkah (page 219) or Crispy Fennel-Spiced Crumbs (page 228).

1 teaspoon **coriander seeds**

1 teaspoon **cumin seeds**

½ teaspoon **caraway seeds** (or use more cumin or coriander)

2 tablespoons **extra-virgin olive oil**

2 pounds (910 g) skinny **carrots**, scrubbed but not peeled (see Ingredient Note)

Kosher salt and freshly ground **black pepper**

8 **Medjool dates** (135 g), pitted and chopped (optional)

1. Preheat the oven to 425°F (220°C).

2. Lightly crush the coriander, cumin, and caraway seeds in a mortar with a pestle or add to a spice grinder and pulse once. They don't need to be finely crushed, just opened up a bit. For alternative methods, see page 74. Add the seeds to a small bowl and whisk in the olive oil.

3. Spread out the whole carrots on a rimmed sheet pan, or two sheet pans, depending on the size of your carrots (don't overcrowd them, otherwise they will steam).

4. Drizzle the spiced oil over the carrots and season generously with salt and pepper. Roast for 15 to 25 minutes (depending on how skinny the carrots are), until fork-tender. Take the pan out, stir the carrots, and add the dates (if using). Roast for 7 to 10 more minutes, until the carrots are tender and deeply browned in spots and the dates are chewy and a little charred on the bottom.

Jammy Zucchini

Serves 4 | GF, SF, NF

You might associate zucchini with meh flavor, or with "zoodles" (which are decidedly *not* the same as pasta, though some folks may try to convince you otherwise). But when you cook it in a hot pan with olive oil and garlic, zucchini can be exquisite—meltingly tender, jammy, and unctuous.

Ingredient Note: The best season for zucchini is summer through midfall.

Tip: If your cast-iron skillet isn't big enough to fit all the zucchini, cook in two batches.

Big-Flavor Meals: For a lighter meal or appetizer, serve on a bed of Mint Yogurt Sauce (page 213), garnish with cilantro and mint, and serve with warm pita (as shown here). Pair with the Whipped Tofu Ricotta (page 206) or Whipped Feta (page 209) and layer on open-faced sandwiches. Or serve with Pomegranate-Glazed Tofu (page 277) and Buttery Brown Rice with Warm Spices (page 309) or Pearl Couscous & Chickpea Salad with Preserved Lemon (page 323) for a gourmet dinner.

1½ pounds (680 g) ripe **zucchini** (about 3 medium or 5 to 6 small)

3 tablespoons **extra-virgin olive oil**

1 teaspoon **kosher salt**, plus more to taste

6 **garlic cloves**, thinly sliced

1. Cut each zucchini lengthwise into quarters, then cut each quarter crosswise into ¾-inch (2 cm) chunks.

2. Heat an 11- or 12-inch (28 or 30 cm) cast-iron skillet over medium-high heat for 2 minutes, then add the olive oil and wait until it's shimmering, about 30 seconds. Add the zucchini, coating all the pieces in the oil. Season with the salt and spread out in a single layer as much as possible. Cook without stirring for 4 minutes to allow some browning. Toss well, then add the garlic. Stir occasionally and cook until the zucchini starts to break down, 3 to 4 minutes.

3. Reduce the heat to medium-low. Cook, stirring every 2 to 3 minutes (reduce the heat a touch as needed to prevent too much sticking), until the zucchini is soft and jammy, 15 to 20 minutes.

Garlicky Kale

Serves 4 | GF, SF, NF

This is my easy go-to method for getting leafy greens into my diet when it's too cold to eat a salad. And while kale stems are basically horse roughage in a salad, when they're thinly sliced and sautéed, they are delightful and crunchy.

Ingredient Note: Feel free to swap rainbow or Swiss chard for the kale.

Big-Flavor Meals

× Kale needs something fatty to make it shine. Serve over a schmear of Whipped Feta (page 209) as shown here or Yogurt Sauce with Chile Oil (page 213). Top with Roasted Chickpeas (page 236) or Wildly Crunchy Cornmeal Beans (page 240) and any quick-pickled vegetables (page 168) or sauerkraut. Round out the meal with pan-fried slabs of crispy bread.

× Serve over a generous dollop of a tahini sauce (page 197) with pan-fried tofu (page 268), or over Mint Yogurt Sauce (page 213) with Masala Baked Tofu (page 271).

1 large bunch (or 2 small bunches) **lacinato kale** (see Ingredient Note)

1½ tablespoons **extra-virgin olive oil**

4 **garlic cloves**, chopped

1½ teaspoons **Aleppo pepper** (or ½ to ¾ teaspoon red pepper flakes)

Kosher salt

1 **lemon** (optional)

1. Hold each kale leaf vertically, top facing down. Pinch your thumb and index finger together and grab the stem, then move in a downward motion to strip the middle rib away from the leaves. Slice the kale ribs thinly. Tear the leaves into pieces, about 2 inches (5 cm) each, and set apart from the ribs. Wash the leaves well, then dry in a salad spinner. Do the same for the stems.

2. In a large sauté pan, heat the olive oil over medium heat. Once it is warm but not hot, add the garlic and cook until it's just barely turning golden, 1½ to 2 minutes. Add the Aleppo pepper and stir for 30 seconds, then add the kale stems. Cook for 1 to 2 minutes, then add the kale leaves and season with a few pinches of salt. Toss to coat and cook until the kale leaves are a bit softer and the stems are still a bit crunchy, 1 to 2 minutes. If desired, zest some lemon peel and squeeze a bit of lemon juice on top before serving.

Lemon-Garlic Brussels Sprouts with Rosemary

Serves 6 | GF, SF, NFO

Roasted Brussels sprouts are always good but even better when tossed with gently fried aromatics. Thinly sliced lemon peel breathes new life into sprouts with its supremely tart and citrusy flavors, rosemary lends a pleasing woodsy aroma, and shallots and garlic add a flavor-rich backbone. Finishing with flaky salt, balsamic, and toasted walnuts brings salty savoriness, a sweet zing, and a nutty crunch.

Ingredient Note: If you're using medium to large sprouts, you should be able to fit everything on one sheet pan. If your sprouts are small, use two sheet pans and arrange a second rack in the bottom of your oven (spreading the sprouts out allows them to roast instead of steam). Brussels sprouts are best in fall and winter.

Tip: A well-worn sheet pan makes for superior (and quicker) browning (the sprouts should be done in 20 to 22 minutes).

Big-Flavor Meals: Serve over farro or brown rice with the Spiced Lentil Salad with Fresh Herbs (page 257), Marinated Chickpeas (page 243), or Wildly Crunchy Cornmeal Beans (page 240).

2 pounds (910 g) **Brussels sprouts**, trimmed and halved (see Ingredient Note)

5½ tablespoons (83 g) **extra-virgin olive oil**

Kosher salt and freshly ground **black pepper**

1 large **lemon**

½ cup (56 g) **walnuts** (sub pepitas or sunflower seeds if nut-free)

2 large **shallots**, thinly sliced into rounds

8 **garlic cloves**, thinly sliced

½ teaspoon **red pepper flakes**

1 tablespoon + 1 teaspoon finely chopped **fresh rosemary**

Flaky sea salt

2 to 3 teaspoons **aged balsamic vinegar**

1 large handful **fresh flat-leaf parsley** leaves and tender stems, chopped

1. Arrange a rack in the top third of the oven. Preheat the oven to 425°F (220°C).

2. In a large bowl, toss the Brussels sprouts with 4 tablespoons of the olive oil, 2 teaspoons kosher salt, and a generous amount of black pepper.

recipe continues

3. Arrange the sprouts cut side down on a sheet pan (see Tip) in a single layer, including any loose leaves. Roast for 15 minutes, then check the bottoms to see if they're nicely browned. If so, stir or toss and roast for 5 to 10 more minutes (well-worn sheet pans should need only 5 to 6 minutes). If the sprouts are not yet browned, rotate the pan by 180 degrees and roast for 10 more minutes. Remove from the oven.

4. Use a vegetable peeler to peel the lemon into strips, but don't peel the white pith underneath. Slice the lemon peel strips into very thin matchsticks.

5. Heat a medium skillet over medium-low heat for a couple of minutes. Add the walnuts and toast, shaking the pan frequently to prevent burning, until nutty, 3 to 5 minutes. For oven toasting instructions, see page 115. Roughly chop the walnuts.

6. In the same skillet, heat the remaining 1½ tablespoons oil over medium heat. Once it is warm but not hot, add the shallots with a pinch of kosher salt. Cook, stirring occasionally, until the shallots start to turn golden, 3 to 5 minutes. Add the garlic and cook, stirring frequently, until it just turns golden, 2 minutes. Add the pepper flakes, rosemary, lemon peel, and a few pinches of flaky salt, and cook for 1 minute, stirring almost constantly. Remove from the heat and transfer to a serving bowl.

7. Add the roasted sprouts to the serving bowl with the aromatics. Drizzle with 2 teaspoons of the balsamic vinegar and add a pinch of flaky salt. Toss well to coat the sprouts. Add the parsley and walnuts and gently toss again. Taste, adding more balsamic or flaky salt as desired. Serve immediately.

Roasted Butternut Wedges

Serves 4 to 6 | GF, SF, NF

Hefty wedges of squash are roasted in spices and maple syrup until browned for a sweet-spicy-earthy flavor profile. Keeping the skin on butternut squash not only saves time and food waste but also adds textural interest: you get soft, creamy flesh with a slightly crisp and chewy caramelized exterior.

Ingredient Note: Swap with kabocha squash, acorn squash, or other winter squash. For a smoky flavor, use chipotle chile flakes instead of red pepper flakes. Butternut squash is available year-round but is best in fall and winter.

Big-Flavor Meals

× Pair with Saucy Black Beans in Sofrito (page 250) or Wildly Crunchy Cornmeal Beans (page 240) and a bed of brown rice.

× For lighter meals or sides, spoon Avocado Crema (page 204) or Chipotle Crema on top (page 205); scatter with toasted pepitas (shelled pumpkin seeds). Or serve with Preserved Lemon Salsa (page 184) and vegan feta.

1 medium-large **butternut squash** (2½ to 3 pounds/1.1 to 1.3 kg)

1½ tablespoons **avocado oil** or **neutral-flavored oil** of choice

1 tablespoon + 1 teaspoon **pure maple syrup**

1½ teaspoons **ground cumin**

1 teaspoon **ground coriander**

½ teaspoon **red pepper flakes** (see Ingredient Note)

1½ teaspoons **kosher salt**

Freshly ground **black pepper**

1. Preheat the oven to 450°F (230°C). Line two rimmed sheet pans with parchment paper (for easier cleanup).

2. Wash and scrub the squash (you'll be eating the peel) and cut the stem off. Use a sharp knife to slice the squash in half crosswise. If you have trouble, microwave the whole squash for 2 minutes to soften. Cut the top skinny neck in half lengthwise, and then cut into spears that are 1 to 1½ inches (2.5 to 3.75 cm) wide. Cut the bottom fat part of the squash in half lengthwise, scoop out the seeds and stringy bits from the cavity, and cut into 1- to 1½ inch-wide (2.5 to 3.75 cm) wedges. Transfer the squash pieces to a large bowl.

3. In a small bowl, combine the oil and maple syrup. In another small bowl, stir together the cumin, coriander, pepper flakes, salt, and a generous amount of black pepper.

4. Drizzle the butternut squash with the oil and maple syrup mixture, then sprinkle it with the spice mixture. Toss with your hands to ensure the squash is well coated. Transfer the squash wedges to the prepared pans and spread out so they have space to brown. Roast for 25 minutes, or until the squash is tender and nicely browned on the edges (no need to flip).

Jammy Roasted Eggplant

Serves 4 | GF, SF, NF

Eggplant can be hard to get right and is often either dry and rubbery or oil-drenched, but this method has convinced more than one eggplant-hater that eggplant can be marvelous. When roasted at high heat with just the right amount of fat, it becomes impossibly tender and almost custard-like.

Ingredient Note: This low-fuss method works with skinny eggplants, like Japanese or Chinese (or anything your farmers' market sells), as they break down easily and have a creamy flesh. Skip the large, seed-heavy globe eggplants. Eggplant is best from summer through midfall.

Big-Flavor Meals

× Serve on a bed of Yogurt-Tahini Sauce (page 215) and garnish with mint and pomegranate seeds, as shown here. Scatter Crunchy Roasted Chickpeas (page 236) on top and serve with hunks of bread.

× Pair with the Marinated White Beans & Fennel with Spiced Za'atar Oil (page 245), Marinated Chickpeas (page 243), or Spiced Lentil Salad with Fresh Herbs (page 257).

2 pounds (910 g) skinny **eggplants** (see Ingredient Note)

¼ cup (56 g) **avocado oil**, **grapeseed oil**, or **neutral-flavored high-heat oil** of choice

1 teaspoon **kosher salt**

Freshly ground **black pepper**

1. Arrange one rack in the bottom of the oven and one in the top third. Preheat the oven to 450°F (230°C). Line two sheet pans with parchment paper.

2. Using a peeler, peel the eggplant in alternating strips from top to bottom (or peel entirely). Cut into wedges 3 inches long and ¾ to 1 inch wide (8 cm long and 2 to 2.5 cm wide). In a large bowl, combine the eggplant wedges with the oil, salt, and pepper to taste. Toss well, then divide across the two prepared sheet pans, arranging the wedges flat side down.

3. Roast for 25 minutes, then flip a piece over to see if it's done: it should be charred on the outside but tender and jammy when pierced with a knife. If not done, roast for another 10 minutes, until deeply golden brown and charred on the outside but tender and soft on the inside (it will cook faster on well-worn sheet pans; fatter eggplant varieties will need 40 to 45 minutes total).

Collard Greens with Sesame–Miso Cream

Serves 4 | GF, NF

When I first went vegan, several folks tried to convince me that collard green wraps were just as good as regular wraps. They were wrong, and I was left underwhelmed (and hungry). But *cooked* collard greens, I can get down with.

Here, the greens are thinly sliced and sautéed with aromatics, then steam-braised with toasty, sweet, and umami-rich flavors until they're tender-chewy, with an almost buttery texture. Finishing with dollops of a creamy, nutty, tangy tahini sauce adds a little indulgence, while sesame seeds play up all the toasty sesame flavors and add a delicate crunch.

Ingredient Note: Collard green season varies by location, but they're often good year-round.

Big-Flavor Meals: Serve with white or brown rice and seasoned edamame or Crispy Sesame Baked Tofu (page 270). For a more gourmet meal, pair with rice and Sticky Coconut Milk–Braised Tofu (page 278).

1½ pounds (680 g) **collard greens** (2 large or 3 medium bunches)

2 tablespoons **toasted sesame oil**

1½ teaspoons **pure maple syrup** or **agave nectar** (or Spicy "Honey" with Candied Jalapeños, page 176)

1 tablespoon **tamari** or **soy sauce** (use tamari to keep GF)

¼ teaspoon **red pepper flakes**

1 tablespoon **grapeseed oil** or **neutral-flavored oil** of choice

3 **scallions**, sliced on a bias (reserve dark green tops for garnish)

2 **garlic cloves**, thinly sliced

1-inch (2.5 cm) piece **fresh ginger**, julienned (cut into very thin strips)

2 tablespoons well-stirred **tahini**

1 tablespoon **rice vinegar** (or freshly squeezed lime juice)

1 tablespoon **white miso paste**

1 tablespoon **roasted black or white sesame seeds**

1. Cut out and discard the thick middle rib from each collard leaf. Stack the leaves and roll them up like cigars, like you would do for basil. Slice the leaves into ribbons. Wash the leaves well, then dry in a salad spinner.

2. In a small bowl, stir together the sesame oil, maple syrup, tamari, and pepper flakes.

3. Heat a large, deep sauté pan for which you have a lid over medium heat. Add the oil, and once it's warm, add the white and light green parts of the scallions, garlic, and ginger and cook until the garlic turns golden, stirring occasionally to prevent burning, 2 to 3 minutes.

4. Add the greens in batches, pushing them down as you add each batch to create space. Once they're all in, add the sauce, toss to combine, and cover the pan. Cook until the greens are tender but still retain a bit of chew, 7 to 10 minutes. Use tongs or a slotted spoon to lift the greens onto a serving plate, leaving the excess liquid behind in the pan.

5. In a small bowl (you can use the same bowl from step 2), whisk together the tahini, rice vinegar, and miso. Add a couple of spoonfuls of water until the texture is thick but pourable.

6. To serve, drizzle the miso tahini on top of the greens and scatter on the sesame seeds and reserved scallion greens. Gently toss to combine.

Quick Roasted Cauliflower

Serves 4 | GF, SF, NF

Roasted cauliflower is quite possibly the most versatile vegetable side dish, and all you need is a hot oven, olive oil, salt, and twenty minutes.

Big-Flavor Meals

× Drizzle with a tahini sauce (page 197); scatter with toasted pine nuts, parsley, capers, and chopped dates. Top with Hazelnut Dukkah (page 219), as shown here.

× Use a second sheet pan to make the Crunchy Roasted Chickpeas (page 236) or Wildly Crunchy Cornmeal Beans (page 240). Top with Spicy Mint & Cilantro Sauce (page 189).

× For a lighter meal or side, spoon Herby Shallot-Garlic Confit (page 163) on top and sprinkle with any of the Crispy & Crunchy Things from chapter 5.

1 large head **cauliflower** (about 1½ pounds/680 g florets)

3 tablespoons **extra-virgin olive oil**

1½ teaspoons **kosher salt**

Freshly ground **black pepper**

1. Arrange an oven rack in the top third of the oven. Preheat the oven to 450°F (230°C).

2. Cut out the core from the cauliflower and remove any leaves. Cut into medium-size florets, ideally cutting the florets in half through the stem so you end up with a flat surface on one side (these brown better).

3. Transfer the florets to a rimmed sheet pan (ideally a well-worn one for better browning) and drizzle on the olive oil. Rub the oil up in the nooks and crannies of the florets, then season with the salt and several cracks of pepper. Spread out, flat sides facing down, and roast for 10 minutes. Don't toss the cauliflower but rotate the pan 180 degrees for even browning. Roast for 10 to 12 more minutes, until the cauliflower is nicely browned and tender. If the florets seem stuck to the pan, let rest for a few minutes, then remove from the pan.

Charred Sweet Potato Wedges

Serves 8 | GF, SF, NF

Leaving the skin on sweet potatoes saves on prep time and adds texture, while charring the potatoes instead of just roasting introduces more flavor dimension beyond pure sweetness.

Big-Flavor Meals

× Serve with Tandoori Roasted Chickpeas (page 238) or Tandoori-flavored Wildly Crunchy Cornmeal Beans (page 240). Top with Mint Yogurt Sauce (page 213).

× Drizzle with any tahini sauce (page 197) and serve with Marinated Chickpeas (page 243).

× For a crowd-pleasing appetizer or side, serve over a bed of Whipped Feta (page 209) and lightly drizzle with Spicy "Honey" with Candied Jalapeños (page 176).

5 to 6 medium **sweet potatoes**, ideally long, skinny ones (3 pounds/1.4 kg)

¼ cup (56 g) **grapeseed oil** or **neutral-flavored oil** of choice

1½ teaspoons **kosher salt**

Freshly ground **black pepper**

Flaky sea salt

1. Arrange one rack in the bottom of the oven and one in the top third. Preheat the oven to 425°F (220°C). When hot, transfer two rimmed sheet pans to the racks for 10 minutes.

2. Wash and scrub the potatoes but don't peel them. Cut each potato in half lengthwise, then into wedges 2 to 3 inches long and ¾ inch wide (5 to 7.5 cm long and 2 cm wide). Transfer to a large bowl and drizzle with the oil and season with the salt and lots of pepper. Toss with your hands to evenly distribute the oil.

3. Using oven mitts, remove the pans from the oven. Spread the potatoes out across both pans, flesh side down. Roast for 20 minutes, then rotate the pans by 180 degrees and swap their rack positions. Roast for 10 to 20 more minutes, until charred in some spots and completely tender when tested with a paring knife (the potatoes cook faster on well-worn sheet pans). Transfer to a serving platter and sprinkle with a pinch of flaky salt.

How to Use Chapters 5 Through 8 for Meal Planning

× ×

In my own weeknight cooking, I often turn to a flavor-packed condiment to help with meal planning for the next few days. Below are six examples of how to start with a condiment from chapter 5 and build several meals around it.

#1

Starting Sauce

Mint-Pistachio Pesto (page 178)

Meal Prep

- ○ Make the Mint-Pistachio Pesto.
- ○ Cook a big pot of white or brown rice.
- ○ Make a double batch of the Tandoori Spice Blend (page 238).

Meals to Make During the Week

MEAL #1: Make the Tandoori Roasted Chickpeas (page 238) and the Jammy Roasted Eggplant (page 339). Drizzle with the pesto and serve with rice and/or a simple green salad.

MEAL #2: Make the Maple-Roasted Squash & Chickpeas with Mint-Pistachio Pesto (page 404). Serve over rice.

MEAL #3: Make the Tandoori-flavored Crunchy Cornmeal Beans (page 240) and Charred Sweet Potato Wedges (page 345). Drizzle with the pesto and serve with a simple green salad.

#2

Starting Sauce

Avocado Crema (page 204)

Meal Prep

- ○ Make the Avocado Crema.
- ○ Make a batch of quick-pickled onions (page 168).

Meals to Make During the Week

MEAL #1: Dollop the crema on charred corn or flour tortillas. Spoon Saucy Black Beans in Sofrito (page 250) and Quick Roasted Cauliflower (page 342) on top. Serve with pickled onions.

MEAL #2: Dollop crema on charred tortillas. Nestle the Classic Roasted Chickpeas (page 236) and Roasted Butternut Wedges (page 337) on top. Serve with pickled onions.

> *Note:* You can roast the chickpeas and butternut wedges at the same time, both at 450°F (230°C); check the chickpeas at 20 minutes. Cut the butternut wedges into small pieces after roasting.

MEAL #3: Serve cooked rice with leftover Saucy Black Beans and leftover roasted cauliflower or butternut wedges. Serve with the crema and pickled onions.

#3

Starting Sauce

Life-Changing Homemade Chili Crisp (page 187)

Meal Prep

- ○ Make the chili crisp.
- ○ Cook a big pot of white or brown rice.
- ○ Freeze and defrost tofu.

Meals to Make During the Week

MEAL #1: Make the Edamame Salad with Chili Crisp (page 249) and Garlicky Kale (page 333). Serve with rice.

MEAL #2: Make the Crispy Sesame Baked Tofu (page 270). Serve with rice and steamed broccoli or green beans, and drizzle chili crisp on top.

MEAL #3: Make the Korean BBQ–Flavored Saucy Glazed Pan-Fried Tempeh (page 294). Drizzle chili crisp on top of stir-fried bok choy or snap peas and rice.

#4

Starting Sauce

Cashew Cream (page 201)

Meal Prep

- ○ Make the Cashew Cream.
- ○ Cook a big pot of farro or quinoa.

Meals to Make During the Week

MEAL #1: Make the Everyday-flavored Wildly Crunchy Cornmeal Beans (page 240) and Charred Sweet Potato Wedges (page 345). Drizzle with cashew cream. Serve with a kale salad and farro or quinoa on the side.

Note: You can roast the beans and sweet potatoes at the same time if you halve the sweet potato recipe.

MEAL #2: Make the Crunchy Spiced Tofu Nuggets (page 274) and Garlicky Kale (page 333). Serve over a bed of cashew cream with farro or quinoa on the side.

MEAL #3: Make an open-faced sandwich: use cashew cream as the spread and top with leftover Tofu Nuggets or pan-fried tofu (page 268) and heirloom tomatoes flecked with sea salt. Serve with a kale salad on the side.

#5

Starting Sauce

Tahini Sauce (any variety, page 197)

Meal Prep

- ○ Cut cauliflower into florets.
- ○ Make the tahini sauce.

Meals to Make During the Week

MEAL #1: Make the Classic Roasted Chickpeas (page 236) and Quick Roasted Cauliflower (page 342). Generously spoon on tahini sauce and serve with warm pita.

Note: You can roast the chickpeas and cauliflower at the same time, both at 450°F (230°C); check the chickpeas at 20 minutes.

MEAL #2: Make the Marinated Chickpeas (page 243) and Spice-Roasted Whole Carrots (page 329). Drizzle with tahini sauce and serve with warm pita.

MEAL #3: Make the Masala Baked Tofu (page 271) and cook a pot of farro or grain of choice. Serve with leftover roasted cauliflower or carrots. Drizzle with tahini sauce.

#6

Starting Sauce

Mint Yogurt Sauce (page 213)

Meal Prep

○ Make the yogurt sauce but double or triple the recipe.

○ Cook a big pot of white or brown rice (or make the Buttery Brown Rice with Warm Spices, page 309).

Meals to Make During the Week

MEAL #1: Make the Crispy Lentils (page 253) and Jammy Zucchini (page 330). Spoon with yogurt sauce and serve with rice.

MEAL #2: Make the Spiced Lentil Salad with Fresh Herbs (page 257) and toss it with arugula or salad greens of choice. Spoon with yogurt sauce and serve with rice.

MEAL #3: Make the Jammy Roasted Eggplant (page 339) and Tandoori Roasted Chickpeas (page 238). Spoon with yogurt sauce and serve with rice. Serve with an arugula salad.

If you're looking for even more meal planning and meal prep ideas, you can download a free weekly vegan meal plan at **rainbowplantlife.com /BVF-mealplan.**

Wow-Worthy

PART 3

Meals

While the recipes in part 2 can easily be mixed and matched into weeknight dinners, the recipes that follow are designed to be wow-worthy meals in their own right. They're hearty enough for omnivores, packed with exciting flavors and fun textures, and feature a mix of nutrient-dense ingredients with a side of indulgence.

And while they take a bit more time and effort, most of the recipes can be partially made ahead of time (look for the **Make Ahead** note).

9

Big–Personality Salads

I'm a firm believer that salads can be magical. But all too often they are haphazard affairs born out of a last-minute realization that we should probably "eat something green" (and often that means using a sad, almost-wilted bag of greens from the back of the crisper drawer).

Here's my promise to you: Once you know how to make magical salads, your life will be forever changed. Your food will be more fun and flavorful, but you'll also be eating more vegetables, and this will make you feel (rightfully) superior to everyone else in your life.

In this chapter, you'll find salads that are elegant but also a little unique, and always packed with freshness, brightness, and pleasing textures. Crunchy produce is usually featured prominently, as are perky, fresh herbs and flavor-packed dressings. These salads are not second chair to an entrée or just a side-dish afterthought. These are big-girl salads with big personality! (And many are hearty enough to work as a main course.)

Some of these salads will be their shiniest selves during summer, but many of them are wonderful any time of year. While a few of the recipes have multiple components, almost everything (aside from the fresh produce) can be prepared ahead of time.

Read this chapter, make some magical salads, and go forth into this world and spread the joy of being a salad person.

If you want to master making great salads *without* a recipe, you can download a printable guide at **rainbowplantlife.com /salad-guide.**

My Weekly Herby Green Salad

Serves 2 as a meal, 4 to 6 as a side | GFO, SF, NFO

This is my go-to green salad. Quick but a little fancy, with lots of fun flavors and textures. Two different kinds of salad greens add textural interest, tiny crispy things pepper each bite, pickled onions add tang, and handfuls of fresh herbs elevate it above ordinary green salad territory. For a main meal, add any bean or lentil, such as the Crunchy Roasted Chickpeas (page 236) or Wildly Crunchy Cornmeal Beans (page 240), and serve with crusty bread.

Easy Variations: If you don't have a crunchy topper in the pantry, make the super-quick Crispy Seed Crumbs below. No pickled onions or cukes? Use sauerkraut and another crunchy veg in your crisper. Only have one kind of herb? Also fine. For extra veggies, add shredded cabbage or a thinly shaved raw beet or fennel bulb. The one nonnegotiable: use your best-quality olive oil and vinegar, as there's no actual vinaigrette.

GF Option: Use gluten-free panko in the Savory Walnut Crunch or Crispy Seed Crumbs, or sub Hazelnut Dukkah (page 219).

NF Option: Omit the Savory Walnut Crunch and Crispy Fennel-Spiced Crumbs and top with the Crispy Seed Crumbs recipe that follows.

3 cups (135 g) chopped **Little Gem or romaine lettuce**

3 cups (70 g) finely shredded or slivered **lacinato kale**

1 cup (12 g) tender **fresh herb leaves**, such as parsley, dill, basil, mint, and/or tarragon, torn or chopped if the leaves are large

Fine sea salt and freshly ground **black pepper**

2 tablespoons best-quality **extra-virgin olive oil**

1½ tablespoons best-quality **champagne vinegar**, **white wine vinegar**, or **red wine vinegar**, plus more to taste

1 small (or ½ of a large) **English cucumber**, thinly sliced on a diagonal

1 medium ripe **avocado**, torn into chunks or diced

½ cup (60 g) **quick-pickled onions** (page 168; see Easy Variations)

½ heaping cup (60 g) **Savory Walnut Crunch** (page 220) or **Crispy Fennel-Spiced Crumbs** (page 228); or 1 recipe **Crispy Seed Crumbs** (recipe follows)

1 **lemon**

1. In the bowl of a salad spinner, combine and gently rinse the lettuce, kale, and herbs. Run the spinner and dry the greens (do this in a couple of batches as needed) or dry on dish

recipe continues

towels. Transfer to a large bowl and season lightly with salt and pepper.

2. Drizzle the greens with the olive oil and vinegar. Use your hands to toss gently. Add the cucumber, avocado, and pickled onions and toss gently. Add the walnut crunch and toss again. Finish with a couple of squeezes of lemon juice. Taste, adding more lemon juice or vinegar and salt and pepper as needed.

Crispy Seed Crumbs

Makes ½ heaping cup (75 g) | GFO, SF, NF

1 tablespoon **extra-virgin olive oil**

⅓ cup (45 g) **pepitas** (shelled pumpkin seeds) and/or **shelled sunflower seeds**

Kosher salt and freshly ground **black pepper**

⅓ cup (25 g) **panko bread crumbs**

1. In a medium skillet, heat the oil over medium heat. Add the seeds with a few pinches of salt and grinds of pepper. Cook for 2 minutes, stirring occasionally. Add the panko and cook, stirring frequently, until the panko and seeds are golden brown, 1½ to 2 minutes. Remove from the heat and set aside to cool slightly.

2. Store any leftovers in a jar in the pantry for a few weeks.

Heirloom Tomato Salad with Ricotta & Chile Oil

Serves 4 | GF, NF

Come tomato season, there is no wrong way to make a tomato salad, but this one is exceptional. Dollops of creamy "ricotta" gently swaddle meaty wedges of heirloom tomatoes, while shallots and garlic add a piquant bite. Everything gets drizzled with a mild chile oil and finished with tomato's best friends: fresh basil, balsamic vinegar, and flaky sea salt. It's so simple (and fantastic), there's no excuse to not make it once tomatoes roll into season. I'd be remiss if I didn't mention that this salad served with grilled bread is one of life's finest summer pleasures.

Bonus: The human body can better absorb the lycopene in tomatoes when it's paired with a healthy fat, such as olive oil. So enjoy the heck out of that chile oil.

Ingredient Note: Heirloom tomatoes are in season from summer through fall. If you don't have access to them, use the best-quality tomatoes you can find, including a mix of grape or cherry tomatoes with larger tomatoes.

Tip: You may have leftover tofu ricotta, but it stays good in the fridge for at least 1 week and is great on many things (check out page 206 for ideas).

Make Ahead: You can make the tofu ricotta several days ahead of time.

2 tablespoons best-quality **extra-virgin olive oil**

½ to 1 tablespoon **Aleppo pepper** or **Urfa biber**, or a mix of both (use lower range for very mild heat)

1½ pounds (680 g) **heirloom tomatoes**, sliced into wedges (see Ingredient Note)

1 large **shallot**, very thinly sliced

2 **garlic cloves**, minced

½ heaping teaspoon **fine sea salt**

Freshly ground **black pepper**

½ to 1 cup (110 to 225 g) **Whipped Tofu Ricotta** (page 206)

1 to 2 tablespoons **aged balsamic vinegar**

½ cup (8 g) **fresh basil** leaves, slivered

Flaky sea salt

1. In a small saucepan, heat the olive oil and Aleppo pepper over low heat. Simmer very gently for 5 minutes. Remove from the heat.

2. In a large bowl, combine the tomatoes, shallots, garlic, sea salt, and some cracks of black pepper. Gently toss to combine, taking care to not smush the tomatoes.

3. Add a few dollops of the ricotta to a serving platter. Arrange the tomato mixture on top and add a dollop more ricotta around the tomatoes. Drizzle with the chile oil and 1 tablespoon of the balsamic vinegar. Garnish with basil. Taste, adding more balsamic as needed, and season with flaky salt and black pepper.

The Fancy Caesar Salad

Serves 4

Like a classic Caesar, this one is intensely savory, salty, and a little tangy, with each bite punctuated by the crunch of romaine and homemade croutons. An umami-heavy Caesar dressing, parmesan-like Cheesy Crunchies, and nuggets of nori-flecked croutons make this just as good as if not better than the original. While there are multiple components, this salad is easy to prep in advance.

Ingredient Notes: For the croutons, you want day-old (or two-day-old) bread. If you don't have day-old bread, a sourdough baguette works fine. If you have sensitive teeth, remove the crust before tearing.

Tips: To save time and/or if you don't have a spice grinder, make Classic Torn Croutons (page 229). If you don't have time to make the Cheesy Crunchies, sub with ½ cup (50 g) store-bought vegan parmesan.

Make Ahead: The dressing stays good in the fridge for up to 1 week and makes enough for two batches; the croutons stay fresh on the counter for 1 week; the Cheesy Crunchies keep for at least 1 month in the pantry. Store your chopped lettuce and chickpeas in a large container, store all other components separately, and assemble a fantastic salad in minutes.

Easy Variation: Replace the lettuce with thinly sliced and massaged kale or finely shredded Brussels sprouts.

Nori Croutons (see Tips)

8 to 10 ounces (230 to 280 g) **day-old sourdough bread, Italian bread,** or **country bread** (see Ingredient Notes)

2 sheets (6 g) **roasted nori**

3 tablespoons **extra-virgin olive oil**

½ teaspoon **fine sea salt**

½ teaspoon **garlic powder**

Salad

12 to 14 ounces (340 to 400 g) **romaine hearts** or **Little Gem lettuce**

½ recipe **All Hail Caesar Dressing** (page 155), or to taste

½ cup (55 g) **Cheesy Crunchies** (page 223; see Tips)

1 (15-ounce/425 g) can **chickpeas**, drained and rinsed (optional, to make this a main meal)

1. Preheat the oven to 375°F (190°C).

2. **Make the nori croutons.** Tear the bread into bite-size pieces (¾ to 1 inch/2 cm) and add to a large bowl. Tear each nori sheet into small pieces. Add one sheet to a spice grinder and blitz into crumbs. Transfer to a small bowl and repeat with the other nori sheet. Drizzle the

recipe continues

bread with the olive oil and sprinkle with the ground nori, salt, and garlic powder, tossing well with your hands. Spread out on a rimmed sheet pan and bake for 10 minutes. Use a spatula to flip or shake the pan back and forth several times. Rotate the pan by 180 degrees and bake for 5 more minutes, or until toasted and golden brown. The croutons should be crunchy with a slight chew. Let cool slightly before using. If you have a lot of nori crumbs on the sheet pan, sprinkle some over your salad when serving.

3. Separate the leaves from the lettuce and tear any large leaves with your hands. If you prefer a chopped Caesar, chop the lettuce first.

4. **Assemble the salad.** Add the lettuce to a large bowl. Pour on some of the dressing and toss to combine. Sprinkle on the cheesy crunchies (reserve a few for garnish) and toss again. Add the chickpeas (if using) and croutons and toss again. Taste, adding more dressing as needed. Add an extra sprinkle of cheesy crunchies before serving.

Smashed Cucumbers with Yogurt-Tahini Sauce & Spicy "Honey"

Serves 4 to 6 | GF, SF, NFO

Come summer, I cannot resist a smashed cucumber salad. Here, crunchy cucumbers are torn into craggy chunks, then dragged through a luscious yogurt-tahini sauce for the ultimate crisp-crunchy-creamy pairing. An easy jalapeño "honey" with candied jalapeños adds an irresistible sweet-and-spicy flair, while roasted almonds play up tahini's nuttiness and add extra crunch.

Ingredient Notes: Small Persian cukes, found at many grocery stores, are easiest to smash. I also love this with Japanese cucumbers, available at farmers' markets during the summer. If you can't find either, English cukes are fine, but pass on the pole cucumbers, as they're seedy and not as crisp.

To get a schwoopable consistency for the sauce, a creamy yogurt is required. For my recommended yogurt brands, flip back to page 61. You can also use Whipped Feta (page 209) if you have it on hand.

Make Ahead: You can make the Yogurt-Tahini Sauce a few days in advance, and the Spicy "Honey" with Candied Jalapeños well in advance—it lasts a month in the fridge.

1¼ to 1½ pounds (570 to 680 g) **Persian cucumbers** (about 6 to 8) or **English or Japanese cucumbers** (about 2 medium; see Ingredient Notes)

Kosher salt

½ to 1 recipe **Yogurt-Tahini Sauce** (page 215)

¼ cup (30 g) **roasted almonds**, chopped (use sunflower seeds if nut-free)

1 to 3 tablespoons **Spicy "Honey" with Candied Jalapeños** (page 176)

1. Slice the ends off the cucumbers, then cut them in half lengthwise. Using your largest, heaviest knife (or a cleaver if you have one), smash the cukes by pressing the flat side of the knife against them, using the heel of your palm to press down (similar to smashing down on a garlic clove to remove the peel). If you are using larger Japanese or English cucumbers, chop them into 2- to 3-inch (5 to 7.5 cm) segments, then turn them on their sides to smash them.

2. Tear the smashed cucumbers into bite-size chunks, discarding any loose seeds or watery

recipe continues

membranes. Transfer to a colander fitted over a bowl or in the sink. Sprinkle the cucumbers with ½ teaspoon salt, mixing with your hands to ensure all the cucumbers are evenly coated.

3. Place a bag filled with ice and cold water (or a bag of frozen peas) on top of the cucumbers to weight them down and keep them cold. Let rest for 30 minutes on the counter, or up to 4 hours in the fridge. Discard any accumulated liquid and shake off excess water from the cukes to avoid a watery salad.

4. Grab a large shallow bowl and schmear on a generous amount of the yogurt-tahini sauce. Top with the smashed cucumbers, followed by the almonds. Drizzle with a bit of the spicy "honey" (include candied jalapeño slices for extra heat). Taste, adding more spicy "honey" as desired. If keeping leftovers, plate what you plan to serve and store the components separately.

Shaved Fennel Salad with Pears & Grapefruit–Shallot Vinaigrette

Serves 6 to 8 | GF, SF, NFO

About once a month in college, I'd splurge on a few specialty groceries and cook a bougie dinner. One afternoon, I watched my teenage idol Ina Garten make a fennel-orange salad on her show, which inspired me to purchase my very first bulb of fennel. I sliced it as best as I could with my college-budget knife collection in my 4-foot by 8-foot kitchen, and I made myself a very fancy fennel salad.

These days, I'm the proud owner of a mandoline and my kitchen is more spacious, but I still love a citrusy fennel salad. This one features feathery shavings of fennel, a zingy grapefruit-shallot vinaigrette, juicy pears, cooling mint, and buttery avocado. It's wonderfully refreshing, with great texture. *Now how bad could that be??* (Cue laughter from fellow Ina fans.)

To make this a heartier dish, add French green or black beluga lentils, Crispy Lentils (page 253), or Crunchy Roasted Chickpeas (page 236). You can also double the avocado. Serve with crusty bread.

Ingredient Note: Fennel is in season during fall, winter, and early spring, but depending on the region where it's grown, it may be in season in summer.

Tips: No mandoline? Cut the bulbs into wedges and push them through the feed tube of your food processor, using the thinnest slicing blade. Or use your sharpest knife. Slice the pears just before serving, or if you are slicing ahead of time, squeeze with lemon juice to prevent browning. If you have a little leftover pear, Microplane or grate it into the vinaigrette for added sweetness and body. And if you have leftover grapefruit from the vinaigrette, feel free to layer a few slices into the salad.

Make Ahead: You can make the vinaigrette 3 to 4 days ahead of time.

3 medium-large **fennel** bulbs with fronds (each 9 to 10 ounces/275 g)

Fine sea salt and freshly ground **black pepper**

½ cup (8 g) **fresh mint** leaves

Grapefruit-Shallot Vinaigrette (page 166)

2 large ripe but firm **pears**, thinly sliced

½ cup (65 g) **shelled roasted pistachios or almonds**, roughly chopped (omit if nut-free)

1 medium-large ripe **avocado**, thinly sliced

1. Cut the stalks and fronds off the fennel. Measure out ⅓ cup (about 7 g) fennel fronds and roughly chop; save the stalks for broths or stews. For the bulbs, slice in half lengthwise and remove the tough outer layer after cutting off the bottom core. Use the thinnest setting on your mandoline to slice the bulb (see Tips).

recipe continues

Add the fennel to a large bowl and season with a few pinches of salt and pepper.

2. To avoid blackening, tear the mint leaves with your hands or roughly chop them just before serving.

3. Pour one-half to three-quarters of the vinaigrette on the fennel and toss to combine. Gently fold in the fennel fronds, pears, mint, and nuts. Sprinkle the salad with salt and pepper and dress with more vinaigrette. Add the avocado and toss very gently to avoid smushing. This salad is best fresh, but if you are keeping leftovers, dress only the amount of salad you plan to eat and add the avocado directly to the serving plates.

FLAVOR BOOSTERS FOR GREAT SALADS

- Raw produce is sweetest and freshest (and most nutritious) when in season, so shop locally and in season when you can, especially if an ingredient is the star in a salad.

- Pair two contrasting salad greens for more interest, for example, something crunchy like romaine with something bitter like radicchio. Or mild mesclun with something peppery like arugula.

- For tougher greens like kale and Swiss chard, shred them thinly to make them more enjoyable to chew.

- Sprinkle salt and black pepper on greens before dressing to directly infuse them with flavor.

- Not every salad has to include salad greens! Make your base thinly sliced raw vegetables or roasted or grilled vegetables. Or use large handfuls of soft fresh herbs as your base (e.g., cilantro, mint, parsley, dill, basil, tarragon), or combine salad greens with herbs. In winter, replace dainty lettuces with kale, thinly sliced fennel, roasted root vegetables, blanched potatoes, grains, beans, or lentils.

- Don't rely just on raw veggies. Experiment by adding pickled radishes or carrots, roasted tubers, blanched green beans, or grilled peppers and zucchini.

- Salads are a good exercise in balance. If your dressing has some fruity sweetness, pair it with a bitter or peppery lettuce, or give it something salty, like vegan feta, olives, or capers. Using bitter greens? Add something with umami and acidity. If your salad feels too light, add in avocado chunks.

- If adding nuts or seeds, toast them first for richer flavor and better texture.

- Always taste for salt and acidity before serving, and add more as needed. A flat salad can usually be livened up with a squeeze of lemon.

Shaved Carrot Salad with Pickled Shallots & Fresh Herbs

Serves 4 | GF, SF, NF

Thinly shaved carrot ribbons and handfuls of fresh herbs make this an elegant salad you'll want to serve at dinner parties. The avocado is a creamy contrast to the crisp carrots, a whole lemon and sumac-pickled shallots add a refreshing tartness, and a jalapeño brings a kick you don't often get in salads. For a heartier salad, add French green lentils, chickpeas, or white beans, or double the avocado. Toss in some toasted almonds or Crispy & Crunchy Things from chapter 5, and/or serve over a bed of Lemon Tahini Sauce (page 197) for extra richness.

Ingredient Note: Carrots are usually good year-round but best from late spring through late fall. If yours are very sweet, you can skip the maple syrup or use less of it.

Tip: You can also pulse the herbs, scallions, and jalapeño in a food processor until finely chopped. It's less gorgeous but quicker.

Easy Variations: Replace the cilantro with more parsley or mint. Add chopped oranges or a thinly shaved apple or beet for a little sweetness; if fresh peas are in season, they'd be lovely here.

1 large **shallot**, sliced as thinly as you can (a mandoline helps)

3 tablespoons best-quality **champagne vinegar**, **white wine vinegar**, or **red wine vinegar**

1 tablespoon **sumac** (for extra-bright lemony flavor; omit if you don't have it)

Fine sea salt and freshly ground **black pepper**

1 pound (455 g) **carrots** (use rainbow carrots for the prettiest presentation)

1 large **lemon**

1 loosely packed cup (12 to 14 g) **fresh cilantro** leaves and tender stems, finely chopped

1 cup (16 g) **fresh mint** leaves, finely chopped

¾ loosely packed cup (9 g) **fresh flat-leaf parsley** leaves, finely chopped

6 **scallions**, sliced very thinly on a bias

1 **jalapeño pepper**, sliced as thinly as possible (remove membranes and seeds for mild heat)

1 tablespoon **pure maple syrup**

3 tablespoons best-quality **extra-virgin olive oil**

1 large **avocado** (or 2 small), diced or thinly sliced

recipe continues

1. In a small bowl, mix the shallots, vinegar, sumac, and a pinch of salt with your hands. Macerate for 15 to 30 minutes while you prep everything else.

2. Using a Y-shaped vegetable peeler, peel the carrots vertically in ribbons until you get to the point where you can't peel anymore (laying the carrot flat on a cutting board helps you get more ribbons). Save the inner pieces that can't be ribboned to quick pickle (see page 168) or for snacks.

3. Zest the lemon. Now, using a paring knife, peel the white pith and remaining skin; discard. Chop the peeled lemon flesh into small pieces, discarding the seeds and fibrous white membranes.

4. In a serving bowl, combine the chopped lemon, lemon zest, fresh herbs, scallions, and jalapeño. Add the carrot ribbons and pickled shallots and sprinkle with a pinch or two of salt.

5. In a small bowl, whisk together the maple syrup and olive oil and season with a pinch or two of salt and pepper. Drizzle on the salad and toss gently. Add the avocado and toss very gently. Taste, adding salt and pepper as needed.

Spicy, Crunchy Kale Salad with Preserved Lemon Vinaigrette

Serves 4 | GFO, SF, NF

Yes, this is a kale salad blah blah blah, but it's not the kind of kale salad you force down your gullet just because it's good for you. It's a *fantastic* kale salad with a zingy and garlicky preserved lemon vinaigrette; sweet-hot-tangy pickled chiles and shallots; buttery, crunchy croutons; and creamy avocado. Try topping this salad with chickpeas or lentils, or the Crunchy Spiced Tofu Nuggets on page 274, for a complete meal.

Make Ahead: You can make the Preserved Lemon Vinaigrette ahead of time (it stays good for 2 weeks in the fridge), as well as the croutons (they stay fresh in a sealed bag on the counter for up to 1 week). Store the shredded kale and the pickled mixture separately in the fridge.

Easy Variations: Use a mix of kale and romaine. Already have pickled chiles or onions in the fridge? Use those instead. Sub Savory Walnut Crunch (page 220) for the croutons.

GF Option: Instead of croutons, make Crunchy Roasted Chickpeas (page 236), Hazelnut Dukkah (page 219), or Cheesy Crunchies (page 223).

2 medium **shallots**, thinly sliced

1 **Fresno or jalapeño pepper**, thinly sliced (remove membranes and seeds for mild heat)

¼ cup (60 ml) **distilled white vinegar**

1 tablespoon **pure maple syrup**

1 teaspoon **Aleppo pepper** or ¼ teaspoon **red pepper flakes** (optional, for more heat)

Fine sea salt and freshly ground **black pepper**

2 heads **lacinato or curly kale** (around 1 pound/ 455 g total)

Preserved Lemon Vinaigrette (page 164)

Classic Torn Croutons (page 229)

1 medium ripe **avocado**, torn into chunks or diced (optional, for a creamy element)

1. In a shallow bowl or small jar, combine the shallots, chile pepper, vinegar, maple syrup, and Aleppo pepper (if using). Sprinkle with a pinch of salt and set aside to macerate, for 10 minutes (or longer), stirring once or twice.

2. Slice out or strip away the middle rib from each kale leaf. Roll up the leaves like a cigar and slice very thinly, then rinse and dry in a salad spinner. Transfer to a large bowl and spoon on most of the vinaigrette. Massage the kale with your hands for about 1 minute.

3. Spoon the shallot mixture over the kale, leaving behind the excess liquid (it's okay if a little gets in, it's tasty). Taste, adding the rest of the vinaigrette as desired, and toss to combine. Scatter the croutons on top, add the avocado (if using), and gently toss. Season with salt and black pepper as needed.

Creamy & Crunchy Beet Salad with Crispy Fennel Crumbs

Serves 4 to 6 | GFO, SF, NFO

Beets are best when paired with bright, tangy flavors and creamy textures, and here, a creamy and citrus-forward vinaigrette is the perfect tart-sweet foil for earthy beets (as well as peppery arugula). To make them easier to chew (and to save time), beets are pulsed in a food processor until finely diced, then layered with fresh herbs and fennel-spiced crumbs. It's a very fun blend of creamy, crisp, crunchy, and chewy textures that even the beet haters in my life have enjoyed. Add cooked chickpeas or green lentils to make this salad extra hearty, and serve with a hunk of bread.

Ingredient Note: Beet season varies regionally, but they're usually best in spring, summer, and fall.

Tip: If using golden beets, shred right before assembling to avoid browning, or soak in ice water (or ignore this because they taste the same even if they have browned a bit and are safe to eat).

Make Ahead: Combine beets, arugula, and herbs in a container; refrigerate for 1 to 2 days. Make the vinaigrette up to 1 week in advance. Make Crispy Fennel-Spiced Crumbs in advance and store in a jar in the pantry for a few weeks.

Easy Variations: If you already have Hazelnut Dukkah (page 219) or Savory Walnut Crunch (page 220), use ½ to ¾ cup (55 to 80 g) of those instead of the Fennel-Spiced Crumbs. If your beet greens look good, use a few cups in place of arugula.

GF Option: Use gluten-free panko in the Crispy Fennel-Spiced Crumbs or substitute with Hazelnut Dukkah (page 219).

NF Option: Use more pepitas or sunflower seeds in place of hazelnuts in the Crispy Fennel-Spiced Crumbs.

5 medium (or 3 large) **red or golden beets** (20 ounces/570 g)

4 ounces (115 g) **arugula** or **watercress** (about 8 cups), chopped well

¾ cup (12 g) **fresh dill**, tough stems removed and finely chopped

1 cup (12 g) **fresh flat-leaf parsley** leaves, chopped

Fine sea salt and freshly ground **black pepper**

Citrus-Date Vinaigrette (page 171)

Crispy Fennel-Spiced Crumbs (page 228)

1 large ripe **avocado**, cut into small chunks (optional, for extra creaminess)

1. Scrub, peel, and roughly chop the beets. Add them to a food processor and blend for a few seconds to break them up, then pulse in short bursts until very finely diced.

2. In a large serving bowl, add roughly one-third each of the arugula, dill, parsley, and beets. Season with a pinch or two of salt and several cracks of pepper. Repeat the layers

recipe continues

until you run out of ingredients. Toss well using tongs.

3. If planning to serve all the salad now, add most of the vinaigrette and toss to combine. If you are keeping leftovers, dress only the amount of salad you plan to eat. Refrigerate the remaining salad and dressing separately to avoid sogginess.

4. Before serving, add the fennel-spiced crumbs and toss. If using avocado, gently combine. Add the rest of the vinaigrette, as desired. Finish with a pinch of salt.

Garlicky Asparagus & Beans with Lemon-Infused Olive Oil

Serves 3 as a main, 6 to 8 as a side | GF, SF

This salad-but-not-salad features a classic flavor pairing of asparagus, lemon, and olive oil, but with a few special bonuses, like crunchy fried garlic chips and gently fried lemon zest. Basil adds a sweet anise flavor, chile flakes a kick, and pistachios a buttery crunch. Blanching the asparagus and beans, instead of steaming or roasting, keeps them crisp, making them a perfect picnic or al fresco lunch option.

Ingredient Notes: Some folks say you should always cook edamame, even though it's been blanched before being frozen. I am not one of those people, but if your bar for food safety is higher, boil the edamame when you add the green beans. If your pistachios are raw, toast them first (see page 115 for instructions). Asparagus is at its peak in spring and early summer.

Tip: Skip the "bend and snap method" when trimming asparagus, as it wastes a lot. Instead, slice where the spears start to get tough, 1 to 2 inches (2.5 to 5 cm) from the ends. Line up the spears and lop off the ends in one fell swoop.

Easy Variations: Use chickpeas or lentils instead of edamame. If basil isn't in season, use parsley. Sub walnuts for pistachios, or add capers for a salty pop. For a heartier meal, toss with pasta (coated in vegan butter or olive oil) and finish with the Cheesy Crunchies on page 223.

Kosher salt

8 ounces (227 g) **haricots verts** (French green beans) or **regular green beans**, trimmed

1 bunch **asparagus** (12 to 16 ounces/340 to 455 g), trimmed (see Tip)

12 ounces (340 g) **shelled edamame**, thawed if frozen (see Ingredient Notes)

½ cup (65 g) **shelled roasted pistachios**, finely chopped (or pulsed in a food processor; see Ingredient Notes)

1 cup (16 g) **fresh basil** leaves, finely chopped

Flaky sea salt

3 tablespoons good-quality **extra-virgin olive oil**, plus more to taste

5 large **garlic cloves**, thinly sliced

1 medium-large **lemon**, zested and juiced

½ to 1 teaspoon **red pepper flakes** (½ teaspoon for a mild heat)

Freshly ground **black pepper**

1. Bring a large pot of water to a boil (8 to 12 cups/2 to 3 L). Salt generously (about 1½ tablespoons kosher salt).

recipe continues

2. Cut the green beans in half on a bias (if they are skinny and small, keep them whole). If you are using regular green beans, cut them into 2-inch (5 cm) pieces. Slice the trimmed asparagus on a sharp bias into 1½- to 2-inch (4 to 5 cm) pieces. Fill a large bowl with ice water.

3. Add the green beans to the pot. Once the water returns to a boil, cook for 2 minutes (3 minutes for regular green beans). Add the asparagus and, once the water returns to a boil, cook for 2 minutes. Use a slotted spoon to immediately transfer the veg to the ice bath. Once cold, drain, transfer to dish towels, and dry as well as you can so the vegetables don't taste watery. Transfer to a large serving bowl, add the edamame, and sprinkle with a few pinches of kosher salt.

4. In a small bowl, combine the pistachios and basil. Sprinkle with a few pinches of flaky salt.

5. In a medium skillet, heat the olive oil over medium-low heat. Once it is warm but not hot, add the garlic and cook, swirling the pan or stirring frequently and separating the slices, until it just turns golden (don't wait until it browns), 2 to 2½ minutes. Add the lemon zest and pepper flakes and cook for 30 seconds, swirling often. Season with a pinch of kosher salt and black pepper and remove from the heat.

6. Drizzle the warm garlic oil on top of the asparagus and beans. Add 2 tablespoons lemon juice, ¼ teaspoon flaky salt, and several cracks of black pepper and toss well. Add the pistachio-basil topping and toss to coat. Taste, adding a drizzle of olive oil or more lemon juice as desired.

Indian-Spiced Charred Corn Salad

Serves 4 to 6 | GF, SF, NFO

My father grew up humbly in a two-room apartment in Mumbai, where he and his siblings slept on the floor. When he moved to the US in the 1980s, he was forced to repeat his medical residency because, despite it being prestigious back home, it was not accepted by American hospitals. He did so without complaint, frequently working seventy-two-hour shifts for a $700 monthly paycheck.

Even though he has, by all definitions, "achieved the American Dream," he still carries the curiosity and gratitude of the boy he once was. He's not a religious man, but every day he says one prayer: "Thank you, God. For everything." He's never cared what anyone else thinks (as evidenced by his choice to wear socks with sandals), and he still marvels in awe at ripe summer produce, year after year.

Sweet corn is a favorite of his, and each summer, he serves us a new rendition of corn salad. Some years, he does a Mexican-inspired version with black beans, lime, and jalapeños; other years, red onions, cilantro, and Indian spices abound. The first time he met Max's parents, he prepared one such corn salad, and his parents still rave about it years later.

This tangy, slightly sweet, Indian-spiced corn salad is an ode to my father. To both his delicious corn salads and to his unwavering gratitude and zest for life. I love you, Dad.

Ingredient Note: Corn is in season in summer through early fall.

4 ears **fresh corn**, husked

3 **scallions**, trimmed

3 tablespoons **extra-virgin olive oil**

½ cup (8 g) **fresh mint** leaves, chopped

¾ cup (12 g) **fresh cilantro** leaves and tender stems, chopped

3 **garlic cloves**, grated or finely minced

2 medium **limes** (zest 1 lime and juice both of them)

½ teaspoon **ground cumin**

¼ teaspoon **ground coriander**

⅛ teaspoon **ground cardamom**

¼ teaspoon **garam masala**

¼ teaspoon **Indian red chile powder** (or 1 small jalapeño pepper, finely diced), plus more as needed

Kosher salt and freshly ground **black pepper**

3 tablespoons **dry-roasted peanuts**, chopped (omit if nut-free; if using unsalted peanuts, add a pinch more salt)

1. Position an ear of corn upright over a sheet pan. Use a chef's knife in a downward direction to shave the corn, allowing the kernels to drop into the pan. Repeat with the remaining corn.

recipe continues

2. Thinly slice the dark green tops of the scallions on a bias and save for the garnish. Finely chop the remaining light green and white parts.

3. Heat a large cast-iron skillet over medium-high heat, ideally over a burner with a wide flame. Add 1 tablespoon of the olive oil, and once hot, add half of the corn kernels. If the kernels start popping up violently, reduce the heat to medium. Cook for about 8 minutes, until nicely charred in spots, stirring only every 2 minutes to allow charring. Transfer the corn to a serving bowl and repeat the process with 1 more tablespoon of oil and the remaining corn. The second batch will cook in just 4 to 6 minutes, as the pan will be hot.

4. To the bowl of charred corn, add the mint, cilantro, light green and white parts of the scallions, garlic, lime zest, 2 tablespoons lime juice, the cumin, coriander, cardamom, garam masala, and chile powder. Season with ¼ teaspoon kosher salt and several cracks of pepper. Toss to combine. Drizzle in the remaining 1 tablespoon oil and toss to coat.

5. Taste, adding more salt (about ¼ teaspoon), lime juice, or chile powder as needed. Serve with peanuts and the reserved scallion greens on top.

Swiss Chard & Carrot Slaw with Crispy Bread Crumbs

Serves 6 | GFO, SF

Swiss chard is one of those vegetables I wish I ate more often. It's rich in iron, fiber, and a bajillion vitamins. Every time you eat it, you pretty much add a month to your life expectancy.

So how do you get yourself to actually eat it more often? Shred it thinly so it's easier to chew, blanket it with a buttery and lemony dressing, add pops of juicy fruit, and shower it with delightfully crispy bread crumbs. I promise this salad is one of the most delicious things you will ever make with this leafy green superstar.

To turn this into a main meal, add cooked or roasted chickpeas or lentils and serve with bread or over your favorite grain.

Ingredient Note: Swiss chard is best in summer and fall, though available year-round.

Tips: This salad tastes best with chilled vinaigrette. Use leftovers with other salads or vegetables (it's especially good with broccoli). If you are using whole carrots, grate about 4 medium carrots on a box grater, with a julienne peeler, or with the shredding disc of your food processor. To speed things up, buy pre-shredded carrots.

Make Ahead: You can make the vinaigrette 3 to 4 days ahead of time.

Easy Variation: If persimmons or pomegranates are in season, use instead of tangerines.

10 ounces (285 g) **Swiss chard** or **rainbow chard** (1 large head)

8 ounces (227 g) shredded **carrots** (3 scant cups; see Tips)

½ cup (60 g) **quick-pickled onions or cabbage** (page 168), or store-bought sauerkraut

3 **tangerines** or **mandarins**, peeled and each segment cut in half (or 1 large navel orange, peeled and chopped)

Fine sea salt and freshly ground **black pepper**

1 tablespoon **extra-virgin olive oil**

½ cup (40 g) **panko bread crumbs** (use gluten-free panko for GF)

About ½ recipe **Buttery Caper–Pine Nut Dressing** (page 174; see Tips)

1. Cut the middle rib from each chard leaf; discard or set aside to pickle later using the brine on page 168. Stack and roll the leaves up like cigars, like you would do for basil. Slice into ribbons as thinly as you can. Use a salad spinner

recipe continues

to wash and dry the leaves, or dry them on towels.

2. In a large bowl, combine the chard, carrots, pickled onions, and tangerine pieces. Sprinkle with ½ teaspoon salt and lots of pepper and toss gently. If you have lemon zest remaining from making the dressing, add that in.

3. In a medium or large skillet, heat the olive oil over medium heat. Add the panko with a few pinches of salt and cracks of pepper. Cook, tossing frequently, until golden brown, 3 to 5 minutes.

4. Pour some vinaigrette on the salad, tossing to coat. Add more vinaigrette as desired and fold in the bread crumbs, tossing again. Taste and add more salt as needed. Store leftover bread crumbs in a jar at room temperature for a few weeks.

Radicchio Salad with Ranch & Smoky Seed Sprinkle

Serves 4 to 6 | GF, SFO, NF

Radicchio is bossy and bracingly bitter, so this is a salad for adventurous eaters. But the combination of flavors—resplendent radicchio leaves that are aggressively seasoned in a salty, slightly tangy, creamy ranch and punctuated by the crunch of warmly spiced, smoky seeds—is so intriguing it will keep you coming back for more. To make this a hearty meal, add cooked chickpeas or the Classic Roasted Chickpeas (page 236) and fold in roasted winter squash or sweet potatoes.

Tips: To tame some of the bitterness of radicchio, (1) slice it thinly on a diagonal and (2) lightly massage it with some salt. If it's your first time with radicchio, swap half of it for romaine (you can use a bit less salt).

If you have other Crispy & Crunchy Things from chapter 5 in your pantry, use instead of the seed sprinkle. If you have leftover dill from making the ranch, use in place of parsley.

Make Ahead: You can make the ranch 3 to 5 days ahead of time. Make the seed sprinkle a week or two ahead of time.

1 medium head **radicchio** (about 10 ounces/300 g; see Tips)

Fine sea salt and freshly ground **black pepper**

About ½ cup (120 g) **Throwback Ranch Dressing** (page 203), or to taste

1 medium ripe **avocado**, torn into chunks

1 cup (12 g) **fresh flat-leaf parsley** leaves, torn or chopped (see Tips)

Smoky Seed Sprinkle (page 216)

1. Slice the radicchio thinly on a diagonal. For a nicer presentation, save a few radicchio leaves and tear them into bite-size pieces.

2. Add the radicchio to a large bowl and season quite generously with salt. Drizzle ¼ to ⅓ cup (60 to 80 g) of the ranch around the sides of the bowl and use your hands to coat the leaves.

3. Transfer to a serving platter. Add the avocado and parsley. Drizzle on a bit more ranch and toss to combine. Scatter several handfuls of the smoky seed sprinkle on top. Taste, adding a pinch of salt or pepper as needed. Serve with more ranch on the side if desired.

Rainbow Veggie Slaw with Green Goddess Dressing

Serves 6 | GF, SF, NF

I have spent the last two decades encouraging my mom to eat more salad. It is a losing battle. Every time I serve her salad, she makes a face that says, *But why do you hate me so much?* And when she finally agrees to eat some, she just covers it up with other food to pretend she's eaten it.

To my surprise, she ate an entire plate of this slaw. When she asked for seconds, I looked upward and told the gods, "My work here is done. You can take me now."

Crisp raw vegetables are ribboned or shredded, then bathed in a creamy, herby dressing. Mango is the secret star, adding a sweet contrast to the slightly tangy, herb-heavy dressing and a velvety texture.

Tips: Depending on the vegetables you're using, either peel them with a Y-shaped peeler to get ribbons, thinly slice with a sharp knife or mandoline, or shred with a box grater or food processor slicing disc. When peeling ribbons, if you get to the point where you can no longer shave long peels, slice the remaining vegetables thinly for a crunchy contrasting texture.

You'll use about two-thirds of the dressing for this salad. Use the leftovers to make a killer chickpea salad sandwich, or use it as a dip for crudités. I find it easiest to peel ripe mangoes when they're chilled.

6 to 8 cups or big handfuls of **ribboned, thinly sliced, or shredded vegetables** (see Tips), such as:
- **Carrots**, ribboned with a Y-shaped peeler
- **Zucchini**, ribboned with a Y-shaped peeler
- **Asparagus** (use large spears), ribboned with a Y-shaped peeler
- **Red cabbage**, shredded with a box grater or food processor slicing disc, or thinly sliced with a mandoline or knife
- **Golden or red beets**, thinly sliced with a mandoline or knife
- **Fennel**, thinly sliced with a mandoline or knife
- **Red, yellow, or orange bell peppers**, thinly sliced

Fine sea salt and freshly ground **black pepper**

1 medium or large ripe **mango**, peeled and thinly sliced (see Tips)

4 **scallions** (white and light green parts only), thinly sliced on a bias

1 cup (240 g) **Green Goddess Dressing** (page 182)

⅓ cup (45 g) **roasted sunflower seeds** (or pepitas)

1 medium ripe **avocado**, sliced or cubed

1. Add the vegetables to a large serving bowl. Season with salt and pepper and toss to coat. Add the mango and scallions.

2. Pour on the dressing and gently toss to coat. Before serving, scatter the sunflower seeds on top and gently fold in the avocado. Taste, adding more dressing as desired. If you are not planning to serve the whole salad, store the undressed salad in the fridge for up to 3 days.

10

Vegetables Are the Main Event

I used to come home from the farmers' market and toss every vegetable I bought onto a sheet pan and hope for the best. The end result was always edible, sometimes even nice. But it was never spectacular.

Going vegan, though, changed that. Once I stopped paying so much attention to what I thought was the "centerpiece" of the dish (e.g., the meat), I was able to devote that time and energy to making sure the vegetables tasted not just edible but excellent.

Eating a plant-based diet opened my eyes to a new world of techniques for coaxing out the most flavor from vegetables. It taught me new ways to enliven the familiar flavors of carrots and broccoli, how to caramelize winter squash, and even how to turn beet haters into beet fanatics.

And it helped me realize that cauliflower and leeks and fennel deserve more than just being thrown together in the same pan. They each deserve a chance at the spotlight.

The recipes in this chapter seek to do that, treating individual vegetables as the main event. Like the salads in chapter 9, they are packed with fun textures and flavors, but these recipes are warming, a bit heartier, and wonderfully cozy. All the recipes are flexible enough to work as a main meal or as a side dish to serve a crowd.

Glazed Torn Beets with Pistachio Butter & Mint

Serves 3 as a main, 6 as a side | GF, SF

Beets get the full luxe treatment here. First, they're roasted, then torn into chunks and cooked in a sticky maple-Dijon-balsamic glaze until lightly charred. The craggy crevices of the torn beets allow them to absorb all the flavors of the tangy glaze, which mellows some of their natural sweet earthiness. The char brings a subtle smokiness, adding a dynamic twist. Once glistening, the beets are plated on a schmear of dreamy and fatty pistachio butter, which slices right through any earthy funkiness. Finally, they're dappled with fresh mint to brighten them up.

This is my all-time favorite beet dish, and it's guaranteed to win over even the biggest beet skeptics. You can make this a heartier meal by serving with the optional cooked lentils and a hunk of seeded whole-grain bread. Or serve it over farro or crispy quinoa (see method on page 315).

Ingredient Notes: Golden beets are less earthy than red beets, making them a great option for beet skeptics. Beet season varies regionally, but they're usually best in spring, summer, and fall.

Make Ahead: You can make the pistachio butter a week or two in advance (or make it while the beets roast). Roast the beets and cook the lentils up to 3 days ahead.

1½ to 2 pounds (680 to 910 g) medium **red or golden beets** (about 6 beets)

2 tablespoons **extra-virgin olive oil**, plus more for roasting

Kosher salt

½ cup (100 g) **French green lentils** or **black beluga lentils** (optional)

Glaze

2½ tablespoons **pure maple syrup**

1½ tablespoons **Dijon mustard**

1 tablespoon **aged balsamic vinegar**

1½ teaspoons **apple cider vinegar**

⅛ to ¼ teaspoon **cayenne pepper** (⅛ teaspoon for the mildest kick)

1 teaspoon **kosher salt**

Freshly ground **black pepper**

recipe and ingredients continue

For Serving

¼ to ½ cup (65 to 130 g) **Pistachio Butter** (page 194), at room temperature

½ cup (8 g) **fresh mint** leaves, chopped

Flaky sea salt

A few squeezes of fresh **lemon juice**

1. Preheat the oven to 425°F (220°C.) Trim any beet greens and most of their attached stalks (leave some stalk intact to prevent the beets from "bleeding" in the oven). To keep the beets juicy, do not trim any skinny beet tails. Wash and scrub the beets well.

2. **Roast the beets.** Rub the beets with a bit of olive oil so they have a thin coating and transfer to a baking dish or ovenproof pan with a tight-fitting lid. Pour in 1 cup (240 ml) of water and cover tightly with foil (or the lid). Roast for 45 to 60 minutes, until fork-tender (medium beets usually take 60 minutes; smaller beets, 45 minutes).

3. **Meanwhile, make the lentils (if using).** Bring a medium saucepan of water to a boil and season with several pinches of salt. Add the lentils and cook at a decent simmer until tender but still a bit al dente, 17 to 20 minutes. Drain well and set aside to dry off.

4. **Make the glaze.** In a small bowl, whisk together the maple syrup, mustard, both vinegars, cayenne, kosher salt, and several cracks of black pepper. Add 2 tablespoons of water, stir, and set aside.

5. When the beets are cool enough to touch, run them under cool water and peel off the skins (wear food-safe gloves if you don't want pink hands for a few hours). Cut off any stems and tough bottoms. Use your hands to tear the beets into roughly 1-inch (2.5 cm) pieces.

6. **Glaze the beets.** In a 12-inch (30 cm) skillet, heat the 2 tablespoons olive oil over medium-high heat. Once shimmering, add the torn beets and cook undisturbed for 2 minutes. Flip and cook until nicely charred in spots, turning only every 2 minutes, 6 to 8 more minutes. Remove the pan from the heat and pour in the glaze (stand back to avoid splatter). Return the pan to medium heat. Cook, gently stirring the beets into the glaze, until thick enough to coat the back of a spoon, 2 to 3 minutes. Remove from the heat and let cool for 5 minutes.

7. **To serve,** schmear the pistachio butter on a large serving plate. Spoon the glazed beets on top, adding the reserved glaze if desired. If adding lentils, spoon them around the plate. Garnish with mint and season with a bit of flaky salt and a couple of squeezes of lemon juice.

Citrus-Braised Fennel with White Beans

Serves 2 as a main, 4 to 6 as a side | GF, SF, NFO

This is an easy yet impressive restaurant-quality dish that spotlights one of my favorite underrated vegetables. Fennel bulbs are sliced into thick wedges, seared in a hot pan, then braised in freshly squeezed orange juice and vegetable broth until silky soft and melt-in-your-mouth tender. Finishing with zingy orange zest accents the fennel's sweetness, while olives and walnuts add a salty, savory, meaty bite.

Tip: Dial up the flavor by replacing half of the broth with a citrusy, mineral white wine like Sancerre or Albariño.

Big-Flavor Meals: Serve with a crusty hunk of bread or alongside your favorite grain or a simple lemon and olive oil pasta. Also excellent with Herby Shallot-Garlic Confit (page 163) on the side. For a heartier meal, serve with the Pasta & Chickpeas with Fried Capers & Tomato-Shallot Butter (page 501).

2 large **fennel bulbs** (each 10 to 12 ounces/290 g to 340 g), ideally with fronds attached

2 tablespoons **extra-virgin olive oil**

1 teaspoon **kosher salt**

Freshly ground **black pepper**

1 medium-large **orange**, zested and juiced (about 1 tablespoon zest and ¼ cup/60 ml juice)

1 cup (240 ml) **vegetable broth** (see Tip)

¼ cup (30 g) **walnuts**, roughly chopped (omit if nut-free)

1 (15-ounce/425 g) can **cannellini beans**, drained and rinsed

Flaky sea salt

¼ cup (35 g) pitted **Castelvetrano or other green olives** (about 8 to 10 olives), sliced

1. Cut the stalks and fronds off the fennel. Reserve the wispy fronds and chop 2 tablespoons; save the stalks for soups or broths. Slice the fennel bulbs in half lengthwise through the core. Slice each half into quarters so you have eight pieces per bulb (try to slice as evenly as possible). If your bulbs are small, cut into fourths instead of eighths.

recipe continues

2. In a 12-inch (30 cm) sauté pan, heat the olive oil over medium-high heat. Once shimmering, add the fennel. Cook undisturbed for 2 to 3 minutes, then flip and cook for 2 to 3 more minutes. Flip the fennel onto its side (there should be at least one flat side on each wedge) and cook for 2 minutes, until all sides are somewhat browned, 6 to 8 minutes total.

3. Reduce the heat to medium. Add the kosher salt and pepper to taste and gently toss. Pour in the orange juice (not zest), scraping up any browned bits from the bottom. When the juice has mostly boiled down, add the broth. Cover and cook for 15 minutes, reducing the heat as needed to maintain a rapid simmer.

4. **Meanwhile, toast the walnuts.** Heat a small skillet over medium-low heat for a couple of minutes. Add the walnuts, shaking the pan frequently to prevent burning, and toast until nutty in aroma, 3 to 5 minutes. Or toast them in the oven on a sheet pan at 350°F (175°C) for 7 to 10 minutes.

5. Uncover the pan and add the beans, stirring gently to incorporate. Cover and cook until the fennel is tender, about 5 minutes.

6. Increase the heat to a rapid boil and cook, uncovered, until the liquid has reduced and slightly thickened, 3 to 5 minutes. Remove from the heat. Add most of the fennel fronds and the orange zest, reserving a bit of each, and gently combine. Taste for seasonings, adding a pinch of flaky salt.

7. To serve, plate the fennel and beans in shallow bowls. Top with the reserved fennel fronds and orange zest, several cracks of pepper, sliced olives, and walnuts.

Buttery Charred Cabbage in Spiced Tomatoes with Tahini

Serves 4 | GF, SF, NF

One of my favorite party tricks is showing folks that cabbage—a cruciferous vegetable most often used in coleslaw—can get gloriously sweet and buttery. Here, cabbage wedges are seared in a hot cast-iron pan until charred, releasing cabbage's natural sugars. Next, they're nestled into a tangy, spiced tomato sauce and braised until they are meltingly tender and take on a nutty flavor. Finally, they're doused in a creamy tahini sauce, which takes the dish to new indulgent heights.

Ingredient Note: Using good-quality canned tomatoes makes the sauce juicier and less acidic (see page 58 for recommended brands).

Tips: While you shouldn't cook acid-heavy tomatoes in a raw cast-iron pan for a long time, it's fine for quick-cooking applications like this recipe. However, if your cast-iron pan is new and not well seasoned, use a stainless steel, enameled cast-iron, or nonstick pan in steps 4 and 5. Save your leftover half cabbage to quick pickle (page 168) or make a really great slaw (page 511 or 529).

Big-Flavor Meals: Add a can of chickpeas and ½ teaspoon salt after adding the tomatoes in step 5; simmer for 10 to 12 minutes, adding a splash of broth or water as needed. Or serve with the Marinated Chickpeas (page 243) or Wildly Crunchy Cornmeal Beans (page 240). Pair with any cooked grains hanging out in your fridge or with slabs of bread.

Make Ahead: You can make either tahini sauce several days in advance (it stays good for at least 1 week).

½ medium **green (or red) cabbage** (a medium cabbage weighs about 2 pounds/910 g)

3 tablespoons **extra-virgin olive oil**

1 teaspoon **kosher salt**

1 tablespoon **pure maple syrup**

1 (14.5-ounce/410 g) can **diced tomatoes** (or ½ of a 28-ounce/800 g can whole peeled tomatoes, crushed by hand)

1½ teaspoons **cumin seeds**

2 medium **shallots**, sliced

3 **garlic cloves**, finely chopped

½ teaspoon **ground coriander**

1 teaspoon **sweet or hot paprika**

¼ teaspoon **ground cinnamon**

⅛ teaspoon **freshly grated nutmeg**

1 tablespoon **Aleppo pepper** or **Urfa biber** (or about ½ teaspoon red pepper flakes)

½ cup (8 g) **fresh cilantro** (or flat-leaf parsley) leaves and tender stems, chopped

Freshly squeezed **lemon juice**

½ recipe **Lemon Tahini Sauce** or **Pomegranate Tahini Sauce** (page 197), or to taste

recipe continues

1. Cut the cabbage half lengthwise through the core to get four wedges.

2. Heat a large cast-iron skillet or heavy-bottomed pan for which you have a lid over medium-high heat. Add 2 tablespoons of the olive oil. Once shimmering, add the cabbage, cut side down, and season with ½ teaspoon of the salt. Using tongs, move the wedges back and forth gently to ensure they're evenly coated in the oil, and cook until browned on the bottom, 5 to 7 minutes. Carefully flip, sprinkle with the remaining ½ teaspoon salt, and cook until browned on the other side, 5 to 7 minutes. Transfer the wedges to a plate. Take the pan off the heat to cool down for 5 to 10 minutes (do some prep or cleanup in the meantime).

3. Stir the maple syrup into the canned tomatoes. Set aside.

4. Heat the remaining 1 tablespoon oil in the same pan over medium heat. Add the cumin seeds and cook, tossing frequently, until they are aromatic and darker in color, 1 minute. Add the shallots and garlic and cook for 2 minutes. Add the coriander, paprika, cinnamon, nutmeg, and Aleppo pepper and cook for 1 minute, stirring frequently.

5. Reduce the heat to medium-low. Pour in the tomato–maple syrup mixture with all the juices, stir, and carefully nestle the wedges back into the pan. Cover and simmer until the cabbage is tender and the tomatoes have thickened a bit, 8 to 10 minutes, opening the pan once to check if the tomatoes are drying up (if so, add a few splashes of water).

6. Serve the cabbage straight from the pan. Top with cilantro and a squeeze of lemon juice. Spoon some tahini sauce generously on top and serve more on the side.

Maple-Roasted Squash & Chickpeas with Mint-Pistachio Pesto

Serves 4 | GF, SF

This caramelized, sweet-salty winter squash is so delicious you'll want to make it every week of fall and winter. When sliced very thinly and roasted in a hot oven, squash becomes chewy and even crispy, its sweetness further coaxed out by maple syrup. Roasting chickpeas gives them a nice crunch, and plating these crispy, chewy morsels over creamy mint pesto makes for a harmonious medley of textures.

Ingredient Note: Winter squash may be good year-round but is best in fall and winter.

Tip: If you don't have time to make Hazelnut Dukkah, toast some chopped pistachios and white sesame seeds in a skillet until aromatic and toasty while the squash is roasting.

Big-Flavor Meals: Serve with slabs of crusty bread or a pot of grains. If you have more time, this is excellent with the Buttery Brown Rice with Warm Spices (page 309) or Customizable Grain Salad with Garlicky Spiced Oil & Fresh Herbs (page 305).

Make Ahead: This is a great dinner to meal prep. The pesto will stay good in the fridge for up to 5 days; the dukkah can be made a week or two ahead.

1½ to 2 pounds (680 to 910 g) **delicata squash**, **acorn squash**, or **butternut squash**

1 (15-ounce/425 g) can **chickpeas**, drained and rinsed

2½ tablespoons **extra-virgin olive oil**

1 tablespoon **pure maple syrup**

1 teaspoon **ground cumin**

Kosher salt and freshly ground **black pepper**

⅓ to ½ cup (80 to 120 g) **Mint-Pistachio Pesto** (page 178), or to taste

1 small handful **fresh mint and/or cilantro** leaves, chopped

2 to 3 tablespoons **Hazelnut Dukkah** (page 219; optional; see Tip)

Aleppo pepper (optional, for mild heat)

1. Arrange one rack in the bottom of the oven and one in the top third. Preheat the oven to 450°F (230°C). Once hot, add two rimmed sheet pans (ideally well-worn pans) to preheat for 10 to 15 minutes.

recipe continues

2. If you are using butternut squash, peel it first; for delicata or acorn squash, keep the skin on but wash it.

3. Use a large, sharp knife to slice your squash in half vertically, then scoop out the seeds with a spoon. Thinly slice the squash crosswise into ¼-inch (0.5 cm) half-moon slices.

4. Dry the chickpeas very well, gently rubbing in a dish towel to pat dry (or transfer to a salad spinner for a few rounds, then pat dry).

5. Transfer the squash and chickpeas to a large bowl. Add the olive oil, maple syrup, cumin, 1½ teaspoons kosher salt, and a generous amount of black pepper. Toss well to combine.

6. Using oven mitts, remove the pans from the oven and divide the squash and chickpeas between the pans. Arrange the squash pieces so they make contact with the pan and overlap as little as possible; it's okay if some chickpeas rest on top of squash.

7. Roast for 15 minutes, then flip the squash over and toss the chickpeas. Return to the oven, but change the position of each pan on the racks and rotate them by 180 degrees for even baking. Roast for 12 to 15 more minutes, until the squash is tender and deeply browned (some charring is good) and the chickpeas are browned in some spots and a bit crunchy.

8. To assemble, smear some pesto on a serving plate. Top with squash and chickpeas. For a drizzleable consistency, stir a little water into the pesto and drizzle more pesto on top. Garnish with mint and/or cilantro, a nice handful of dukkah, and a few sprinkles of Aleppo pepper (if desired).

Crispy Smashed Potatoes with Lots of Saucy Options

Serves 6 to 8 | GF, SF, NF

Crispy smashed potatoes are the complete potato package: creamy and fluffy on the inside but with flaky, crispy skins and craggy, crunchy edges. While they're delicious on their own, my favorite way to serve them is with a mega-flavorful sauce for drizzling or dipping, so I've given you a chart for customizable sauces and toppings.

Ingredient Note: Baby golden or yellow potatoes are the Goldilocks of potatoes: waxy enough to get crispy on the outside but starchy so their interiors stay fluffy and creamy. You can use small Yukon Gold potatoes in a pinch, but they don't get as crispy.

Tip: To use a bit less oil, use a pastry brush to brush the oil onto the potatoes.

Big-Flavor Meals: Serve as a hearty side with your sauce and topping of choice, or alongside a protein for a complete meal. Check out the chart on the next page for mix-and-match options.

Sauce of choice (see chart on page 409)

Toppings of choice (see chart on page 409)

3 pounds (1.4 kg) **baby golden potatoes** (see Ingredient Note)

¼ cup (36 g) **kosher salt** (or 2 tablespoons fine sea salt), plus more to season

4 to 5 tablespoons (60 to 75 g) **extra-virgin olive oil**

Freshly ground **black pepper**

1. Choose your desired sauce and topping combo from the chart and prepare in advance or while the potatoes are cooking.

2. Preheat the oven to 450°F (230°C). Arrange one rack in the bottom of the oven and one in the top third.

3. Add the potatoes to a large saucepan. Cover with cold water and season with the salt (yes, it's a lot, but potatoes are dense and need it; it won't be overly salty). Bring to a boil, then reduce the heat to maintain a decent simmer and cook until fork-tender but not soft, 12 to 14 minutes. Don't overboil or they'll become mushy. Drain the potatoes and allow to dry out in the colander for 5 minutes.

4. Transfer the potatoes to two rimmed sheet pans. Use the bottom of a glass or mug to gently but firmly smash the potatoes. If the potatoes stick to the glass, lightly rub some oil on the bottom of the glass. Drizzle some of the olive oil on top and coat the top sides; gently flip, add more oil, and coat the other side. If the

recipe continues

potatoes feel dry, add a bit more oil. Spread them out on the pans so they have space to breathe. Season fairly generously with kosher salt (less if using sea salt) and a few twists of pepper.

5. Roast for 15 minutes. Then, without flipping the potatoes, rotate the pans by 180 degrees and swap their rack positions. Roast for 15 more minutes, or until crispy and browned.

6. Transfer the potatoes to a serving platter. Drizzle or spoon some of your sauce on top of the potatoes, scatter with the toppings, and serve the remaining sauce as a dip on the side.

Crispy Smashed Potatoes—Saucy Pairings

SAUCE	TOPPINGS	MAIN MEAL PAIRING (OPTIONAL)
Avocado Crema (page 204) or Chipotle Crema (page 205)	1 handful fresh cilantro, chopped + a few thinly sliced scallions	Serve with Saucy Black Beans in Sofrito (page 250) or scatter black or pinto beans on top of the potatoes.
Herby Shallot-Garlic Confit (page 163)	1 handful fresh dill, chopped + 1 small handful toasted almonds, finely chopped	Scatter simply cooked French green lentils alongside the potatoes or serve with Spiced Lentil Salad with Fresh Herbs (page 257).
Italian Basil & Parsley Salsa Verde (page 181)	1 small handful toasted pine nuts	Coat cannellini beans in the salsa verde, then spoon on top of the potatoes.
Turkish-Spiced Tahini Sauce (page 198)	1 handful each fresh mint and parsley, chopped + 1 small handful toasted almonds or walnuts, finely chopped	Scatter Crunchy Roasted Chickpeas (page 236) alongside the potatoes or serve with Marinated Chickpeas (page 243).
Mint Yogurt Sauce (page 213)	1 handful fresh cilantro, chopped + 2 to 3 tablespoons chopped peanuts + a dusting of chaat masala or garam masala	Scatter Tandoori Roasted Chickpeas (page 238) alongside the potatoes.
Throwback Ranch Dressing (page 203)	1 handful fresh chives, finely chopped	Scatter BBQ Roasted Chickpeas (page 239) alongside the potatoes.
Preserved Lemon Salsa (page 184)	A few dollops of unsweetened coconut yogurt or vegan sour cream	Serve with cannellini beans dressed with olive oil, lemon zest, and lemon juice.
Spicy Mint & Cilantro Sauce (page 189) or Pomegranate Molasses Vinaigrette (page 165)	A few dollops of unsweetened coconut yogurt + 1 handful fresh mint or cilantro, chopped	Scatter simply cooked French green lentils alongside the potatoes.
Life-Changing Homemade Chili Crisp (page 187)	1 handful fresh cilantro, chopped + a few thinly sliced scallions	Serve with Edamame Salad with Chili Crisp (page 249).

Baingan Bharta

Serves 2 as a main, 4 as a side · GF, SF, NF

Baingan bharta has a special place in my heart because it was the first dish that convinced my deeply eggplant-averse partner that eggplant is actually really delicious. And as anybody who's been in a long-term relationship knows, those little moments where you get to show your partner that you were right the whole time . . . well, those are big victories.

This dish hails from the Punjab region of India and is traditionally made by roasting a whole eggplant over an open flame or tandoor oven to infuse it with a smoky aroma. Luckily, if you have a gas stove, you can achieve nearly the same results at home.

Whole roasting the eggplant over an open flame on the stove infuses it with a rich, smoky char *and* transforms rubbery eggplant into something so tender that it melts in your mouth. When combined with a simple mix of Indian spices and aromatics (the bharta), it takes on a spicy, tangy flavor that is irresistible.

Ingredient Notes: Choose a medium globe or Italian eggplant that weighs about 1 pound (400 to 455 g) and is relatively uniform in girth from top to bottom so it cooks evenly. For moderate (but not mild) heat, use 1 to 1½ teaspoons Kashmiri chile powder and omit the serrano pepper.

Tips: To minimize the eggplant cook time, choose a ripe eggplant (one that is fairly soft to the touch but not mushy or bruised), or wait until your eggplant is ripe. Your stove will get dirty, so use a grease-cutting soap, baking soda paste, or a distilled vinegar and water solution and a tough sponge to clean up afterward. If you don't have a gas stove, follow the sauté method instructions below, though you won't get the smoky flavor. For a touch of richness, stir in a few teaspoons of melted vegan butter in step 10.

Big-Flavor Meals: Serve with Simple Flatbread (page 535) or Indian flatbread like roti or vegan naan. Top with Mint Yogurt Sauce (page 213) or a dollop of coconut yogurt. Or serve as a side dish to My Favorite Dal Tadka (page 497) or Tofu 65 (page 477).

Make Ahead: You can cook and mash the eggplant 3 to 5 days ahead of time (store in the fridge). You can also make the bharta a few days in advance and store it separately.

Baingan

1 medium **eggplant** (about 1 pound/455 g; see Ingredient Notes)

Neutral-flavored oil of choice

Bharta

1½ tablespoons **neutral-flavored oil** of choice

1 teaspoon **cumin seeds**

1 medium **red or yellow onion**, finely diced

Kosher salt

4 **garlic cloves**, finely chopped

1-inch (2.5 cm) piece **fresh ginger**, grated or minced

1 small **serrano pepper**, finely chopped (optional, for *spicy!*; omit for mild heat)

½ teaspoon **ground turmeric**

1 teaspoon **ground coriander**

recipe and ingredients continue

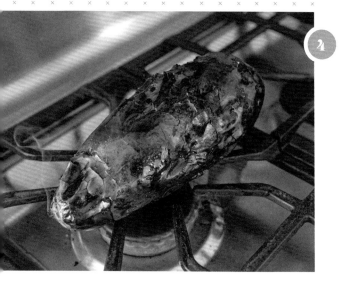

2 medium **Roma or plum tomatoes**, finely chopped

½ teaspoon **Kashmiri chile powder**
(see Ingredient Notes)

1 teaspoon **garam masala**

1 cup (16 g) **fresh cilantro** leaves and tender stems, chopped

For Serving

Roti, vegan naan, Simple Flatbread (page 535),
or **cooked rice**

Baingan

1. Ventilate your kitchen and open the windows. Peel any leaves from the top of the eggplant to prevent them from burning. Using a pastry brush or your hands, brush just a light coating of oil on the eggplant.

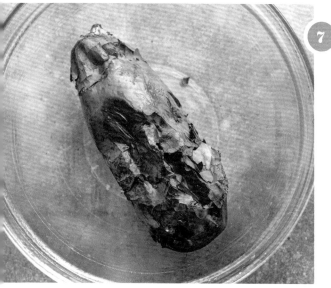

2. Turn a gas burner on your stove to medium-low heat. Use tongs to hold the eggplant upright (vertically) and hold the bottom of the eggplant over the flame for 3 to 6 minutes to char the bottom, until a paring knife can pierce the bottom without much resistance.

3. Flip the eggplant 180 degrees with the tongs. Char the top of the eggplant for 2 to 3 minutes, making sure the stem doesn't directly touch the flame to avoid burning.

4. Place the eggplant on its side (lying flat, horizontally), positioning the fatter bottom part directly over the flame. Every 2 minutes, gently rotate the eggplant using the tongs.

5. Once deeply charred and very wrinkly, insert a paring knife into the fattest part of the eggplant. The eggplant needs to be very soft, so the knife should slide in easily with minimal

or no resistance. This should take about 8 minutes for a ripe eggplant; firmer eggplants need about 15 minutes.

6. Now insert the knife into the skinnier, top part of the eggplant. If there is a bit of resistance, cook for 4 to 6 minutes, rotating every 2 minutes, until charred and wrinkly. If it has no resistance, carefully use tongs to transfer the eggplant to a medium or large bowl.

7. Cover the eggplant with a plate and steam for 5 minutes. Dip your hands in water and peel off the charred papery black flakes (it's okay if tiny black spots remain). Transfer the eggplant to a cutting board and slice off the head. Using a knife, mash the eggplant as if you were mincing garlic.

Bharta

1. In a medium skillet, heat the oil over medium-high heat. Add the cumin seeds and cook for 1 minute, tossing frequently. Add the onions with a pinch of salt and cook until softened but not browned, 4 to 5 minutes. Add the garlic, ginger, serrano (if using), and turmeric and stir frequently for 60 to 90 seconds. Add the coriander, 1½ teaspoons salt, and tomatoes and cook until the oil starts to release from the tomatoes and the tomatoes are soft, about 5 minutes.

2. Add the mashed eggplant and chile powder. Toss well to combine. Reduce the heat to medium or medium-low and cook for 3 to 5 minutes, stirring often and mashing it all together.

3. Add the garam masala and cilantro and season with a couple of pinches of salt. Serve warm with flatbread or rice of choice.

Sauté method

1. Peel the eggplant and cut into ½-inch (1 to 1.5 cm) pieces.

2. In a large nonstick skillet, heat 2½ tablespoons of oil over medium-high heat. Once shimmering, add the eggplant, season with salt, and cook, tossing occasionally, until the eggplant starts to break down, about 6 minutes. Reduce the heat to medium and cook until the eggplant is soft and jammy and there's no resistance, about 20 minutes. Use a knife to mash the eggplant as if you were mincing garlic. Make the bharta and serve as written above.

"Cream"-Braised Leeks with Crispy Bits

Serves 4 as a main, 8 or more as a side | GFO, SF

When braised, leeks become impossibly tender and almost meaty, and when braised in "cream," they become truly indulgent and melt in your mouth. To finish, the leeks are blanketed with buttery bread crumbs and fried leek greens for that creamy-crispy textural wonderland, while lemon zest and pepper flakes awaken the richness. This is a fabulous cold-weather main dish or side for your next cozy dinner party.

Ingredient Notes: Don't use extra-virgin olive oil instead of vegan butter in the bread crumbs, as it will cause them to burn under the broiler. I suggest choosing a dry white wine like Sauvignon Blanc, Sancerre, Pinot Grigio, Pinot Gris, Albariño, or Chablis to braise the leeks. Typically, leeks are best in the fall through early spring.

Tips: You'll end up with excess dark green leek tops, so feel free to make a double batch of the Crispy Leek Tops (they're a great zero-waste topping for any savory bowl). Or freeze them for broths or soups.

Big-Flavor Meals: You can toss the remaining half of the beans from step 6 with a bit of lemon juice, olive oil, salt, and pepper flakes; pour it over arugula or salad greens to serve on the side. Serve with crusty bread.

Make Ahead: You can make the "cream" and buttery bread crumbs 3 days ahead of time.

Braised Leeks

6 medium (or 3 very large) **leeks** (3¼ to 3½ pounds/ 1.5 kg; see Tips)

2 tablespoons **extra-virgin olive oil**, plus more as needed

Kosher salt and freshly ground **black pepper**

⅓ cup (80 ml) **dry white wine** (see Ingredient Notes)

1 cup (240 ml) **vegetable broth**, plus more as needed

6 to 10 **thyme** sprigs

Bread Crumbs

¾ cup (60 g) **panko bread crumbs** (use gluten-free panko for GF)

1½ tablespoons melted **vegan butter** or **high-heat oil**, such as avocado oil (see Ingredient Notes)

"Cream"

½ cup (70 g) **raw cashews**, soaked or quick soaked, drained, and rinsed (see page 106)

½ of a 15-ounce (425 g) can **cannellini beans**, drained and rinsed (see Big-Flavor Meals)

1 teaspoon **kosher salt**, plus more to taste

1¼ teaspoons **Dijon mustard**, plus more to taste

Extra-virgin olive oil

recipe and ingredients continue

Crispy Leek Tops (recipe follows)

1 small handful **fresh flat-leaf parsley** leaves and tender stems, chopped

1 medium-large **lemon**, zested

½ to ¾ teaspoon **red pepper flakes** (¾ teaspoon for a noticeable kick)

Flaky sea salt

Crusty bread, for serving (highly recommended)

1. **Start the braised leeks.** Peel the leeks' papery outer layers and trim the roots. Cut off the dark green tops and slice thinly into rounds, as evenly as possible; set aside for the crispy leek tops recipe that follows.

2. Slice the remaining white and light green leek portions into ¾-inch (2 cm) coins and add to a bowl of cold water. Weight down with a smaller bowl to submerge the leeks for 5 minutes. Very gently loosen any dirt, trying to keep the slices intact. Scoop the leeks with your hands out onto a towel-lined surface and pat dry. Dump the dirty water and refill with cold water for the Crispy Leek Tops.

3. **While the leeks soak, make the bread crumbs.** In a medium bowl, mix together the panko and melted butter until well combined.

4. Heat a 12-inch (30 cm) cast-iron skillet or other ovenproof sauté pan over medium heat. Add the olive oil, and once shimmering, add the leek slices in a single layer as much as possible. Cook undisturbed for 2 minutes,

then shake the pan. Cook, shaking the pan occasionally, until they are browned on the bottom, 2 to 4 more minutes. Flip the leeks with tongs or a wide spatula. Cook, stirring only occasionally, until nicely browned on the other side, 3 to 5 minutes.

5. Season the leeks with kosher salt and pepper, then pour in the wine and simmer for 3 to 4 minutes. Add the broth and nestle in the thyme sprigs. Bring to a boil, then reduce to a simmer and cook for 10 minutes, stirring occasionally.

6. **While the leeks simmer, make the "cream."** Add the soaked and drained cashews to a high-powered blender or food processor. Add ½ cup (120 ml) of water, the half can of beans, the kosher salt, and mustard. Blend until smooth and creamy, stopping to scrape down the sides as you go. Taste, adding more salt or mustard as desired, or a drizzle of olive oil for richness.

7. Fish out the thyme sprigs from the leeks. Pour the "cream" into the leeks and simmer, stirring occasionally to prevent sticking, until the leeks are very tender (lower the heat as needed to maintain a simmer), 5 to 7 minutes. If the mixture gets too thick, add a splash or two of broth or water.

8. Position an oven rack on the second shelf below the broiler and preheat the broiler to high. Sprinkle the buttered bread crumbs on top of the leeks. Broil for 2 minutes, or until the top is golden brown (keep a close eye to prevent burning).

9. Top the braised leeks with the crispy leek tops and parsley. Sprinkle with lemon zest, pepper flakes, and a bit of flaky salt. Taste and add more lemon zest or salt as needed. Dig in with hunks of crusty bread.

Crispy Leek Tops

Serves 4 to 8 | GF, SF, NF

Dark green leek tops are almost always tossed, but when you gently fry them, they become not just edible but incredibly delicious and crispy-chewy. Reducing food waste has never tasted so good.

1 cup (65 g) **dark green leek tops**, thinly sliced into rounds

2 tablespoons **avocado oil**, **extra-virgin olive oil**, or **oil of choice**

Flaky sea salt

1. In a large bowl of cold water, place the sliced leek tops, submerging and swishing them with your hands to remove any sand. Dry as instructed in step 2 on page 416. Line a plate with a few paper towels.

2. In a small saucepan, heat the oil over medium to medium-high heat. To test if it's hot enough, add one piece of leek; if it bubbles at the surface, the oil is ready. Fry the leek tops, stirring frequently, until crisp but still quite green, 4 to 5 minutes. If they start browning quickly, reduce the heat a touch. Remove with a slotted spoon to the paper towel–lined plate to blot excess oil. Sprinkle with a pinch of flaky salt.

Braised Carrots & Chickpeas with Dill Gremolata

Serves 5 to 6 | GF, SF, NF

Whole carrots are seared and caramelized with spices, then oven-braised with chickpeas in olive oil. The carrots become meltingly tender and silky and the chickpeas plump, each infused with the sweetness of braised shallots and the warmth of toasted spices and chile flakes. Finishing with dill gremolata and sweet balsamic brightens all the cozy flavors.

The prep and active cook time are pretty minimal, and the 50-minute braise is hands-off, which makes this a great weeknight dinner if you can start early.

Ingredient Notes: Use skinny carrots, which are sweeter than large carrots and can be left whole. If you can't find them, cut your carrots in half lengthwise. You won't be able to sear them all at once, so do step 3 in two batches before adding the spices.

Tip: If you don't have a braising pan or wide Dutch oven, cut the carrots crosswise first and do step 3 in two batches.

2 teaspoons **cumin seeds**

2 teaspoons **coriander seeds**

¼ cup + 2 tablespoons (84 g) **extra-virgin olive oil**, plus more as needed

1½ pounds (680 g) skinny **carrots**, scrubbed but not peeled (see Ingredient Notes)

Kosher salt and freshly ground **black pepper**

½ to 1 teaspoon **red pepper flakes** (use ½ teaspoon for milder heat)

10 **garlic cloves**, smashed

⅓ cup (80 ml) **dry white wine** (optional; or more veg broth)

1 cup (240 ml) **vegetable broth**, plus more as needed

4 medium **shallots**, thinly sliced into rings

2 (15-ounce/425 g) cans **chickpeas**, drained and rinsed

1 to 1½ cups (190 to 285 g) uncooked or 3 to 4½ cups (425 to 650 g) cooked **brown or white rice**, or grains of your choice

½ to 1 cup (8 to 16 g) **fresh dill** (tough stems removed), chopped (dill lovers, use 1 cup/16 g)

1 large **lemon**, zested

¼ teaspoon **flaky sea salt**

2 to 3 teaspoons **aged balsamic vinegar**

recipe continues

1. Preheat the oven to 325°F (165°C).

2. Roughly grind the cumin and coriander seeds in a mortar with a pestle or add to a spice grinder and pulse just once or twice. For alternative methods, see page 74.

3. In a braising pan or a wide Dutch oven, heat 2 tablespoons of the olive oil over medium-high heat. Once shimmering, add the carrots in a single layer (a little overlap is okay) and season with a few pinches of kosher salt. Cook undisturbed for 4 minutes. Turn with tongs, and cook until they are starting to brown in spots, 5 to 7 more minutes.

4. Add the lightly crushed cumin and coriander, pepper flakes, and garlic. Cook until the garlic is golden and the carrots are starting to caramelize, about 3 minutes. If the pan starts to dry out, add a splash of water or a bit more oil.

5. Pour in the wine (or broth if not using wine) and use some elbow grease to deglaze the pot, scraping up the browned bits. Cook until the smell of alcohol cooks off, about 3 minutes. If there are a lot of bits stuck to the pan, pour in some of the broth and deglaze again.

6. Turn off the heat. Add the shallots and chickpeas. Pour in the broth and the remaining ¼ cup (56 g) oil. Season generously with kosher salt (about 1½ teaspoons) and lots of black pepper. Stir to combine. Cover the pan with its lid or tightly cover with foil. Transfer to the oven to braise for 50 minutes, or until the carrots are easily pierced with the tip of a sharp knife. Uncover and let cool for 10 minutes. While the dish braises, cook your rice or grains using your preferred method (see pages 303–4), or get out your leftover cooked rice or grains.

7. In a small bowl, combine the dill, lemon zest, and flaky salt. Sprinkle over the carrots. Before serving, drizzle with 2 teaspoons balsamic vinegar. Taste, adding more vinegar, flaky salt, and/or black pepper as needed. Serve with cooked rice or grains.

Cauliflower Steaks with Italian Basil & Parsley Salsa Verde

Serves 4 as a main, 8 as a side | GF, SF, NFO

Slicing vegetables unconventionally is a simple way to make them more exciting. These "steaks" are browned and caramelized in a hot oven, then any loose florets are pureed into a deceptively indulgent "cream." Each bite of creamy tenderness is peppered with the salty, garlicky heat from Italian salsa verde. Adding white beans makes this a versatile dish you can serve as an entrée for a few, or a side dish for many (great for holiday gatherings).

Tips: Roast the cauliflower on an unlined, well-worn sheet pan for the best browning.

You should get three steak-style cuts from a large cauliflower, but if you only get two, don't worry, because the florets are just as tasty.

If you have preserved lemons, fold a few teaspoons of chopped lemon peel into the cream instead of the lemon zest (and go easy on the salt).

Make Ahead: You can make the salsa verde a few days ahead of time. Store leftovers in the fridge for up to 1 week.

Cauliflower

2 large heads **cauliflower**

3 tablespoons **extra-virgin olive oil**, plus more as needed

Kosher salt and freshly ground **black pepper**

Cauliflower Cream

2 cups (210 g) reserved **roasted cauliflower florets**

1 (15-ounce/425 g) can **cannellini beans**, drained and rinsed

3 tablespoons well-stirred **tahini**

2 **garlic cloves**, roughly chopped

1 medium **lemon**, zested

2 tablespoons freshly squeezed **lemon juice**

2 tablespoons plain **plant-based milk** of choice, plus more as needed

1 tablespoon **extra-virgin olive oil**, plus more as desired

1 teaspoon **red wine vinegar** or **champagne vinegar**

¼ teaspoon **red pepper flakes**

Kosher salt and freshly ground **black pepper**

For Serving

⅓ to ½ cup (80 to 120 g) **Italian Basil & Parsley Salsa Verde** (page 181), or to taste

¼ cup (35 g) toasted **pine nuts** (omit if nut-free)

1. Preheat the oven to 425°F (220°C).

2. **Roast the cauliflower.** Remove any cauliflower leaves and trim the bottom stems

recipe continues

that jut out, but keep the cores intact (this is essential for getting steak-style cuts). Slice each cauliflower in half lengthwise. Now slice each half into ¾-inch (2 cm) thick slabs. Cut loose pieces into small florets.

3. Arrange the cauliflower steaks on two rimmed sheet pans in a single layer (no parchment paper). Drizzle with about 2 tablespoons of the olive oil, rubbing it into the crevices, and sprinkle generously with salt and black pepper. Flip and rub in the remaining 1 tablespoon oil and season with salt and pepper. Toss loose florets with a bit of oil, salt, and pepper and add to empty spaces in the pans.

4. Roast undisturbed for 25 minutes. Remove from the oven and use a wide spatula to carefully flip the steaks. Toss the florets. Roast for 10 to 15 more minutes, until the steaks are nicely browned on both sides.

5. **Make the cauliflower cream.** Transfer 2 cups (210 g) of the roasted florets to a blender or food processor. Add half of the cannellini beans (about ¾ cup/120 g beans; reserve the rest for serving), the tahini, garlic, lemon zest and juice, milk, olive oil, vinegar, and pepper flakes. Puree until smooth. Season with salt and black pepper to taste. If the mixture is too thick, add another spoonful of milk. For more richness, add more olive oil.

6. **To serve,** spoon a generous amount of the cauliflower cream across a platter. Top with the cauliflower steaks and spoon the reserved beans and any leftover roasted florets around the steaks. Add several generous spoonfuls of salsa verde on top. Scatter on the pine nuts and serve.

HOW TO PICK THE IDEAL COOKING METHOD FOR VEGETABLES

The best cooking method depends on not only your vegetable's characteristics (is it sturdy or delicate?) but also the role you want it to play in the dish (is it the hero or a supporting character?) and the type of dish you're going for (light and bright for summer, or comforting and rich for winter?).

These three-ish methods are the ones I use most often that don't require specialty equipment yet yield great flavor and texture.

Roasting

When in doubt, roasting a vegetable is a solid bet, as it coaxes out the vegetable's natural sugars. Generally, the sweet spot, temperature-wise, is 400° to 450°F (200° to 230°C).

For the most browning and caramelization, (1) roast vegetables on a naked rimmed sheet pan that is well worn (not lined with parchment paper or foil), and (2) spread the veg out as much as you can to avoid steaming. Don't be afraid of a little char; especially with naturally sweet vegetables, charring adds amazing complexity. Avoid roasting vegetables with different water content levels together (e.g., potatoes and zucchini).

BEST VEGETABLES TO ROAST: root vegetables (e.g., beets, carrots), cruciferous vegetables (e.g., cauliflower, cabbage), tubers, squash family (e.g., pumpkin), sturdy mushrooms (e.g., oysters), eggplant, cherry tomatoes.

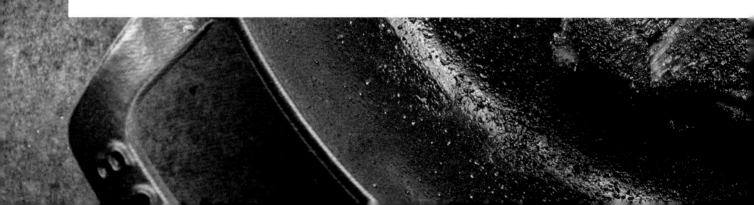

Braising

Great for when you're feeling fancy and/or want something that feels hearty. Braising involves first pan-searing the vegetable, then cooking it in a small amount of flavorful liquid in a covered pan until tender.

Experiment with different braising liquids, including vegetable broth, white or red wine, East Asian cooking wines like mirin or Shaoxing wine mixed with soy sauce, beer, cider, citrus or other fruit juices, olive oil, coconut milk, or canned tomatoes. Punch up the flavor by adding a splash of vinegar or soy sauce, or infuse complementary whole spices (e.g., cinnamon sticks) and aromatics (e.g., lemongrass) into the braising liquid.

BEST VEGETABLES TO BRAISE: root vegetables, tubers, alliums (e.g., onions, leeks), celery, cabbage, hearty leafy greens and lettuces. Avoid juicy veg like tomatoes or summer squash.

Pan-Frying and Sautéing

Easy methods when you want vibrant yet slightly crisp vegetables with lots of flavor. Cook over relatively high heat with some amount of fat (less for sautéing, a bit more with pan-frying).

For the most caramelization, (1) wait until the oil is shimmering before adding the veg, (2) use cast-iron or stainless steel pans, and (3) don't overcrowd the pan. When pan-frying, coat the bottom side of the vegetable in oil, then cook undisturbed for a bit before flipping so it can sear.

BEST VEGETABLES TO SAUTÉ OR PAN-FRY: most work well.

11

Weekend Brunch

I lived in New York City from the ages of twenty-four to thirty-two. Which is to say I ate a lot of brunch.

I love the frivolity of brunch. No one *needs* to eat an enormous plate of pancakes alongside a Bloody Mary at noon, but it sure is fun. And isn't that sort of the point of life? To have fun? Otherwise, you're just stuck in an endless loop of paying taxes and doing laundry.

But going out to *vegan* brunch can be hard. The first time I tried doing it, I was served approximately three ounces of a smoothie bowl dusted with a light coating of puffed brown rice cereal masquerading as "artisanal granola." For sixteen dollars.

That's why I prefer to brunch at home these days. Plus, there's something so delightfully indulgent about whipping up a fancy-ish meal midday on a Saturday or Sunday.

So what you'll find in this chapter is a mix of savory and sweet weekend brunch recipes that are exciting, varied, and above all, delicious. Pour yourself your weekend beverage of choice, invite a few friends over, and enjoy this very special invention we call brunch.

Hannah's Carrot Lox

Makes enough for 8 open-faced bagels | GF, SF, NF

At the start of the pandemic, I left isolation for two things: (1) toilet paper and (2) NYC bagels. Halfway across the world in the Netherlands, my soon-to-be culinary assistant, Hannah, filled her spare time (in between nursing a newborn) with carrot lox experiments. When she shared this recipe with me, I was blown away by how carrots—*sweet and crunchy carrots*—could taste so similar to smoked salmon.

Slow baking carrots in a mountain of salt dries them out, concentrates their flavor, and transforms them into a wholly different entity. Once marinated, they take on the salty, smoky flavors you love about lox and soften into something velvety and almost meaty.

Pile this onto a bagel schmeared with vegan cream cheese (or better yet, my Whipped Feta) and dot with briny capers and feathery wisps of dill, and enjoy a life-changing brunch experience.

Ingredient Notes: Use small-medium carrots that are fairly skinny. Large/chubby carrots don't dry out and they taste like steamed carrots. You need an obscene amount of salt for this recipe, but you can save it to clean dirty pots and pans or to make a couple of batches of future lox (just break up the salt clumps with your hands).

14 ounces (400 g) small-medium **carrots** (about 8 to 10; see Ingredient Notes)

2 to 2½ cups (280 to 350 g) **kosher salt**

3 tablespoons good-quality **extra-virgin olive oil**

2 tablespoons chopped **fresh dill**

1 teaspoon **Dijon mustard**

1 tablespoon **caper brine**

¼ teaspoon **ground white pepper** (or freshly ground black pepper)

¼ teaspoon **liquid smoke**

½ teaspoon **umeboshi paste** (optional; adds more savory, tangy depth of flavor)

¼ teaspoon **smoked sea salt**

For Serving

Whipped Feta (page 209) or store-bought vegan cream cheese

4 **everything bagels**, or bagels of choice, toasted

Capers

Dill sprigs, chopped

recipe continues

1. Arrange a rack in the middle of the oven. Preheat the oven to 350°F (175°C). Wash and scrub the carrots very well, but do not peel them or remove their nubby tops (remove any leafy greens). Pat dry with a towel.

2. In a 13 × 9-inch (3 L) casserole pan (or another baking dish that will fit the carrots in a single layer without touching), add ¾ to 1 cup (105 to 140 g) of kosher salt, enough to cover the bottom. Gently shake back and forth to even out the salt. Arrange the carrots in a single layer on top of the salt, leaving enough room so they don't touch each other. Pour the remaining salt on top of the carrots, arranging the carrots snugly in the salt and using your hands to cover the carrots in salt (they must be encased in it in order to bake properly).

3. Bake for 2 hours. If the carrots are very skinny, start checking 15 minutes earlier.

4. **Make the marinade.** In a small or medium bowl, whisk together the olive oil, dill, mustard, caper brine, pepper, liquid smoke, umeboshi paste (if using), and smoked sea salt. Set aside.

5. Remove the carrots from the oven. They should be crusted in salt and look shriveled, smaller, and dried out. Let rest until cool enough to handle.

6. Break the crusted salt with your hands and gently remove the carrots. Very gently rinse them under running water and pat dry with a towel. Using a very sharp knife, slice off the top nub and slice each carrot on a hard bias, as thinly as you can. If any skinny bottoms have blackened or hardened, cut off and discard them.

7. Add the carrots to a quart-size (1 L) resealable bag, pour in the marinade, seal, and massage to coat the carrots. Refrigerate for at least 1 day, preferably 2 days. Massage the carrots in the marinade once a day.

8. When ready to eat, let rest on the counter for 15 to 20 minutes to bring the oil to room temperature. Stir before using to incorporate the oil.

9. Schmear the whipped feta or vegan cream cheese on the bagels, pile on some lox, and dot each bagel with a few capers and a sprinkling of dill. Store leftover lox in its marinade in a lidded jar in the fridge for up to 2 weeks.

Mushroom Bacon

Serves 4 to 6 | GF, NF

I've tried several iterations of plant "bacon," and my favorite version features very thinly sliced king oyster mushrooms coated in a smoky, salty, slightly sweet, hickory-forward marinade and baked in the dry heat of an oven. The flavor is startlingly bacon-like: the thinner pieces get super crispy, while thicker pieces get a little chewy.

Ingredient Note: If you can't find king oyster mushrooms, use shiitakes: remove the stems and slice the caps into ⅛-inch (0.3 cm) slices; bake for 20 minutes, flip, then check after 10 to 15 minutes.

Tip: For even mushroom slices, use a mandoline.

Use It for Big Flavor: Layer on toast or a bagel with Shallot-Garlic Confit (page 163) or smashed avocado. Make an epic breakfast burrito with the Eggy Tofu Scramble (page 439), Extremely Easy Queso Sauce (page 199) or shredded vegan cheese, salsa, hot sauce (page 190), and avocado. For lunch, make an avocado BLT.

1 pound (455 g) **king oyster mushrooms** (see Ingredient Note)

2 tablespoons **tamari** or **soy sauce** (use tamari to keep GF)

1 tablespoon **extra-virgin olive oil**, **avocado oil**, or **oil of choice**, plus more for the pan

1 tablespoon **toasted sesame oil**

1 teaspoon **liquid smoke**

1 tablespoon **pure maple syrup**

1½ teaspoons **smoked paprika**

½ teaspoon **kosher salt**

Freshly ground **black pepper**

Smoked sea salt (recommended) or **flaky sea salt**, for finishing

1. Slice off about ¼ inch (0.5 cm) from the tough bottom of the mushroom stems (you can save them for broth). Cut the caps off; slice them thinly (they don't have the same "bacon-like" texture but are still tasty).

2. Using a mandoline or sharp knife, slice the stems lengthwise from top to bottom into ⅛-inch (0.3 cm) slices. When you get to the last part of the stem, you may not be able to cut the same-size pieces, but these are still good!

recipe continues

3. In a shallow dish or pie plate, whisk together the tamari, olive oil, sesame oil, liquid smoke, maple syrup, and paprika. Add the mushrooms and stir gently to combine. Marinate at room temperature for at least 20 minutes, or up to 1 hour.

4. Arrange one rack in the bottom of the oven and one in the top third. Preheat the oven to 350°F (175°C). Line two rimmed sheet pans with parchment paper. Brush the parchment paper with a bit of oil.

5. Divide the mushrooms between each pan in a single layer, leaving behind the excess marinade. Sprinkle with ¼ teaspoon of the kosher salt and lots of pepper.

6. Bake for 20 minutes. Remove the pans and carefully flip the mushrooms using a thin spatula (or your hands, but be careful!). Sprinkle the remaining ¼ teaspoon kosher salt on the second side. For more flavor, brush the tops with excess marinade. Bake for 15 to 20 more minutes, until well browned and chewy but crisp. The mushrooms should reduce in size by 60 to 70 percent.

7. Transfer the mushrooms to a paper towel–lined plate to drain. Sprinkle very lightly with the smoked sea salt or flaky salt.

Scrambled Shakshuka

Serves 4 | GF, NF

Shakshuka was my favorite savory brunch before going vegan, so I really wanted to create an egg-free version. Sami Tamimi's scrambled red shakshuka in *Falastin* is the inspiration for this dish, and I have to admit, I like it even better than the one I used to make with eggs.

Soft, scrambled tofu is ensconced in a richly spiced tomato sauce with a slight smokiness from harissa and a punchy brightness from preserved lemons. When baked in the tomato sauce, the tofu becomes melt-in-your-mouth creamy. Finishing with vegan feta and kala namak adds the shakshuka flavors you love: tanginess, salty cheesiness, and egginess.

Ingredient Notes: I love Violife and Trader Joe's brand vegan feta. If soft tofu is not available, use firm tofu. You can sub ¾ teaspoon each ground cumin and coriander for the cumin and coriander seeds; add with the paprika.

Tip: For a thick, layered shakshuka, use a 10-inch (25 cm) ovenproof pan (it might seem like the veg won't all fit, but it will cook down). A 12-inch (30 cm) pan works, but the dish won't be as deep.

Make Ahead: You can cook the tomato sauce a few days ahead of time.

Easy Variations: Stir in chopped greens toward the end of step 4 to wilt. Nestle leftover cooked potatoes or white beans into the sauce before baking. To take this to the next level, drizzle with Spicy Mint & Cilantro Sauce (page 189) or chile oil (page 213).

2 tablespoons **extra-virgin olive oil**

1½ teaspoons **cumin seeds** (see Ingredient Notes)

1 teaspoon **coriander seeds** (see Ingredient Notes)

1 large **red or yellow onion**, thinly sliced

1 large **red bell pepper**, thinly sliced

Kosher salt

5 **garlic cloves**, minced

½ teaspoon **smoked paprika**

1 teaspoon **Aleppo pepper**, plus more as needed

3 tablespoons **harissa sauce or paste** (I use Mina Spicy Harissa sauce)

1 tablespoon **preserved lemon peel** (page 157), finely chopped (optional)

1 tablespoon **coconut sugar** or **organic brown sugar**

1 (28-ounce/800 g) can **whole peeled tomatoes**

1 (14-ounce/400 g) block **soft tofu** (see Ingredient Notes)

3 tablespoons **nutritional yeast**

½ teaspoon **ground turmeric**

3 ounces (85 g) **vegan feta** (optional but highly recommended; see Ingredient Notes)

½ cup (8 g) **fresh flat-leaf parsley or cilantro** leaves and tender stems, chopped

Kala namak (Indian black salt), for serving

Crusty bread, **warm pita**, or **Simple Flatbread** (page 535), for sopping up the sauce

recipe continues

1. Preheat the oven to 375°F (190°C).

2. In a 10-inch (25 cm) ovenproof sauté pan, heat the oil over medium-high heat. Once hot, add the cumin and coriander seeds and swirl frequently for a minute, until they are darker in color and aromatic.

3. Add the onions and bell pepper with a pinch of salt and cook until the onions are lightly browned, 5 to 7 minutes. Add the garlic, paprika, and Aleppo pepper and cook for 60 seconds, stirring frequently. Add the harissa, preserved lemon peel (if using), and sugar. Stir vigorously for 30 seconds.

4. Using your hands, crush the whole tomatoes into the pan, adding the juices. Season with 1½ teaspoons salt. Bring to a rapid simmer and cook, stirring occasionally, until thickened, 15 minutes. For a smoother texture, run an immersion blender through some of the sauce. Taste, seasoning with a bit more salt or Aleppo pepper as needed (I usually add ½ teaspoon of each).

5. While the sauce simmers, drain the tofu and line a cutting board with paper towels or a dish towel. Crumble the tofu into chunks. Add the tofu on top of the towels, gently press down with another towel, and let rest for 10 to 15 minutes. Remove the wet towels and gently press the tofu with dry towels to remove more water. Transfer the tofu to a bowl and toss with the nutritional yeast and turmeric.

6. When the tomato sauce is done, add the seasoned tofu on top, followed by the feta. Transfer to the oven and bake for 10 to 12 minutes, until the sauce is bubbling and the tofu starts to meld into the dish. Garnish with parsley or cilantro and a few sprinkles of Aleppo pepper. Before serving, sprinkle with a few dashes of kala namak for an eggy taste. Serve warm with bread of choice.

Brunch Tacos

Serves 4 | GF, NFO

If I were running for mayor of any city, my central campaign pillar would be that every restaurant serving brunch must have brunch tacos on the menu. They're fun, easy to customize, and small enough that you can have several before getting full. Until I become mayor of your city, though, make these protein-packed and flavor-packed tacos at home for a fabulous weekend brunch.

Tip: Pickled onions do some heavy lifting here, adding a one-two punch of brightness and crunch. If you don't have any in your fridge, make the quickest of quick-pickled onions: Slice 1 small red onion (or 3 shallots) very thinly and add to a jar. Cover with ¼ cup (60 ml) boiling water, ¼ cup (60 ml) red wine vinegar or distilled white vinegar, ¼ teaspoon kosher salt, and ½ teaspoon sugar or maple syrup. Shake well and macerate while you make everything else.

Make Ahead: You can make your sauce of choice 3 to 4 days ahead of time; you can make the scramble 1 day ahead; the pickled onions can be made a week or two in advance.

NF Option: Use the Avocado Crema (page 204) as your sauce of choice.

Eggy Tofu Scramble

1 (14-ounce/400 g) block **firm tofu**, drained

¼ teaspoon **ground turmeric**

½ teaspoon **garlic powder**

½ teaspoon **onion powder**

¼ teaspoon **sweet or hot paprika**

½ teaspoon **chipotle chile flakes** (or ¼ teaspoon red pepper flakes)

½ teaspoon **kala namak** (Indian black salt), plus more to finish

Kosher salt and freshly ground **black pepper**

1 heaping tablespoon **tahini**

2 tablespoons **nutritional yeast**

½ cup (120 ml) plain **plant-based milk** of choice, such as oat, cashew, or soy

1½ tablespoons **extra-virgin olive oil**

1 (15-ounce/425 g) can **black beans**, drained and rinsed

1 juicy **lime**

For Serving

12 **corn tortillas** or small **flour tortillas**

Sauce of choice: **Chipotle Crema** (page 205), **Avocado Crema** (page 204), or **Extremely Easy Queso Sauce** (page 199)

Quick-pickled onions (page 168, or see Tip)

1 handful **fresh cilantro** leaves, chopped

recipe continues

1. **Make the tofu scramble.** Cut the tofu vertically into four slabs. Press the tofu for 15 minutes (see page 265).

2. In a medium bowl, whisk together the turmeric, garlic powder, onion powder, paprika, chipotle flakes, kala namak, several cracks of black pepper, tahini, and nutritional yeast. Pour in the milk gradually and whisk until you have a nice sauce.

3. Crumble the pressed tofu with your hands into chunks, not too big or too small.

4. In a large nonstick skillet, heat the olive oil over medium-high heat. Once the oil is hot, add the tofu. Cook, stirring occasionally (but not too often), until lightly browned, 5 to 7 minutes. Break up any large chunks of tofu with your spatula but don't break it up too finely.

5. Add the spiced milk sauce and fold to combine, using a silicone spatula to coat each piece of tofu with the sauce. Add the beans, a few squeezes of lime juice, and a few pinches of salt and black pepper. Cook until the scramble is no longer runny, 2 minutes. Finish with a couple more dashes of kala namak for eggy flavor.

6. **Char the tortillas.** If you have a gas stove, turn a burner to medium-low and use tongs to place the tortilla directly over the flame until charred in spots, 15 to 30 seconds per side. Or add each tortilla to a cast-iron skillet over medium-high heat for 20 to 40 seconds per side. Stack and wrap the tortillas in a dish towel to keep warm.

7. Top each tortilla with a dollop of your sauce of choice, followed by the scramble and beans, pickled onions, and cilantro. If desired, squeeze a bit of lime juice on top.

Crispy & Savory Moong Dal Pancakes (or Crepes)

Makes about 10 pancakes or crepes | GF, SF, NF

These pancakes are loosely inspired by a moonglet, a mashup of a fluffy Indian pancake and an eggless omelet. The batter is made from moong dal, and while you might be feeling skeptical about "lentil pancakes," you should know these are my favorite pancakes ever. They have a robust savory flavor redolent with spices and a subtle egginess, and the tangy-sweet tomato chutney intensifies these flavors. For an East Asian twist, serve with Life-Changing Homemade Chili Crisp (page 187). PS: With a few tweaks, you can turn these into uber-crispy crepes.

Ingredient Notes: Moong dal is also sold as "split yellow mung beans" or "split yellow lentils." If you don't have time to make chutney, use a store-bought version like Brooklyn Delhi's tomato achaar.

Tips: Use a cast-iron skillet for the crispiest exterior. If you don't have one, use a nonstick pan: heat over medium to medium-high heat and use ½ teaspoon oil per pancake.

Make Ahead: You can make the batter 2 days ahead of time and refrigerate it. Before cooking, add the batter to a bowl and whisk very well to incorporate.

1½ cups (300 g) **yellow moong dal** (see Ingredient Notes), soaked in cool water for at least 4 hours, or overnight

¼ cup (56 g) **neutral-flavored oil** of choice, plus more for cooking the pancakes

1 teaspoon **ground turmeric**

1½ teaspoons **ground cumin**

½ heaping teaspoon **ground coriander**

½ heaping teaspoon **garlic powder**

¼ teaspoon **cayenne pepper**

2 to 2½ teaspoons **kosher salt**

Freshly ground **black pepper**

¼ teaspoon **organic cane sugar**

¼ cup (20 g) **nutritional yeast**

¼ cup (38 g) **potato starch**

For Finishing

Garam masala

Kala namak (Indian black salt)

For Serving

Mom's Tomato-Garlic Chutney (page 192) or **store-bought chutney** or **achaar**

recipe continues

To make pancakes

1. Drain the soaked dal and rinse with water. Add the dal to a high-powered blender along with 2½ cups (600 ml) of water. Blend on medium or high speed until relatively smooth, stopping to scrape down the sides as needed. Transfer the batter to a bowl.

2. To the batter, add the oil, turmeric, cumin, coriander, garlic powder, cayenne, 2½ teaspoons salt, several cracks of black pepper, the sugar, nutritional yeast, and potato starch. Whisk well to combine.

3. Heat a cast-iron skillet over medium heat. Add about ¾ teaspoon oil, tilting the pan to coat the bottom. Once the oil is hot, ladle in ½ cup (120 g) batter, using the bottom of the measuring cup to spread out the batter from the center to the edges.

4. Once air bubbles start to form, about 2 to 3 minutes, sprinkle the top with ¼ teaspoon garam masala and a nice pinch of kala namak. Carefully flip and swirl the pan around to use all the oil on the outer edges. Cook until golden brown on both sides, 1½ to 2 more minutes.

5. Repeat with the remaining batter, adding just a touch of oil for each pancake and lowering the heat a bit if the batter starts to cook too quickly.

6. Serve with chutney on the side. Store leftover pancakes tightly wrapped in the fridge. Reheat in a hot skillet, flipping occasionally, until warmed through.

To make crepes

1. Drain the soaked dal and rinse with water. Add the dal to a high-powered blender along with 2 cups (480 ml) of water. Blend on medium or high speed until relatively smooth, stopping to scrape down the sides as needed. Fit a fine-mesh sieve over a bowl and strain the batter into the bowl, pushing down with a silicone spatula to get all the liquid into the bowl. You will need to scrape the bottom of the sieve to get it all. Discard the thick pulp left in the sieve and use only the thin batter. For reference, you should have about 1¾ cups (400 g) of the leftover thick pulp and slightly more of the thin batter, about 2¼ cups (500 g). You can see the desired texture of the thin crepe batter in the bowl on the right in the photo—it should be like a thin pancake batter.

2. To the batter, add the oil, turmeric, cumin, coriander, garlic powder, cayenne, 2 teaspoons of the salt, several cracks of black pepper, the sugar, nutritional yeast, and potato starch. Whisk well to combine.

3. Heat a cast-iron skillet over medium heat. Add about ¾ teaspoon oil. Once the oil is hot, ladle in ¼ cup (56 g) batter, using the bottom of the measuring cup to spread out the batter from the center to the edges.

4. Once air bubbles start to form, about 2 to 3 minutes, sprinkle the top with ¼ teaspoon garam masala and a nice pinch of kala namak. Carefully flip and swirl the pan around to use all the oil on the outer edges. Cook until golden brown on both sides, 1½ to 2 more minutes.

5. Repeat with the remaining batter, adding just a touch of oil for each crepe and lowering the heat a bit if the batter starts to cook too quickly.

6. Serve with chutney on the side. Store leftover crepes tightly wrapped in the fridge. Reheat in a hot skillet, flipping occasionally, until warmed through.

Discard

Crepe Batter

Diner-Style Buttermilk Waffles

Makes 6 to 7 hearty Belgian-style waffles | SFO, NFO

One summer, I lived near a Manhattan diner whose specialty was crispy yet fluffy waffles with generous pats of butter. After going vegan, I assumed I'd see these waffles only in my dreams. After many years of dreaming, though, I cracked the code for buttery and rich, fluffy yet crispy vegan waffles.

A mixture of vegan sour cream and homemade "buttermilk" adds the tang and richness necessary for diner-style waffles, melted vegan butter and a mixture of sweet spices add lovely flavor, and a generous amount of baking powder makes the interior fluffy and pillowy.

Ingredient Notes: I have tried this recipe with four different brands of vegan sour cream, and each batch was great (Follow Your Heart sour cream was *the* best). Plain vegan yogurt also works, as long as it's thick (standard thin yogurts won't cook through in the batter); flip to page 61 for my recommended yogurt brands. Be sure to use aluminum-free baking powder to avoid any metallic taste.

Tips: Use about ¾ cup (145 g) batter for a standard Belgian waffle maker, but adjust if your machine is smaller or bigger.

Store leftover waffles wrapped in the fridge and reheat on a wire rack fitted on a sheet pan at 250°F (120°C) for 15 minutes, flipping halfway through.

Make Ahead: This batter stays fresh for at least 4 days, so midweek waffles can definitely be a thing. Cold batter takes longer to cook, so bring the batter to room temperature or adjust the heat level or cook time to prevent undercooking.

Easy Variations: While this recipe is best with all-purpose flour, you can still get good results with 100 percent whole wheat flour (just increase the milk to 2¼ cups/540 ml). For lemon poppy seed waffles, add the zest of 2 large lemons to the wet ingredients and 1½ tablespoons poppy seeds to the dry ingredients.

SF and NF Option: Choose soy-free vegan butter (I like Violife Plant Butter and Earth Balance Soy Free Buttery Sticks) and soy-free sour cream (I like the ones from Follow Your Heart and Kite Hill). There are many nut-free vegan butters and sour creams, but be sure to read labels carefully.

¾ cup (170 g) **vegan sour cream** (see Ingredient Notes)

2 cups (480 ml) **full-fat oat milk**

1½ tablespoons freshly squeezed **lemon juice** (or apple cider vinegar)

2 cups (250 g) **all-purpose flour**

2 tablespoons (25 g) aluminum-free **baking powder** (see Ingredient Notes)

½ teaspoon **fine sea salt**

2 tablespoons **organic cane sugar**

1 teaspoon **ground cinnamon**

½ teaspoon **freshly grated nutmeg**

¼ teaspoon **ground cardamom**

1 teaspoon **pure vanilla extract**

1 tablespoon **orange zest** (from about 1 large orange)

3 tablespoons **vegan butter**, melted (or refined coconut oil), plus more for serving

recipe and ingredients continue

Topping Options

Pure maple syrup + **vegan butter**

Vegan whipped cream or **nut butter** + **fresh berries**

Raspberry Compote (page 577) or **Macerated Berries with Basil & Mint** (page 549)

1. Let the sour cream sit at room temperature for 15 to 30 minutes.

2. In a medium bowl, combine the milk and lemon juice. Stir and set aside until it curdles slightly, 5 to 10 minutes. This is your vegan buttermilk.

3. In a large bowl, whisk together the flour, baking powder, salt, sugar, cinnamon, nutmeg, and cardamom.

4. To the buttermilk, add the sour cream, vanilla, and orange zest and whisk until well combined. Drizzle in the melted butter and stir until just combined. Pour over the flour mixture and whisk until just combined. Do not overmix—lots of little lumps are fine. Rest for 10 minutes. The batter will be thick and fluffy with lots of air bubbles.

5. **If you are using an electric waffle iron,** preheat it. It should beep when hot enough; if not, add a small drop of water; if it sizzles, it's ready. Depending on your waffle maker material and age, you might need to grease the plates.

Scoop about ¾ cup (145 g) batter (see Tips) and pour into the center of the mold. Use a silicone spatula to spread it out evenly to cover the grates, but don't overfill, as the waffles will rise.

Close and set the timer. Most machines need 4 to 6 minutes. Once nicely golden brown and cooked through, use an offset spatula or chopstick to nudge the waffle out. If your timer beeps sooner than 4 minutes, gently pull a piece of the first waffle apart to see if it's cooked through. If you see wet batter, cook for a few more minutes.

6. **If you are using a stovetop waffle iron,** preheat both sides. Grease the plates. Pour the batter into the iron to uniformly cover the grates but don't overfill. Cook for 2 to 4 minutes, flip, and repeat until golden brown and crisp on both sides.

7. For extra-crispy waffles (or to keep the waffles warm), heat your oven to 250°F (120°C). Fit a wire rack on a sheet pan and arrange freshly cooked waffles on the rack in a single layer. Bake for 10 minutes.

8. Serve each waffle with a pat of vegan butter and drizzle with maple syrup, or serve with desired toppings of choice.

Chickpea Pancake with Sesame Greens

Serves 2 | GF, SF, NF

When I want an easy but fancy-ish brunch for just two, I lean on this savory baked chickpea pancake. It's inspired by socca, the thin fried chickpea-flour pancake that's popular along the French and Italian coasts, but is a little heartier and is topped with herby sesame-flavored greens. My very loose interpretation of "salad pizza."

Preheating the cast-iron pan before pouring in the chickpea batter lends a nice crispy texture and devilishly delicious crunchy edges. Infusing the batter with nutritional yeast amps up the savoriness, and kala namak adds a subtle eggy flavor.

Tips: You need a well-seasoned cast-iron skillet to prevent the chickpea flour from sticking; if you don't have one, use another ovenproof 10-inch (25 cm) skillet. If you're feeding more than two, double the chickpea pancake batter and salad. Cook the pancakes in two rounds.

Chickpea Pancake

1 cup (105 g) **chickpea flour**

1 cup (240 ml) **lukewarm water**

¾ teaspoon **kosher salt**

Freshly ground **black pepper**

2 generous tablespoons **extra-virgin olive oil**

½ teaspoon **kala namak** (Indian black salt), plus more for finishing (optional)

3 tablespoons **nutritional yeast**

¼ to ½ teaspoon **red pepper flakes** (¼ teaspoon for mild heat)

Sesame Greens

6 cups (or large handfuls) **soft salad greens** of choice

1 heaping cup (12 g) **fresh cilantro** leaves, torn if large

½ cup (8 g) **fresh mint** leaves, torn (or more cilantro)

Fine sea salt or **kosher salt** and freshly ground **black pepper**

1 large juicy **lime**

2 teaspoons **rice vinegar**

1 tablespoon **toasted sesame oil**

1 heaping tablespoon **roasted black or white sesame seeds**

For Serving (optional but recommended)

Mint Yogurt Sauce (page 213)

1. **Make the chickpea pancake.** Add the chickpea flour to a medium bowl. Slowly add the warm water, whisking to get rid of lumps and until the mixture is foamy. Whisk in the kosher salt, a generous amount of black pepper, and 1 generous tablespoon of the olive oil. Cover the batter and let rest at room temperature for at least 45 minutes, or up to 4 hours.

recipe continues

2. Arrange a rack in the middle of the oven. Preheat the oven to 475°F (245°C). Once preheated, add a well-seasoned 10-inch (25 cm) cast-iron skillet or other ovenproof skillet to the oven and heat for 10 minutes.

3. When the batter is done resting, whisk in the kala namak, nutritional yeast, and pepper flakes.

4. Using oven mitts, remove the pan from the oven and pour in the remaining 1 generous tablespoon olive oil and swirl to coat the entire surface. Carefully pour the chickpea batter into the pan and swirl it around to cover the bottom in an even layer.

5. While the batter is still sizzling, return the pan to the oven. Bake for 20 minutes, or until golden brown and crisp around the edges and set in the middle. To prevent sticking, let the pancake rest in the pan for 5 minutes, then use tongs or a thin spatula to lift it out of the pan and onto a serving plate or cutting board. If desired, dust a little kala namak on top.

6. **While the pancake bakes, make the sesame greens**. In a large bowl, combine the salad greens, cilantro, and mint and sprinkle with just a pinch of salt and black pepper. Add 2 tablespoons lime juice, the vinegar, and sesame oil and gently toss with your hands. Season to taste with salt and several cracks of pepper and add the sesame seeds. Add more lime juice as desired.

7. To serve, pile the greens on top of the pancake and slice into wedges, pizza style. Or use your hands to tear the pancake apart, dip into yogurt sauce, and scoop up the greens.

French Toast Casserole with Black Sesame Butter

Serves 8 to 10 | NFO

While most of my food memories from Southeast Asia are about savory food, there was one dessert I ate with abandon: Chinese black sesame dumplings and pastries. There's something transcendent about roasted black sesame seeds with sugar, and that flavor pairing is what shines in this French toast casserole.

Roasted black sesame seeds are pureed into a magical concoction with sugar and vegan butter, dolloped on top of craggy bread pieces, then covered with a milky spiced custard before being baked in the oven. The result is a deconstructed French toast casserole that's sweet, nutty, and full of textural variety: some bread pieces are chewy, others soft, and the tops get crispy and caramelized. It's a seriously decadent, special-occasion brunch that can be assembled the night before and is 100 percent worth all the sugar and butter.

Ingredient Notes: You're looking for a loaf of bread, not a baguette, ideally about 2 days old. Fresh bread will get soggy, so dry it out first: tear it into bite-size pieces and bake on a sheet pan at 275°F (135°C) for 10 to 12 minutes.

The sesame butter makes this French toast pretty sweet. I don't serve it with maple syrup, but if you do, add it sparingly.

If your sesame seeds are raw, roast them using the stovetop or oven methods (see page 115).

NF Option: Choose a nut-free vegan butter and use coconut flakes instead of nuts in the topping in step 5.

Black Sesame Butter

½ cup + 1 tablespoon (80 g) **roasted black sesame seeds**

¼ cup + 2 tablespoons (80 g) **organic cane sugar**

10 tablespoons (140 g) **vegan butter**, cubed and softened at room temperature

Pinch of **fine sea salt** (about ¹⁄₁₆ teaspoon)

1 loaf **stale Italian- or French-style bread**, or a **sourdough boule** (about 14 ounces/400 g), torn into bite-size pieces (see Ingredient Notes)

Batter

2 cups (480 ml) **full-fat oat milk**

8 ounces (227 g) **silken soft tofu**

1 tablespoon **pure maple syrup**, **organic brown sugar**, or **organic cane sugar**

¼ teaspoon **fine sea salt**

1½ teaspoons **ground cinnamon**

1½ teaspoons **freshly grated ginger** (or ½ teaspoon ground ginger)

½ teaspoon **freshly grated nutmeg**

½ medium **orange**, zested (about 1½ teaspoons zest)

2 teaspoons **pure vanilla extract**

1 teaspoon aluminum-free **baking powder**

1 tablespoon **arrowroot powder** or **cornstarch**

recipe and ingredients continue

½ cup **fat coconut flakes** (30 g) or **pecans** or **walnuts** (60 g), chopped

Fresh raspberries, for serving

1. Make the black sesame butter. In a food processor, add the sesame seeds and sugar and blend until mostly pulverized and quite fine (it should take 30 to 60 seconds, depending on the strength of your food processor). Add the softened butter pieces and salt and blend until a thick paste forms.

2. Grease a 13 × 9-inch (3 L) baking pan or 12-inch (30 cm) cast-iron pan with a bit of vegan butter or oil. Add the bread pieces to the pan. Dollop spoonfuls of the black sesame butter on top, trying to cover as much of the bread as you can. Set aside.

3. Make the batter. In a blender, combine the milk, tofu, maple syrup, salt, cinnamon, ginger, nutmeg, orange zest, vanilla, baking powder, and arrowroot powder. Blend until the mixture is completely smooth and no lumps remain. If you have a large-capacity food processor, you can do this in the food processor you used for the sesame butter.

4. Slowly pour the batter around the edges of the pan, making your way to the middle. Repeat until the batter is used up and the bread is soaked. Cover the pan tightly and refrigerate for at least 30 minutes, or up to 14 hours.

5. When ready to bake, arrange an oven rack in the middle. Preheat the oven to 350°F (175°C). Sprinkle the top of the casserole with the coconut flakes or nuts. Bake, uncovered, for 35 to 45 minutes, until the top bread pieces are nicely golden. Keep an eye on the pan during the last 10 minutes—if it starts browning too much, loosely tent the pan with foil. Let rest for 5 minutes before slicing. Serve slices with fresh raspberries.

6. Store leftovers covered in the fridge for up to 6 days. Reheat in an ovenproof pan at 350°F (175°C) for 15 minutes, or until warmed through and slightly crisp.

Scrambled Chickpeas with Chile Yogurt Sauce and Za'atar Pita

Serves 5 to 6 | GFO, SF, NF

The combo of garlicky spiced "scrambled" chickpeas, a creamy mint-flecked yogurt sauce, chewy and crunchy toasted za'atar pita, and crisp salad greens makes this Middle Eastern–inspired brunch plate an unforgettable experience. The chile oil adds slightly fruity, earthy notes and a subtle heat, while the yogurt sauce brings a luxurious quality to the meal.

I make this plate about once a month on Sundays, per my partner's request ("Who needs eggs when you can have this?" is something he's actually said when eating this).

Ingredient Note: Use your favorite store-bought plain-flavored hummus. Of course, if you use homemade hummus, this dish will be even more delicious.

Tips: If you're feeding just two people, halve the chickpeas, salad, and pita. You'll have leftover yogurt and chile oil, but these are great multipurpose condiments. Or make the full recipe and store the components separately; don't dress the salad in advance. That way, you can assemble weekday lunches that taste like weekend brunch in 5 minutes. Keep the yogurt sauce and chile oil separate until needed.

Make Ahead: You can make the yogurt sauce and chile oil a few days in advance. Scramble the chickpeas 1 day in advance.

GF Option: Serve with roasted potatoes in lieu of pita.

Spice Blend (or 4½ teaspoons store-bought ras el hanout)

1½ teaspoons **ground cumin**

1½ teaspoons **ground coriander**

1 teaspoon **sweet or hot paprika**

¼ teaspoon **ground cinnamon**

¼ teaspoon **ground cloves**

2 pinches **ground cardamom**

2 pinches **freshly grated or ground nutmeg**

¼ teaspoon **kosher salt**

Freshly ground **black pepper**

1 teaspoon **kala namak** (Indian black salt), plus more for finishing (optional)

Scrambled Chickpeas

2 (15-ounce/425 g) cans **chickpeas**, drained and rinsed

2½ tablespoons well-stirred **tahini**

¼ cup (20 g) **nutritional yeast**

3 tablespoons **extra-virgin olive oil**

recipe and ingredients continue

⅔ cup (180 g) **hummus** of choice (see Ingredient Note)

Kosher salt and freshly ground **black pepper**

1 cup (16 g) **fresh cilantro** (or flat-leaf parsley) leaves and tender stems, chopped

2 medium **lemons**, zested and juiced (about 6 tablespoons/90 ml juice)

For Serving

5 to 6 vegan-friendly **pita** breads

Yogurt Sauce with Chile Oil (page 213; see Tips)

8 to 10 cups (or large handfuls) **soft salad greens** of choice

1 small **English cucumber**, sliced in half-moons (optional)

1 handful **fresh mint or cilantro** leaves, torn (optional)

About 1 tablespoon **Za'atar** (page 179 or store-bought)

1. Preheat the oven to 325°F (165°C).

2. **Make the spice blend.** In a small bowl, mix together the cumin, coriander, paprika, cinnamon, cloves, cardamom, nutmeg, salt, several cracks of pepper, and kala namak (if using).

3. In a large bowl, add the chickpeas and stir in the spice blend, tahini, and nutritional yeast. Divide the chickpea mixture in half.

4. **Make the scrambled chickpeas.** In a 12-inch (30 cm) skillet, heat 1½ tablespoons of the olive oil over medium heat. Add the first half of the chickpeas. Cook until hot and a little crisp, 3 to 4 minutes. With the back of a spatula or spoon, mash some chickpeas,

but not so much they turn into a big mushy pile. Add in half of the hummus and 2 tablespoons of water and stir to combine. Cook until the liquid starts to evaporate and the mixture thickens a bit, 2 to 4 minutes. For a looser consistency, add an extra tablespoon of water. Transfer to the large bowl used in step 3. Repeat with the remaining oil, chickpeas, and hummus and 2 more tablespoons of water. When done, add to the large bowl. Add a pinch of salt to taste, keeping in mind the other components will have salt. For an eggier flavor, add a pinch of kala namak.

5. To the scrambled chickpeas, add the cilantro, lemon zest, and 2 tablespoons of the lemon juice (reserve the rest for the salad and yogurt sauce if you haven't already made it).

6. Add the pitas to a sheet pan (or two if needed) and heat in the oven for 6 to 7 minutes, until warmed through.

7. Before serving, spoon some but not all of the chile oil over the yogurt sauce. In a large bowl, combine the salad greens and cucumber (if using) with 1 tablespoon of lemon juice and most of the remaining chile oil (save a tiny bit for step 8); season with salt and pepper and top with herbs (if using). Toss gently. Taste, adding more lemon juice as needed.

8. When the pitas are done, brush them with the remaining chile oil and sprinkle generously with za'atar. Slice the pita in halves (for pita pockets) or into wedges (for scooping and dipping). Serve the scrambled chickpeas with yogurt sauce, salad, and pita.

Cheesy Herb Bread Pudding with Caramelized Leeks

Serves 6 to 8 | SF, NF

Featuring a rich milky bread and maple-caramelized leeks, this savory bread pudding hits all the indulgent weekend brunch notes: creamy with crunchy and chewy bits throughout plus cheesy, sweet-and-salty, buttery flavors. Or as my sister has said on many occasions, "This is one of the most delicious things I've ever put in my mouth."

Come November, bring this to the Thanksgiving table instead of the same-old stuffing.

Ingredient Notes: If you prefer a crunchy texture with just a few soft pieces, use a sourdough baguette instead of a loaf or boule-style bread. I love Follow Your Heart vegan parmesan. If you can't find vegan parm, it's still great without it.

Tip: If you don't have an 11- or 12-inch (28 or 30 cm) cast-iron pan, use a large skillet for the leeks, then transfer the leeks and bread to an 8-inch (20 cm) or 9-inch (23 cm) square baking pan.

Make Ahead: You can do steps 1 through 4 one to two days ahead of time; store the infused milk and caramelized leeks separately in the fridge, and store the bread in a reusable plastic bag on the couter. Or, you can refrigerate the bread pudding overnight instead of for 30 minutes (don't add the parm now) and cover it. Before baking, scatter the parm on top. The texture will be a bit softer but still great, or use a baguette to retain some crunch.

2 cups (480 ml) **full-fat oat milk**

1 medium **yellow onion**, quartered

6 to 8 **thyme** sprigs

1 large **rosemary** sprig

1 **bay leaf**

Kosher salt and freshly ground **black pepper**

10 ounces (285 g) **day-old or stale sourdough loaf or boule**, chopped into ¾- to 1-inch (2 to 2.5 cm) pieces (see Ingredient Notes)

1½ tablespoons **extra-virgin olive oil**

¾ cup (78 g) **vegan parmesan** (optional but recommended; see Ingredient Notes)

2 to 3 tablespoons finely chopped **fresh chives** (or scallions)

Caramelized Leeks

2 medium-large **leeks** (each about 12 ounces/340 g before trimming)

¼ cup (56 g) **extra-virgin olive oil**

4 **garlic cloves**, minced

Kosher salt

¼ to ½ teaspoon **red pepper flakes** (½ teaspoon for a kick)

2 tablespoons **pure maple syrup**

recipe continues

1. In a medium saucepan, combine the milk, onion, thyme and rosemary sprigs, and bay leaf along with 1 teaspoon salt and several cracks of black pepper. Bring to a gentle simmer over medium-low heat. Remove from the heat and let cool. Strain the milk in a fine-mesh sieve, discarding the herb sprigs, bay leaf, and onion.

2. Preheat the oven to 350°F (175°C). Spread the bread pieces out on a rimmed sheet pan. Drizzle with the olive oil, season with a pinch or two of salt, and toss. Bake for 10 minutes, or until lightly golden and dried out (if your bread is stale, it may need only 5 to 8 minutes; if soft, 12 to 15 minutes). Remove the pan and turn off the oven.

3. **Make the caramelized leeks.** Peel and discard the leeks' tough outer layers, along with any wilted tops. Using a mandoline or large, sharp knife, slice the leeks into fairly thin rounds, about ⅛ inch (0.3 cm) thick, including the dark green tops. Add the leeks to a large bowl and cover with cold water. Run your hands in the water to loosen the dirt, then scoop the leeks out using your hands or a slotted spoon. Pat dry.

4. In an 11- or 12-inch (28 to 30 cm) cast-iron skillet, heat the ¼ cup (56 g) olive oil over medium heat. Once hot, add the leeks and cook until quite soft, 7 to 9 minutes. Add the garlic, ½ teaspoon salt, and the pepper flakes and toss to coat for 1 minute. Stir in the maple

syrup, reduce the heat to medium-low, and cook until sticky, 5 to 7 minutes.

5. Remove from the heat and add the toasted bread, tossing well to combine. Pour the herbed milk on top and allow it to soak in, gently pressing down so some of the bread gets submerged. Let rest for 30 minutes on the counter, pressing down on the bread a few times.

6. Preheat the oven to 350°F (175°C). Sprinkle the top with the parmesan (if using) and cover the pan with foil. Bake for 30 minutes. Uncover, and bake for 30 more minutes, until the top pieces are golden brown and the pudding is set. For a browner top, preheat your broiler to high and arrange an oven rack on the second shelf. Broil for 60 to 90 seconds (but keep a close eye to prevent burning). Let cool for 10 minutes, then sprinkle with the chopped chives and serve.

7. Store leftovers in the fridge for up to 5 days. Reheat in an ovenproof pan at 350°F (175°C) for 15 to 25 minutes, until warmed through and slightly crisp.

12

Next-Level Dinners

When I first went vegan, most of my dinners came in the form of "the vegan bowl." A grain topped with veggies, a simple protein, and maybe a simple sauce. I had a lot of quinoa-broccoli-chickpea bowls back in 2016.

I still appreciate a vegan bowl on busy days, especially when it has a few flavorful condiments (the kind you'll find in chapter 5). But I also know that vegan food can be much more than "bowl food."

And that's where this chapter comes in. It's packed with dinner recipes that will wow your taste buds, as well as your family and friends. There are some dinners for weeknights, and some for fancier times and weekends. The chapter is divided into four mini chapters: (1) noodles and stir-fries, (2) curries and stews, (3) glorious carbs, and (4) magical mushrooms. What they have in common are bold flavors, very fun textures, and global inspiration.

If you tend to gravitate toward "bowl food" on weeknights, you can always find lots of inspiration using the condiments, proteins, grains, and vegetables in chapters 5 through 8 (and the section following them on meal planning). But when you have more time in your schedule or special occasions to celebrate, the dinners here are guaranteed to seriously impress.

Spicy Noodle Stir-Fry with Salt & Pepper Tofu

Serves 4 | GFO, NF

This is my favorite-ever stir-fry. It hits all the comfort food take-out notes with its combo of salt-and-pepper tofu, blistered green beans, and a tangle of silky noodles, all coated in a deeply savory, garlicky, salty, and spicy sauce.

Ingredient Notes: Shaoxing wine adds a rich, nutty, and salty but slightly sweet depth of flavor to Chinese stir-fries. You can find it at pan-Asian grocery stores or online. You can sub with mirin or dry sherry; if using mirin, use just 1 tablespoon of brown sugar instead. Fruity and bright white pepper is essential for Chinese salt-and-pepper flavors; you can find it at most grocery stores. The Chinese five-spice powder is optional, but it makes this dish taste even more amazing.

Tips: If you don't have a small fine-mesh sieve for coating the tofu in step 4, add the spices, arrowroot powder, and salt to a gallon-size (2 L) resealable plastic bag, shake to combine, and add the tofu. Hold the bag from the top, and gently shake so that the tofu slides around until evenly coated.

If you don't have a wok, you can use a 12-inch (30 cm) nonstick skillet. In step 7, heat over medium-high for 2 minutes, then add the oil and heat for 2 more minutes. Add the tofu for 4 to 5 minutes, then toss and cook for 6 to 7 minutes, shaking the pan every 1 to 2 minutes.

Make Ahead: You can slice the tofu, prep the aromatics, and make the sauce 1 to 2 days ahead.

GF Option: Use tamari instead of soy sauce. Sub the Shaoxing wine with dry sherry or mirin. Skip the noodles and serve over rice, or use rice noodles.

Sauce

3½ tablespoons (60 g) **soy sauce** or **tamari**

2½ tablespoons **Shaoxing wine** (see Ingredient Notes)

2 tablespoons **organic brown sugar**

1 to 2 tablespoons **chili-garlic sauce** or **sambal oelek** (2 tablespoons for *spicy!*)

3 tablespoons **vegetable broth** (or water)

Salt & Pepper Tofu

1 (14-ounce/400 g) block **extra-firm tofu**, ideally previously frozen and thawed (see page 266)

½ teaspoon **ground white pepper** (see Ingredient Notes)

½ teaspoon **onion powder**

¼ teaspoon **garlic powder**

½ teaspoon **Chinese five-spice powder** (optional)

3 tablespoons **arrowroot powder** or **cornstarch**

¾ teaspoon **kosher salt**

3 tablespoons **neutral-flavored high-heat oil** of choice, such as avocado oil

Noodles

6 ounces (170 g) **noodles**, such as ramen, udon, or egg-free wheat noodles

1 tablespoon **toasted sesame oil**

recipe and ingredients continue

Green Beans

1 tablespoon **neutral-flavored high-heat oil**

12 ounces (340 g) **green beans**, cut in half

Kosher salt

2-inch (5 cm) piece **fresh ginger**, peeled and thinly sliced, then sliced into matchsticks

4 **garlic cloves**, finely chopped

6 **scallions**, thinly sliced on a bias (reserve dark green tops for garnish)

½ cup (8 g) **fresh cilantro** leaves and tender stems, roughly chopped

1 tablespoon **roasted black or white sesame seeds**

1. **Make the sauce.** In a small jar, combine the soy sauce, Shaoxing wine, brown sugar, chili-garlic sauce, and vegetable broth.

2. **Make the tofu.** Drain the tofu, wrap it in a thin dish towel, and gently squeeze it using the palms of your hands to remove excess water (see page 265). If you're not using thawed tofu, press it for 15 minutes instead.

3. Cut the tofu into ¼- to ⅓-inch-thick (0.5 to 0.75 cm) squares (see tofu squares, page 267). Gently press down with a towel to get the water out and repeat a few times.

4. In a small bowl, combine the white pepper, onion powder, garlic powder, five-spice powder (if using), and arrowroot powder. Transfer the mixture to a small fine-mesh sieve (see Tips).

5. Arrange the tofu tightly spaced on a cutting board. Sprinkle the top with half of the salt, then dust with half of the spice mixture. Flip the tofu, sprinkle with the rest of the salt, and dust with the rest of the spice mixture.

6. Line a cutting board or large plate with paper towels.

7. Heat a flat-bottomed wok over medium-high heat until it just starts to smoke. Then add the oil and tilt the pan to coat the lower sides. Reduce the heat to medium and add the tofu, standing back to avoid splatter. Cook for 5 to 6 minutes, shaking the pan every minute for even cooking, until golden brown on the bottom. Flip the tofu and repeat this process for 3 to 4 minutes, until golden brown but not charred on the bottom. Transfer to the paper towel–lined surface. Wipe out the pan.

8. **Make the noodles.** While the tofu fries, cook the noodles for 1 minute less than the package instructions call for. Drain and toss with the sesame oil.

9. **Make the green beans.** Heat the wok over high heat until it just starts to smoke, then add the oil. Add the green beans with a tiny pinch of salt and spread in a single layer as much as possible. Cook undisturbed until some beans start to blister, 1 minute. Toss and cook undisturbed for 90 seconds. Add the ginger, garlic, and white and light green parts of the scallions and toss frequently until aromatic, 1 minute.

10. Pour in the sauce, standing back to avoid splatter. Stir-fry until the beans are crisp-tender, another 2 minutes.

11. Turn off the heat and add the noodles, reserved scallion greens, cilantro, and sesame seeds. Use tongs to toss the noodles in the sauce. Add the fried tofu and use a spatula to gently incorporate.

Malaysian Curry Noodle Soup

Serves 4 | GFO

Curry meets noodle soup in this fragrant brothy dish, a vegan version of Malaysian curry laksa (or curry mee, as it's called in northern Malaysia) and my all-time favorite soup. I adore its blend of flavors and cultures, from the hallmark citrusy flavors of lemongrass found in Southeast Asian cuisine to the warm heat of Indian cumin and curry leaves to the deep savoriness of Chinese cooking.

Homemade laksa paste adds an unmatched depth of flavor, while sugar and lime juice lend that sweet-and-tart flavor that makes Southeast Asian curries so dang good. Coconut milk brings a silky consistency, and each bite is punctuated by chewy noodles and spongy fried tofu puffs.

Ingredient Notes: You can find kombu and wakame at Asian markets and well-stocked grocers. Don't have Chinese soy sauce? Use ¼ cup (68 g) supermarket soy sauce in the broth and 1½ tablespoons in the laksa paste.

If you have time, toast the coriander and cumin seeds in a skillet over medium heat for a few minutes to release more flavor. Galangal can have a hard exterior, so use a sharp knife and cut off any hard knobs. No need to peel it as long as you slice it very thinly. If it's not available, use ginger.

For mild heat: Use 3 *mild* dried red chile peppers in the laksa paste. For *spicy!*: Use 3 to 4 fresh chiles in the paste and garnish with 1 to 2 thinly sliced peppers, or top with Life-Changing Homemade Chili Crisp (page 187).

For instructions on how to prep lemongrass, see page 472. You can use the tough stalks in the soup. Just smash down on them with a rolling pin or mallet, then add them to the soup in step 4 and discard before serving.

Not a fan of mushrooms? Replace with snap peas, snow peas, or chopped baby bok choy and add along with the spinach in step 5.

Make Ahead: Laksa paste can be refrigerated in a jar for 1 to 2 weeks. Or you can double or triple it and freeze it for up to 3 months.

GF Option: Use rice noodles; use tamari instead of Chinese soy sauce, using the amount listed in the Ingredient Notes.

Broth

3 sheets (about 12 g) **kombu** (see Ingredient Notes)

1 tablespoon **wakame seaweed** (optional; adds a subtle sealike flavor; see Ingredient Notes)

2½ tablespoons (43 g) **Chinese light soy sauce** (see Ingredient Notes)

1 tablespoon freshly squeezed **lime juice**

Laksa Paste

1½ teaspoons **coriander seeds** (see Ingredient Notes)

1 teaspoon **cumin seeds** (see Ingredient Notes)

3 **shallots**, roughly chopped

4 **garlic cloves**

2-inch (5 cm) piece **galangal** (or ginger), very thinly sliced (see Ingredient Notes)

1-inch (2.5 cm) piece **fresh turmeric**, peeled and roughly chopped (or ¾ teaspoon ground turmeric)

recipe and ingredients continue

1 to 4 **Thai chiles**, stemmed (or 3 to 5 dried red chiles, such as bird's eye, cayenne, chile de arbol, or guajillo; see Ingredient Notes)

2 **lemongrass** stalks, finely chopped (see page 472), tough stalks reserved for the soup if desired (see Ingredient Notes)

2 tablespoons **raw or roasted cashews or peanuts**

1 tablespoon **Chinese light soy sauce**

1 small handful (5 g) **fresh cilantro** leaves and tender stems

1 teaspoon **lime zest**

2 teaspoons freshly squeezed **lime juice**

1 to 2 tablespoons **neutral-flavored oil** of choice

Soup

2 tablespoons **neutral-flavored oil** of choice

8 ounces (227 g) **oyster, maitake, beech, shiitake, or cremini mushrooms**, torn or sliced

Kosher salt

1 (13.5-ounce/400 ml) can **full-fat coconut milk**

5 **fresh curry leaves** (or 10 dried; see Ingredient Notes on page 192)

1 (8-ounce/227 g) package **fried tofu puffs** or **soy puffs** (or store-bought baked tofu)

2 to 4 cups (40 to 80 g) **baby spinach**, roughly chopped (optional)

1 to 2 teaspoons **coconut sugar** or **organic brown sugar**, as needed

6 to 8 ounces (170 to 230 g) **ramen noodles** (or noodles of choice)

Toppings (optional)

1 to 2 cups (60 to 120 g) **bean sprouts**

Fresh mint and/or cilantro leaves

Thinly sliced **Thai chiles** (for *spicy!*)

Fried Shallots (page 224)

Lime wedges

1. **Make the broth.** Cut a few slits in the kombu to release the flavor. In a small saucepan over medium heat, bring 5 cups (1.2 L) of water, the kombu, wakame (if using), and soy sauce to a simmer. Simmer for 10 minutes, then remove from the heat and stir in the lime juice. The broth should taste like the sea. Fit a bowl underneath a colander and strain the broth, discarding the kombu and wakame.

2. **Make the laksa paste.** In a food processor or small-capacity high-powered blender (a 32-ounce/1 L or smaller blender cup), add the coriander seeds, cumin seeds, shallots, garlic, galangal, turmeric, chiles, lemongrass, cashews, soy sauce, cilantro, lime zest, and lime juice. Blend until a paste forms, stopping to scrape down the sides as you go. Add the oil

gradually, 1 tablespoon at a time, until a paste comes together (it won't be completely smooth). Don't stick your eyeballs directly over the blender or they'll water!

3. **Make the soup.** In a Dutch oven or soup pot, heat the 2 tablespoons oil over medium-low heat. Once hot, add the laksa paste and cook, stirring frequently to prevent sticking, until it just starts to dry out, 5 to 6 minutes.

4. Pour in the broth from step 1, scraping up any browned bits stuck to the bottom. Add the mushrooms, ½ teaspoon kosher salt, and the leftover lemongrass stalks (if using; see Ingredient Notes). Bring to a boil, then lower the heat and simmer rapidly for 10 minutes.

5. Use a slotted spoon to discard the whole lemongrass pieces, if used. Add the coconut milk, curry leaves, tofu puffs, and spinach (if using). Simmer for 5 minutes. Taste for seasonings, adding more salt as needed; if the soup is too acidic, add the sugar to taste.

6. While the soup simmers, cook the noodles according to the package directions. Drain and keep warm.

7. **Assemble.** Divide the noodles among four bowls. Ladle hot curry on top and add desired garnishes. Squeeze fresh lime juice on top, if desired.

HOW TO PREP LEMONGRASS

1. Remove the papery and tough outer layers from the lemongrass stalk until you get to the slightly soft interior layers.

2. Use a large, sharp knife to slice off the bottom tough root from the stalk, as well as the top green stalks. You should be left with the pale lower part of the lemongrass, which is tender.

3. Using a rolling pin, mallet, the back of a heavy knife, or a wine bottle, smash down on the lemongrass to bruise it and release its aroma.

4. Now mince, finely chop, or very thinly slice the lemongrass, or pound it finely in a mortar with a pestle (depending on the recipe directions). If you have leftover lemongrass, cut the stalks into 1- or 2-inch (2.5 or 5 cm) pieces, then wrap in foil and freeze in freezer-safe bags.

Vietnamese Rice Noodle Bowls with Crispy Tofu & Mushrooms

Serves 6 | GFO, NFO

In the month we backpacked through Vietnam, one of our staple dishes was bún chả, a northern dish featuring grilled meat over rice noodles, served with abundant fresh herbs and a sweet-and-sour fish sauce called nước chấm.

Tofu and mushrooms, which get surprisingly chewy and crispy in the oven, stand in place for meat with delectable results. Big-flavor condiments like soy sauce, Bragg liquid aminos, agave nectar, and umeboshi paste help mimic the perfectly savory-sweet-tart flavor of nước chấm. Like the original, these noodle bowls are finished with piles of cooling herbs for a lovely contrast of flavors and textures.

Ingredient Notes: I don't recommend using cornstarch with the baked tofu, as it can leave a subtle chalky aftertaste. Bragg liquid aminos resemble fish sauce slightly better than soy sauce does, but you can use soy sauce (or vegan fish sauce if you have it). You can find Thai basil at most Asian markets; if not, use cilantro and mint.

Tips: If you are keeping leftovers, don't add all the herbs at once; instead add fresh herbs when serving. For extra heat, serve with Life-Changing Chili Crisp (page 187).

Make Ahead: You can make the sauce, chop the tofu, and tear the mushrooms 1 to 3 days ahead; you can prep the salad ingredients 1 day ahead.

Tofu and Mushrooms

1 (14-ounce/400 g) block **extra-firm tofu**, ideally previously frozen and thawed (see page 266)

2 tablespoons **neutral-flavored oil** of choice

2 teaspoons **toasted sesame oil**

1 tablespoon **soy sauce** or **tamari** (use tamari for GF)

1 tablespoon **pure maple syrup**

Kosher salt and freshly ground **black pepper**

1 tablespoon **arrowroot powder** or **potato starch** (see Ingredient Notes)

1½ tablespoons **panko bread crumbs** (use gluten-free panko for GF)

1 tablespoon **roasted black or white sesame seeds**

1 pound (455 g) **oyster mushrooms** or **shiitakes**

10 ounces (285 g) **thin rice noodles** (a.k.a. bún noodles in small or medium thickness)

Sauce

3 **garlic cloves**, grated or finely minced

1 to 3 **Thai chiles**, finely minced (omit for mild heat; use 3 for *spicy!*)

⅓ cup (80 ml) freshly squeezed **lime juice** (about 3 medium limes)

1 tablespoon **rice vinegar**

¼ cup (68 g) **tamari** or **soy sauce** (use tamari for GF)

2 tablespoons Bragg **liquid aminos** (see Ingredient Notes)

recipe and ingredients continue

¼ cup (84 g) **agave nectar**

½ teaspoon **umeboshi paste** (optional, for extra savoriness)

Salad

2 cups (140 g) shredded **carrots**

1 small or medium **English cucumber**, julienned or cut into thin half-moons

2 cups (120 g) **bean sprouts** (or more carrots)

6 **scallions**, sliced on a bias

2 cups (about 32 g) **fresh Thai basil, cilantro, and/or mint** leaves (see Ingredient Notes)

⅓ cup (45 g) **dry-roasted peanuts or cashews**, chopped (optional; omit if nut-free)

1. Arrange one rack in the bottom of the oven and one in the top third. Preheat the oven to 425°F (220°C). Line two rimmed sheet pans with parchment paper.

2. **Make the tofu and mushrooms.** Slice the tofu vertically into four slabs and press for 10 minutes (20 minutes if you're not using thawed tofu), changing the towels in between if you can (see page 265). Chop the tofu into ½- to ¾-inch (about 1.5 to 2 cm) cubes (½-inch/1.5 cm pieces get extra crunchy).

3. Place the tofu in a large bowl. Add 1 tablespoon of the oil, the sesame oil, soy sauce, maple syrup, and ¼ teaspoon salt (if not using thawed tofu, add a bit more salt). Toss gently with a silicone spatula or your hands. Add the arrowroot powder, panko, and sesame seeds. Gently toss. Spread the tofu out on one prepared pan.

4. Brush off any dirt patches on the mushrooms with a dry towel. Slice off the woody ends of the oyster mushrooms, then tear each cluster in half, thirds, or quarters (thinner strips get crispier). For shiitakes, thinly slice the caps; discard the stems. Add the mushrooms to the bowl from step 3 and toss with the remaining 1 tablespoon oil; season with ½ teaspoon salt and pepper to taste. Spread out on the other prepared pan as much as you can.

5. Bake the pans in the oven for 15 minutes. Remove the pans, toss the mushrooms, and flip the tofu. Change rack positions and bake for 12 to 15 minutes more, until the tofu and mushrooms are crispy and browned (the mushrooms may need an extra 5 minutes).

6. **Prepare the noodles.** Cook the noodles according to the package instructions. Drain and rinse under cold water, using a fork to fluff and separate the strands. Let drain in the colander for 10 minutes.

7. **Make the sauce and salad.** In a jar, combine the garlic, chiles (if using), lime juice, vinegar, soy sauce, liquid aminos, agave, umeboshi paste (if using), and ¼ cup (60 ml) of water. Seal and shake vigorously until well combined. In a large bowl, combine the carrots, cucumber, bean sprouts, and scallions. In a separate bowl, combine the fresh herb leaves, tearing any large leaves.

8. **Assemble.** Divide the noodles among four deep bowls. Drizzle a generous amount of sauce on top and toss to combine. Divide the tofu and mushrooms among the bowls, then top each with some salad, handfuls of fresh herbs, and peanuts. Just before eating, drizzle more sauce on and serve more sauce on the side.

Tofu 65

Serves 3 to 4 | GF, NF

Chicken 65 is a spicy deep-fried dish popular in South India, but tofu makes a great stand-in for chicken. When soaked in salted boiling water, it not only develops a crackly crust after frying but is also better able to absorb the tantalizing flavors of this stir-fry. Coating the fried tofu in garlic and tamari adds savory depth while cumin seeds and curry leaves add warmth and punchiness.

If I haven't sold you yet, let's just say several people have told me this "tastes like popcorn fried chicken, but Indian!" Here it's served with rice and stir-fried snap peas for dinner, but you can also double the recipe and serve the tofu solo as an appetizer. To double the tofu, batter the tofu in two stages and fry in three to four batches.

Ingredient Notes: When fried, firm tofu gets a crunchy exterior and a slightly soft, melt-in-your-mouth interior, but if you don't have it, use extra-firm tofu. Rice flour yields the crispiest coating, but you can sub with ⅓ cup (42 g) all-purpose flour.

Tips: Open windows and ventilate your kitchen before starting the stir-fry, as the capsaicin in the chili sauce will circulate quickly once it hits the hot oil. You may also want to wear a mask when cooking the stir-fry to prevent coughing.

Big-Flavor Meals: You can serve the tofu with virtually any stir-fried vegetable. For something a little lighter, serve with steamed or blanched green beans, snap peas, bok choy, or broccoli.

Make Ahead: You can fry the tofu and store it in a paper towel–lined airtight container in the fridge for 1 to 2 days. To reheat, transfer the tofu to a wire rack–fitted sheet pan; bake at 375°F (190°C) for 12 to 15 minutes, until hot and crispy. Store the stir-fry separately. Toss the tofu with the stir-fry when ready to serve.

Tofu

1 (14-ounce/400 g) block **firm tofu**, drained (see Ingredient Notes)

Kosher salt

1½ teaspoons grated **fresh garlic** (2 to 3 cloves)

1½ teaspoons grated **fresh ginger** (no need to peel)

½ teaspoon freshly ground **black pepper**

2 teaspoons **Kashmiri red chile powder** (or ½ teaspoon cayenne pepper)

1 teaspoon **ground coriander**

½ teaspoon **ground turmeric**

½ teaspoon **garam masala**

3 tablespoons **unsweetened coconut yogurt**

24 to 32 ounces (0.7 to 1 L) **vegetable oil** or other **neutral-flavored high-heat oil** of choice, for deep-frying

¼ cup (32 g) **cornstarch**

⅓ cup (60 g) **white rice flour** (see Ingredient Notes)

1½ cups (285 g) uncooked or 4½ cups (650 g) cooked **basmati rice**

recipe and ingredients continue

Stir-Fry

1½ tablespoons **neutral-flavored oil** of choice

1 teaspoon **cumin seeds**

4 **garlic cloves**, chopped

½ small **serrano pepper**, chopped (remove membranes and seeds for mild heat; use the full pepper for *spicy!*)

10 to 12 **fresh curry leaves** (or 25 dried; see Ingredient Notes on page 192)

2 tablespoons **sambal oelek** or **chili-garlic sauce**

1 tablespoon + 1 teaspoon **tamari** or **soy sauce** (use tamari to keep GF)

For Finishing

12 ounces (340 g) **sugar snap peas** or **green beans**

¼ teaspoon freshly ground **black pepper**

1. In a saucepan or kettle, bring a few cups of water to a boil.

2. Slice the tofu lengthwise into four slabs, then cover them with a thin dish towel. Gently press down to remove some water. Using your hands, tear the tofu into 1½-inch (4 cm) chunks. Gently press down on the chunks with a dry towel.

3. Combine 2 cups (480 ml) of the boiling water and 2 teaspoons salt in a medium bowl. Add the tofu and soak for 10 minutes. Drain well and spread the tofu out on a towel for at least 5 minutes.

4. **Marinate the tofu.** In a small bowl, stir together 1 teaspoon salt, the garlic, ginger, black pepper, chile powder, coriander, turmeric, garam masala, and yogurt. Transfer the tofu to a medium bowl, add the

marinade, and use a silicone spatula or your hands to gently coat the tofu (don't smush or break it). Marinate for 15 minutes to 1 hour at room temperature, or for a few hours in the fridge.

5. Meanwhile, cook the rice using your preferred method, or get out your leftover cooked rice.

6. **Make the stir-fry.** Open a window for ventilation (see Tips). Heat a skillet or wok over medium-high heat for a minute or two. Add the 1½ tablespoons oil (if using a wok, wait until the pan smokes to add the oil). Once shimmering, add the cumin seeds and cook for 30 to 45 seconds, swirling often. Add the garlic and serrano and cook, stirring frequently, until the garlic is golden but not browning, 60 to 90 seconds. Add the curry leaves (cover the pan immediately if using fresh curry leaves to avoid splatter) and cook for 30 seconds. Add the sambal oelek and tamari and sizzle briefly to thicken. Remove from the heat and transfer to a bowl. Let cool to room temperature. A room-temperature stir-fry is essential; if hot, it will dampen the tofu's crispiness.

7. **Heat the frying oil**. Add enough oil to a heavy-bottomed saucepan for deep-frying, no more than half-full to prevent bubbling up. Heat on medium-high heat until it reaches 350° to 370°F (175° to 188°C)—it should take 10 to 12 minutes (see Note in step 9). Line a large plate with a few paper towels.

8. **While the oil is heating, batter the tofu.** In a gallon-size (2 L) resealable plastic bag, add the cornstarch and rice flour with a pinch of

salt, seal, and shake to combine. Add the marinated tofu, seal, and gently shake to coat but don't massage or smash the tofu.

9. Once the oil reaches temperature (see Note below), add just a few pieces of tofu to a spider or slotted spoon, trying to space them apart so they're not lumped together. Carefully lower into the oil; repeat until you've added half of the tofu. Cook undisturbed for 2 minutes, then use a chopstick to stir and gently separate the pieces. Fry, stirring once or twice, until golden brown all over, 4 to 6 more minutes.

Note: To test the oil temperature without a thermometer, stick a wooden spoon or chopstick in the oil: it's ready if you see a steady swirl of moderate bubbles. If the bubbles are vigorous, it's a bit too hot; if you don't see any bubbles, the oil isn't hot enough.

10. Scoop up the tofu with the spider and gently shake up and down to get rid of excess oil. Transfer to the paper towel–lined plate and sprinkle with a tiny pinch of salt. Keep the heat at medium-high and heat the oil until it reaches 350°F (175°C) again (it takes 1 to 2 minutes). Fry the second batch of tofu.

11. **Cook the snap peas.** Heat the skillet or wok used for the stir-fry over high heat. Add a drizzle of oil, and once hot, add the snap peas. Cook, stirring occasionally, until charred and crisp-tender, about 5 minutes.

12. Add the fried tofu to the room-temperature stir-fry from step 6 and season with the black pepper. Toss to coat all the tofu. Serve with the rice and snap peas.

Sweet & Sour Tempeh Peanut Stir-Fry

Serves 6 | GF

Inspired by the Indonesian dish kering tempeh (deep-fried tempeh and peanuts in a sweet-and-spicy glaze), this is a recipe that will win over even tempeh haters.

Here, tempeh is very thinly sliced and pan-fried until crispy (it tastes deceptively deep-fried), while roasted peanuts and snap peas add crunch. Lemongrass and lime leaves add intoxicatingly citrusy aromas, and the sweet-and-sour, salty-and-savory sauce makes you forget you're eating nutrient-dense tempeh.

Ingredient Notes: Tamarind paste and concentrate are sold at Asian and Indian grocery stores, in the Asian or Latin aisle of well-stocked supermarkets, or online; in a pinch, you can sub with more lime juice. Fresh makrut lime leaves are sold at Southeast Asian markets and some pan-Asian markets like H Mart, or order dried lime leaves online and lightly tear or crush with your hands.

Tips: If you can't find lemongrass or lime leaves, this stir-fry is still lovely without them but feels more peanut-heavy, so use ½ cup (70 g) peanuts. If you are using a wok, in step 3, heat over high until it just starts to smoke, then add the oil and swirl up the sides.

Make Ahead: You can prep the tempeh, aromatics, and sauce 1 to 3 days ahead; refrigerate separately.

Easy Variations: Sub snap peas with shredded napa cabbage, green beans, or thinly sliced bell peppers or bok choy. Allergic to peanuts? Use almond butter or cashew butter and replace the peanuts with roasted cashews.

1½ cups (285 g) uncooked or 4½ cups (650 g) cooked **jasmine rice** or **sticky white rice** (glutinous rice)

2 (8-ounce/227 g) blocks **tempeh**

¼ cup (56 g) **neutral-flavored high-heat oil** of choice

Kosher salt

¾ cup (105 g) **salted or unsalted dry-roasted peanuts** (see Tips)

Sauce

3 tablespoons freshly squeezed **lime juice**

3 tablespoons (50 g) **tamari** or **soy sauce** (use tamari to keep GF)

1 tablespoon **sambal oelek** or **chili-garlic sauce,** plus more as needed

1 tablespoon **tamarind paste or concentrate** (see Ingredient Notes)

3 tablespoons **organic brown sugar** or **pure maple syrup**

2 tablespoons no-sugar-added creamy **peanut butter**

Stir-Fry

1½ tablespoons **neutral-flavored oil** of choice

6 **scallions**, thinly sliced on a bias (reserve dark green tops for garnish)

recipe and ingredients continue

4 **garlic cloves**, minced

1½-inch (3.75 cm) piece **fresh ginger**, grated or minced

1 to 3 **Thai chiles** (or ½ serrano pepper), thinly sliced or minced (omit for mild heat; 3 for *spicy!*)

1 **lemongrass** stalk, minced (see page 472 for prep tips)

4 to 5 **fresh makrut lime leaves**, minced (or 10 to 12 dried lime leaves; see Ingredient Notes)

½ teaspoon **ground coriander**

12 to 16 ounces (340 to 455 g) **sugar snap peas**, halved (large pieces cut into thirds)

For Serving

A few squeezes of fresh **lime juice**

1. Start by cooking the rice using your preferred method, or get out your leftover cooked rice.

2. Cut the tempeh into matchsticks following the instructions on page 292. The matchsticks yield the best texture, but if you want to save time, you can roughly slice the tempeh and add it to a food processor; pulse repeatedly until it's in small crumbles.

3. Heat a 12-inch (30 cm) nonstick skillet over medium-high heat (see Tips if using a wok). Add the oil and heat for a few minutes until shimmering. Add the tempeh with a few pinches of salt and stir to coat in the oil. Cook undisturbed for 2 minutes, then flip. Repeat this process for 10 more minutes—cooking undisturbed for 2 minutes, then stirring—until most of the tempeh is browned and crispy.

4. Transfer the tempeh to a paper towel–lined surface to absorb excess oil and season with a few pinches of salt.

5. **Make the sauce.** In a medium bowl, whisk together the lime juice, tamari, sambal oelek, tamarind paste, brown sugar, and peanut butter.

6. **Make the stir-fry.** Return the pan to medium heat for a minute or two. Add the oil and once hot, add the white and light green parts of the scallions, the garlic, ginger, and chiles (if using). Fry until aromatic and the garlic begins to turn golden, 2 to 3 minutes. Add the lemongrass, lime leaves, and coriander and cook for 30 seconds, stirring or shaking the pan frequently. Increase the heat to medium-high and add the snap peas. Cook until crisp-tender, 2 to 3 minutes.

7. Pour in the sauce and bring to a boil, scraping up any stuck bits. Once the sauce thickens, about 1 minute, add the tempeh and peanuts. Toss the tempeh until fully coated, then remove from the heat. Remove the dried lime leaves, if used.

8. Squeeze a bit of lime on and taste, adjusting the seasonings. Garnish with scallion greens and serve over rice. When reheating leftovers, finish with a squeeze of lime and add more sambal oelek for heat, if desired.

Creamy Chickpea Spinach Masala with Tadka

Serves 4 to 6 | GF, SF, NF

I think of this as a spin on a North Indian chana masala with the addition of spinach and coconut milk and a South Indian–flavored tadka to finish. It has everything you want in a creamy Indian-restaurant-style gravy dish, including the depth of flavor you typically get only after a slow simmer, but it's ready from start to finish in under an hour.

Ingredient Notes: All the spices, including fresh curry leaves for the tadka, can be found at Indian grocers.

Make Ahead: Prep the onions, aromatics, tomatoes, and spinach 1 to 3 days ahead; refrigerate separately.

¼ teaspoon **cardamom seeds** (from 4 to 5 green cardamom pods)

2 teaspoons **coriander seeds**

1½ teaspoons **cumin seeds**

2 tablespoons **neutral-flavored oil** of choice

1 (2-inch/5 cm) **cinnamon stick**

1 large **yellow or red onion**, finely diced

Kosher salt and freshly ground **black pepper**

6 **garlic cloves**, minced

2-inch (5 cm) piece **fresh ginger**, grated or minced

1 to 3 **serrano peppers**, diced (1 for mild; 3 for *spicy!*)

1 teaspoon **ground turmeric**

2 tablespoons **tomato paste**

1 pound (455 g) **Roma or plum tomatoes**, finely chopped

1 (13.5-ounce/400 ml) can **full-fat coconut milk**

2 (15-ounce/425 g) cans **chickpeas**, drained and rinsed

2 tablespoons no-sugar-added creamy **almond butter**

1 teaspoon **organic brown sugar** or **coconut sugar**

6 cups (120 g) **baby spinach**, chopped

2 teaspoons **garam masala**

1½ teaspoons freshly squeezed **lime or lemon juice**, plus more to taste

1 cup (16 g) **fresh cilantro** leaves and tender stems, chopped

1 small handful **fresh mint** leaves, chopped (optional)

Tadka (recipe follows)

1. Roughly grind the cardamom, coriander, and cumin seeds in a mortar with a pestle or add to a spice grinder and pulse just a few times. For alternative methods, see page 74.

2. In a 12-inch (30 cm) deep sauté pan, heat the oil over medium-high heat. Once hot, add the cinnamon stick and toss for 30 seconds. Add the roughly crushed spices and cook for 1 minute, tossing frequently.

recipe continues

3. Add the onions with a pinch of salt and cook until they begin to get some color, 5 to 7 minutes. Add a splash of water to prevent browning. Add the garlic, ginger, serrano, turmeric, and tomato paste and cook for 90 seconds, stirring frequently.

4. Add the tomatoes and their juices and 1½ teaspoons salt. Cook until the tomatoes start to break down and soften, 4 to 5 minutes. Pour in a few spoonfuls of coconut milk, scraping up any browned bits with a spatula. Add the rest of the coconut milk, the chickpeas, almond butter, and brown sugar. Stir well and bring to a simmer. Cover and simmer for 15 minutes, uncovering to stir occasionally.

5. Add the spinach and garam masala and simmer until the spinach wilts. Discard the cinnamon stick. Turn off the heat, stir in the lime juice, cilantro, and mint (if using), and season to taste with salt and pepper. Taste, adding more lime juice or salt as needed.

6. Just before serving, prepare the tadka. Pour the tadka on top of the chickpea masala. If freezing leftovers, pour tadka only on top of the amount you plan to eat now.

Tadka

Serves 4 to 6 | GFO, NF, SF

Perhaps my favorite and most-used flavor-infusion technique from Indian cooking is tadka, the process of blooming spices (and sometimes aromatics) in a fat source like oil (for more, see page 72). Drizzling it on top of the chickpea masala just before serving takes it from great to excellent. For tadka cooking tips, see page 193.

1½ to 2 tablespoons **coconut oil** or **neutral-flavored oil** of choice

1½ teaspoons **black or brown mustard seeds**

1 teaspoon **cumin seeds**

1 or 2 pinches **asafetida** (a.k.a. hing; optional; omit if gluten-free)

10 to 12 **fresh curry leaves** (or 20 to 25 dried; see Ingredient Notes on page 192)

½ teaspoon **Indian red chile powder**

1. Heat your smallest skillet or a tempering pan over medium heat. Add the oil and once shimmering, add the mustard seeds. Shake the pan occasionally. Once they start sputtering, add the cumin seeds and cook for 30 seconds. Add the asafetida (if using) and swirl for 10 seconds. Add the curry leaves (cover the pan immediately if using fresh curry leaves to avoid splatter) and keep swirling until very aromatic and the leaves have shriveled, about 20 seconds.

2. Remove from the heat immediately and stir in the chile powder.

Ethiopian Red Lentil Stew with Spiced Butter

Serves 4 │ GF, SFO, NF

When I lived in New York City, I had the luxury of ordering a yetsom beyaynetu (a vegetarian Ethiopian platter) to my doorstep any night of the week. Here, I share a spin on my favorite item on that platter, misir wot, a richly spiced red lentil stew.

My version includes a homemade berbere blend with spicy, citrusy, smoky notes and an Indian flair in the form of a tadka. The tadka is in turn inspired by nit'r qibe, a clarified butter infused with herbs and spices that's used across many Ethiopian dishes. The mishmash results are uniquely delicious.

Ingredient Notes: I once heard Chef Marcus Samuelsson say that berbere is Ethiopians' version of salt and pepper, so I've offered my homemade blend for maximal flavor (it makes a generous amount, so you can make this stew more quickly the next time). If you have access to good-quality berbere (I like the one from the Spice House), feel free to use that.

Tip: Finely dice the onions; otherwise, they stay a bit crunchy.

Make Ahead: You can make the berbere well in advance; store in the pantry. Prep the onion and aromatics 1 to 3 days ahead; refrigerate separately.

1 cup (180 g) **red lentils** or **split red lentils**

1 tablespoon **neutral-flavored oil** of choice

2 medium **red onions**, finely diced (see Tip)

Kosher salt

4 **garlic cloves**, chopped

1 tablespoon grated or minced **fresh ginger**

2 tablespoons **tomato paste**

2 tablespoons **Berbere Spice Blend** (recipe follows; or store-bought)

2½ cups (600 ml) **low-sodium vegetable broth** (or water)

½ cup (8 g) **fresh cilantro** leaves and tender stems, chopped

Spiced Butter

4 tablespoons (56 g) **vegan butter** (use soy-free butter as needed)

½ teaspoon **fenugreek seeds**

½ teaspoon **coriander seeds**

½ teaspoon **cumin seeds**

½ teaspoon **dried oregano**

¼ teaspoon **ground turmeric**

For Serving

Flatbread of choice (or cooked rice)

Unsweetened coconut yogurt (optional)

1. Soak the lentils in cold water while you prep everything else. Then drain and rinse them until the water runs mostly clear.

recipe continues

2. In a large, deep sauté pan, heat the oil over medium-high heat. Once shimmering, add the onions and a pinch of salt. Cook until a bit browned, stirring occasionally, 6 to 7 minutes. Reduce the heat to medium and add the garlic and ginger. Stir frequently for 1 to 2 minutes. Add the tomato paste and 1½ tablespoons of the berbere. Stir frequently for 2 minutes, adding a splash of water to prevent burning.

3. Pour in the broth to deglaze, scraping up any bits stuck to the bottom of the pan. Add the lentils and 1½ teaspoons salt and stir to combine.

4. Bring the stew to a boil, then reduce the heat to low, cover, and simmer for 25 minutes, stirring occasionally. Uncover and simmer for 10 to 15 more minutes, until the lentils are very soft and meld into the stew (the lentils might look cooked after the first 25 minutes, but they need more time to break down). If you want a creamier texture, run an immersion blender through a portion of the lentils.

5. When the stew is done, make the spiced butter. In a medium skillet, heat the butter over medium heat. Once melted and foamy, add the fenugreek, coriander, and cumin seeds. Cook for 1 minute, swirling or shaking the pan frequently. Add the oregano and turmeric and cook for 20 to 30 seconds, swirling frequently. Remove from the heat.

6. Pour the butter over the stew. Add the remaining ½ tablespoon berbere and the cilantro. Serve with flatbread or rice and dollop the stew with yogurt, if desired.

Berbere Spice Blend

Makes 4 to 5 tablespoons (25 to 30 g) | GF, SF, NF

¾ teaspoon **fenugreek seeds**

½ teaspoon **whole black peppercorns**

1½ teaspoons **coriander seeds**

4 **black or green cardamom pods**, slightly cracked

3 **allspice berries** (or ¼ teaspoon ground)

2 **whole cloves** (or ⅛ teaspoon ground)

3 to 4 **chiles de arbol** (or other medium-hot dried red chiles)

1½ teaspoons **kosher salt**

2 tablespoons + 1 teaspoon **sweet or hot paprika**

½ teaspoon **ground or freshly grated nutmeg**

¼ teaspoon **ground cinnamon**

¼ teaspoon **ground ginger**

1. In a small skillet over medium heat, add the fenugreek seeds, peppercorns, coriander seeds, cardamom pods, allspice berries, and cloves. Cook, swirling the pan frequently for 2 minutes. Add the chiles and cook for 1 minute. Remove from the heat and let cool. Crack open the cardamom pods to get the seeds; discard the shells.

2. Transfer the toasted spices to a spice grinder or mortar and pestle. Grind into a fine powder. Add the salt, paprika, nutmeg, cinnamon, ginger (and ground allspice and cloves if you didn't use the whole versions). Stir well. Store in a sealed jar in the pantry for up to 6 months.

Thai Red Curry with Tofu

Serves 6 | GFO, NF

I ate the best food of my life when traveling in Thailand, so I wanted to bring you a small sliver of those delicious memories. This version has all the flavors you crave in a Thai curry: savory, salty, sweet, sour, and spicy, all wrapped up in a silky, creamy broth dotted with soft yet chewy tofu and crisp-tender vegetables.

A few ingredients like makrut lime leaves and Thai basil require a visit to your local Asian grocery store, but I promise the results are worth it.

Ingredient Notes: Maesri makes my favorite vegan curry paste (sold at Asian markets and online). It's spicier than standard grocery store curry paste.

Fresh makrut lime leaves add the fresh and zesty fragrance characteristic of Thai curries. If you can't get them, order dried lime leaves online, or omit if you must.

Thai soy sauce is also known as light, or thin, soy sauce. It's much saltier than standard grocery store soy sauce. If your brand has sugar, use a bit less coconut sugar. You can sub with 2½ tablespoons standard soy sauce or tamari (use tamari for GF).

Make Ahead: Prep the aromatics and veg and boil the tofu 1 to 3 days ahead; refrigerate separately.

Easy Variations: Use baby bok choy, bell peppers, snap peas, or small cauliflower florets.

1½ to 2 cups (285 to 380 g) uncooked or 4 to 6 cups (650 to 900 g) cooked **jasmine rice**

1 (14-ounce/400 g) block **extra-firm tofu**, drained

1 tablespoon **kosher salt** (or 1½ to 2 teaspoons fine sea salt)

2½ tablespoons **unrefined coconut oil** or **neutral-flavored oil** of choice

2-inch (5 cm) piece **fresh galangal** (or ginger), grated or minced (see Ingredient Notes on page 468 for tips)

6 **garlic cloves**, minced

3 medium **shallots**, thinly sliced into rings

1 to 3 **Thai chiles**, sliced (omit for mild heat; 3 for *spicy!*)

2 **lemongrass** stalks, minced (see page 472 for prep tips)

6 tablespoons (100 g) **red curry paste** (see Ingredient Notes)

2 (13.5-ounce/400 ml) cans **full-fat coconut milk**

6 **fresh makrut lime leaves**, torn in a few places (or 12 dried, lightly crushed; see Ingredient Notes)

2½ tablespoons **coconut sugar**, plus more to taste (see Ingredient Notes)

1½ tablespoons **Thai soy sauce** (see Ingredient Notes), plus more to taste

3 cups (180 g) small-cut **broccoli florets**

1½ cups (140 g) halved **snow peas** or **sugar snap peas**

½ tablespoon freshly squeezed **lime juice**, plus more to taste

½ to 1 cup (8 to 16 g) **fresh Thai basil leaves**, plus more for garnish if desired

recipe continues

1. Start by cooking the rice using your preferred method, or get out your leftover cooked rice.

2. Bring a medium saucepan of water to a boil. Slice the tofu vertically into four slabs, then gently press down on them with a dish towel to remove some water. Cut the tofu into ½- to ¾-inch (1.5 to 2 cm) cubes. Once the water is boiling, add the salt, followed by the tofu. When the water returns to a boil, set a timer for 2 minutes. Use a slotted spoon to transfer the tofu to a bowl and set aside.

3. In a 12-inch (30 cm) deep sauté pan, heat the oil over medium heat. Once hot, add the galangal, garlic, shallots, chiles (if using), lemongrass, and curry paste. Cook, stirring frequently, until the paste dries out, 2½ to 4 minutes. The curry paste might sputter, so stand back.

4. Pour in a few spoonfuls of the coconut milk, let it bubble, then scrape up any browned bits. Stir in the rest of the coconut milk, the lime leaves, sugar, and soy sauce. Increase the heat a bit so the mixture comes to a rapid simmer. Cook until the curry just starts to thicken, about 5 minutes.

5. Add the boiled tofu to the curry and gently toss. Add the broccoli, peas, and ½ cup (120 ml) of water, using your spatula to submerge the veg. Partially cover the pan and simmer rapidly until the veg is tender but still crisp and bright green, 4 to 6 minutes.

6. Turn off the heat. Add ½ tablespoon of the lime juice. Taste for seasonings, adding more soy sauce, lime juice, or sugar as needed. Remove the lime leaves and stir in the Thai basil.

7. Divide the curry among six bowls and garnish with a few Thai basil leaves, if desired. Serve with the rice.

Velvety White Bean & Tomato Stew

Serves 6 to 8 | GF, SF, NF

Come winter, you need a stew that'll make you feel cozy inside but is also nutrient dense. This one features a rich tomatoey flavor, brothy beans, and a generous amount of kale. It has an incredible savory depth and surprisingly creamy texture. Plus, it makes a generous quantity, is great for meal prep, and is freezer friendly. All in all, it checks off every box for a great stew. Serve with hunks of seeded bread for a heartier meal.

Ingredient Notes: Use the best-quality canned tomatoes you can afford, as they're a key part of the stew. See page 58 for my preferred brands. I love using beans cooked from scratch, but canned beans work, too (see instructions below).

Tip: I always soak my dried beans overnight, as it aids with digestion and yields fewer split skins, but if you don't have the time, try a 30-minute soak. If you're using unsoaked beans, they will take longer to cook.

Make Ahead: You can soak the beans, drain, and refrigerate for up to 4 days. You can prep the veggies 1 to 3 days ahead; refrigerate separately.

Easy Variations: Use thyme in place of sage or rosemary, or Swiss chard for kale. Add a fennel bulb into the mix, or swap parsnips for carrots.

1 pound (455 g) **dried navy beans** (or other small white beans) or 4 (15-ounce/425 g) **cans navy beans**, drained and rinsed

Kosher salt and freshly ground **black pepper**

2 teaspoons **baking soda** (for dried beans only)

⅓ cup (75 g) + 1 tablespoon **extra-virgin olive oil**, plus more for finishing

4 medium **carrots**, scrubbed and finely chopped

2 large **shallots**, sliced into rings (¼ scant inch/0.5 cm thick)

6 **garlic cloves**, thinly sliced

4 cups (960 ml) **vegetable broth**

1 (28-ounce/800 g) can good-quality **whole peeled tomatoes** (see Ingredient Notes)

2 **sage** sprigs

1 large or 2 small **rosemary** sprigs

2 **bay leaves**

1½ teaspoons **porcini mushroom powder** (optional but recommended, for more savory oomph; see Ingredient Notes on page 187)

1 large bunch **lacinato kale**, center ribs removed and thinly sliced

½ cup (8 g) **fresh flat-leaf parsley** leaves and tender stems, chopped (optional)

Crusty bread, for serving (optional)

recipe continues

To make with dried beans

1. **Soak the beans.** In a large bowl, cover the dried beans with 8 cups (2 L) cold water. Stir in 1 tablespoon kosher salt and the baking soda. Soak for 8 hours, or overnight (see Tip). Drain and rinse with cold water.

2. In a Dutch oven or large ovenproof soup pot, heat 1 tablespoon of the oil over medium heat. Add the carrots with a pinch of salt and cook until just starting to soften, 4 to 5 minutes. Add the shallots and garlic and cook until the shallots have softened, 2 to 4 minutes.

3. Pour in a splash of broth and deglaze the pan, scraping up any browned bits. Add the rest of the broth and the soaked beans. Pour 2 cups (480 ml) of water on top and season with 2 teaspoons kosher salt.

4. Bring to a boil and boil the beans for 10 minutes, using a spoon to skim off any thick foam that rises to the surface. Reduce the heat to low. Partially cover the pot and gently simmer until the beans are tender, 45 to 50 minutes. If you're on the lowest heat but it's simmering rapidly, move the pan to your smallest burner. If a lot of liquid evaporates during simmering, add enough boiling water to just cover the beans. Toward the end of cooking, use the back of a spoon to smash some beans for extra creaminess.

5. Preheat the oven to 450°F (230°C).

6. When the beans are tender, pour in the tomato juices from the canned tomatoes. Crush the whole tomatoes by hand (no large pieces) and add to the beans. Using kitchen twine, make an herb bundle (bouquet garni) out of the sage, rosemary, and bay leaves and nestle it in the pan. Add the mushroom powder (if using), 1 teaspoon salt, lots of pepper, the remaining ⅓ cup (75 g) oil, and the kale. Stir to combine. If the stew looks too thick, add up to ½ cup (120 ml) of water.

7. Transfer to the oven and bake, uncovered, for 25 to 30 minutes, until the beans are creamy. Remove the bouquet garni. Season with salt and pepper to taste and drizzle with a glug of olive oil. If desired, garnish with parsley and serve with bread.

To make with canned beans

1. In a Dutch oven or large ovenproof soup pot, heat 1 tablespoon of the oil over medium heat. Add the carrots with a pinch of salt and cook until just starting to soften, 4 to 5 minutes. Add the shallots and garlic and cook until the shallots have softened, 2 to 4 minutes.

2. Pour in a splash of broth and deglaze the pan, scraping up any browned bits. Add the canned beans and the rest of the broth and season with 2 teaspoons kosher salt. Crush in the tomatoes and add the juices. Using kitchen twine, make an herb bundle (bouquet garni) out of the sage, rosemary, and bay leaves and nestle it in the pan. Add the mushroom powder (if using), 1 teaspoon salt, and lots of pepper.

3. Simmer until starting to thicken, about 15 minutes. Toward the end of cooking, use the back of a spoon to smash some of the beans.

4. Meanwhile, preheat the oven to 450°F (230°C).

5. Add ¼ cup (56 g) of the oil and the kale to the beans. Stir to combine. Bake, uncovered, for 15 to 20 minutes, until the beans are creamy. Remove the bouquet garni. Season with salt and pepper to taste and drizzle with a glug of oil. If desired, garnish with parsley and serve with bread.

My Favorite Dal Tadka

Serves 4 | GFO, SF, NF

Dal is a deeply spiced, aromatic lentil stew. Every region of India, and even every family, has their own variation. Tadka, a hallmark of Indian cooking, refers to a tempered oil in which spices, herbs, and/or aromatics are briefly fried in oil (see page 72).

In dal tadka, the dal is finished by pouring the tadka on top just before serving. My version combines tips I learned from Mom, along with my own spins. It's super creamy and finished with a tadka resplendent with crunchy mustard seeds, earthy cumin seeds, glistening red chiles, and crisp curry leaves.

Ingredient Notes: You can sub red lentils or masoor dal (split red lentils) for moong dal.

To puree tomatoes, add them to a food processor. If tomatoes are out of season, use a 14.5-ounce (400 g) can of diced tomatoes.

Asafetida is a staple Indian spice, though it's actually a gum resin from a plant. It smells pungent and eggy but works wonders and adds a classically Indian je ne sais quoi to the tadka (it also aids with digesting legumes). If you don't have it or are allergic to gluten, skip it.

Tips: When making the tadka, use your senses of sight and smell. If the spices seem to change color very quickly, reduce the heat. If the spices burn, start over (it's very quick). For more cooking tips, see page 193. I like to make a fresh batch of tadka for leftovers to dial up the flavors.

Make Ahead: You can soak the lentils, drain, and refrigerate them for 1 to 3 days. You can prep the onions, aromatics, and tomatoes 1 to 3 days ahead; refrigerate separately.

1 cup (200 g) **moong dal** (split yellow lentils; see Ingredient Notes)

1 tablespoon **coconut oil** or **neutral-flavored oil** of choice

1 medium **yellow onion**, chopped

Kosher salt and freshly ground **black pepper**

4 **garlic cloves**, minced

1-inch (2.5 cm) piece **fresh ginger**, grated or minced

1 **serrano pepper**, diced (omit for mild heat)

1 teaspoon **curry powder**

1 teaspoon **garam masala**

¼ teaspoon **ground coriander**

¼ teaspoon **ground turmeric**

1½ cups (300 g) finely diced or pureed **fresh tomatoes** (10 to 12 ounces/280 to 340 g; see Ingredient Notes)

½ cup (8 g) **fresh cilantro** leaves and tender stems, chopped, plus more for garnish if desired

recipe and ingredients continue

Tadka

1½ to 2 tablespoons **coconut oil** or **neutral-flavored oil** of choice

1 teaspoon **black or brown mustard seeds**

½ teaspoon **cumin seeds**

1 to 2 dried **red chiles**, such as chiles de arbol (optional, for *spicy!*)

1 or 2 pinches **asafetida** (a.k.a. hing; see Ingredient Notes; optional; omit if gluten-free)

4 to 6 **fresh curry leaves** (or 10 to 12 dried; see Ingredient Notes on page 192)

For Serving

Cooked **basmati rice** or **Indian flatbread**

Plain vegan yogurt or **Mint Yogurt Sauce** (page 213)

Thinly sliced **red onions** or **pickled red onions** (page 168)

1. Soak the lentils in cold water for 15 minutes, then drain.

2. **Meanwhile, prep the aromatics.** In a deep sauté pan, heat the oil over medium-high heat. Once shimmering, add the onions and season with a pinch of salt. Cook until softened and the edges are starting to turn golden brown, 5 to 7 minutes.

3. Add the garlic, ginger, and serrano (if using). Cook until the garlic is lightly browned and very fragrant, 60 to 90 seconds. Add the curry powder, garam masala, coriander, and turmeric and stir to coat into the onions. Cook for 30 seconds, stirring almost constantly.

4. Deglaze the pan with water—I use 2 to 2½ cups (480 to 600 ml) at this stage (for a looser dal, use 3 cups/720 ml)—and scrape up any browned bits on the bottom of the pan. Add the lentils, 1 teaspoon salt, and several cracks of black pepper. Stir to combine.

5. Bring the dal to a boil, then lower the heat and partially cover the pan (if your lid has a hole on top to vent steam, you can fully cover the pan). Simmer until the lentils are fully cooked through, about 30 minutes. You will need to stir occasionally and add more water as it evaporates.

6. Add the tomatoes and cook until they are cooked down and blended into the dal, 4 to 5 minutes. I prefer a creamier dal, so I run an immersion blender through part of it (keep in mind dal thickens as it rests). Finally, stir in the cilantro. Season to taste with salt and black pepper.

7. **When the dal is done, make the tadka.** Heat your smallest skillet or a tempering pan over medium heat. Add the oil and once shimmering, add the mustard seeds. Once they start popping, add the cumin seeds and cook for a few seconds until they start to change color. Add the dried chiles (if using), asafetida (if using), and curry leaves (cover the pan immediately if using fresh curry leaves to avoid splatter). Stir or swirl the pan to cook evenly and prevent burning, 20 to 30 more seconds, until very aromatic. The curry leaves should be shriveled and the chiles and cumin seeds darker in color. Remove from the heat immediately to prevent overcooking.

8. Pour the tadka over the dal right before serving and stir to combine. If desired, garnish with cilantro. Taste for salt and pepper. Serve with rice or flatbread and toppings of choice.

Pasta & Chickpeas with Fried Capers & Tomato-Shallot Butter

Serves 4 | GFO, SF, NF

This is a hearty, creamy pasta dinner that feels fancy but is weeknight friendly, especially if you make the tomato-shallot butter in advance. The tomato-shallot butter is subtly sweet yet savory and its creamy texture lovingly cradles the ridged pasta and chickpeas. Lemon zest, basil, and parsley add freshness, while fried capers add a fantastically salty and crunchy finish.

Tip: For the most efficient use of time, make the fried capers while the pasta cooks.

Big-Flavor Meals: If you have Cheesy Crunchies (page 223) in your pantry, use as a topper instead of Fried Capers. Serve with a green salad, or with Jammy Zucchini (page 330), Quick Roasted Cauliflower (page 342), or Jammy Roasted Eggplant (page 339).

Make Ahead: You can make the Tomato-Shallot Butter 3 to 4 days ahead of time.

Kosher salt or **fine sea salt**

8 ounces (227 g) medium-size ridged **pasta**, such as penne rigate, cavatappi, or rigatoni (use gluten-free pasta for GF)

Tomato-Shallot Butter (page 173)

1 (15-ounce/425 g) can **chickpeas**, drained and rinsed

2 tablespoons **nutritional yeast**

1 medium **lemon**, zested

Freshly ground **black pepper**

1 handful **fresh basil** leaves, slivered

1 large handful **fresh flat-leaf parsley** leaves, chopped

Fried Capers (page 167; optional)

Freshly squeezed **lemon juice**, as needed

1. Bring a large saucepan of water to a boil. Once boiling, add 1 tablespoon kosher salt (or 1½ to 2 teaspoons sea salt) and the pasta and cook according to the box instructions until just al dente, no longer. Before draining, reserve a ladleful of pasta water.

2. Add the tomato-shallot butter to the pan used for the pasta and bring to a simmer over medium heat. Add the chickpeas and toss to coat for 1 minute. Add the hot cooked pasta and nutritional yeast and use tongs to coat the pasta, adding a splash of pasta water as needed to bring everything together.

3. Reduce the heat to low. Add about half of the lemon zest and crack in a generous amount of pepper. Cook for 2 minutes, stirring occasionally.

4. Remove from the heat and finish with basil, parsley, and fried capers (if using). Taste for seasonings, adding more salt and lemon zest as needed. For brightness, squeeze a bit of the lemon juice on top.

Lemony Pasta with Sausage & Broccoli

Serves 4 to 5 | SF, NF

This is my idea of a perfectly balanced pasta: vegan sausage and rigatoni make it robust, while the lemon sauce, broccoli, and herbs are light and fresh. Pairing three types of acid—lemon, capers, and Dijon—adds zingy brightness, and the broccoli stems and florets bring fun textures: the seared stems get slightly crisp, and the florets break down in the pasta water and help thicken the sauce.

Ingredient Note: Beyond Meat hot Italian sausage crumbles and clings to the pasta perfectly. Field Roast Italian sausage also works nicely. If your sausage doesn't crumble, slice it thinly and cook until browned.

Make Ahead: Prep the broccoli, make the lemon sauce, and crumble the sausage 1 to 2 days ahead; refrigerate separately.

Easy Variations: Not a fan of sausage? Pan-fry chickpeas in olive oil until crisp, then add the garlic and broccoli stems. Sub 1-inch (2.5 cm) pieces of asparagus or green beans for the broccoli, or dill for the basil.

1 pound (455 g) **broccoli**

Kosher salt and freshly ground **black pepper**

12 ounces (340 g) **rigatoni** or **cavatappi** (or other medium-size ridged pasta)

4 links **vegan sausage** (12 to 16 ounces/340 to 455 g; see Ingredient Note)

6 **garlic cloves**, thinly sliced

¼ to ½ teaspoon **red pepper flakes** (½ teaspoon for a kick)

3 tablespoons **nutritional yeast**

½ cup (8 g) **fresh flat-leaf parsley** leaves and tender stems, chopped

½ cup (8 g) **fresh basil** leaves, slivered

2 tablespoons **capers**, drained

Lemon Sauce

3 medium **lemons**

¼ cup (56 g) **extra-virgin olive oil**

1 teaspoon **Dijon mustard**

1 teaspoon **kosher salt**

Freshly ground **black pepper**

recipe continues

1. Slice off the tough bottom 1 to 2 inches (2.5 to 5 cm) of the broccoli stalks, then peel the first outer layer of the stalks with a vegetable peeler. Slice the stalks thinly into coins with a mandoline or sharp knife. Cut the crowns into florets, not too big or too small.

2. Bring a large pot of water to a boil. Don't use too much water; otherwise, the pasta water won't be starchy. I recommend 10 to 12 cups of water (2.4 to 2.9 L).

3. **Make the lemon sauce.** Zest the lemons and set aside. Juice the lemons into a mason jar (you should have about 9 tablespoons/135 ml). Add the olive oil, mustard, salt, and several cracks of black pepper. Shake until emulsified.

4. Once the water is boiling, add 1 tablespoon salt, followed by the pasta. Cook according to the package directions' minimum time for al dente, stirring occasionally. Three minutes before the pasta should be done, add the broccoli florets (not the stems). Cook until the pasta is barely al dente (a little undercooked is okay) and the florets are crisp-tender and bright green, 2½ to 3 minutes. Before draining, scoop out a big ladlefull of pasta water into a bowl and reserve. Drain the pasta and broccoli but do not rinse.

5. While the pasta cooks, heat a large skillet over medium-high heat. Crumble the sausage with your hands, add to the pan, and cook until a bit browned (if it sticks, add a touch of oil), 2 to 3 minutes. Add the garlic and reserved broccoli stems with a few pinches of salt. Cook until the stems start to turn golden brown, 4 to 6 minutes. Add the pepper flakes and cook for 30 seconds. Take the pan off the heat and set aside.

6. **Assemble.** Return the hot cooked pasta and broccoli florets to their pot. Add the sausage mixture, lemon sauce, nutritional yeast, and ½ cup (120 ml) pasta water. Return to medium-high heat. Use tongs to vigorously toss everything together until the pasta is al dente and the sauce clings to the pasta, about 2 minutes. If needed, add a few more spoonfuls of pasta water.

7. Stir in the parsley, basil, capers, and half of the reserved lemon zest. Toss again and cook for 1 minute. Taste, adding more lemon zest as desired. Sprinkle with a pinch or two of salt and black pepper before serving.

Jammy Plantains and Black Beans in Charred Poblano Sauce

Makes 8 to 10 tacos | GF, SF, NF

My first taste of plantains was in the form of deep-fried plantain chips, made by my aunt Anie, who grew up in the tropical Indian state of Kerala. The sweet-salty contrast hooked me instantly, and it's what I love about this dish. Ripe, sweet plantains are seared until deeply browned, then simmered with black beans in a savory, spicy, smoky, and tangy Mexican-ish sauce made from charred poblanos, jalapeños, garlic, and tomatoes. Folded into tortillas, this taco filling tastes entirely indulgent but is secretly fiber packed.

Ingredient Note: You can find plantains at well-stocked grocery stores, or Latin, African, and Asian markets. You're looking for ripe yellow plantains with lots of black spots (they should be only slightly firm to the touch). If yours are not ripe, leave them on the counter for several days. Green plantains can take 8 to 12 days to ripen, but you can speed up the process by storing them in a brown paper bag with an apple or banana (don't seal tightly).

Easy Variations: Instead of tacos, serve the plantains and black beans over rice with vegan sour cream. If you have Avocado Crema (page 204) in your fridge, use that instead of the avocado mash. For a spicy topping, serve with Quick Miso-Chile Hot Sauce (page 190).

2 tablespoons **avocado oil** or **neutral-flavored oil** of choice, plus more for the aromatics

1 **poblano pepper**, quartered and seeded (keep the top cap but discard the stem)

2 **jalapeño peppers**, kept whole with stem on (use 1 for moderate heat)

4 large **garlic cloves**, peeled

1 pint **cherry or grape tomatoes** (10 ounces/285 g)

2 medium-large ripe **yellow plantains** (slightly more than 1 pound/500 g; see Ingredient Note)

Kosher salt and freshly ground **black pepper**

1 teaspoon **ground cumin**

½ teaspoon **ground coriander**

½ teaspoon **Mexican oregano** (or regular oregano or marjoram)

¾ cup (180 ml) **low-sodium vegetable broth** (or water)

1 (15-ounce/425 g) can **black beans**, drained and rinsed

1 large juicy **lime**, juiced (you'll need 2½ to 3 tablespoons total)

1 cup (16 g) **fresh cilantro** leaves and tender stems, chopped

8 to 10 **corn tortillas**

Quick-pickled onions (page 168) and **vegan sour cream** (optional)

Avocado Mash

2 large (or 4 small) ripe **avocados**

1 tablespoon freshly squeezed **lime juice** (use remaining lime juice from above)

Fine sea salt or **kosher salt**

recipe continues

1. **Char the aromatics.** Heat a 12-inch (30 cm) cast-iron skillet over medium-high heat with a touch of oil. Open a window for ventilation. Once the pan is hot, add the poblanos and jalapeños. Cook undisturbed for 4 minutes, then turn with tongs. Add the garlic and tomatoes to open areas of the pan. Cook, turning everything occasionally, until charred in spots and the tomatoes have shriveled a bit, 5 to 6 more minutes. If the garlic starts to burn, turn down the heat. As the aromatics start to blacken in spots, use tongs to transfer them to a plate and allow to cool. Remove the jalapeño stem.

2. **Prepare the plantains.** Cut the ends off each plantain. Use a sharp knife to slice the peel along the length of each plantain without cutting into the flesh (after peeling the first side with a knife, I switch to using my hands). Cut each plantain into ½-inch (1.5 cm) slices on a bias.

3. **Cook the plantains.** Wipe out the pan, then heat the 2 tablespoons oil over medium heat until shimmering. Add the plantains and sear until the bottoms are deeply golden brown, 3 to 4 minutes (very ripe ones may need only 2 minutes). Flip and sear on the second side (some pieces will brown more quickly). Once done, transfer to a plate or cutting board. Use a fork to gently smash about halfway down on each plantain, then sprinkle them with a couple of pinches of kosher salt. Wipe out excess oil from the pan.

4. **Make the sauce.** Add the charred aromatics to a blender (or food processor). If sensitive to spicy food, start with half of the jalapeño(s). Add the cumin, coriander, oregano, 1 teaspoon kosher salt, and several cracks of black pepper. Blend until well combined. Taste for seasonings, adding more kosher salt as needed.

5. Transfer the sauce to the skillet. Bring to a simmer and cook for 3 minutes. Pour in the broth, then add the plantains, nestling each piece in the sauce. Add the black beans and cover the pan with a lid.

6. Simmer rapidly until there is little resistance when the plantains are poked with a fork, about 5 minutes. If the sauce hasn't thickened, uncover and simmer rapidly for 3 to 4 minutes. Turn off the heat and add 1½ tablespoons lime juice and most of the cilantro (set aside a bit for the garnish). Stir to combine. Taste, adding salt or more lime juice as needed.

7. **Make the avocado mash.** In a bowl, roughly mash the avocados with a fork. Add the remaining 1 tablespoon lime juice and several pinches of sea salt. Mash together and taste, adding more lime juice or sea salt as needed.

8. **Char the tortillas.** If you have a gas stove, turn a burner to medium-low and use tongs to place each tortilla directly over the flame until charred in spots, 15 to 30 seconds per side. Or add each tortilla to a cast-iron skillet over medium-high heat for 20 to 40 seconds per side. Stack and wrap charred tortillas in a dish towel to keep them warm.

9. To assemble, spread some avocado mash on top of each tortilla. Spoon the plantains and beans on top and garnish with reserved cilantro. Serve with pickled onions and sour cream (if using).

Korean BBQ Jackfruit Sandwiches with Creamy Sesame Slaw

Makes 6 sandwiches (or 10 to 12 sliders) | GFO, NF

This is my favorite faux meat sandwich and my go-to entrée for BBQs or potlucks because it's so remarkably meaty that it takes everyone by surprise. Jackfruit is shredded, seared in spices, and simmered in a sweet-salty-spicy Korean BBQ sauce until it's sticky, chewy, and legit meaty. Then it's paired with a creamy sesame cabbage slaw and piled on toasted buttered buns for an explosion of flavors and textures.

Make Ahead: You can make the BBQ sauce and/or BBQ jackfruit several days in advance. For the slaw, refrigerate the veggies and dressing separately, then combine on the day of serving.

GF Option: Make the gluten-free alternative to the Korean BBQ Sauce (see page 175). Serve the BBQ jackfruit with gluten-free buns if available, or serve on top of white rice with the Creamy Sesame Slaw (recipe follows) for an epic rice bowl.

Vegan butter, for toasting the buns (can sub with extra-virgin olive oil)

6 vegan-friendly **hamburger buns** of choice (or 10 to 12 ciabatta rolls or dinner rolls for sliders)

Vegan mayo, for spreading on the rolls

Korean BBQ Jackfruit (recipe follows)

Creamy Sesame Slaw (recipe follows)

1. Add a pat of butter to the cut sides of each bun (or drizzle with olive oil). Toast in a warm skillet, buttered sides down, until golden, a few minutes.

2. To serve, add a bit of mayo to each bottom bun. Add a scoop of jackfruit, followed by a few tablespoons of slaw. Top with the remaining bun. Serve sandwiches with extra slaw on the side.

recipe continues

Korean BBQ Jackfruit

Serves 6 | GFO, NF

Shredding jackfruit and slow-cooking it in a thick sauce makes it meaty and chewy yet tender with a sticky, saucy consistency, remarkably similar to BBQ pulled pork.

Ingredient Note: If your jackfruit comes in 14-ounce (400 g) cans, use 3 cans. Some jackfruit brands have a modest amount of sodium (e.g., the 20-ounce/570 g cans at Trader Joe's), but other brands have a dizzying amount (e.g., 90 percent of your daily value of sodium in a 14-ounce/400-g can!). If your brand contains the latter, you need to soak it; otherwise, it will be too salty. Once the jackfruit is shredded, cover it with boiling water and soak for 1 hour. Drain and rinse very well with cold water, then transfer to dish towels and wrap tightly. Dry well before tossing with the spices in step 3.

Tip: If you don't have a large nonstick pan, you can use another pan, but stir often to prevent sticking.

2 (20-ounce/570 g) cans young **jackfruit** in water or brine (not in syrup), drained (see Ingredient Note)

2 teaspoons **gochugaru** (Korean chile flakes)

1 teaspoon **smoked paprika**

Korean BBQ Sauce (page 175)

1½ to 2 tablespoons **grapeseed oil** or **neutral-flavored oil** of choice

1. Drain and rinse the jackfruit very well. Use your fingers to pull the pieces apart so it resembles shredded meat. The tough cores will become edible once cooked, but discard large pods, as they don't soften.

2. Transfer the shredded jackfruit to a large bowl, cover with cold water, and agitate with your hands. If the water turns murky from the brine, drain and rinse again. Transfer to several dish towels to dry. Squeeze out excess water.

3. In a small bowl, stir together the gochugaru and paprika. Sprinkle over the shredded jackfruit and toss to coat each piece with your hands.

4. Scoop out 3 tablespoons of the Korean BBQ sauce and set aside for step 6.

5. Heat a 12-inch (30 cm) nonstick sauté pan over medium-high heat (see Tip). Add the oil, and once shimmering, add the jackfruit. Cook for 2 minutes, undisturbed. Toss, then cook for about 6 minutes, tossing just occasionally. Pour in the BBQ sauce (minus the reserved 3 tablespoons) and ½ cup (120 ml) of water. Stir to coat the jackfruit, then reduce the heat and simmer for 30 minutes, stirring every 5 minutes or so to avoid sticking.

6. Stir in the reserved 3 tablespoons BBQ sauce and toss to coat, then remove from the heat. Depending on the brand of jackfruit, it might taste a bit salty, but once paired with the mayo and coleslaw, the flavors will be well rounded.

Creamy Sesame Slaw

Serves 6 to 8 | GF, NF

This slaw features an addictive mix of sweet-savory-salty-nutty sesame notes and a surprising creaminess. For the best texture, finely grate the cabbage (see page 529 for tips).

Ingredient Note: Asian or Korean pears are in season from August through winter and can be found at Asian supermarkets and well-stocked grocery stores, though you can easily sub with Bosc pears or Fuji apples. You'll likely need 2 pears—one for the Korean BBQ sauce, one for the slaw.

4 cups (300 g) shredded **red cabbage**

½ large (or 1 small) **Asian pear**, grated
(or a Bosc pear or Fuji apple; see Ingredient Note)

¾ cup (12 g) **fresh cilantro** leaves and tender stems, chopped

3 **scallions**, thinly sliced (white and light green parts only)

3 tablespoons freshly squeezed **lime juice**
(or rice vinegar)

1 tablespoon **toasted sesame oil**

1 tablespoon + 1 teaspoon **pure maple syrup**

1 teaspoon **soy sauce** or **tamari**, plus more as needed (use tamari to keep GF)

3 tablespoons (42 g) **vegan mayo**

1½ tablespoons **roasted black or white sesame seeds**

Kosher salt, as needed

In a large bowl, mix together the cabbage, pear, cilantro, and scallions. In a small bowl, whisk together the lime juice, sesame oil, maple syrup, soy sauce, mayo, and sesame seeds. Pour over the cabbage mixture and toss well to combine. Season with salt or soy sauce as needed. Refrigerate leftovers for 3 to 4 days.

Oven-Baked Polenta with Tomatoes & White Beans

Serves 4 to 6 | GF, SF, NF

I adore polenta, but it's tiring to hang around the stove and stir for 45 minutes (I have dainty wrists). But *baked* polenta is hands-off and just as good, especially when you add fresh corn kernels for sweet, buttery notes and chewy, juicy bites. Vegan butter and nutritional yeast add savory richness, while the tomatoes and white beans and the basil gremolata topping make this rustic Italian comfort food taste like a fresh summer meal.

Ingredient Note: This meal is best in summer when fresh corn, tomatoes, and basil are at their finest. If you don't have fresh corn, use 1½ cups (225 g) thawed frozen corn kernels.

Tip: To reheat polenta, add some water or plant milk, stir, and reheat gently on the stove to loosen.

Make Ahead: You can make the Tomatoes & White Beans 1 to 2 days ahead; refrigerate, then reheat on the stove.

Extra-virgin olive oil, for greasing and drizzling

1 large **garlic clove**, grated or crushed with a press

2 medium ears **fresh corn** (see Ingredient Note)

Kosher salt and freshly ground **black pepper**

1 cup (160 g) **polenta**, **corn grits**, or **coarse-grind cornmeal** (not tube polenta)

3 tablespoons **vegan butter**, cut into cubes (or extra-virgin olive oil)

¼ cup (20 g) **nutritional yeast**

1 teaspoon **lemon zest**

Tomatoes & White Beans (recipe follows)

Basil Gremolata (recipe follows)

1. Arrange a rack in the middle of the oven. Preheat the oven to 350°F (175°C).

2. Rub the bottom of an ovenproof 10-inch (25 cm) or 12-inch (30 cm) sauté pan with some olive oil. Add 5 cups (1.2 L) of water and the garlic and bring to a simmer over medium-high heat.

recipe continues

3. Meanwhile, position an ear of corn upright over a sheet pan. Use a chef's knife in a downward direction to shave the corn, allowing the kernels to drop into the pan. Repeat with the remaining ear of corn. Now run a spoon along the shaved cobs to extract the corn "milk."

4. Add the corn kernels and corn milk to the simmering water along with 2 teaspoons kosher salt and a generous amount of pepper. Gradually pour in the polenta, whisking constantly. Bring to a boil, whisking almost constantly. Using oven mitts, transfer the pan to the oven and bake, uncovered, for 25 minutes, or until tender.

5. Remove from the oven and add the butter, nutritional yeast, and lemon zest. Whisk well, scraping the bottom of the pan, until thick and smooth. Bake, uncovered, for 5 minutes, until the liquid is absorbed and the polenta is creamy. If runny, bake for 5 more minutes.

6. Remove from the oven and let rest for 5 minutes, then whisk again. If a skin starts to form on top, whisk again.

7. While the polenta bakes, make the tomatoes and white beans and basil gremolata.

8. To serve, spoon the tomatoes and white beans on top of the polenta. Generously spoon gremolata on top of each serving and drizzle with a bit of olive oil.

Tomatoes & White Beans

Serves 4 to 6 | GF, SF, NF

A slightly sweet and tart mixture of cherry tomatoes and shallots intensifies the natural sweetness of corn, while white beans bulk up this dish without weighing it down.

1½ tablespoons **extra-virgin olive oil**

1 large **shallot**, thinly sliced

3 **garlic cloves**, chopped

¼ to ½ teaspoon **red pepper flakes** (½ teaspoon for a kick)

1 pint **cherry or grape tomatoes** (10 ounces/285 g), halved

Kosher salt and freshly ground **black pepper**

1 (15-ounce/425 g) can **navy beans** or other **white beans**, drained and rinsed

2 teaspoons **red wine vinegar**

Pinch of **organic cane sugar** (only as needed)

1. In a large skillet, heat the olive oil over medium heat. Add the shallots and garlic and cook until golden and aromatic, about 3 minutes. Add the pepper flakes and tomatoes and season with a bit of salt. Cook until the tomatoes start to soften, about 3 minutes.

2. Add the beans, ½ teaspoon salt, and several cracks of black pepper. Reduce the heat to medium-low and cook undisturbed for 2 minutes, then stir. Cook, stirring occasionally, until the tomatoes are mostly broken down and the beans are very soft, 7 minutes.

3. Add the vinegar and cook for 30 seconds, then remove from the heat. Taste for salt and pepper. If it's a bit acidic, stir in the sugar.

Basil Gremolata

Serves 4 to 8 | GF, SF, NF

A classic Italian gremolata tastes even better with the addition of fresh basil. Here, it peppers the polenta with subtly sweet lemony notes and layers of summer freshness.

¾ cup (12 g) **fresh flat-leaf parsley** leaves and tender stems

¾ cup (12 g) **fresh basil** leaves

2 large **garlic cloves**, peeled

2 medium **lemons**

Flaky sea salt

Finely chop the parsley and basil. Using a Microplane, grate the garlic and zest the lemons on top of the herbs, taking care to not zest the white pith of the lemons. Mix the garlic and lemon zest into the herbs and chop again until finely minced. Sprinkle with a bit of flaky salt.

Adult Grilled Cheese with Chili Crisp

Makes 4 mega grilled cheeses

Grilled cheese may not be conventional dinner fare, but these are so unreasonably good—and a serious upgrade on the classic lunch staple—that I had to include them. They feature my two possibly all-time favorite condiments—fermented cashew cheese and chili crisp—in a melty grilled cheese designed for adult palates.

Sticky, spicy caramelized bits slice through the one-note richness of a standard grilled cheese, while the double hit of umami leaves this version lingering on your taste buds in the best way possible. If that hasn't sold you, multiple omnivores have told me this is the best thing they've ever eaten.

Tips: Both condiments take some time to prepare, but they last weeks to months, so bookmark this recipe for when you've got both in your fridge.

Use the chart to choose your grilled cheese adventure, or pick several toppings and host the world's finest grilled cheese bar.

I use shredded vegan cheese instead of sliced cheese because it melts easier (I like Chao Creamery shredded cheese). If you don't have access to a good variety, skip it and use 4 tablespoons of fermented cashew cheese per sandwich.

3 tablespoons **vegan butter**, softened at room temperature

8 slices **sourdough sandwich bread** (or soft sandwich bread of choice)

12 to 16 tablespoons **Fermented Cashew Cheese** (page 210; see Tips)

4 tablespoons **Life-Changing Homemade Chili Crisp** (page 187) or store-bought, or to taste

Mix-and-Match Toppings (see chart on page 518)

1 cup (85 g) **shredded vegan cheese**, more as desired (optional; see Tips)

1. Butter one side of each slice of bread, a generous teaspoon per slice.

2. On half of the bread slices, on the unbuttered side, spread a generous amount of fermented cashew cheese, 3 to 4 tablespoons (enough to generously cover each slice).

recipe continues

salty, tangy, and crisp

sweet and savory

spicy, tangy, and crisp

salty, tangy, and crisp

spicy, tangy, and crisp

sweet and savory

3. Add 1 tablespoon chili crisp (less for mild heat) on top, but strain it first so you get the crispy stuff and minimal oil; use a clean spoon each time you dig in so you don't contaminate it. Add your toppings of choice, followed by the shredded cheese (if using), about ¼ cup (21 g) per slice.

4. Top with the remaining slices of bread, buttered side facing up. Flip the sandwich over so that the side with the shredded cheese faces down.

5. Add one sandwich to a **cold** medium skillet, or two sandwiches to a cold large skillet (starting with a cold pan helps with slow, even cooking so your bread doesn't burn before the cheese melts). Turn the heat to medium, cover with a lid, and cook for 4 to 5 minutes (the steam helps the cheese melt better, but check the bottom occasionally—if the bread is browning but the shredded cheese isn't near melting, reduce the heat). Flip, cover, and continue to cook until the other side is golden brown, 2 to 3 minutes. If not done yet, flip again, and cook, uncovered, until the second slice of bread is golden brown on the bottom, 1 to 2 minutes.

6. For the next sandwiches, wipe out the pan and reduce the heat to medium-low to prevent burning and cook for about 3 minutes per side.

7. Transfer the grilled cheeses to a sheet of parchment paper to prevent sogginess. Serve warm.

Adult Grilled Cheese—Mix & Match Toppings

FLAVOR PROFILE/TEXTURE	ADD-INS
Sweet and savory (my favorite)	Chopped Medjool dates (1 large date per sandwich) or Fig jam (a thin layer per sandwich)
Salty, tangy, and crisp	2 to 4 tablespoons pickled red onions (page 168), drained, or sauerkraut
Spicy, tangy, and crisp	1 to 2 tablespoons pickled chiles (page 168), drained, or store-bought pickled jalapeños
Fresh, sharp, and oniony	2 to 3 scallions, thinly sliced
Spicy, tangy, and funky	Spread 1 teaspoon gochujang (per sandwich) on top of the cashew cheese

The Sexy Skillet Lasagna

Serves 8 | NF

Since going vegan, I've had many lasagnas—raw zucchini lasagna, lasagna with lentils, deconstructed lasagna. Some have been good, but not many have been great.

The exception is this very classic, very sexy lasagna, which is easily the best one I've had, vegan or not. Each layer is packed with a serious savory depth of flavor, thanks to an umami-rich red sauce, creamy ricotta, vegan parm, and vegan sausage. Baking it in a cast-iron skillet gives you ample caramelized and crunchy edges, which contrast beautifully with the layers of saucy, melty, gooey cheesiness.

Ingredient Notes: You can easily use fresh spinach instead of frozen—chop 1 pound (455 g) baby spinach and cook in a skillet until just wilted, then squeeze dry.

There are two types of no-boil lasagna noodles: (1) noodles with wavy edges (you'll need 10 ounces/285 g, and a 55-minute bake time) and (2) thinner, shorter lasagna sheets (you'll need 7 to 8 ounces/200 to 225 g, and a 40-minute bake time). The former make the lasagna feel more substantial, but both work great.

Make Ahead: Like any great lasagna, this is a labor of love, but the red sauce and ricotta can be made up to 4 days in advance.

Easy Variations: If vegan "meat" isn't your thing, sub with Jammy Roasted Eggplant (page 339), Jammy Zucchini (page 330), or sautéed mushrooms.

Outrageously Good Red Sauce (but Not Marinara) (page 161)

1 (10-ounce/285 g) box **frozen chopped spinach**, thawed (1 to 1½ cups; see Ingredient Notes)

Whipped Tofu Ricotta (page 206)

¼ cup (60 ml) plain **plant-based milk** of choice

1 cup (105 g) **vegan parmesan**

Kosher salt and freshly ground **black pepper**

⅛ teaspoon **freshly grated or ground nutmeg**

½ cup (8 g) **fresh basil** leaves, finely chopped, plus more for serving

4 links **vegan sausage**, such as Beyond Meat (12 to 16 ounces/340 to 455 g)

7 to 10 ounces (200 to 280 g) **no-boil lasagna noodles** (see Ingredient Notes)

1. Prep the ingredients. In a large bowl, combine the red sauce with 1½ cups (360 ml) of water and stir well (thinning it out is necessary to cook no-boil noodles). You should end up with 4½ to 5 cups (1.2 kg) of sauce.

2. Wrap the thawed spinach in a dish towel and squeeze it over the sink to wring out as much water as you can.

recipe continues

3. In a medium bowl, mix together the ricotta, milk, ⅓ cup (35 g) of the parmesan, lots of pepper, the nutmeg, and basil. Fold in the spinach with a spatula.

4. Preheat the oven to 400°F (205°C).

5. Heat a large skillet over medium-high heat. Crumble the sausage with your hands into the hot pan and cook until a bit browned (if it sticks, add a touch of oil). Set aside.

6. **Assemble and bake the lasagna.** Lightly grease a 12-inch (30 cm) cast-iron skillet or a deep 12-inch (30 cm) ovenproof sauté pan with oil or cooking spray.

7. Pour one-third of the red sauce (about 1⅔ cup/400 g) in the bottom of the pan. Top with 3 or 4 lasagna noodles, breaking the noodles to fit the shape of the pan, but don't overlap them (they won't cook through).

8. Top with half of the cooked sausage. Dollop half of the ricotta mixture in spoonfuls, schmearing it out with a silicone spatula (it might bleed into the red sauce, but that's okay because it's all going in your belly). Add a layer of noodles, followed by another third of the red sauce.

9. Add the rest of the sausage and the rest of the ricotta mixture, spreading it out. Add the final layer of noodles, followed by the last of the red sauce. Sprinkle with the remaining ⅔ cup (70 g) parmesan and a few pinches of salt and pepper.

10. Lightly spray a piece of foil and cover the lasagna but don't press down. Bake, covered, for 30 minutes. Uncover and bake for 10 minutes for lasagna sheets (25 minutes for wavy lasagna noodles), or until a paring knife inserted in the noodles comes out with little resistance, almost like al dente pasta.

11. To brown the top, pop the pan under the broiler for 1 to 2 minutes. Let rest for 10 minutes before slicing. Garnish with basil. Leftovers can be frozen for 2 to 3 months.

An Ode to Mushrooms

Mushrooms are one of the most magical foods on the planet. With their naturally high umami content and chewy texture, they are particularly convincing meat replacements.

Mushrooms are also nutrient-rich: they contain powerful antioxidants that protect our brains and lower our stress, are rich in energy-boosting B vitamins, and contain anti-inflammatory and immune-boosting compounds.

Mushrooms even play a key role in forest health, decomposing toxic pollutants and generating new life.

So when I meet folks who don't like mushrooms or describe them as "slimy" or "rubbery," my mind is boggled.

I guess I shouldn't be surprised, though, given how poorly mushrooms are treated. Raw button mushrooms haphazardly dot pizzas in countless restaurants and sit out in plastic vats in salad bars until browned and soggy.

But if you give them a little extra love and consideration, you can transform these fungi into foods we all love and crave: taco meat, shawarma meat, burger meat, carnitas, pulled pork, steak, fried chicken, scallops, and crab cakes.

In the next few pages, you'll find recipes that treat mushrooms as the A-list stars they deserve to be: they get seared and browned, pressed, shredded, brined, and yes, even deep-fried.

PS: Even if you consider yourself a mushroom hater like my partner, I am 99 percent certain that at least one of these recipes will change your tune on mushrooms.

How to Boost the Flavor of Mushrooms

Get the excess water out. Shrooms are watery, so I prefer to clean them by wiping off dirt patches with a dry towel instead of submerging them in water. When grilling or searing larger cuts, like portobellos or big clusters of oyster mushrooms, weight them down with a heavy skillet to extract more water.

Give them room to breathe. Adding a mountain of shrooms to your skillet will yield steamed mushrooms. Instead, cook them in a couple of batches if needed so they can sear.

Use high heat. To help them shed their rubberiness, use medium-high to high heat. But don't stir too frequently or else they won't get browned. Instead, stir or flip every few minutes.

Embrace the diversity. White button mushrooms cooked properly can be tasty, but there are so many more delicious and meaty options to explore. Check out your local Asian market or farmers' markets, which typically have more varieties than standard supermarkets. I'm partial to **oyster mushrooms**, which can mimic fried chicken or be torn and baked until crispy; **shiitake mushrooms** in stir-fries and soups, particularly dried shiitakes to add a savory depth to liquids; **maitake mushrooms**, which taste a bit like chicken and crisp up so well; **king oyster or trumpet mushroom** stems, which can be shredded to mimic meat; and **cremini mushrooms**, when I need an inexpensive mushroom that still has great flavor.

Buttermilk Fried "Chicken" with Cornbread & Dilly Slaw

Serves 6 to 8 | GFO, SF, NF

According to many of my southern-bred friends, this mushroom fried chicken is just as good as actual fried chicken, but without the heaviness. You might not think that squidgy mushrooms could deliver an earth-shattering crunch, but with a double dredge and deep-fry, they do just that. Plus, the natural savory meatiness of mushrooms makes them a great alternative to chicken.

And when served with a buttery, crispy-crusted cornbread and a dilly slaw, it's a whole out-of-this-world gourmet southern comfort food experience. This meal takes some time to put together, so bookmark it for special occasions.

Ingredient Notes: Oyster mushrooms mimic fried chicken the best, particularly those with bunched clusters (not loose stringy pieces). In a pinch, you can sub with shiitake mushroom caps (no stems) for smaller "chicken wings." They fry in 1½ to 3 minutes. Two teaspoons of cayenne may sound like a lot, but deep-fried food needs a lot of seasoning (it's only mildly spicy).

Tips: To test the oil temperature without a thermometer, add a small piece of a battered shroom: if it sizzles almost immediately, the oil is ready. Or stick a wooden spoon or chopstick in the oil: it's ready if you see a steady swirl of moderate bubbles. If the bubbles are vigorous, it's a bit too hot; if you don't see any bubbles, the oil isn't hot enough. For a 4-quart (3.8 L) saucepan, it takes about 15 minutes for the oil to reach 350°F (175°C); for a 3-quart (2.8 L) saucepan, 10 minutes.

You can reuse frying oil a few times, but strain out any debris using a fine-mesh sieve. When ready to toss, pour cooled oil into a disposable container, seal tightly, and put in the trash.

For leftovers, layer the fried shrooms in a container between layers of paper towels to avoid sogginess. To reheat, bake on a sheet pan at 350°F (175°C) for 20 minutes, until warm and crisp.

Easy Variations: You can also serve this fried "chicken" solo as an appetizer with Throwback Ranch Dressing (page 203) and BBQ sauce. For a sweet-and-salty kick, drizzle with Spicy "Honey" with Candied Jalapeños (page 176).

12 to 14 ounces (340 to 400 g) **oyster mushrooms** (see Ingredient Notes)

Kosher salt

Buttermilk

1½ cups (360 ml) plain **oat milk**

3 tablespoons freshly squeezed **lemon juice** or **apple cider vinegar**

2 tablespoons **hot sauce**, such as Cholula or Tabasco

1 tablespoon **liquid smoke** (optional, for a subtle smoky flavor)

recipe and ingredients continue

Breading

1 cup **white rice flour** (160 g) or **all-purpose flour** (125 g) (use rice flour for GF)

2 tablespoons **cornstarch**

¼ teaspoon aluminum-free **baking powder**

1 tablespoon **garlic powder**

2 teaspoons **cayenne pepper**

2 teaspoons freshly ground **black pepper**

1½ teaspoons **onion powder**

1½ teaspoons **sweet or hot paprika**

¾ teaspoon **mustard powder** (optional)

1½ teaspoons **kosher salt**

2 tablespoons **nutritional yeast**

Canola oil, **vegetable oil**, **sunflower oil**, or **grapeseed oil**, for deep-frying

For Serving

Lemon wedges

Buttery Vegan Cornbread (recipe follows)

Dilly Slaw (recipe follows)

1. **Prep the mushrooms.** Separate the oyster mushrooms into small to medium clusters (see photo for reference).

2. **Make the buttermilk.** In a medium bowl, stir together the milk and lemon juice. Set aside until it curdles slightly, 5 to 10 minutes.

3. **Make the breading.** In another medium bowl, stir together the flour, cornstarch, baking powder, garlic powder, cayenne, black pepper, onion powder, paprika, mustard powder (if using), salt, and nutritional yeast.

4. Stir the hot sauce and liquid smoke (if using) into the buttermilk.

5. Arrange your breading station: mushrooms, buttermilk, breading, and a large sheet pan.

6. Using your nondominant hand, dip a mushroom cluster into the buttermilk, lightly shaking off the excess. Using your dominant hand, dredge the mushrooms in the breading and coat on all sides and in the nooks and crannies; shake off excess flour. Set on the sheet pan and repeat with the remaining shrooms.

7. Dip the breaded clusters in buttermilk again, lightly shaking off the excess, then dip into the breading again, shaking off excess flour. Transfer back to the sheet pan.

8. Pour enough oil in a heavy-bottom saucepan for deep-frying, about 1½ (4 to 5 cm), but don't fill more than halfway to prevent bubbling over. Heat the oil over medium-high heat until a thermometer registers 350°F (175°C) (see Tips). Meanwhile, grab another sheet pan, line it with a few paper towels, and set it near the stove.

9. Fry the "chicken." Once the oil reaches temperature, use a spider or slotted spoon to carefully lower a few of the clusters into the hot oil. You'll need to fry in a few batches (about three batches for a 4-quart/3.8 L saucepan). Fry for about 6 minutes, gently flipping them over halfway through cooking, until deeply golden brown. Use the spider to transfer the clusters to the towel-lined pan and sprinkle with salt.

recipe continues

Return the oil back to 350°F (175°C) (it should take 3 to 5 minutes) and fry the next batches (they may take just 4 to 5 minutes).

10. Serve fried "chicken" with lemon wedges on the side, along with cornbread and dilly slaw.

Buttery Vegan Cornbread

Serves 8 to 10 | GFO, SFO, NF

After twenty tests (yes, twenty!), this epic crispy-crusted, buttery, and moist vegan cornbread was born. It's glorious with fried "chicken," as well as chili, soups and stews, and any holiday meal.

Ingredient Notes: Avoid standard boxed fine-ground cornmeal, which is too finely ground and yields a cornbread with muted corn flavor and a less interesting texture. Bob's Red Mill medium-grind yellow cornmeal works great and is widely available. If you have good-quality stone-ground white cornmeal (the type traditionally used in southern cornbread), it's also lovely. Spoon and level the cornmeal, as you would flour. Don't sub "lite" oat milk for the full-fat version.

Tip: If you don't have a cast-iron skillet, use a 9-inch (23 cm) square pan; use just 1 tablespoon of butter in step 6; and bake for an extra 5 minutes if needed to get a golden-brown crust.

GF Option: Replace the flour with ¾ cup (94 g) gluten-free all-purpose flour (ideally, with xanthan gum), add an extra ¼ cup (60 ml) milk, and let the cornbread rest for at least 30 minutes before slicing.

1½ cups (360 ml) **full-fat oat milk** (see Ingredient Notes)

2 teaspoons **apple cider vinegar**

1½ cups (195 g) **stone-ground cornmeal**, plus more for the pan (see Ingredient Notes)

¾ cup (94 g) **all-purpose flour**

1 tablespoon + 1 teaspoon aluminum-free **baking powder**

½ heaping teaspoon **fine sea salt**

4 tablespoons (56 g) **vegan butter**, melted + 2 tablespoons for greasing the skillet (use soy-free butter as needed), plus more for serving

¼ cup (56 g) **extra-virgin olive oil** or **neutral-flavored oil** of choice

¼ cup (40 g) **organic brown sugar**

¼ cup (84 g) **agave nectar**

1 heaping tablespoon finely chopped **fresh rosemary**

1. Arrange a rack in the middle of the oven. Preheat the oven to 400°F (205°C).

2. In a medium bowl or measuring cup, stir together the milk and vinegar. Set aside until it curdles slightly, 5 to 10 minutes. This is your vegan buttermilk.

3. In a large bowl, combine the cornmeal, flour, baking powder, and salt. Whisk well to break up any clumps.

4. Make a well in the center and pour in the 4 tablespoons melted butter, oil, brown sugar, agave, and buttermilk. Gently whisk until just smooth, taking care to not overmix—lumps are normal! Fold in the rosemary.

5. Rest the batter for 10 minutes, or up to 1 hour. It should look a bit like pancake batter.

6. Meanwhile, transfer a 9-inch (23 cm) or 10-inch (25 cm) cast-iron skillet to the preheated oven for 10 minutes. Use oven mitts to remove the hot pan and add the 2 tablespoons butter. It will start melting quickly. Dust the pan lightly with a sprinkle of cornmeal, about 1 teaspoon.

7. Gradually pour the batter into the hot skillet (not too quickly or the butter will pool up at the top). Bake for 25 to 28 minutes (check at 25 minutes), until a toothpick inserted in the center comes out clean and the top is golden brown.

8. Let the pan cool on a wire rack for 15 to 20 minutes. Slice and serve warm, or with a pat of softened butter on top of each slice. This cornbread is best on day one, but leftovers stay good on the counter for 3 days. Store in an airtight container instead of in a reusable bag for the best texture. To reheat, transfer cornbread slices to a sheet pan or baking dish and bake at 375°F (190°C) for 10 to 15 minutes (for moister results, wrap in foil).

Dilly Slaw

Serves 6 to 10 | GF, SFO, NF

A dill-forward slaw that's perfect for fried "chicken" (or any picnic or BBQ spread).

Tips: I prefer finely grated cabbage, as it feels less cruciferous-y. To finely grate, quarter the cabbage (with the core intact) and grate along the large holes of a box grater in a downward sliding motion. This requires more muscle than using a mandoline or food processor shredding disc, so I leave the trade-off up to you. If making in advance, store the cabbage mix and dressing separately in the fridge, then combine on the day of serving.

½ cup (112 g) **vegan mayo** (use soy-free mayo as needed)

⅓ cup (84 g) **dill pickle relish** (if using sweet relish, omit the maple syrup)

½ teaspoon **garlic powder**

½ cup (12 g) **fresh dill**, finely chopped (omit tough stems)

¼ cup (60 ml) freshly squeezed **lemon juice**, plus more to taste

1 tablespoon **pure maple syrup** (or Spicy "Honey" with Candied Jalapeños, page 176, for a kick)

2 teaspoons **celery seeds** (or celery salt)

Kosher salt or **fine sea salt** (omit if using celery salt)

Freshly ground **black pepper**

5 cups (375 g) shredded **red or green cabbage** (see Tips)

2 cups (140 g) shredded **carrots** (store-bought or 3 to 4 medium carrots, grated on a box grater)

1 medium **Granny Smith apple**, peeled (or not) and cut into matchsticks

In a large bowl, whisk together the mayo, relish, garlic powder, dill, lemon juice, maple syrup, and celery seeds. Season to taste with salt and pepper. Add the cabbage, carrots, and apple and toss to combine. Taste for seasonings, adding more salt or pepper or lemon juice as needed. Leftovers can be refrigerated for 3 to 4 days.

Loaded Mushroom Shawarma Flatbreads

Serves 4 | GFO, SF, NF

When I worked at a Manhattan law firm, there was always a halal cart nearby. And when I needed to forget about the job I hated, I'd treat myself to their deeply seasoned shawarma meat, wrapped in fluffy bread with spicy sauce and creamy white sauce. This recipe re-creates those special memories, but in a homemade, plant-based way.

Naturally meaty oyster mushrooms are coated in a shawarma spice blend and seared until deeply browned. Pressing them with a heavy skillet—a technique that comes from mushroom kings Derek and Chad Sarno of Wicked Healthy—compacts them into crispy, umami-supercharged vessels. They're then tossed in a bright, tangy marinade and briefly baked until the natural sugars caramelize. The result is shawarma "meat" that's juicy and tender on the inside with a flaky, crackly skin.

Once thinly sliced, they're tucked into flatbreads and blanketed with a creamy yogurt-tahini sauce, spicy mint sauce, vegetables, and herbs for the ultimate shawarma experience.

Tips: To streamline this recipe, you can skip the homemade flatbreads and buy a thin Lebanese bread, like lavash, or pita. Instead of the Yogurt-Tahini Sauce, squeeze some lemon into vegan yogurt and season with salt, then drizzle tahini on the wrap before serving.

Make Ahead: You can make the Yogurt-Tahini Sauce and Spicy Mint & Cilantro Sauce 3 to 4 days in advance and refrigerate.

GF Option: Make a shawarma plate instead of serving with flatbread (it's ridiculously good with the Buttery Brown Rice with Warm Spices on page 309).

Yogurt-Tahini Sauce (page 215; see Tips)

4 to 6 **Simple Flatbreads** (recipe follows) or store-bought vegan-friendly pita or lavash bread (see Tips)

Mushroom Shawarma (recipe follows)

¼ to ⅓ cup (60 to 80 g) **Spicy Mint & Cilantro Sauce** (page 189), or to taste

Optional Toppings

Quick-pickled vegetables, such as cabbage, red onions, carrots, or chiles (page 168)

Raw vegetables, such as sliced cucumber, halved cherry tomatoes, shredded cabbage or lettuce, or thinly sliced chiles for *spicy!*

Fresh cilantro, parsley, or mint leaves

Lemon wedges

recipe continues

Slather a generous amount of yogurt-tahini sauce on top of the flatbreads. Divide the shawarma among each, add your desired pickled and/or raw vegetables, and drizzle on some spicy mint and cilantro sauce. Spoon a bit more yogurt-tahini sauce on top, if desired. Top with fresh herbs and a squeeze of lemon juice, if desired.

Mushroom Shawarma

Serves 4 | GF, SF, NF

Like shawarma meat, oyster mushrooms get juicy and tender on the inside, with a crispy exterior and sticky bits, thanks to (1) the Maillard reaction and (2) caramelization, which occurs when they're basted with the natural sugars from pomegranate molasses. Sprinkling them with a homemade shawarma spice blend during searing infuses them with a big punch of the warming flavors you expect from traditional shawarma.

Ingredient Note: This is best with oyster mushroom clusters, but if you can't find them, use 4 large (or 5 to 6 small) portobello mushroom caps.

Tip: In place of homemade seasoning, you can use 2½ tablespoons of a store-bought shawarma blend (the Spice House makes a good one).

16 to 18 ounces (450 to 520 g) **oyster mushrooms**, left whole in clusters (see Ingredient Note)

4 tablespoons **neutral-flavored oil** of choice, plus more as needed

Kosher salt

Shawarma Seasoning (see Tip)

1½ teaspoons **sweet or hot paprika**

1½ teaspoons **sumac**

1 teaspoon **ground coriander**

½ teaspoon **ground cumin**

½ teaspoon **ground turmeric**

½ teaspoon **garlic powder**

½ teaspoon **ground cardamom**

½ teaspoon freshly ground **black pepper**

¼ teaspoon **ground cinnamon**

¼ teaspoon **ground ginger**

¼ teaspoon **ground cloves**

¼ teaspoon **ground allspice**

Marinade

3 tablespoons **extra-virgin olive oil**

1 tablespoon freshly squeezed **lemon juice**

1½ tablespoons **pure pomegranate molasses**

1 teaspoon **kosher salt**

½ teaspoon **garlic powder**

1. **Prep the mushrooms.** If any of the mushroom clusters have stems that jut out, trim them, but make sure the cluster stays intact. If any clusters are much bigger than the others, cut them in half vertically.

2. **Make the shawarma seasoning.** In a small bowl, mix together the paprika, sumac, coriander, cumin, turmeric, garlic powder, cardamom, pepper, cinnamon, ginger, cloves, and allspice.

3. **Make the marinade.** In another small bowl, whisk together the olive oil, lemon juice, pomegranate molasses, salt, and garlic powder. Set aside.

4. Grab oven mitts, a clean dish towel, a 12-inch (30 cm) cast-iron skillet for cooking,

recipe continues

and another heavy skillet that's slightly smaller (another cast-iron pan, if you have it).

5. Preheat the oven to 400°F (205°C). Open the kitchen windows, as it will get smoky.

6. Heat the 12-inch (30 cm) cast-iron pan over medium-high heat for several minutes until very hot. Add 2 tablespoons of the oil, swirling the pan to evenly coat. Heat until very hot (add a drop of water; if it sizzles immediately, it's ready). Add the mushroom clusters, stem side down. Use tongs to push them around in the oil.

7. **Press the mushrooms ("Pressing Method").** Wearing oven mitts, carefully lower the other heavy pan ("Pan 2") on top of the mushrooms. Use a dish towel to press down on Pan 2 until you hear a sizzle; press for 20 seconds. Remove your hands but keep Pan 2 on the shrooms for 1 to 2 minutes.

Lift up Pan 2 and use the towel to wipe off liquid from the bottom of the pan and set aside.

Cook the shrooms uncovered for 1½ to 2 minutes and push them around in the oil. If they are blackening on the bottom, lower the heat a bit.

8. Once the water from the mushrooms has mostly evaporated, season the mushrooms generously with salt and with half of the shawarma seasoning. Add the remaining 2 tablespoons oil to open spaces in the pan, pushing the shrooms around to coat.

9. Standing a distance away, use tongs to carefully flip the clusters (they should be golden brown on the bottom). Repeat the Pressing Method.

10. Season the shrooms with the remaining shawarma seasoning and a bit more salt. If the pan looks like it's getting dry or sticking, add a bit more oil and swirl it around.

11. Use tongs to flip the shrooms again, and repeat the Pressing Method (the third press). Now, flip once more and repeat the Pressing Method (the fourth press). The mushrooms should be deeply browned and charred in some spots and quite flat and crispy. If your clusters were very large, you may need to repeat the pressing technique once more.

12. Transfer the shrooms to a large bowl. Pour the marinade on top and gently coat all over with a silicone spatula, flipping over to get both sides. Wipe out any stuck bits from the skillet.

13. Transfer the mushrooms back to the skillet and pour the excess marinade on top. Bake in the preheated oven for 10 minutes. Remove, flip the clusters over, and bake for 5 more minutes, until sticky, the skin is crispy, and the juices are bubbling. Once cool enough to handle, remove from the skillet and slice the clusters into strips on a bias.

Simple Flatbread

Makes 6 | SF, NF

This no-yeast flatbread is surprisingly simple, with just a 15-minute rest time. It's a little fluffy, light but surprisingly buttery, and has a pleasant tang from the yogurt.

1¾ cups + 2 tablespoons (235 g) **all-purpose flour**, plus more for dusting

¾ teaspoon **fine sea salt**

1½ teaspoons aluminum-free **baking powder**

1 teaspoon **organic cane sugar**

⅔ cup (150 g) good-quality **unsweetened coconut yogurt** (see page 61 for recommended brands)

Warm water, as needed

3 tablespoons **extra-virgin olive oil**, plus more for drizzling

Avocado oil, **grapeseed oil**, or other **high-heat oil**, for cooking

For Serving

Za'atar (optional; page 179 or store-bought)

Flaky sea salt

1. Very lightly flour a work surface. In a large bowl, whisk together the flour, sea salt, baking powder, and sugar. In a medium bowl, whisk together the yogurt and 3 tablespoons olive oil (it will get fluffy).

2. Make a well in the flour. Add the yogurt mixture and use your hands to gradually mix the flour into the yogurt. When just mixed, transfer the dough to a work surface. Gently knead into a ball until mostly smooth, about 30 seconds. If the dough is a bit crumbly, add a teaspoon of warm water at a time and mix to combine. Don't overknead or add too much flour, as it will toughen the bread.

3. Add a bit of olive oil to the bowl and roll the dough in it to coat it on all sides. Cover the dough with a dish towel and let rest for 15 minutes.

4. Using a bench scraper, cut the dough into six equal portions. Place one dough round on the counter and use one palm to roll it into a ball (this is best done with one hand instead of two). Cover the other dough balls to prevent drying out.

5. Using a rolling pin, roll the dough ball into a thin round ⅛ to ¼ inch (about 0.5 cm) thick and 6 to 7 inches (15 to 18 cm) in diameter. To prevent sticking, roll outward and off instead of back and forth over the same spot.

6. Open nearby windows for ventilation. Heat a cast-iron skillet over medium-low heat for 5 minutes. Add a teaspoon or two of high-heat oil and increase the heat to medium-high.

7. Carefully pick up a dough round and transfer it to the hot pan. Cook until slightly puffed on top and the bottom is charred in some spots, about 1 minute (the first one usually takes a bit longer). Flip and cook for 1 minute.

8. While each flatbread cooks, roll out another dough round. Wipe out the pan as needed and add a touch more oil to the pan before cooking another flatbread. You may need to reduce the heat a bit as you go.

9. Sprinkle each hot flatbread with za'atar (if using), a drizzle of olive oil, and a sprinkle of flaky salt.

Miso Butter–Seared King Oyster "Scallops"

Serves 3 to 4 | GF, NF

I first saw mushroom "scallops" in Candice Hutchings's *The Edgy Veg* cookbook and was intrigued. Once I tried it myself, I was amazed by the uncannily similar appearance and texture they have to traditional scallops.

Here, king oyster mushrooms are given the full spa treatment. They're first bathed in a salty brine to tenderize their fibers (the meditative salt room meets a deep tissue massage). Then they're marinated in a savory, ocean-y Japanese dashi-style broth made with umami superstars (the seaweed body wrap). Finally, they're seared in miso butter until caramelized and charred on the outside and tender on the inside (the hot stone treatment and sauna phase).

You can enjoy these mushroom scallops for an elegant dinner (see below), but they also make a fun appetizer served on toasted crostini slathered with Sriracha-Ginger Cashew Cream (page 201).

Ingredient Notes: You can find king oyster mushrooms and kombu at Asian markets and well-stocked grocery stores. If you can't get umeboshi paste, use 2 teaspoons white miso paste. If you can't get ume plum vinegar, sub with 1½ tablespoons red wine vinegar and a pinch of salt.

Big-Flavor Meals: Serve over simple buttered noodles with roasted cherry tomatoes and fresh parsley (as shown here). Or serve with Lemongrass Ginger Rice (page 321); cold noodles tossed with soy sauce and Life-Changing Homemade Chili Crisp (page 187); polenta (page 513); or farrotto (page 311).

7 to 9 **king oyster mushrooms** or **king trumpet mushrooms** (1¼ to 1½ pounds/570 to 680 g; see Ingredient Notes)

Kosher salt

Brine

¼ cup + 3 tablespoons (63 g) **kosher salt**

1 cup (240 ml) **boiling water**

Broth

2 sheets (8 g) **kombu** (see Ingredient Notes)

1 tablespoon + 1 teaspoon **tamari** or **soy sauce** (use tamari to keep GF)

1 teaspoon **umeboshi paste** (see Ingredient Notes)

2 tablespoons **ume plum vinegar** (see Ingredient Notes)

8 **garlic cloves**, peeled and smashed

1 tablespoon + 1 teaspoon **rice vinegar** (or freshly squeezed lime juice)

recipe and ingredients continue

Miso Butter

3½ tablespoons (49 g) **vegan butter**, softened at room temperature

1 tablespoon **white miso**, softened at room temperature (or 1½ teaspoons umeboshi paste)

1. **Prep the mushrooms.** Cut the mushroom stems into ¾-inch-thick (2 cm) rounds (three to four slices per stem). Dab off any dirt patches with a dry towel. Save the caps for another use or freeze to make vegetable or mushroom broth.

2. **Brine the mushrooms.** In a large bowl, combine the salt and boiling water and stir until dissolved. Pour in 4 cups (960 ml) of cold water, then add the mushroom slices.

Place a smaller bowl or heavy lid on top to submerge the shrooms. Let rest for 10 minutes, then drain. Return the shrooms to the bowl.

3. **Meanwhile, make the broth.** Using scissors, make a couple of slits in the kombu. In a small saucepan over medium heat, add 2 cups (480 ml) of water, the kombu, tamari, umeboshi paste, ume plum vinegar, and garlic. Bring to a simmer, cover, and simmer for 10 minutes. Taste the broth—it should be quite salty and savory. The garlic may turn a little blue from the acidity, but it's harmless. Scoop out and discard the kombu. Stir in the rice vinegar.

4. Pour the broth over the mushrooms in the bowl. Again, cover with the smaller bowl to submerge. Marinate for at least 30 minutes, or

up to 2 hours at room temperature (or overnight in the fridge).

5. Remove the mushrooms from the broth, leaving behind the excess liquid, and transfer to a cutting board. Using a paring knife, score the top and bottom of each slice with a few shallow cuts but don't slice all the way through—this allows more flavor to seep into them during cooking.

6. Make the miso butter. In a small bowl, combine the softened vegan butter and miso. Cream with a fork until well combined.

7. Cook the oyster scallops. Open a window or turn on a fan for ventilation. Heat a large cast-iron skillet or heavy-bottomed skillet over medium heat for just a few seconds, then add the miso butter. Once melted, add the mushrooms to the pan and use tongs to arrange each piece with a flat side facing up. Cook for 4 to 5 minutes, using tongs to rub the scallops in the melted butter and to pick up any browned bits (tilt the pan back and forth occasionally to evenly distribute the butter).

8. Once the bottoms are golden brown with a charred exterior ring, flip each piece. Cook until the bottom sides are seared, 4 to 5 minutes. Use tongs to transfer the "scallops" to a serving plate and very lightly sprinkle with salt.

8

Mushroom Carnitas Tacos
(Beachside Fiesta Tacos)

Makes 10 tacos | GF, SF, NF

When I take a bite of these tacos, I'm transported to a classy but festive Caribbean beach resort where frosty margaritas are in no short supply. They're smoky and spicy yet citrusy with a cooling tang from avocado crema and very fun to eat.

And while these mushrooms aren't nearly as high-fat as the pork in carnitas, shredding and baking them until crispy and chewy, then tossing them in a smoky spice blend and wrapping them in corn tortillas with all the fixings, is a pretty great way to re-create the carnitas tacos experience.

I love serving these "carnitas" under a tangle of pickled onions with avocado crema, but feel free to make a taco bar and pick your fave toppings.

Shredding mushrooms is therapeutic but takes some time, so solicit a helper or turn on your favorite podcast.

Make Ahead: You can tear the shrooms, mix the spice blend, and make the crema 2 to 3 days in advance.

10 corn (or flour) taco-size **tortillas**

½ recipe **Avocado Crema** (page 204), or to taste

Mushroom Carnitas (recipe follows)

Quick-pickled red onions (page 168) or **salsa** of choice, such as pico de gallo

Other Taco Bar Fixings (go wild!)

Vegan sour cream

Grilled or charred **corn**

Fresh cilantro leaves or sliced **scallions**

Quick Miso-Chile Hot Sauce (page 190) or store-bought **hot sauce**

1. **Char the tortillas.** If you have a gas stove, turn a burner to medium-low and use tongs to place the tortilla directly over the flame until charred in spots, 15 to 30 seconds per side. Or add each tortilla to a cast-iron skillet over medium-high heat for 20 to 40 seconds per side. Stack and wrap the tortillas in a dish towel to keep warm.

2. **Assemble.** Dollop avocado crema on each prepared tortilla. Top with a few spoonfuls of mushroom carnitas. Add pickled onions or salsa, and other toppings of choice!

recipe continues

Mushroom Carnitas

Serves 4 | GF, SF, NF

Tearing the mushrooms thinly and roasting them makes them surprisingly crispy while retaining some chewy meatiness, and also concentrates their deeply savory flavor. Tossing them with toasted spices *after* roasting prevents the spices from burning, and finishing with lime and orange juice awakens the smoky, spicy flavors.

Ingredient Notes: If you are using king oyster mushrooms, slice the caps off; grip each stem with one hand and start shredding with a fork in the other hand. Once you get a decent amount of shredding done, switch to shredding with your hands. Slice the caps about the same width as the stems. You can sub with maitakes and tear them.

2 pounds (910 g) **oyster mushrooms** or **king oyster mushrooms** (see Ingredient Notes)

4 tablespoons (56 g) **avocado oil** or **extra-virgin olive oil**

3 teaspoons **kosher salt**

Freshly ground **black pepper**

1 (15-ounce/425 g) can **pinto beans**, drained, rinsed, and dried well

2 to 3 tablespoons freshly squeezed **orange juice**

4 to 6 teaspoons freshly squeezed **lime juice**

¾ cup (12 g) **fresh cilantro** leaves and tender stems, finely chopped

Spice Blend

1½ teaspoons **ground cumin**

1½ teaspoons **smoked paprika**

1½ teaspoons **chipotle chile flakes**

1½ teaspoons **dried oregano**

1 to 2 teaspoons **chili powder** (2 teaspoons for *spicy!*)

½ teaspoon **garlic powder**

½ teaspoon **onion powder**

1. Arrange a rack in the bottom of the oven and one in the top third. Preheat the oven to 425°F (220°C).

2. Cut off the tough stem at the bottom of the oyster mushrooms. Use your hands to tear the mushrooms into thin strips (see photo opposite for reference). The thinner they are, the crispier they get, but you'll need to pay closer attention to prevent burning.

3. Transfer the shrooms to a large bowl and add 2 tablespoons of the oil, tossing well to coat. If they seem dry, add a touch more oil. Add 2 teaspoons of the salt and a generous amount of black pepper and toss to coat. Divide between two lightly oiled rimmed sheet pans, trying to space them out with little overlap. Bake for 15 minutes.

4. Meanwhile, in the same bowl used for the shrooms, toss the drained beans with 1 tablespoon of the oil, the remaining 1 teaspoon salt, and black pepper to taste.

5. Remove the shrooms from the oven and stir. Scatter the beans across both pans, dividing roughly evenly. Rotate the pans by 180 degrees, switch oven rack positions, and bake for 15 more minutes, or until the shrooms are browned and crispy and the beans are also crispy.

6. **Make the spice blend.** In a small bowl, mix together the cumin, paprika, chipotle flakes, oregano, chili powder, garlic powder, and onion powder.

7. In a large sauté pan, heat the remaining 1 tablespoon oil over medium-low heat. Once warm, add the spice blend and cook until aromatic, about 30 seconds, stirring frequently to prevent burning (it will turn into a paste). Add the mushrooms and beans and toss until there are no more spice clumps. Transfer to a large bowl and add 2 tablespoons of the orange juice, 4 teaspoons of the lime juice, and the cilantro. Toss well. Taste, adding a few pinches of salt and the additional lime or orange juice as needed.

8. To reheat leftovers, transfer the mushrooms and beans to a sheet pan and roast at 350°F (175°C) for 10 minutes, or until warmed through and crisp.

13

Sweet Treats

The month my nephew turned one, I made my crispy spiced cobbler cake for Christmas dessert. My sister gave him just a taste, but the instant the sweetness hit his baby tongue, his eyes lit up.

More! He moved closer in his high chair, lunging his baby neck out toward us. After a few bites, I figured, *He's so tiny. How much more can he eat?* The second I went to grab two adult spoons for my sister and me, he started squeaking in protest.

Clearly, the human brain is wired to love sugar.

And if that's the case—if our love for sugar is coded into our DNA from the time we are babies, an inevitable consequence of evolution—then I think we should enjoy it.

In moderation, yes, of course. Not every day and not in the form of highly processed candies and sodas. But if you're going to eat dessert from time to time, I think it should be a really great dessert, one that you can savor and truly enjoy with good company.

And that's what you'll find in this chapter. Really great desserts that will remind you that life is sweet and meant to be enjoyed, from fruit-forward desserts to rich chocolatey treats.

NISHA'S BAKING TIPS

Invest in precision. We all use measuring cups differently, but a digital scale never lies (also, fewer dishes to wash!). And get an oven thermometer, because home ovens are wild places and can vary a lot from their stated display.

Spoon and level. If you don't have a scale, don't scoop your flour straight out of the bag—this compacts it and causes you to overmeasure. Instead, spoon the flour out with a spoon, add it to your measuring cup a spoon at a time, and level it off with a butter knife.

Keep canned chickpeas handy . . . When whipped, chickpea liquid, a.k.a. aquafaba, adds tenderness and fluffiness to vegan baked goods in lieu of eggs. If your canned chickpeas have a fair amount of salt, use a pinch less salt than the recipe calls for. Save the actual chickpeas for the savory recipes in this book.

. . . And apple cider vinegar. Many vegan baked goods can be dense or dry. Mixing plant milk with an acid like ACV (or lemon juice) to make "buttermilk" tenderizes baked goods and gives them some lift.

When in doubt, don't overmix. Mix just as much as needed to bring the dough or batter together, or until no dry ingredients can be seen. Overmixing can cause gluten strands to overdevelop, which leads to dense and gummy textures.

Don't skimp on fat. When you take eggs, full-fat milk or cream, and butter out of the equation, you're left with very little fat. If you don't compensate, you'll end up with stereotypically vegan cardboard-esque baked goods. Bring some fat back in with vegan butter or oil, plant-based milks that are relatively high in fat, and/or nut butters.

- Earth Balance buttery sticks is a **vegan butter** that works well in most applications and is widely available.

- When baking with **coconut oil**, opt for *refined* coconut oil to avoid a coconutty taste. Bring cold ingredients to room temperature first, or coconut oil will seize up into chunks.

- When replacing full-fat milk, my usual preference is **full-fat oat milk**, like the one from Oatly, or a barista-style oat milk. Its fat content is about the same as dairy milk; plus, its natural sugar content helps baked goods brown nicely. Soy milk is usually a good option too.

Baking is a science. Baking is not the time to experiment all willy-nilly, so if you need to make substitutes or changes, start slowly. Try reducing the sugar in a recipe by 25 percent, not by 50 percent. Replace one-third of the oil with almond butter, or one-third of the flour with almond or oat flour, not all of it. And remember: Just because oat flour is marketed as flour, it doesn't mean it's actually flour (it most certainly does not behave like flour!).

Macerated Berries with Basil & Mint

Serves 6 | GF, SF, NFO

This is the fruit salad for anyone who loves fruit but hates "fruit salad." No more large chunks of mealy cantaloupe and honeydew—this elevated fruit salad has delicately sweet berries that are perfumed with the aromas of fresh mint and basil, zippy and floral orange zest, and sweet-tart balsamic vinegar.

It's the easiest dessert to throw together, yet still impressive enough to serve to guests.

How to serve: As a light dessert on its own, or spoon on top of vegan vanilla ice cream or cake. For breakfast, spoon over coconut yogurt or pancakes, French toast, or waffles (page 446).

Ingredient Notes: If using strawberries, halve small ones and quarter larger ones. If your berries aren't very sweet, add a bit more maple syrup. A good-quality aged balsamic vinegar is key (check out page 47 for my go-to brands).

3 pints (36 ounces/1 kg) fresh **raspberries, blackberries, blueberries,** and/or **strawberries** (see Ingredient Notes)

3½ teaspoons good-quality **aged balsamic vinegar** (see Ingredient Notes)

¼ teaspoon **pure almond extract** (use vanilla for nut-free)

2 tablespoons **pure maple syrup,** plus more to taste

10 large **fresh mint** leaves, thinly sliced (¼ scant cup/3 g)

6 to 8 large **fresh basil** leaves, slivered (¼ scant cup/3 g; or use more mint)

1 small **orange**, zested

1. Gently rinse and dry the berries in a salad spinner with gentle pressure. If still a bit wet, transfer to dish towels and spread out. Once dry, transfer the berries to a large serving bowl.

2. In a small bowl, combine the balsamic vinegar, almond extract, and maple syrup. Pour over the berries and gently stir to combine. Refrigerate, covered, for 1 hour.

3. When ready to serve, add the mint, basil, and orange zest and gently toss. This is best on day one, but leftovers will stay good in the fridge for 1 to 2 days.

Spiced Wine–Poached Figs with "Honey"

Serves 8 | GF, SF, NF

When figs are in season, this is a fun way to dress them up, especially if your fancy friends are coming over. They're briefly poached in white wine, maple syrup, citrus peels, spices, ginger, and chiles, resulting in plump, juicy figs with a citrusy, subtly spicy, sunshiny warmth. The poaching liquid is boiled down until magically honey-like, then drizzled on top before being served with vanilla ice cream.

Ingredient Notes: When figs are out of season, use firm-ripe pears (3 to 4 Bosc or Anjou). Just before poaching, peel them, keeping the stems intact. Gently lower into the liquid on their sides, cover, and simmer until tender but not too soft, 15 to 25 minutes. Chill, then pour the syrup on top.

Tips: Add leftover vanilla bean pod, citrus peels, cinnamon, ginger, and jalapeño to a tea infuser and steep in boiling water with black tea leaves or bags for 10 minutes for a delicious spiced tea. Use leftover syrup to make spiced rum or bourbon cocktails, drizzle over ice cream, or use instead of maple syrup for waffles (page 446).

2 cups (480 ml) dry (but not bone-dry) **white wine**, such as Sauvignon Blanc, Pinot Grigio, or Pinot Gris

¼ cup (80 g) **pure maple syrup**

½ cup (100 g) **organic cane sugar**

Zest of 1 large **lemon**, peeled into strips with a vegetable peeler

Zest of 1 large **orange**, peeled into strips with a vegetable peeler

1 **vanilla bean**, split

1 large (or 2 small) **cinnamon stick**

1½-inch (3.75 cm) piece **fresh ginger**, thinly sliced (peel on is fine)

1 large **Fresno or jalapeño pepper**, thinly sliced

15 to 20 **fresh figs** (12 to 14 ounces/340 to 400 g), halved

For Serving

1 or 2 pints (½ or 1 L) **vegan vanilla ice cream**

1 handful **fresh mint** leaves, finely slivered (optional)

1. In a wide saucepan or Dutch oven (large enough to hold the figs in a single layer), combine the wine, maple syrup, sugar, citrus

recipe continues

peels, vanilla bean, cinnamon, ginger, chile pepper, and 1 cup (240 ml) of water. Bring to a boil, then reduce the heat and simmer for 10 minutes.

2. Use a slotted spoon to gently lower the figs into the pan, arranging them in a single layer as much as possible. Simmer until tender but not falling apart, 7 to 8 minutes. Transfer the figs to a bowl and chill in the fridge.

3. Strain the poaching liquid and return it to the pan. Scrape the seeds from the vanilla bean into the liquid. Discard the pod and the other aromatics (or save them—see Tips). Bring the liquid to a boil over high heat and cook until it reduces into a darker syrup-like consistency, 15 to 20 minutes (20 minutes makes it really viscous, like honey). Let cool slightly.

4. Spoon ice cream into individual dessert glasses. Top each with several figs. Spoon a bit of syrup on top (not too much, as it's very sweet) and serve the syrup on the side. If desired, garnish each glass with a sprinkling of mint.

Soft & Chewy Ginger Cookies with Cardamom Sugar

Makes 22 to 24 small cookies (or 8 to 9 jumbo cookies) | SFO, NF

The fact that ginger cookies are reserved for Christmastime is very unfair because, in my universe of cookie rankings, they're second only to a chocolate chip cookie. I'm on a mission to change that with these soft yet chewy ginger cookies you'll want to eat year-round. They're subtly nutty from using half whole wheat pastry flour and feel like a warm hug from the molasses and spices. Rolling the cookie dough in cardamom sugar adds heady, sweet warmth and a subtle sugary crunch.

Ingredient Note: Whole cardamom seeds are best, but can be subbed with ½ teaspoon ground cardamom. If you have leftover cardamom sugar, it's lovely in tea.

Tips: You can make these cookies small or jumbo. Small cookies are great for gifting; jumbo ones are great for devouring at home. See instructions for each option below.

If your kitchen is warm, try to work quickly when shaping the dough so it doesn't get too soft. If it does, refrigerate it for 30 minutes.

Make Ahead: Chill the dough for up to 5 days; rest it at room temperature for 15 minutes before baking.

1 tablespoon **flaxseed meal**

¾ cup (94 g) **all-purpose flour**

¾ cup (94 g) **whole wheat pastry flour** (or more all-purpose flour)

1½ teaspoons aluminum-free **baking powder**

1½ teaspoons **ground ginger**

½ teaspoon **ground cinnamon**

¼ teaspoon **ground cloves**

½ scant teaspoon **freshly grated nutmeg**

¼ teaspoon **fine sea salt**

¼ loosely packed cup (40 g) **organic brown sugar**

2 tablespoons **organic cane sugar**

4 tablespoons (56 g) **vegan butter** (use soy-free butter as needed), softened at room temperature

¼ cup (56 g) **sunflower oil** or **neutral-flavored oil** of choice

¼ cup (78 g) **molasses** (avoid blackstrap molasses, as it's bitter)

1 teaspoon **pure vanilla extract**

Cardamom Sugar

¾ teaspoon **cardamom seeds** (from green cardamom pods; see Ingredient Note)

3 tablespoons **organic cane sugar**

recipe continues

1. In a small bowl, mix together the flaxseed meal with 2½ tablespoons of warm water; whisk well and set aside for 15 minutes to gel. This is your flax egg.

2. **Make the cardamom sugar.** Add the cardamom seeds to a spice grinder and blitz until finely ground. Transfer to a small bowl and mix in the sugar. For ground cardamom, mix with sugar in a bowl. Set aside.

3. In a medium bowl, whisk together both flours, the baking powder, ginger, cinnamon, cloves, nutmeg, and salt until well combined.

4. In a large bowl, add both sugars and the softened butter. Using an electric mixer on medium or high speed, cream until well combined, stopping to scrape down the sides as you go, 1 to 2 minutes. Add the flax egg, oil, molasses, and vanilla. Mix again until combined.

5. Working in four batches, gradually beat the flour mixture into the wet mixture until it's smooth and thick but easily scoopable. Cover the dough and refrigerate for 2 hours, or longer (refrigerating the dough is necessary to prevent the cookies from spreading).

6. Preheat the oven to 350°F (175°C). Line two sheet pans with parchment paper.

7. **For small cookies:** Scoop 1 tablespoon (19 g) of chilled dough into your palm. Keeping your bottom palm still, use your top hand to make circular motions until a ball is formed. Use your top hand to gently roll back and forth to form a tall, cylindrical-shaped ball (it should look like a fat Tootsie Roll); don't roll them into round balls, as those make for dry cookies. Repeat with the remaining dough. Roll each ball in the cardamom sugar.

Arrange the dough balls on the prepared pans, 10 to 12 per pan. Stand the tall balls upright, not lying flat. Bake for 10 to 12 minutes, rotating the pans 180 degrees halfway through (bake 10 minutes for softer cookies). The edges should be just barely set and the cookies will look a little soft, but they'll firm up more while cooling. Let the pans cool on wire racks for 10 minutes, then enjoy. Store leftovers in an airtight container on the counter for up to 1 week.

8. **For jumbo cookies:** Scoop 3 tablespoons (57 g) of chilled dough into your palm and roll into tall, cylindrical balls as described above or classic round balls (round balls will make flatter, crispier cookies), then roll each ball in the cardamom sugar.

Space the dough balls 3 inches (7.5 cm) apart on the pans, 4 to 5 per pan. Bake for 15 to 16 minutes, rotating the pans 180 degrees halfway through, until the edges are barely set (they might look underbaked). Let the pans cool on wire racks for 20 minutes, then enjoy. Store leftovers in an airtight container on the counter for up to 1 week.

Caramelized Stone Fruit Crisp with Tahini Custard

Serves 10 │ GF, SF

A fruit crisp is like pie's lower-maintenance little sister, which makes it a great choice for easy breezy entertaining. Here, stone fruit is briefly caramelized in spices and maple syrup to deepen its sweet, juicy flavor, then topped with a nutty crumble. Baking it in a cast-iron skillet lends those sexy caramelized edges and crystallized sugar bits that make for a texture-rich dessert. It's delicious on its own, but even better when drizzled with a creamy spiced tahini custard before serving.

Ingredient Note: Peaches and nectarines are in season from summer through early or mid-fall. Ripe (but not overly ripe) fruit that has been refrigerated makes for the cleanest fruit slices.

Tips: If your fruit isn't sweet, add 1 to 3 tablespoons more sugar in step 2. Don't have a 12-inch (30 cm) cast-iron skillet? Use another 12-inch (30 cm) ovenproof pan, or caramelize the fruit in a skillet, then transfer to a 2-quart (2 L) baking dish.

Make Ahead: You can caramelize the fruit and make the tahini custard a day ahead of time.

Easy Variations: Use plums, pluots, or apricots. Sub minced almonds or pistachios for the shredded coconut, or use walnuts or hazelnuts for pecans. Serve with vegan vanilla ice cream instead of tahini custard.

Caramelized Fruit

2½ pounds (1.1 kg) **peaches** or **nectarines** (6 to 8 peaches or nectarines; see Ingredient Note)

3 tablespoons **coconut sugar** (or organic brown sugar)

2 tablespoons **pure maple syrup**

1¼ teaspoons **ground cinnamon**

½ teaspoon **ground ginger**

¼ teaspoon **ground allspice**

¼ teaspoon **freshly grated nutmeg**

¼ cup (50 g) **coconut oil** (either refined or unrefined), melted (or melted vegan butter)

2 tablespoons **arrowroot powder** or **cornstarch**

2 tablespoons **cold water**

Crisp

3 tablespoons **pure maple syrup**

2 tablespoons **coconut sugar** (or organic brown sugar)

¼ cup (50 g) **coconut oil** (either refined or unrefined), melted (or melted vegan butter)

1 teaspoon **pure vanilla extract**

½ teaspoon **almond extract** (or more vanilla)

¾ teaspoon **fine sea salt**

recipe and ingredients continue

½ cup (50 g) **old-fashioned rolled oats** (use certified gluten-free oats as needed)

¾ cup (75 g) blanched **almond flour**

¼ cup (20 g) **shredded unsweetened coconut**

2 tablespoons **flaxseed meal**

½ cup (60 g) chopped **pecans** (can sub almonds, hazelnuts, or walnuts)

For Serving

Tahini Custard (optional; recipe follows)

Pinch of **flaky sea salt** (optional)

1. Arrange a rack in the middle of the oven. Preheat the oven to 350°F (175°C).

2. **Make the caramelized fruit.** Slice the fruit into ½- to ¾-inch-wide (about 1.5 cm) segments. You should end up with about 5 cups (about 750 g) fruit. In a small bowl, stir together the coconut sugar, maple syrup, cinnamon, ginger, allspice, and nutmeg.

3. In a 12-inch (30 cm) cast-iron skillet (see Tips), heat the coconut oil over medium-low heat. Once the oil is melted and warm, add the maple-spice mixture. Bring to a gentle simmer, then add the fruit, using a silicone spatula to gently toss the fruit. Gently simmer until the fruit is just tender, 3 minutes.

4. Remove from the heat and let cool for 3 to 4 minutes (to avoid the mixture getting gloopy in step 5). In a small bowl, whisk together the arrowroot powder and cold water until well combined and no clumps remain.

5. Return the pan with the fruit to medium heat and gradually pour the arrowroot slurry in. Use a spatula to stir the slurry around the fruit. Cook briefly, just until the juices have thickened and coated the fruit (60 to 90 seconds for arrowroot powder, 2 to 3 minutes for cornstarch). Remove from the heat and set aside.

6. **Make the crisp.** In a small bowl or jar, whisk together the maple syrup, coconut sugar, coconut oil, vanilla and almond extracts, and salt until the salt is dissolved. In a medium bowl, toss together the oats, almond flour, shredded coconut, flaxseed meal, and pecans. Pour the liquid on top and mix together with a fork or your hands until it's a crumbly, sandy mix. Scatter evenly over the caramelized fruit. A few large clumps are fine.

7. Transfer the skillet to the oven and bake, uncovered, for 35 to 40 minutes, until the fruit juices are bubbling around the edges and the top is golden brown. Let cool on a wire rack for 10 to 15 minutes.

8. Right before serving, drizzle each serving with tahini custard (if using). Sprinkle with a pinch of flaky sea salt, if desired.

Tahini Custard

Makes ¾ heaping cup (200 g) | GF, SF, NF

This rich and creamy spiced tahini-based "custard" makes for an unexpected but delightful fruit-crisp topping. Store leftover tahini custard in the fridge to use as a dipping sauce for dates, a filling for crepes, or a topping for brownies, waffles, and oatmeal.

½ cup (120 ml) **full-fat oat milk**

1 tablespoon + 1 teaspoon **pure maple syrup**

1 teaspoon **pure vanilla extract**

½ teaspoon **ground cinnamon**

¼ teaspoon **freshly grated nutmeg**

Pinch of **fine sea salt**

1 tablespoon **arrowroot powder**

3 tablespoons **cold water**

3 tablespoons well-stirred good-quality **tahini** (see page 196 for recommended brands)

1. In a small saucepan, combine the milk, maple syrup, vanilla, cinnamon, nutmeg, and salt. Bring to a boil, then reduce the heat to maintain a gentle simmer for 2 minutes.

2. In a small bowl, whisk together the arrowroot powder and cold water until well combined and no clumps remain.

3. Reduce the heat to the lowest setting. Whisk the arrowroot slurry again, then gradually add it to the pan (don't add all at once!), whisking continuously until the mixture is thickened, about 1 minute. Remove from the heat and whisk in the tahini until smooth.

Lemon Corn Cake with Lavender & Rosemary

Serves 10 | SF, NF

I love any lemon cake, but there's no lemon cake quite as addictive as this one, which is infused with three fun ingredients that will intrigue and wow your taste buds. Rosemary brings its characteristic lemony herbaceousness, lavender highlights the floral notes of citrus zest, and cornmeal adds a subtle crunch and warm corn flavor. It's like the cornbread–lemon cake mashup you didn't know you needed in your life.

Ingredient Note: Use culinary lavender (it's not soapy like the kind used in perfumes). It's sold online and at spice and tea shops, health food stores, even Walmart. If you are using fresh edible lavender, double the amount. Do NOT use lavender essential oil (not safe!). If you can't find lavender, the cake is still excellent without it.

Tips: To collect the aquafaba, shake your can of chickpeas before opening to evenly distribute the starches. Set a bowl beneath a colander and drain the chickpeas to collect their liquid.

Finishing with a lemony icing enhances all the sweet-yet-tart flavors, but the icing may be omitted for a less sweet dessert.

½ cup (120 ml) **full-fat oat milk**, at room temperature

2 medium-large **lemons**, zested and juiced to get 6 tablespoons (90 ml) juice

1¼ cups (156 g) **all-purpose flour**

½ cup (70 g) **fine cornmeal**

¼ teaspoon **baking soda**

1 teaspoon aluminum-free **baking powder**

¼ teaspoon **fine sea salt**

⅔ cup (140 g) **organic cane sugar**

½ cup (112 g) **sunflower oil** or **neutral-flavored oil** of choice

¼ cup (60 ml) **aquafaba** (liquid from a can of unsalted chickpeas; see Tips)

1 tablespoon finely chopped **fresh rosemary**

1½ teaspoons culinary/edible **dried lavender** (see Ingredient Note)

1½ teaspoons **pure vanilla extract**

Lemon Glaze

¾ cup (90 g) **organic powdered sugar**

1½ tablespoons **unsweetened coconut yogurt** (or 2 to 3 teaspoons plant-based milk)

2 teaspoons freshly squeezed **lemon juice**, plus more as needed

recipe and ingredients continue

A few pinches of **lemon zest**

1 or 2 pinches finely chopped **fresh rosemary** (optional)

1. Arrange a rack in the middle of the oven. Preheat the oven to 350°F (175°C). Line a 9 × 5-inch (23 × 13 cm) loaf pan with parchment paper so there is some overhang on the sides.

2. In a small bowl or measuring cup, stir together the milk and lemon juice. Set aside until it curdles slightly, 5 to 10 minutes. This is your vegan buttermilk.

3. In a medium bowl, whisk together the flour, cornmeal, baking soda, baking powder, and salt until evenly combined.

4. In a large bowl, combine 1 tablespoon lemon zest and the sugar and rub with your hands until well mixed and the sugar is moist (this releases the zest's essential oils). Add the oil and use an electric mixer (or stand mixer) to beat on medium speed until well incorporated and glossy, about 1 minute. Set aside. Rinse and dry the beaters.

5. Pour the aquafaba into a small bowl. Beat on medium speed until foamy throughout, including at the bottom of the bowl, 30 to 60 seconds. You may need to angle the bowl to whip it.

6. To the sugar-oil mixture, add the whipped aquafaba, buttermilk, rosemary, lavender, and vanilla. Mix until just combined, 15 to 20 seconds.

7. Add half of the dry mixture to the wet mixture, beating on low until just combined, taking care to not overbeat. Add the remaining flour and beat until mostly smooth, then switch to a silicone spatula to finish combining. Once the batter is just combined and no flour pockets remain, stop mixing. It should be light and airy.

8. Pour the batter into the prepared pan and smooth it out on the top. Bake for 40 to 50 minutes, until the top is lightly golden and a toothpick inserted at a 45-degree angle in the center of the cake comes out clean or with a few moist crumbs (inserting at an angle, instead of straight down, is a more reliable test for doneness here). If you get gooey batter, bake for 5 more minutes. If the top starts to brown early, loosely tent the pan with foil.

9. Cool on a wire rack for 15 minutes. Use the parchment paper to lift the cake out of the pan and onto the rack. Cool completely.

10. **Meanwhile, make the lemon glaze**. In a small bowl, whisk together the powdered sugar, yogurt, and lemon juice until you have a thick yet pourable glaze. For a thinner glaze, add more lemon juice (or a spoonful of milk). For more lemon flavor, add more lemon juice or some lemon zest.

11. Once the cake has cooled, drizzle it with the lemon glaze and top with a few pinches of lemon zest and chopped rosemary, if desired.

Crispy Spiced Cobbler Cake with Pears

Serves 8 to 10 | GFO, SFO, NFO

I enjoy a fluffy cake, but a fluffy cake that also has a crunchy exterior is top on my list. And that's what this rustic cake/cobbler mashup is: layers of juicy, spice-soaked pears and berries shimmering in a fluffy, melt-in-your-mouth cake with sweet-and-salty caramelized bits and shatteringly crunchy edges.

Ingredient Notes: No spice grinder? Use ½ teaspoon ground cinnamon, ¼ teaspoon ground cardamom, and ¼ teaspoon ground cloves. As long as your pears aren't rock hard or super ripe, they will work in this recipe. Bosc, Bartlett, and Anjou are all good varieties. If your butter is unsalted, use ½ scant teaspoon fine sea salt.

Easy Variations: Swap raspberries for blueberries or blackberries; in winter, use frozen berries or fresh cranberries. In summer, use 1 pound (455 g) peaches, nectarines, or plums. When Ataulfo mangoes are in season, use 3 medium and slice thinly.

GF Option: Replace the flour with ¾ cup (82 g) oat flour and ¾ cup + 2 tablespoons (116 g) gluten-free all-purpose flour. Use certified gluten-free oats.

2 (3-inch/7.5 cm) **cinnamon sticks** (see Ingredient Notes)

¼ heaping teaspoon **cardamom seeds** (see Ingredient Notes)

4 **whole cloves** (see Ingredient Notes)

½ teaspoon **freshly grated nutmeg**

2 medium **pears**, unpeeled (see Ingredient Notes)

¾ cup (90 g) **fresh berries**, such as raspberries

⅓ cup (56 g) **organic brown sugar**

1 medium **orange**, zested (about 1 tablespoon)

1½ cups (188 g) **all-purpose flour**

⅔ scant cup (60 g) **old-fashioned rolled oats**

1 cup (200 g) **organic cane sugar**

⅛ heaping teaspoon **fine sea salt** (see Ingredient Notes)

2 teaspoons aluminum-free **baking powder**

1⅓ cups (320 ml) **full-fat oat milk,** at room temperature

1½ teaspoons **pure vanilla extract**

¼ teaspoon **pure almond extract** (optional; omit if nut-free and use more vanilla instead)

10 tablespoons (140 g) **vegan butter**, sliced into tablespoon-size pieces (use soy-free butter as needed)

For Serving

Vegan vanilla ice cream or **vegan whipped cream** (optional)

recipe continues

1. Add the cinnamon sticks to a spice grinder and grind into tiny pieces. Add the cardamom and cloves and blend again until mostly ground. Stir in the nutmeg.

2. Slice the pears into ¼-inch-thick (0.75 cm) slices (about 2 heaping cups).

3. In a medium or large bowl, add the pears, berries, spice mix, brown sugar, and orange zest and toss gently to combine. Let rest at room temperature for 30 minutes or refrigerate for up to 3 hours.

4. Arrange a rack in the middle of the oven. Preheat the oven to 375°F (190°C).

5. In a medium or large bowl, whisk together the flour, oats, cane sugar, salt, and baking powder until well combined.

6. When the fruit is done resting, pour the milk, vanilla, and almond extract (if using) into the flour mix. Whisk until well combined. It should be thick and a little chunky but easily pourable.

7. Heat a large cast-iron skillet (11 or 12 inches/28 to 30 cm) over medium heat. Add the butter and use a spatula to spread it across the sides of the pan. Once melted, foamy, and at a bubble (it should take about 3 minutes), heat for another 2 minutes, stirring frequently to prevent burning, then take the pan off the heat (toasting the butter makes it taste nuttier and richer).

8. Using a ladle or measuring cup, dollop the cake batter on top of the butter around the entire pan. Ladling in rounds helps the butter swirl into a ripple pattern. Use your hands to gently arrange the pears on top, then top with the berries and spiced juices, but do not stir. It's a thin batter, so the fruit will sink.

9. Bake for 45 to 50 minutes, until the top is deeply golden brown and bubbling and the edges are caramelized. Transfer the pan to a wire rack for 10 minutes to cool slightly before digging in. Serve warm with ice cream or whipped cream, if desired.

10. Store leftovers, covered, for 3 to 4 days at room temperature, 5 to 6 days in the fridge, or a month in the freezer. Reheat wrapped in foil (to retain moisture) on a sheet pan at 350°F (175°C) until warmed through.

Chai-Spiced Custard Tart with Mango

Serves 12 | GF, SFO

With a custardy filling redolent with chai spices, a slightly nutty crust, and lots of mango, this sweet-tangy tart is perhaps my favorite summer dessert. Raw cashews and coconut cream make for a luxurious filling, while citrus brightens it up and spices add cozy warmth. Mango is layered at two stages, offering a juicy burst of sweetness in each morsel. Make this for special occasions or for any summer get-together where you want to be the most beloved person in the room.

Ingredient Notes: You can buy canned coconut cream, or refrigerate a can of full-fat coconut milk for 24 hours and then scoop out the solidified cream. If available, choose gold-skinned Ataulfo mangoes (a.k.a. honey mangoes) or Indian Alphonso mangoes, which are creamier and less fibrous than larger red-skinned mangoes. Ataulfo mangoes are in season from late February through summer; Alphonsos from April to June.

Tips: If you prefer only mildly sweet desserts, use ¼ to ⅓ cup (80 to 105 g) agave nectar in the filling.

Don't have a tart pan? Use an 8- or 9-inch (20 or 23 cm) springform pan (push the crust up the sides of the pan a bit); before unclasping, run a knife around the edges.

To make mangoes easier to peel and slice, I refrigerate them first.

Make Ahead: This tart can be made 1 to 2 days before serving and refrigerated (don't add berries or mint).

Chai Spice Blend

1½ teaspoons **ground cinnamon**

1 teaspoon **ground ginger**

¼ teaspoon **cardamom seeds**, blitzed in a spice grinder (or ¼ teaspoon ground cardamom)

⅛ teaspoon **ground allspice**

⅛ teaspoon **ground cloves**

Crust

¾ cup + 2 tablespoons (94 g) **oat flour** (use certified gluten-free oat flour as needed)

¾ cup + 2 tablespoons (88 g) blanched **almond flour**

¼ teaspoon **fine sea salt**

4 tablespoons (56 g) **vegan butter**, melted (or melted coconut oil if soy-free)

3 tablespoons (60 g) **pure maple syrup**

¾ teaspoon **pure vanilla extract**

Filling

1 cup (140 g) **raw cashews**, soaked or quick soaked, drained, and rinsed (see page 106)

⅓ cup (80 g) canned **coconut cream** (see Ingredient Notes)

½ cup (160 g) **agave nectar** (or pure maple syrup; see Tips)

recipe and ingredients continue

3½ tablespoons freshly squeezed **lemon juice**

⅛ teaspoon **fine sea salt**

¾ teaspoon **ground ginger**

½ teaspoon **cardamom seeds**

½ cup (100 g) **refined coconut oil**, melted

1 teaspoon **pure vanilla extract**

1 tablespoon **orange zest** (from about 1 large orange)

3 ripe but firm **mangoes** (about 1½ pounds/ 680 g; see Ingredient Notes)

Optional Topping

½ cup (62 g) **fresh raspberries**

1 small handful **fresh mint** leaves

1. Preheat the oven to 350°F (175°C). Grease the sides and bottom of a 9-inch (23 cm) round tart pan with a removable bottom (see Tips) with cooking spray.

2. **Make the spice blend.** In a small bowl, mix together the cinnamon, ginger, cardamom, allspice, and cloves.

3. **Make the crust.** In a medium or large bowl, combine the oat flour, almond flour, salt, and chai spice blend and stir to combine. Drizzle in the melted butter, maple syrup, and vanilla. Stir until the dough comes together and is moist. Add the dough to the prepared pan and first pinch it up the sides into the fluted edges, then press the remaining dough evenly into the bottom of the pan, using a flat measuring cup to smooth out the surface.

4. Prick the crust with a fork all over to prevent it from bubbling up during baking. Place the tart pan on a rimmed sheet pan and bake for 20 minutes, until lightly golden brown on the

edges and somewhat firm. Let cool on a wire rack and turn off the oven.

5. **Make the filling.** Add the soaked and drained cashews to a high-powered blender. Add the coconut cream, agave, lemon juice, salt, ginger, cardamom, coconut oil, vanilla, and orange zest. Blend until smooth and creamy, stopping to scrape down the sides as you go. If using a food processor, blend the cashews first until broken down into tiny bits, then add the remaining ingredients; it will take about 4 minutes to fully blend.

6. Pour a little less than half of the filling (about 1 cup/240 g) into the cooled tart shell, using a silicone spatula to smooth the surface. Refrigerate for 20 minutes.

7. Peel the mangoes and slice into thin strips, about ⅛ to ¼ inch (about 0.5 cm) thick (see Tips).

8. Remove the tart from the fridge and top with half of the sliced mango, arranging it in a flat layer. Pour the remaining filling on top, smooth out, and refrigerate for 20 minutes.

9. Top the tart with the remaining mango in a flat layer, or in fancy curved lines as shown. Refrigerate at least 2 hours or overnight (when chilled longer, it has a firmer custard-like texture).

10. Before serving, top each slice with a few raspberries and mint leaves (if using). Refrigerate leftovers for 3 to 5 days.

Perfectly Sweet–yet–Tart Plum Galette

Serves 8 | SFO, NFO

I believe there is no better galette than a red-skinned plum galette in late summer. When the plums are enveloped in a flaky and buttery crust and then baked, their tart-sweet flavor and juiciness gets ten times better. Flavoring plums with orange zest, fresh ginger, cinnamon, and nutmeg brings a sweet warmth, making this the ideal dessert to bridge summer and fall.

Ingredient Notes: If your fruit is sweet, ⅓ cup (70 g) sugar makes for a perfect tart-yet-sweet galette. To gauge sweetness level, start with ⅓ cup (70 g) sugar and taste the filling in step 6 before adding the cornstarch; add more sugar as needed. Plums and pluots are in season from summer to early fall.

Tips: Don't swap vegan butter with coconut oil, as it solidifies when chilled and makes it hard to roll out the dough.

Cold butter is key for a flaky crust, so cool down your kitchen in advance and don't skip freezing the butter (it keeps the butter in distinct pieces that then steam and create aerated pockets during baking that puff up into flaky layers). When rolling the dough, prep everything else in advance and roll quickly to avoid a warm dough.

Make Ahead: You can make the dough up to 3 days in advance and refrigerate, or freeze for up to 3 months and defrost in the fridge; make the filling a day ahead.

Easy Variations: Feel free to sub with peaches or nectarines. In fall or winter, opt for persimmons or a mix of tart and sweet apples. For apples, slice them no thicker than ¼ inch (0.5 cm) and dot them with 2 tablespoons cubed vegan butter before baking.

Crust

1¾ cups (220 g) **all-purpose flour**, plus more as needed

2 tablespoons **organic cane sugar**

¼ teaspoon **fine sea salt**

1 teaspoon **lemon zest**

8 tablespoons (112 g) **vegan butter** (use soy-free butter as needed), cut into small cubes and frozen for 15 minutes until very firm

2 to 3 tablespoons **ice-cold water**, plus more as needed

2 teaspoons **apple cider vinegar**

Filling

5 to 6 medium **red plums** or **pluots** (20 ounces/570 g)

1½ teaspoons **orange zest**

⅓ to ⅔ cup (70 g to 140 g) **organic cane sugar** (see Ingredient Notes)

1 tablespoon + 1 teaspoon freshly squeezed **lemon juice**

1½ teaspoons freshly grated **ginger** (or ½ teaspoon ground ginger)

1 teaspoon **ground cinnamon**

½ teaspoon **freshly grated nutmeg**

1 teaspoon **pure vanilla extract**

recipe and ingredients continue

½ teaspoon **almond extract** (use more vanilla if nut-free)

⅛ teaspoon **fine sea salt**

2 tablespoons **cornstarch** or **arrowroot powder**

For Finishing

1 to 2 teaspoons plain **plant-based milk** of choice

1 teaspoon **organic cane sugar**

Vegan vanilla ice cream or **vegan whipped topping**, for serving

1. **Make the crust.** Add about half of the flour to a food processor, along with the sugar, salt, and lemon zest. Blend until combined, just a few seconds. Add the cold butter cubes and do 20 to 25 quick pulses, until the dough begins to clump into pea-size pieces. Add the remaining flour and pulse until just incorporated, 5 to 7 pulses. Transfer to a large bowl.

2. Mix 2 tablespoons of the ice water with the vinegar. Sprinkle it over the dough mixture, gently kneading until the dough easily comes together when you squeeze it. You should be able to form a ball that doesn't crumble when you pull it apart. If the dough is crumbly or dry, add a teaspoon of ice water at a time. If the dough gets too wet, mix in a little more flour.

3. Shape the dough into a 5-inch (13 cm) disc. Wrap in plastic wrap and refrigerate for at least 2 hours, or up to 72 hours.

4. Before rolling the dough, rest it on the counter until pliable, 45 to 60 minutes (longer if it was chilled for more than 2 hours).

5. Arrange a rack in the middle of the oven. Preheat the oven to 400°F (205°C).

6. Make the filling. Slice the plums ¾ to 1 inch thick (2 to 2.5 cm) to get 3½ cups. Add to a large bowl. In a medium bowl, combine the orange zest and sugar and rub with your hands until well mixed and the sugar is moist (this releases the zest's essential oils). Add the lemon juice, ginger, cinnamon, nutmeg, vanilla and almond extracts, salt, and cornstarch. Pour on top of the plums, tossing very gently to avoid bruising.

7. Let rest for 5 minutes, then strain the juices into a small saucepan. Heat over medium-low heat, whisking occasionally. Once gently simmering, whisk every 3 to 5 seconds to prevent congealing, until the juices have just thickened (they should be on the heat for a total of 2½ to 3 minutes).

Transfer to a bowl to stop the cooking process. As the juices rest, they will thicken.

8. Place the disc of dough on a large sheet of parchment paper and prep your equipment: rolling pin, paring knife, rimmed sheet pan, and bowl with flour for dusting.

9. Roll out the dough. Press the dough down and out with your palm until you have a round with a 6-inch (15 cm) diameter. Use a rolling pin to roll out an oval or roundish shape that's 12 to 14 inches long (30 to 35 cm) on its longer side and about ⅛ inch (0.3 cm) thick. Dust the rolling pin or surface with flour as needed to prevent sticking. Lightly trim the edges with a paring knife and reserve the scraps. When done rolling, carefully slide the parchment paper and dough onto the sheet pan.

10. Assemble. Gently spoon the fruit on top of the dough, leaving a 1½-inch (4 cm) border. Lift up the edges of the dough and fold them over the filling to form a crust, ensuring the fruit is tucked into the dough. If the dough tears, patch with the reserved dough scraps to prevent leaking in the oven. If the dough is too warm to fold, refrigerate the galette for 10 to 15 minutes before continuing.

11. When done folding, spoon the reserved juices from step 7 on top of the fruit. Brush the dough with the milk, then sprinkle with the sugar.

12. Bake for 40 to 45 minutes, until the crust is golden brown and sturdy and the filling is bubbling a bit. Place the sheet pan on a wire rack to cool for 20 minutes before slicing. Serve warm with ice cream or whipped topping.

Chocolate–Covered Dates with Pistachio Butter

Makes 12 stuffed dates | GF, SF

These chewy, chocolate-covered dates stuffed with velvety homemade pistachio butter are one of my favorite treats to keep on hand. They're nutrient dense but luxurious and rich, so just one (or two) is enough to satisfy even this dessert fiend's cravings. Make a double batch and stash them in the freezer (they thaw in seconds).

Ingredient Notes: To cover the dates fully in chocolate, use 6 ounces (170 g) of chocolate. For partially dipped dates, 3 ounces (85 g) is fine. You can use chocolate chips but they don't melt as smoothly.

Orange zest adds a floral aroma that evokes the citrus-pistachio flavor combo I love in many Middle Eastern desserts, but chocolate purists may want to omit it.

12 large, soft **Medjool dates**

6 tablespoons **Pistachio Butter** (page 194), or to taste

Flaky sea salt

3 to 6 ounces (85 to 170 g) dairy-free **dark chocolate** (65% to 80% cacao), chopped (see Ingredient Notes)

½ teaspoon **orange zest**, plus more for garnishing (optional; see Ingredient Notes)

1. Slice an opening in each date but not all the way through. Remove the pit. Spoon some pistachio butter into each cavity (about ½ tablespoon). Sprinkle a little flaky salt on top. Transfer the dates to a parchment paper–lined plate and freeze for at least 20 minutes.

2. Melt the chocolate using the double boiler or microwave method (see page 576). If using orange zest, stir into the chocolate once melted.

3. Remove the dates from the freezer. Use a fork to dip a date in the melted chocolate, either partially or fully covering the date in chocolate, and transfer back to the lined plate. Immediately sprinkle the date with a pinch of flaky salt and a pinch of orange zest (if using). The chocolate sets quickly, so dip one date at a time. Freeze for 5 minutes (or longer).

4. If you have leftover chocolate, you can drizzle a bit more melted chocolate on top. Store leftover stuffed dates in the freezer for several weeks.

An Ode to (Dark) Chocolate

I live chocolate, I breathe chocolate, I eat chocolate every day. And since going vegan, my love for chocolate has only grown deeper. Without the distraction of milk chocolate, I get to focus on chocolate in its finest form: dark chocolate.

Dark chocolate lingers on your tongue and coats your whole mouth with a rich sensation, longer lasting and more balanced than the cloying sweetness of milk chocolate. It lends unbelievable richness to tarts and frostings and truffles, but also plays nicely with fruits, nuts, aromatics, and spices. It offers varying flavors and cacao content, making it versatile for snacking, cake baking, and tempering.

It's also legitimately good for you and makes you feel fuzzy and warm inside.

If you haven't fallen in love with dark chocolate yet, I hope one of these treats will be your gateway dark chocolate drug.

Melting Chocolate

Classic method: To assemble a **double boiler**, grab a heatproof bowl that can be nestled into a saucepan—it should hover above the bottom of the pan. Fill the pan up with a few inches of water. Keep the water at a rapid simmer. Place the chocolate in the bowl and lower the bowl into the pan, making sure the bottom of the bowl doesn't touch the water and no water comes near the chocolate. Whisk frequently until melted.

Lazy method: Chop chocolate into small pieces and heat in the **microwave** on high power in 30-second intervals, stirring after each round.

Dark Chocolate Mousse with Raspberry Compote

Serves 6 to 8 | GF, NF

The soft yet dense texture of silken tofu—along with the luxe body of melted chocolate and the chewy sweetness of Medjool dates—makes for a creamy, deluxe chocolate mousse. The richness of two kinds of chocolate is brightened and taken to the next level by the tart, orange-laced raspberry compote. It's gourmet but so simple to whip up, making it an ideal low-stress, high-reward dessert for entertaining. The portions may seem small, but this mousse is quite decadent.

Ingredient Notes: If you prefer desserts that are less sweet, use 85% dark chocolate. Don't use chocolate below 70% or the mousse will be too sweet; if that's all you have, start without the maple syrup. Don't sub a block of "soft" tofu for the silken tofu or the mousse will harden.

Tip: If you are using a food processor instead of a high-powered blender, soak the dates in boiling water for 15 minutes, then drain and dry off before blending.

Make Ahead: Both the mousse and compote can be made 3 to 4 days ahead of time.

Chocolate Mousse

5 ounces (140 g) good-quality dairy-free **dark chocolate** (70% to 80% cacao), chopped (see Ingredient Notes)

1 teaspoon **espresso powder** (optional)

12 ounces (340 g) **silken soft tofu** (see Ingredient Notes)

2 soft **Medjool dates**, pitted (see Tip)

¼ cup (80 g) **pure maple syrup**

¼ cup (24 g) **Dutch-process cocoa powder**

1 teaspoon **pure vanilla extract**

¼ teaspoon **ground cinnamon** (optional)

½ to ¾ teaspoon **fine sea salt**

Raspberry Compote

2 cups **raspberries**, fresh (250 g) or frozen (210 g)

2 tablespoons **pure maple syrup**

1½ teaspoons **orange zest**

1 tablespoon freshly squeezed **orange juice**

1 teaspoon **pure vanilla extract**

Fine sea salt

recipe continues

1. **Make the mousse.** Melt the chocolate using the double boiler or microwave method (see page 576).

2. If using espresso powder, whisk it into the warm melted chocolate and allow to cool to room temperature.

3. If using refrigerated tofu, scoop it out of its package and measure out 12 ounces (340 g) into a bowl. Do not remove excess water.

4. In a high-powered blender (or food processor; see Tip), add the tofu with about 3 tablespoons of the water that has accumulated (if no water has accumulated, add about 3 tablespoons filtered water). Add the dates, maple syrup, cocoa powder, vanilla, cinnamon (if using), and ½ teaspoon salt. Blend very well until the dates are fully pulverized and the cocoa has been mixed in, stopping to scrape down the sides as you go.

5. Now add the melted, cooled chocolate and blend until completely smooth and creamy. Taste, adding more salt as desired (I like an extra ¼ teaspoon for sweet-and-salty vibes). Divide among 6 to 8 ramekins or small dessert glasses and chill for at least 1 hour to thicken (don't store all of it in one big container, as it has a tendency to harden).

6. **Make the compote.** In a small or medium saucepan over medium heat, combine the raspberries, maple syrup, orange zest and juice, vanilla, and a pinch of salt. When the mixture starts to bubble quickly, stir almost continuously until the berries break down and start to thicken, 2 to 3 minutes. Reduce the heat and simmer until thickened and jammy, 10 minutes. Let come to room temperature or chill in the fridge.

7. To serve, let the mousse rest at room temperature for a few minutes, then add a few spoonfuls of compote on top of each. Store the mousse in the fridge for 5 to 6 days and the compote for up to 2 weeks.

Fudgy Skillet Brownies with Raspberry Swirl Ice Cream

Serves 12 | GFO, SFO, NF

A few years ago, I shared a recipe on my blog for vegan brownies that I truly think are life changing. They feature three kinds of chocolate (melted dark chocolate, Dutch-process cocoa powder, *and* chocolate chips) and the perfect combo of fudgy richness with a chewy structure. Plus, a blend of whipped aquafaba and sugar brings that irresistible crinkly top so often missing in vegan brownies.

These are those same brownies but in a shiny new package. The brownies are baked in a cast-iron skillet, which means you can eat the brownie (brownie pie?) straight from the pan while they're still warm. No need to wait an hour for them to fully cool, and no need to be civilized and cut them into dainty squares. The brownies are topped with vanilla ice cream swirled with raspberry compote for the perfect tart-yet-sweet balance.

So if you've got company, let your guests assemble their own brownie sundaes. And if you don't, feel free to do what I do: lean against the kitchen counter while you dig spoonfuls of brownie right from the pan into your mouth, then awkwardly slice the leftovers for your friends and family (who will be more than happy to take misshapen brownies off your hands).

Ingredient Note: Brownies are all about the chocolate, so use the best quality you can afford. For sweeter brownies, use dark chocolate that is about 65% cacao. I recommend using Dutch-process cocoa powder over natural cocoa powder for a richer, more intense chocolate flavor.

Tips: To collect the aquafaba, shake your can of chickpeas before opening to evenly distribute the starches. Set a bowl beneath a colander and drain the chickpeas to collect their liquid.

If you don't have a 10-inch (25 cm) cast-iron skillet, you can always bake these the classic way: in a parchment paper–lined 8-inch (20 cm) square metal baking pan. Bake for 34 to 37 minutes.

Short on time? Skip the raspberry compote and just mash fresh raspberries with a fork, then stir those into the ice cream. Or simply serve brownies with plain vegan vanilla ice cream. And if you prefer

a baby scoop of ice cream with your brownies, feel free to use just one pint of ice cream.

GF Option: Replace the flour with ¾ cup (82 g) certified gluten-free oat flour and ¾ cup (100 g) gluten-free all-purpose flour. You might need to bake the brownies for an extra 2 minutes.

1½ cups (180 g) **all-purpose flour**

¼ cup + 3 tablespoons (42 g) **Dutch-process cocoa powder**

½ cup (120 ml) **aquafaba** (liquid from a can of unsalted chickpeas; see Tips)

1½ cups (290 g) **organic cane sugar**

¾ teaspoon **fine sea salt**

recipe and ingredients continue

1 tablespoon **pure vanilla extract**

1 teaspoon **espresso powder**

6 ounces (170 g) dairy-free **dark chocolate** (65% to 75% cacao), roughly chopped (see Ingredient Notes)

8 tablespoons (112 g/1 stick) **vegan butter**, cubed (use soy-free butter as needed)

3 ounces (85 g) dairy-free **dark or bittersweet chocolate chips or chunks** (or finely chopped dark chocolate)

For Serving

Raspberry Swirl Ice Cream (recipe follows)

1. Arrange a rack in the middle of the oven. Preheat the oven to 350°F (176°C). Add 1 teaspoon neutral-flavored oil to a well-seasoned 10-inch (25 cm) cast-iron skillet and spread it out with a paper towel to evenly distribute and absorb excess oil.

2. In a medium bowl, sift the flour and cocoa powder together to prevent any lumps.

3. In a large bowl, add the aquafaba and sugar. Use an electric mixer (you can also use a stand mixer) on high speed and beat the mixture until thickened, glossy, and wavy ribbons frequently appear in the bowl, 2½ to 3 minutes.

4. Add the salt, vanilla, and espresso powder and fold with a silicone spatula until well combined (the espresso will continue dissolving into the mixture as it rests).

5. Assemble a double boiler (see page 576). Add the chopped chocolate and cubed butter to the bowl on top of the saucepan. Allow the chocolate mixture to melt, whisking occasionally until smooth and the chocolate is completely melted. Once the chocolate is completely melted, keep the bowl on the saucepan for an additional 30 to 60 seconds to further warm through.

6. Pour the warm butter-chocolate mixture over the aquafaba-sugar mixture and fold together with the spatula.

7. Add the dry ingredients to the wet ingredients and stir until just combined (stop mixing once the flour traces are gone). Fold in the chocolate chips. Pour the batter into the prepared skillet and smooth out the surface with the spatula.

8. Bake for 32 minutes, or until a toothpick inserted in the middle comes out with a tiny bit of thick batter. If the batter is liquidy or runny, the brownies need a few more minutes.

9. Transfer the skillet to a wire rack to cool for 30 minutes. Then serve with scoops of raspberry swirl ice cream. Dig in with spoons! While warm, the brownie interior will be a little gooey, but it firms up more as it rests.

Raspberry Swirl Ice Cream

Serves 12

GF, SFO, NFO

I know some folks will be on team traditional (brownie + vanilla ice cream = perfection), but I prefer to add a bit of tartness to my brownie sundaes to brighten up all the indulgence. Here, I swirl a quick raspberry compote into softened store-bought vegan vanilla ice cream. Low-stress entertaining at its finest.

Raspberry Compote (page 577)

2 pints or 1 quart (950 ml) **vegan vanilla ice cream** (use soy-free or nut-free vegan ice cream as needed)

1. If you are making the compote now, allow it to cool before using. Let the ice cream sit out at room temperature until softened (but not melty).

2. Line a loaf pan or similar-shaped food storage container with parchment paper so there is some overhang on the sides.

3. Add a generous bed of ice cream to the bottom of the loaf pan, spreading it out with a silicone spatula. Dollop a few small spoonfuls of the compote on top but don't spread it around. Add another layer of ice cream, spread it out, and follow with a few more dollops of compote. Once you get to the top layer, use a spoon to make some swirls. Freeze the ice cream until firm, at least 1 hour.

Celebration Cake with Chocolate Buttercream Frosting

Serves 16 | SFO, NF

To celebrate the end of this book and our culinary journey together, I present you with this celebration cake. It's a classic yellow birthday cake with chocolate frosting, but a little more grown-up and one of my all-time favorite cakes.

Layers of ridiculously fluffy cake with a tender, moist crumb and buttery flavor are draped in a rich, fudgy buttercream frosting. Vegan sour cream does wonders here, lending a pillowy interior, plus a perfectly browned crust and rich flavor.

Make it for birthdays, anniversaries, holidays, and graduations, or anytime good, happy things have been blessed upon you.

Ingredient Note: If you don't have access to vegan sour cream, omit it and double the amount of milk (to 1½ cups/360 ml).

Tips: To collect the aquafaba, shake your can of chickpeas before opening to evenly distribute the starches. Set a bowl beneath a colander and drain the chickpeas to collect their liquid.

To make frosting easier, refrigerate the cakes first. If refrigerating for more than a few hours, carefully wrap in plastic wrap to prevent them from drying out (exercise great caution; the cakes are delicate!).

½ cup (115 g) **vegan sour cream** (see Ingredient Note)

8 tablespoons (112 g/1 stick) **vegan butter** (use soy-free butter as needed), plus more for greasing

¾ cup (180 ml) **full-fat oat milk or soy milk**, at room temperature

2 tablespoons freshly squeezed **lemon juice**

3½ cups (440 g) **all-purpose flour**

2 teaspoons aluminum-free **baking powder**

½ teaspoon **baking soda**

½ teaspoon **fine sea salt**

⅛ teaspoon **ground turmeric** (for color)

¼ teaspoon **freshly grated nutmeg**

¼ teaspoon **ground cardamom** (optional)

1¼ cups (250 g) **organic cane sugar**

1 tablespoon **orange zest** (from about 1 large orange)

½ cup (112 g) **sunflower oil** or **neutral-flavored oil** of choice

½ cup (120 ml) **aquafaba** (liquid from a can of unsalted chickpeas; see Tips)

1 tablespoon **pure vanilla extract**

For Finishing

Chocolate Buttercream Frosting (recipe follows)

Vegan sprinkles or **fresh berries**, for topping (optional)

recipe continues

1. Take the sour cream and butter out of the fridge to soften for at least 20 minutes. Measure out the sour cream and slice the butter into small pieces to soften more quickly.

2. In a small bowl or measuring cup, stir together the milk and lemon juice. Set aside until it curdles slightly, 5 to 10 minutes. This is your vegan buttermilk.

3. Arrange a rack in the middle of the oven. Preheat the oven to 350°F (175°C). Make two parchment paper rounds for two 8-inch (20 cm) round cake pans. Lightly grease the bottoms and sides of each pan, add the parchment paper to each pan, and lightly grease the parchment.

4. In a medium bowl, whisk together the flour, baking powder, baking soda, salt, turmeric, nutmeg, and cardamom (if using) until well combined.

5. In a large bowl, combine the sugar and orange zest and rub with your hands until well mixed and the sugar is moist (this releases the zest's essential oils). Add the softened butter and oil. With an electric mixer (you can also use a stand mixer), beat on low speed until the butter is in small pieces, then increase the speed to medium. Beat until starting to get fluffy and glossy, about 1 minute total. Set aside. Rinse and dry the beaters.

6. In a small bowl, beat the aquafaba on medium speed until foamy throughout, including at the bottom of the bowl, about 1 minute.

7. To the sugar-butter mixture, add the whipped aquafaba, buttermilk, sour cream, and vanilla. Mix on low or medium-low speed until just combined, 15 to 20 seconds.

8. Add half of the dry ingredients into the wet ingredients, beating on low speed until just combined. Add the remaining flour mixture and beat until you have a mostly smooth batter, then switch to a silicone spatula. Fold, stirring the bottom and sides of the bowl to ensure it's well combined. The batter should be thick yet fluffy.

9. Use a digital scale (or measuring cups) to evenly divide the batter between the cake pans (about 24 ounces/700 g per pan). Smooth out the surface with the spatula.

10. Bake for 30 minutes, or until the centers are set and the cakes have puffed up a bit and just started to pull away from the pans. A toothpick inserted in the center should come out with only a few moist crumbs.

11. Let the pans cool on a wire rack for at least 30 minutes. Line the rack with parchment paper, then carefully invert the cakes onto the lined rack. Let cool completely before assembling (see Tips).

12. **Assemble.** Place one cake on a cake platter or plate (bottom side facing up for a leveled cake). Add a generous, thick layer of chocolate frosting on top, spreading to the edges using an offset or icing spatula. Top with the next cake. Add another layer of frosting and spread out. Add the rest of the frosting to the sides of each cake, starting at the bottom,

working your way up to the top. For a clean look, use a bench scraper or straight icing spatula to smooth out the sides. Finally, smooth out the frosting on the top layer. Depending on how much of a frosting person you are, you may have leftover frosting (freeze it for 2 to 3 months; defrost in the fridge, then re-whip).

13. Before serving, garnish with sprinkles or fresh berries, if desired. Store leftover cake covered at room temperature for up to 3 days, then refrigerate, covered, for up to 4 more days.

Chocolate Buttercream Frosting

Makes about 3 cups (750 g)

GF, SFO, NF

Folding melted dark chocolate into the frosting makes it thicker, a little fudge-like, and a richer, more grown-up cake. The more chocolate you add, the fudgier it gets. If you prefer a traditional fluffy buttercream or a sweeter cake, omit it. Either way, you're in for a serious treat.

Make Ahead: Make the frosting 1 week ahead of time and refrigerate. Leave it out at room temperature for several hours, until pliable. Or microwave in 5-second intervals, using a spatula to stir after each round. When it's soft enough, use a mixer and beat briefly until fluffy.

1 to 4 ounces (30 to 110 g) dairy-free **dark chocolate** (65% to 70% cacao), chopped (optional; see headnote)

3 cups (345 g) **organic powdered sugar**, plus more as needed

¾ cup (72 g) **Dutch-process cocoa powder**, plus more as needed

2 sticks (1 cup/224 g) **vegan butter**, at room temperature (use soy-free butter as needed)

2 teaspoons **pure vanilla extract**

3 tablespoons plain **plant-based milk** of choice, plus more as needed

¼ teaspoon **fine sea salt**, plus more as needed

1. If using, melt the chocolate using the double boiler or microwave method (see page 576). Allow to cool a bit.

2. In a large bowl, sift the powdered sugar and cocoa powder together to prevent lumps.

3. Using a stand mixer fitted with the paddle attachment or a handheld electric mixer, beat the butter on medium speed until creamy, 1 to 2 minutes.

4. Add the sifted cocoa-sugar mixture, vanilla, milk, and salt. Beat on low speed for 30 seconds, then gradually increase the speed to high and beat until thick and smooth, another 30 to 60 seconds. If using, add the melted chocolate and mix until well combined.

5. If the frosting is too thick, add more milk, starting with a teaspoon. If too thin, add more cocoa or powdered sugar. If too sweet, add a pinch more salt.

Fancy Time Menus

Holiday Brunch

○ Hannah's Carrot Lox (page 431) with bagels and vegan cream cheese or Whipped Feta (page 209)

○ My Weekly Herby Green Salad (page 357)

○ Diner-Style Buttermilk Waffles (page 446)

Make Ahead

○ 3 to 4 days ahead: Make the lox, Whipped Feta, waffle batter, and Crispy Seed Crumbs for the salad.

Spring Dinner Party

○ Shaved Fennel Salad with Pears & Grapefruit-Shallot Vinaigrette (page 368)

○ Garlicky Asparagus & Beans with Lemon-Infused Olive Oil (page 379)

○ Lemony Pasta with Sausage & Broccoli (page 502)

○ Chai-Spiced Custard Tart with Mango (page 567)

Make Ahead

○ 5 days ahead: Make the vinaigrette.

○ 1 to 3 days ahead: Make the tart and slice the asparagus, green beans, and broccoli.

Summer Lunch with Your Besties

○ Smashed Cucumbers with Yogurt-Tahini Sauce & Spicy "Honey" (page 365)

○ Korean BBQ Jackfruit Sandwiches with Creamy Sesame Slaw (page 508)

○ Caramelized Stone Fruit Crisp with Tahini Custard (page 556)

Make Ahead

○ 1 to 2 weeks ahead: Make the Spicy "Honey" with Candied Jalapeños

○ 1 to 3 days ahead: Make the Yogurt-Tahini Sauce and BBQ jackfruit.

○ 1 day ahead: Prep the veggies for the sandwich slaw; caramelize the fruit and make the tahini custard.

Fall Harvest Party

○ Lemon-Garlic Brussels Sprouts with Rosemary (page 334)

○ Maple-Roasted Squash & Chickpeas with Mint-Pistachio Pesto (page 404)

○ Creamy Baked Wild Rice with Carrots (page 317)

○ Spiced Wine–Poached Figs with "Honey" (page 550)

Make Ahead

○ 3 to 4 days ahead: Make the pesto.

○ 1 day ahead: Make the wild rice; make the figs and refrigerate.

Sweater-Weather Get-Together

○ Spice-Roasted Whole Carrots (page 329) with Pomegranate Tahini Sauce (page 197)

○ The Sexy Skillet Lasagna (page 519)

○ Crispy Spiced Cobbler Cake with Pears (page 563)

Make Ahead

○ 3 to 4 days ahead: Make the tahini sauce; make the "ricotta" and red sauce for the lasagna.

○ 1 to 2 days ahead: Make the cobbler cake.

Mother's Day Brunch

○ Shaved Carrot Salad with Pickled Shallots & Fresh Herbs (page 371)

○ Cheesy Herb Bread Pudding with Caramelized Leeks (page 459)

○ Celebration Cake with Chocolate Buttercream Frosting (page 585)

Make Ahead

○ 1 week ahead: Make the frosting.

○ 1 day ahead: Bake the cake and frost it once cooled; assemble the bread pudding the night before and refrigerate.

Valentine's Day Lovers' Dinner

○ Your choice of a simple green salad with Preserved Lemon Vinaigrette (page 164)

○ Rosemary Farrotto with Cheesy Pine Nuts (page 311)

○ Miso Butter–Seared King Oyster "Scallops" (page 537)

○ Dark Chocolate Mousse with Raspberry Compote (page 577)

Make Ahead

○ 1 week ahead: Make the vinaigrette and raspberry compote.

○ 1 to 2 days ahead: Make the farrotto and mousse.

Easter Lunch

○ Creamy & Crunchy Beet Salad with Crispy Fennel Crumbs (page 377)

○ Cauliflower Steaks with Italian Basil & Parsley Salsa Verde (page 421)

○ Crispy Smashed Potatoes (page 407)

○ Lemon Corn Cake with Lavender & Rosemary (page 561)

Make Ahead

○ 1 to 2 days ahead: Make the salad dressing, crispy crumbs, salsa verde, and lemon cake (ice the cake just before serving).

Summer Picnic in the Park

○ Whipped Tofu Ricotta (page 206) with crudités and crackers

○ Marinated White Beans & Fennel with Spiced Za'atar Oil (page 245)

○ Indian-Spiced Charred Corn Salad (page 383)

○ Macerated Berries with Basil & Mint (page 549)

Make Ahead

○ 1 to 2 days ahead: Make the "ricotta" and Marinated White Beans & Fennel with Spiced Za'atar Oil.

Acknowledgments

I don't even know how to begin to thank the Rainbow Plant Life viewers and readers. Thank you for taking the time out of your busy lives to watch my videos and for placing your trust in me when you choose to make my recipes, whether it's for your weeknight dinners or fancy time dinners. Thank you for helping this passion project of writing a massive cookbook on vegan flavor to come to fruition.

I think about all the afternoons I spent curled up in Barnes & Noble sifting through cookbooks as a teenager. The fact that I get to write one as part of my actual job, and the notion that a young girl might pick it up in a bookstore and find some inspiration in it or might see some part of herself in me . . . the feeling is indescribable and brings a tear to my eyes (okay, fine, I'm bawling right now).

The support from the RPL community has helped me find creativity, greater purpose, and a dream career. I could not be more grateful.

Thank you to my editor, Lucia Watson, who shepherded this book down the right path and patiently waited while I birthed this book over the course of a few years. Your sage big-picture advice helped turn a vague love letter to vegan cooking into reality. If it weren't for you, this project would be a nine-hundred-page encyclopedia.

And to the entire Avery team, thank you for putting so much energy and love into the making of this book: designer/art director Ashley Tucker, production editor Sally Knapp, copyeditor Heather Rodino, and associate editors Suzy Swartz and Isabel McCarthy.

My agent, Sharon Bowers, thank you for supporting and championing my vision for this book and for letting me ramble on calls and then making coherent sense out of those anxious ramblings.

To my recipe testers Claire Breckenridge and Jennifer Bartoli, thank you so much for taking the time to test my recipes and for your invaluable feedback.

Kaitlin Mayfield, thank you for helping to run all things Rainbow Plant Life smoothly while I was head-down writing this massive book.

Callie Vail, you are the most marvelous and organized recipe tester (and unofficial proofreading/grammar queen). Your attention to detail and quality of feedback are unmatched, and they undoubtedly improved the quality of my recipes. It is such a pleasure to work with you.

To Hannah Hairston, who was my culinary assistant extraordinaire and tested nearly every recipe in this book, many of them upward of a dozen times, and who chatted with me in my kitchen about nearly every recipe at *exhaustive* length: thank you for allowing me to be as rigorous and meticulous as possible and for sharing your awesome ideas on a daily basis, including the late-night texts about possible flavor pairings and recipe tweaks. I miss our daily *Gilmore Girls*–esque banter.

Rosana Guay, thank you so much for

editing all of my food photos and making them pop off the page. I am carpal tunnel–free because of you.

Niki Cram, thank you for using your photographic magic to make me look breezy and cool in the kitchen, even though I am actually incredibly clumsy and much better at photobombing than I am at posing for portraits.

To all the chefs who have inspired me and unknowingly given me a free culinary education over the years, a massive thank you!—Ina Garten, Giada De Laurentiis, Alton Brown, Yotam Ottolenghi, Sami Tamimi, Samin Nosrat, Isa Chandra Moskowitz, Harold McGee, Padma Lakshmi, J. Kenji López-Alt, Christopher Kimball, Madhur Jaffrey, Nik Sharma, Joshua McFadden, Joe Yonan, Priya Krishna, Kristen Kish, Ranveer Brar, Bryant Terry, Hetty McKinnon, Amy Chaplin, and many more.

To the wonderful folks at both Burlap & Barrel and Diaspora Co., thank you for helping to bring my food alive with the most incredible spices.

To my mom and dad, you have given me everything in life, and I have no proper way to thank you for the unconditional love you show me day after day, year after year. You were initially terrified when I first left my job as a lawyer (understandable), yet now you are my biggest fans, and it's not lost on me how lucky I am to have such supportive parents.

Dad, your zest for cooking on the fly brings me great joy, and I love that in your semi-retired years you have taken to cooking and baking on a daily basis. I am touched when you insist that everyone you meet must watch one of my YouTube videos (even if it is mildly embarrassing).

Mom, even though your distaste for measuring spoons and cups gives me anxiety, you have taught me so much about Indian cooking, for which I will be forever grateful. Your informal cooking lessons have helped me reconnect with our heritage and embrace my Indian American identity in a way that felt impossible when I was younger. Being able to serve you Indian dishes is one of the greatest joys of my adult life.

To my sister, Puja, thank you for our lifelong friendship and for always giving me extremely positive feedback on literally every dish you try. You are not the most discerning taste tester, but you are the most enthusiastic one.

To my best friends, Lucia, Sonia, and Sravya, thank you for your constant encouragement and love over the years. You are the best cheerleaders.

To my partner, Max, thank you for choosing to build a life (and business) with me. Your quest for living a life worth living has pushed me out of my comfort zone time after time, making me stronger, wiser, and a better version of myself. You put your life on hold in so many ways so that I could finish this book, yet you never complained (and instead washed a lot of dishes). Granted, you ate really well during this time, but you were wonderful throughout it all, and you get more wonderful by the day. I love you so much.

Index

butternut squash
  Maple-Roasted Squash &
    Chickpeas with Mint-
    Pistachio Pesto, 404–6
  Roasted Butternut Wedges, 337
  scraps from, 142
  sweetness found in, 69
Buttery Brown Rice with Warm
  Spices, 308–10
Buttery Caper–Pine Nut Dressing,
  174, 385–87
Buttery Charred Cabbage in Spiced
  Tomatoes with Tahini, 401–3
Buttery Vegan Cornbread, 528–29

C

cabbage
  Buttery Charred Cabbage in
    Spiced Tomatoes with Tahini,
    401–3
  Creamy Sesame Slaw, 508–11
  crisp texture of, 114
  Dilly Slaw, 525–29
  pickled, 170
  Rainbow Veggie Slaw with Green
    Goddess Dressing, 390–91
Caesar salad
  All Hail Caesar Dressing, 155
  Fancy Caesar Salad, 362–64
Cajun aromatics, 90
cakes
  Celebration Cake with Chocolate
    Buttercream Frosting, 584–87
  Crispy Spiced Cobbler Cake with
    Pears, 563–65
  Lemon Corn Cake with Lavender
    & Rosemary, 560–62
Calabrian chili paste, 86, 137
cannellini beans
  Cauliflower Steaks with Italian
    Basil & Parsley Salsa Verde,
    421–23
  Citrus-Braised Fennel with
    White Beans, 398–400
  "Cream"-Braised Leeks with
    Crispy Bits, 414–17
  Marinated White Beans &
    Fennel with Spiced Za'atar
    Oil, 245–47
  as pantry staple, 137
  Wildly Crunchy Cornmeal Beans,
    240–41

capers
  as acid source, 60
  Buttery Caper–Pine Nut
    Dressing, 174
  Cashew Cream, Many Ways, 202
  Fried Capers, 167
  as pantry staple, 137
  Pasta & Chickpeas with Fried
    Capers & Tomato-Shallot
    Butter, 500–501
Caramelized Stone Fruit Crisp with
  Tahini Custard, 556–59, 588
Carnitas Tacos, Mushroom, 540–43
carrots
  Braised Carrots & Chickpeas
    with Dill Gremolata, 418–20
  Creamy Baked Wild Rice with
    Carrots, 317–19
  Hannah's Carrot Lox, 430–32
  pickled, 170
  Rainbow Veggie Slaw with Green
    Goddess Dressing, 390–91
  Shaved Carrot Salad with Pickled
    Shallots & Fresh Herbs,
    371–73
  Spice-Roasted Whole Carrots, 329
  sweetness found in, 69
  Swiss Chard & Carrot Slaw
    with Crispy Bread Crumbs,
    385–87
cashews
  Cashew Cream, Many Ways,
    200–202
  cashew milk, 109
  Cheesy Crunchies, 222–23
  "Cream"-Braised Leeks with
    Crispy Bits, 414–17
  Extremely Easy Queso Sauce,
    199
  Fermented Cashew Cheese,
    210–12
  as pantry staple, 136
  substitutes for, 106–7
  toasting, 115
cast-iron pans, 131
cauliflower
  Cauliflower Steaks with Italian
    Basil & Parsley Salsa Verde,
    421–23
  pickled, 170
  Quick Roasted Cauliflower,
    342–43

scraps from, 142
Celebration Cake with Chocolate
  Buttercream Frosting, 589
celery, 142
Chai-Spiced Custard Tart with
  Mango, 566–69, 588
champagne vinegar, 57, 137
Charred Sweet Potato Wedges,
  344–45
"cheese"
  Adult Grilled Cheese with Chili
    Crisp, 516–18
  Cheesy Crunchies, 222–23,
    362–64
  Cheesy Herb Bread Pudding with
    Caramelized Leeks, 458–61,
    589
  Cheesy Pine Nuts, 311–13
  Extremely Easy Queso Sauce, 199
  Fermented Cashew Cheese,
    210–12
  Whipped Feta, 208–9
cherries, dried, 121
chewy foods, 118–22, 123
"chicken," fried, 524–29
chickpeas
  aquafaba, 122, 205, 561, 580, 585
  BBQ Roasted Chickpeas, 239
  Braised Carrots & Chickpeas
    with Dill Gremolata, 418–20
  Chickpea Pancake with Sesame
    Greens, 449–51
  Classic Roasted Chickpeas,
    236–37
  Creamy Chickpea Spinach
    Masala with Tadka, 483–85
  The Fancy Caesar Salad, 362–64
  Maple-Roasted Squash &
    Chickpeas with Mint-
    Pistachio Pesto, 404–6
  Marinated Chickpeas, 242–44
  as pantry staple, 137
  Pasta & Chickpeas with Fried
    Capers & Tomato-Shallot
    Butter, 500–501
  Pearl Couscous & Chickpea
    Salad with Preserved Lemon,
    323–25
  Scrambled Chickpeas with Chile
    Yogurt Sauce and Za'atar
    Pita, 455–57
  Tandoori Roasted Chickpeas, 238